CONSCIOUSNESS REDUX

CONSCIOUSNESS REDUX

WAKING, SLEEPING, DREAMING, AND STATES IN BETWEEN

by

MARTIN H. STEIN, M.D.

Edited by

BARBARA STIMMEL, Ph.D.

JASON ARONSON INC.
Northvale, New Jersey
London

10 9 8 7 6 5 4 3 2 1

Library of Congress Cataloging-in-Publication Data

Stein, Martin H.
Consciousness redux : waking, sleeping, dreaming, and states in between : by Martin H. Stein, M.D. / Barbara Stimmel, editor
p. cm.
Includes bibliographical references and index.
ISBN 0-7657-0119-7 (alk. paper)
1. Psychoanalysis. 2. Psychoanalytic counseling. 3. Psychoanalytic interpretation. 4. Consciousness. 5. Stein, Martin H. I. Stimmel, Barbara. II. Title.
BF175.S6615 1998
150.19'5—DC21 97-24498

Printed in the United States of America on acid free paper. Jason Aronson offers books and cassettes. For information and catalog write to Jason Aronson Inc., 230 Livingston Street, Northvale, New Jersey 07647-1731. Or visit our website: http://www.aronson.com

Contents

Contributors

Kathy Berkman, M.D.: Assistant Clinical Professor of Psychiatry, Mt. Sinai School of Medicine; Member, New York Psychoanalytic Institute

Frances Cohen, M.D.: Faculty, New York Psychoanalytic Institute

Emily Flint, CSW: Training and Supervising Analyst, Past President, The New York Freudian Society

Manuel Furer, M.D.: Training and Supervising Analyst, Chairman of Educational Committee, New York Psychoanalytic Institute

Marianne Goldberger, M.D.: Clinical Professor of Psychiatry, NYU School of Medicine; Training and Supervising Analyst, The Psychoanalytic Institute, NYU Medical Center

Milton Horowitz, M.D.: Clinical Professor of Psychiatry, NYU School of Medicine; Training and Supervising Analyst, New York Psychoanalytic Institute

Martin H. Stein, M.D.: Training and Supervising Analyst, New York Psychoanalytic Institute

Barbara Stimmel, Ph.D.: Assistant Clinical Professor of Psychiatry, Mt. Sinai School of Medicine; Training and Supervising Analyst, The New York Freudian Society; Associate Secretary, International Psychoanalytical Association; Chair, North American IPA Groups

Introduction

Barbara Stimmel

There are many pleasures in being a psychoanalyst. The privilege of accompanying a person on the profound and illuminating voyage through psychic time and space that is psychoanalysis ranks highest. But there are other relationships and trips that take place in our profession, filled as it is with questioners and navigators, and these have their own rewards. Our friendships, intellectual and personal, with our teachers and mentors provide us with signposts as we make our way through the galaxy of the mind. Martin Stein is one of the quiet but brilliant and revered teachers who has left us a legacy in the classroom and the literature to help guide us on our way.

I begin this introduction with a simple story that demonstrates the generative nature of a true teacher. I met Martin at a party some years ago and I was delighted to learn that he would be my dinner partner. I thought his papers were gems, and his reputation as an erudite and charming conversationalist had preceded him. What I was not yet aware of was his genuine interest in others and his continually probing mind. We soon were talking about a paper of mine, which I was having trouble bringing to light, mostly because it was my first. It was about the written dream. Martin was interested and insightful, and whether or not he intended this to be so, he became my private and immediate ego ideal as a writer. He generously offered to read my paper. I was honored and excited but very nervous. Martin returned my paper to me (a virtual stranger) within two weeks with thoughtful comments containing additions, corrections, and praise. There was now no turning back; I was on the road to authorship. Here was a psychoanalyst/teacher who had—by treating as a commonplace event the writing and publishing of a paper—indirectly and without interpretation helped me work through a classic writing block. He entered the world of my transference figures and I finished working through my conflict with him at my side.

This book is my way of saying thank you.

When considering how to go about doing this, my first thought was a festschrift—papers in honor *of* Martin. We have some wonderful examples on our shelves. But one of Martin's qualities that makes him such a valued colleague is his modesty. He had never published a collection of his own papers. When I realized this I knew that such a book would be a gift not only *for* Martin but also for the rest of us. These papers exemplify Martin's literacy, his incisiveness, and his unusual ability to write beautifully. When read together they produce a lovely tapestry of psychoanalytic thought and wisdom.

There are other people for whom Martin served as an ideal and as a friend. The only way our ego ideals become self—rather than other—representations is through identification and ultimately doing ourselves, and alone, what our ideals appear to do with such ease. It helps us to realize that nothing worth doing is easy and it helps us understand that ideals are meant to be replaced with the ordinary stuff of life. So the other contributors and I would put a book together that would reflect what Martin seems to do so effortlessly—teach and write. We would start by writing about him and his work.

This book begins with short memoirs of three of Martin's students. I invited Kathy Berkman, Frances Cohen, and Emily Flint to write of their experiences under Martin's tutelage. Three of Martin's closest collaborators (Manuel Furer, Marianne Goldberger, and Milton Horowitz) have written short essays introducing their favorite papers of his. These introductions honor Martin and simultaneously offer the reader a glimpse into how his papers inspire others to write and teach. I took the editor's prerogative to reserve for myself two papers to introduce; it should be no surprise that they are the ones about analysts who write and those who don't!

This book includes fifteen of Martin's twenty-four papers. He and I spent some time trying to decide which to include and which to leave out. That conversation alone was worth the doing of the book. Martin's review of his ideas and his ways of presenting them was an instruction in how to be self-critical while retaining a sense of humor about things we wish we had done otherwise. I disagreed with him only insofar as I thought *all* his papers were worthy of inclusion, but his wishes limited us to those presented here.

I save for last a description of the chapter I invited Martin to write: a personal reflection on his life as a clinician and writer. I knew that the book would be enhanced and the reader delighted with a look into the life and mind of this analytic scholar. And he, in his characteristically modest but challenging way, presented me with another paper. It is a kind of summary of what interests him most: the study of consciousness in all its forms. Happily, Martin included a few of his personal experiences.

The introduction to this book is short because the papers speak for themselves. And because Martin has so much to say.

Personal Thoughts

Getting Started

Frances Cohen

My first supervision with Martin Stein took place on a Saturday, in Katonah, New York, after I had insisted upon talking with him before meeting my new analytic patient. Martin greeted me at the train station wearing jeans and drove me to the house to which I would return so happily, a decade later, as a friend. Over coffee and a bagel, he told me that with any luck the patient would be more anxious about beginning the analysis than I was. A few weeks later, I started in earnest working with Martin in his office in Manhattan on East 96th Street, where I arrived one afternoon proudly announcing that my new analytic couch had just been delivered. Martin replied, "Wear it in good health." This was my introduction to Martin's marvelous wry wit, which not only enlivened his teaching but conveyed the mixture of warmth, humor, and charm that characterize his style.

Being supervised by Martin was an education in and of itself. I learned a tremendous amount about analysis and about other things as well. I read or reread bits of history and literature to which references came up in the clinical work or in our discussions, ranging from ancient Greece to Kafka's *Metamorphosis*. It was the beginning of my understanding that psychoanalysis would be a continuing education not only in depth psychology but in other subjects and aspects of life that I would not have encountered under other circumstances. Listening to Martin, I understood that the more I knew about a great variety of subjects, the more I would bring to the understanding of patients. We talked about psychoanalytic theory clinically applied, but my growing knowledge was inseparable from what I learned in Martin's course on dreams. This was a very different but equally important learning experience with Martin, complete with a superb white wine on the evening the class struggled to figure out Chapter VII of *The Interpretation of Dreams*.

Probably the most important thing I learned from my years as Martin's supervisee was what it means to think analytically: how to follow a train of associations, how to derive meaning, how to think about transference and countertransference, how to observe, and when to interpret resistance and defense. But I also got a sense of how Martin worked: that nothing was accepted without further thought, that every statement raised the possibility of its opposite, that no human experience was without conflict. His mind always operated with subtlety, complexity, and an enormous tolerance for ambiguity. One of the clearest examples of this was a continuing discussion we had over the years about a patient's use of reasonableness—not rationalization—as a defense.

There were hard lessons at times, such as when I hoped to hide behind silence some period of confusion and the inability to understand my patient. Martin told me that it was just as much a mistake not to say something that needed to be said as to say something that should not have been said. My inevitable growing pains in dealing with my inexperience, beginner's ignorance, and countertransference were met by Martin with respect, patience, and humor. All this, coupled with his enthusiasm for my progress, made the difficult parts as painless as possible, and the enjoyment substantial. (An occasional excellent piece of dark chocolate from Martin's desk drawer didn't hurt either.) Martin always conveyed the necessity of a sensible view of what we were doing—that the analytic understanding should never depart from connection to the practical world. When a patient was behaving in a potentially self-destructive way, Martin showed me that not vigorously addressing this was taking just as much of an action as doing so; it was only action of a different kind.

Near the end of the years of supervision, there was a time when several difficult events took place in my life, including a personal illness and a death in my family. Martin was particularly generous and kind. He gave me some wise advice and was tenacious in the face of my initial reluctance to accept his help. I will always be grateful. Looking back, I can understand now, in a way that I could not have at the time, how every single aspect of the supervisory experience, not just the discussion of the patient, conveys something about how the supervisor analyzes patients. At the end of this time, Martin declared me ready to work on my own. It was with considerable reluctance that I agreed to this, and only with the promise that our relationship would continue, as it has to this day, as friends.

A Supervisory Moment

Kathy Berkman

Late in 1991, somewhere around the mid-point of my psychoanalytic training, I was trying hard to establish a small population of supervised cases when a colleague called to refer a patient. My advisor asked if I would like Martin Stein as a supervisor for the case, and I leapt at the chance. I had read and greatly admired Dr. Stein's seminal paper, "The Unobjectional Part of the Transference" during my residency, and several years later, I had heard him discuss writing about clinical material at the New York Psychoanalytic Institute. His plain-spoken mode of delivery had impressed me, as had the acuity of his thinking and his ability to use irony and humor to elucidate complex points. Besides that, I had heard his name mentioned in so many contexts for so long, I was very curious to see what this man would be like up close.

My would-be patient agreed to a trial analysis despite having responded to hearing my name from the consultant with the query, "Don't you have any men?" My reaction was to arrange a meeting with Dr. Stein as quickly as possible. At my first supervision appointment, and every time thereafter, he buzzed me into his trim, spare waiting room, and at precisely the time of my hour, he emerged from his office and ushered me in. He was dressed for business and for warmth in wool tweeds, and I was struck by a similarity between him and my long beloved model of literary eloquence, E. B. White. With eyes enlarged by magnifying lenses, he peered at me, and shook my hand with some formality. I followed him inside and he sat down on a sheepskin-covered rocker in the far corner of his compact consulting room. He invited me to sit nearby in the kind of chair often found in a professor's office, black and gold painted wood, but in this case, absent the university insignia. His library, or the part of it housed in his office, contained works of classical literature and reference books—writer's tools, I surmised. The room was made cozy by its smallness and the tastefulness of its appointments; a vase of flowers decorated the top of his antique desk.

Without much ado, he asked me to tell him what I knew of the patient and what I understood about what I knew. The patient had already reported a dream during the initial interview, and I was happy to offer it up to Dr. Stein.

Together we made some preliminary hypotheses. He predicted the patient would be difficult, and I was relieved to be in the company of a clinician who had had a lifetime of experience.

Unfortunately, it soon became obvious that there were not very many unobjectionable parts in this particular patient's transference. The case got stormy early; the patient was either excruciatingly tedious or stonily silent and my own thinking was made murky with the admixture of frustration and fear of failure. But Dr. Stein remained stalwart in the face of it all. His early prediction turned out to be an understatement, and he later revised his initial impression from difficult to impossible—freely acknowledging that he had never actually seen a patient like this himself. Intermittently, he inquired as to whether I wanted to continue with the patient. He never took a position, and I could tell he was being respectful of my feelings and my judgment, although I wondered at times whether he wished I would call it a day and deliver us both from the problems posed by this patient.

Matters were further complicated by the fact that during this early period, I had been grappling with an illness, the treatment for which caused me to lose my hair. I hadn't mentioned it to Dr. Stein, having begun supervision with him when I was already wearing a wig. Several months later, I arrived at his office sporting a half-inch of my own hair. "New hairdo?" he inquired without inflection. I told him the story, and he asked what had transpired with my patients. "No one said anything," I replied with defensive nonchalance. And then I remembered that the patient I'd been presenting to him had been furious with me when he first saw me without the wig, claiming I'd gotten a "radical haircut" because I was too self-centered to care what he would think. Periodically, Dr. Stein revisited the hair business, inquiring about my patients' reactions and inferring explanations for their responses, and each time, I felt irritated with him anew for bringing it up. I had not wanted to attend to it, but it was there in the patient material, and he knew it. We discussed the fact that the patient he was supervising, as well as quite a few others, must have sensed that something was wrong and had been afraid to broach it to me. He encouraged me to look for evidence of this in dreams and associations and to respond more directly to the patients. When I was able to make more appropriate interventions, Dr. Stein suggested I write a paper about my patients' unconscious awareness of my altered state via their veiled references to hair. His method of helping me with the painful subject of my illness was to find something creative for me to do about it.

He counseled directness, honesty, and tact, only infrequently using his own clinical experiences to exemplify the point, preferring to have me provide the examples. Once, however, when we were having a discussion about the problems inherent in receiving gifts from patients, he clearly stated that not accepting a small gift is hurtful. "On the other hand," he said, in a rare instance of reminiscing out loud, "there was the time a patient offered me his entire pornography collection. I just couldn't accept it." He seemed amused by the recollection.

As a supervisor, Dr. Stein was generally all business, but in spite of the terseness of his style and the formality of his demeanor, I always suspected the persistence of a subtle playfulness, seemingly born out of the great elasticity of his mind. As a requirement for my graduation from the institute, he asked me to write a final summary on my difficult patient. In my concluding paragraph I elaborated on what I had learned, particularly about resistance, and expressed my gratitude for having had the opportunity to work with such a challenging young man. "Don't you think you've poured it on a bit thick?" he wryly asked when he read it. Of course he was right, and when I rewrote that paragraph, I found myself chuckling about the manner in which he'd pointed it out to me.

As it turned out, the real opportunity was to have worked with Martin Stein for two and a half years, and it is an experience I will not forget. He enhanced the clarity of my thinking, deepened my empathy for patients, and broadened my knowledge of literature and the arts, with all the "elements of style" E. B. White described so evocatively in his manual for writers.

Teaching and Learning

Emily M. Flint

"Above all he was curious, 'with child'—as he himself put it—to see every strange thing—avid for knowledge and ready to seek for it anywhere, for his was a liberal genius." This description of the seventeenth century diarist Samel Pepys in a biography by Arthur Bryant seems to me to apply also to Martin Stein, a scholar of Pepys's diaries and a man whose far-ranging interests have taken him beyond the confines of the psychoanalytic literature. He is a superb teacher of psychoanalysis because he is interested in everything having to do with the human condition and the way the mind works, and he cares deeply about sharing his interests and knowledge with those who want to learn.

I knew Martin first as a friend and then as a teacher, as leader of a seminar for non-medical analysts on the clinical use of dreams, as a consultant and advisor when I prepared to teach the Dream Theory course for the New York Freudian Society, and as an occasional consultant on a difficult case. In all of these roles he is wholly there with the learner, quiet, listening with an intensity and focus that makes one hear and think differently about the material being discussed and about the person whose material it is. I think of Martin's way of silence as similar to the silences in Mozart's music, giving the repose to hear what has gone before and the time to prepare for what is to come.

In a study group with Martin as leader one is always aware of his superb capacity for free-floating attention and his ability to zero in on what is most important. I recall many times listening to material being presented and wondering how we would be able to learn from it. But Martin was never at a loss to find the point at which teaching and learning converge.

As he listens to dream material Martin encourages more than just getting to the latent meaning behind manifest content. He is always asking "What does this dream tell us that we did not know before? Why is the patient having this dream at this particular moment in the treatment?" Never taken as an isolated phenomenon, a dream is thought of within the context of a particular session and within a particular period in an analysis. This contextual view leads one to see a patient's progression of dreams as a way of charting the progression of analysis. This way of working with dreams made the Stein seminar a place where cases could be followed with the group over a long period of time. As one experienced participant put it, "It's the best supervision one could have."

With Martin as teacher one comes to realize that his knowledge of the world and human experience informs all that he hears and reacts to; he is a walking storehouse of the material that comprises what Harold Bloom calls the Western Canon. The Bible, Shakespeare, other literature and historical writing, art: all are there for him to call on when needed. I remember on one occasion when a patient's dream seemed clearly to be making use of a particularly dramatic operatic reference, although this did not appear in the patient's associations. Not suggesting in any way that our association to the scene from *Rigoletto* be superimposed on the patient's dream, our recognizing this dream source led to a useful piece of interpretative work on the dream.

Martin Stein embodies the concept of the analyst as one who remembers and contains what the patient has brought before and relates it to what is currently active in the analysis. It was touching to know even after I had left the seminar because of my teaching schedule that Martin remembered in great detail a patient whose material I had presented and would occasionally invite me back as a guest participant. His interest in and knowledge of this difficult patient helped tide me over some very rough times in the treatment. At particularly critical moments I would go to Martin for consultation, always finding him attuned and astute.

Through working with Martin Stein as seminar leader and consultant on clinical work and on my own teaching I have developed deep respect for him as a psychoanalytic educator who believes that all who are committed to learning psychoanalysis should have access to the best in the field, whether they are students in his own institute or from some other group. At a time when the divide between medical and non-medical psychoanalysis was even greater than it is today, Martin accepted those who were serious students, regardless of background, and taught with his full capacity. He not only taught about the use of the dream in a clinical setting, he exemplified what it means to be a teacher.

Reminiscence

Martin H. Stein

" . . . the property of being conscious or not is in the last resort our one beacon-light in the darkness of depth psychology"
—Freud, *The Ego and the Id*

In looking over these papers of mine, written over a period of forty years, I have become aware of the persistent theme that reflects my long-standing interests. My first psychoanalytic paper was entitled "Premonition as a Defense"; my latest, so far unfinished, is an attempt to deal with the controversial topic of intuition. I have been preoccupied with shifting levels of consciousness as observed in the analytic situation and in dreams, with illustrations ranging from classical Greek writings about the vicissitudes of transference, the operations of conscience, and the nature of character, especially as it determines modes of conflict solution. I seem always to have returned to my primary question, "How conscious are we at any moment of time and how does this affect our thoughts, feelings, and actions?"

As I wondered what led me to preoccupy myself with questions about consciousness and reality, I recalled a vivid memory from childhood, when I was eight or thereabouts. Walking back from school one day, in a somewhat abstracted state, I asked myself whether the world I experienced was real, with an existence independent of myself, or whether it was, like a dream, the product of my own imagination. I had never heard of Freud, much less Plato, being at the time an avid reader of boys' adventure stories such as G. A. Henty (*With Clive in India, With Nelson at Trafalgar*), a practice that did nothing to encourage introspection.

Nevertheless, I put my question to the test. I tried by force of will to change the location of a building across the street. Even after my most strenuous efforts, it hadn't moved an inch, and I accepted the fact that the world did indeed exist outside myself and I was not its creator. I can still visualize the street on which my experiment took place. Did it occur as I remembered it? Was it a screen memory or perhaps the recall of a dream? I can't say. It was at any rate a profound blow to my infantile narcissism and a good thing for my future sense of reality.

Later, I realized that the question and my naive solution must have been part of the experience of many latency children. Eventually, I became aware that such preoccupations had been the subject of philosophical discourse for thousands of years. Whether my memory is literally accurate or not, I do associate with that experience my persistent curiosity about reality sense, external or psychic, along with my interest in levels of consciousness and dreaming; distinguishing between what we have perceived by way of external sensation, from what we have experienced from within, "outer" from "inner," is the essence of reality testing. In other words, "How awake was I when I saw or heard that?"

It seems altogether appropriate that Freud, after his experience with Charcot, should have become interested in hypnotism, but fortunately for us, he was not very good at it. Had he been able to relieve his patients of their hysterical symptoms as the French master had done so dramatically, he might have achieved a successful practice earlier. No doubt, the history of the treatment of neurosis and the future of psychology and psychopathology would have been very different.

Freud's failure to achieve results led him to develop the technique of free association and so conduct an intensive study of levels of consciousness and their role not only in psychopathology but in day-to-day human behavior as well. His observations of Charcot's spectacular demonstrations and his investigations of his own and his patients' dreams finally convinced him of the existence and importance of unconscious mental processes and contents and to build a hypothesis that would enable him to organize his data in a useful way.

Even though the structural model proved to be far more inclusive and explanatory, the topographic remains alive in the thinking and discussion of many analysts today. To these, an exclusive emphasis on ego psychology tends to result in failure to give sufficient attention to variations in attention and consciousness and their effects on mental processes and behavior. While the structural model does indeed represent a more sophisticated and inclusive hypothesis, it may not be sufficient for all our needs. Many analysts, including myself, keep the topographic in mind for the occasions when it answers the questions we pose.

It is true that viewing the mental apparatus through the medium of the topographic model is only one among the several ways of making sense of our observations; it was the earliest of Freud's attempts to understand the human psyche. Even though the idea of unconscious mental operations had been thought of by earlier psychologists, it was his publication of *The Interpretation of Dreams* that made sense of it. Freud's later work, especially on the defenses, is clearly foreshadowed in *The Interpretation of Dreams*. Nothing could have been accomplished in psychoanalytic practice and theory without understanding the vicissitudes of consciousness, neither *The Ego and the Id* nor the work of Anna Freud, Klein, Hartmann, and everyone who has advanced the subtle understanding of the human mind.

That so much of our mental apparatus is inaccessible to us and at the same time influences, even determines, what we feel and think and do, remains a profound blow to our narcissism. It is never superfluous to remember that the publication of *The Interpretation of Dreams* had an effect on our own view of ourselves comparable to the impacts of Darwin and Marx. It has pervaded modern culture, at least in the West. Understandably, not everyone is pleased.

Certainly, hardly any analysts deny the existence and importance of the "unconscious" as an "agency," or if not that, they agree that much of mental life goes on outside of awareness. Still, I have the impression that even analysts may tend to underestimate the role of changes in levels of consciousness in evaluating our observations of psychic processes and behavior, both in everyday life and in psychoanalytic treatment. The terms *conscious*, *preconscious*, and *unconscious* identify systems in an abstract theoretical model and are quite different from *awake*, *daydreaming*, and *asleep*, which are descriptive and readily observed by anyone.

Clinical reports often describe in detail reactions to interpretation without furnishing a description of the patient's state of consciousness at the time, for example, whether fully alert or rather sleepy, listening carefully and critically, or absorbed in a daydream. Was the patient at a particular time alert or in a state of lesser awareness, perhaps sleepy, which may be characterized as a regression of ego functions, such as impairment of reality testing and critical judgment? It makes a difference.

Ideas achieved and expressed under varying levels of consciousness have varying levels of significance. It is perfectly normal, for example, to hallucinate while asleep, in other words, to dream; it is something else entirely to see visions and believe in them while fully awake. Consciousness is not divided sharply into three distinct states; we do not travel abruptly from unconscious to preconscious to full consciousness. Rather, we traverse a continuum with any number of intermediate steps.

Going to sleep is itself a complex process, more so for some of us than others. During the earliest, hypnogogic period, we experience all sorts of intermediate stages with fleeting images and thoughts, some logical, some bizarre; we are more or less aware of outside stimuli, until swiftly or gradually we fall into a deep slumber during which we may be aware of nothing. Again, as we awaken, we recall and edit dreams, hear the voice or voices of conscience, if we are so inclined, perhaps mistake the sound of the alarm for something else entirely, and only gradually interpret our perceptions accurately. Sometimes this takes place only after the first cup of coffee, if then.

Once wide awake, we go through our days in states of varying alertness, often interspersed with more or less "dreamy" periods, during which we may be engaged in idle fantasy or more productively in creative imagination. We are for all practical purposes more or less awake all day, sometimes fully so, sometimes close to sleep. Our degree of awareness of the outside world varies from time to time, not necessarily in abrupt steps but often incrementally. In topographic terms, we shift between the dominance of the systems Preconscious and Conscious; in descriptive terms, from being wide awake to daydreaming to sleep. We observe these shifts in consciousness most directly in our work with analytic patients on the couch, who often act out sleep rituals as they begin, adjusting the towel, taking off an article of clothing, yawning, even mentioning how sleepy they are. This is often followed by variations in the levels of consciousness throughout the session.

This phenomenon is very common and very striking in patients who have been subjected to general anesthesia in childhood. They tend to reenact on the couch the variations of consciousness associated with that experience, along with sadomasochistic, eroticized fantasies originally stimulated by the surgeon and now expressed in the transference.

For example, a young woman patient, while seemingly perfectly alert, reacted to an interpretation by claiming that she was totally unaware of what I had said, would I repeat it please? It was as if she had been somewhere else. In a sense, she had, for she was caught up with a daydream and was not entirely aware of her surroundings. It took some years to learn the nature of the eroticized images that absorbed her attention during these phases of altered consciousness, in the course of which she became unaware of the outside world, including my presence.

Late in the course of an analysis with another patient, while "working through" before termination, I make an interpretation that I have made a number of times before, in almost the same terms. The patient says, "That's true! But why didn't you tell me that a year ago?" I protest, "But I did, several times." My patient replies, "I don't recall that at all!" Indeed, where was he when I voiced those interpretations? Where was his attention directed—inward perhaps?

This phenomenon must be familiar to anyone who has attempted to get the attention of "normal" adolescents, who may look at first sight as if they were wide awake to their surroundings but are in fact absorbed in fantasy. We have the sense that they are inhabiting a different world with its own rules; when they seem not to hear, they are likely to be listening to other voices, as if in a dream. Yet when the phone rings, they become almost preternaturally alert, thoroughly wide awake to the call of the outside world.

In the analytic situation, other evidence of shifting levels of consciousness is familiar enough. A patient spends the session in bitter attacks on my character, ineptitude, and motives; at the end of the session, she gets up from the couch, smiles most charmingly, and wishes me a good weekend, apparently quite sincerely. It is as if I had been observing two different persons, one awake, one dreaming (Jekyll and Hyde?). The period on the couch represents something akin to a dissociated state. When I describe her behavior to her, she reacts with surprise, as if she had been totally unaware of it. After this, however, it becomes easier for her to express her transference conflicts and fantasies in other, more explicit ways. In a sense, her open attacks had been made during a time when she could imagine herself asleep and dreaming. Like a dreamer, she did not think of herself as altogether responsible for her disturbing thoughts. They belonged to another person, the dreamer. She could put them aside and once again became a friendly young woman. Pointing out her dissociation is the kind of interpretation that "awakens" (as Lewin would say) the patient to a higher, more rational level of consciousness.

Another familiar manifestation of shifting levels of consciousness in patients on the couch consists of momentary feelings of unreality and depersonalization. These can occur in almost anyone under the press of anxiety and unless frequent or severe have little sinister significance and are not necessarily of a psychotic nature. They bear a close resemblance to hypnogogic and dream states, when one is in a sense "outside oneself."

The most extreme change of consciousness in the analytic session is exemplified by falling asleep on the couch. Aside from leaving the treatment altogether, sleep on the couch often constitutes the most dramatic resistance to analyzing. The sleeping patient may awaken spontaneously in a few seconds or minutes or require active intervention by loud speech or otherwise. Occasionally, he or she will mention dreaming but generally has no recollection of the content. I remember best a middle-aged professional man suffering from a depression. My attempt to analyze him was not successful; this was before the days of safe and effective antidepressant medications. Leo Stone has also reported on this phenomenon (his patient, like mine, was quite ill). While it is difficult to confirm, the context of serious depression in these cases gives some support to the speculation that the underlying archaic fantasy was one of joining the analyst in death, the ultimate sleep in the heavenly womb.

Another manifestation of the variability of consciousness is the "creative frenzy" of certain artists visited by the Muse. Samuel Taylor Coleridge, Edgar Allan Poe, and Allen Ginsberg easily come to mind. But many examples abound of artistic activity occurring during altered states of consciousness. The outside world is for the moment shut out and another person takes over, as if it were the dreamer.[1]

[1]The analysts who have contributed most to my understanding of this variable in the psychoanalytic situation have been Otto Isakower and Bertram Lewin. Lewin, particularly, pointed out that the analyst, through his interventions, could raise or lower the patient's state of consciousness (like a hypnotist!).

I have previously suggested and continue to exhort that we devote more interest to variations in the consciousness of the analyst and their effects on his or her work. Sleepiness is far from uncommon even though, if we admit it at all, it is with a certain degree of embarrassment. We are tempted to ascribe our reaction to boredom, implying a profound expression of hostility and withdrawal. It may be the product of some primary response to a disturbance in our own personal lives, having to do with the patient only insofar as something he stands for arouses deep conflict in us. Sometimes it is primarily a response to frustration with a patient who is simply not doing as well as we expect, thus threatening our professional skills and devotion to our work.

Aside from actually falling asleep (which is a serious lapse), sleepiness of the analyst can be a valuable signal, not only for understanding something going on in his mind but also in the detection and analysis of profound transference reactions in the patient. These may consist, for example, in powerful erotic urges, a desire to "sleep with the analyst," more often than not combined with murderous wishes, constituting a kind of Liebestod fantasy, and variations on that theme. The analyst may react to these powerful transferences by sleepiness, "psychic flight," denial, or more appropriately, by forcing him- or herself to face the source of his or her reactions to the patient's transference resistance and deal with them analytically.[2]

But episodes of sleepiness that I have observed in myself and have been reported to me by candidates in supervision (most often by the more gifted and, correspondingly, more candid ones) can occur with a patient who is interesting and not manifestly in a state of severe resistance. In several instances, this reaction turned out to be a response to the hardly perceived (preconscious?) sense of a powerful transference conflict in the patient, producing an echo in me. In the case I reported, the patient "charmed" me into a state of altered consciousness, a few seconds of sleep. It was in many respects the *opposite* of boredom. Embarrassing though this lapse had been, it was to play a useful role in teaching me to understand and put to use variations in my own levels of alertness, especially in the detection of profound transference and countertransference conflicts.

A colleague related the following account of a few sessions in the analysis of a young woman.

> The patient talked somewhat provocatively; that was not unusual, but it produced in me an overwhelming desire to sleep. I could not resist it and fell asleep

---

[2]I heard from a respected colleague many years ago that before the visits of one of his patients, he felt it necessary to take a small dose of Valium. I think he worked out a better solution eventually by returning to his analyst.

for perhaps a minute or two. I awoke and remembered a dream: I saw a slip of paper introduced under the door of my office. It was the slips of paper my patient often brought in to remind her of things she meant to talk about. I don't know if she noticed my lapse. The session continued as before.

The next day the patient began to talk in a mumbling, incoherent way. I could hardly make out the words. She fell asleep and woke up a moment later, saying that she had a dream, which she couldn't recall. She then became much more coherent and began to produce memories of childhood. At the age of five she used to sleep with her older brother. She liked the sense of warmth coming from him. (She did not mention sexual play or explicit excitement.) The patient seems not to have been aware of my lapse of consciousness, of my having "slept with her" the day before.

Freud, in one of his inspired asides, described "Conscious" as "a sense organ for the perception of psychic qualities." Consciousness, from this aspect, is the lens through which we see all we can see of the inner (and outer) world of our experience. It is vital that we remain aware of the nature of that lens, its power, and its capacity for distortion. Consciousness is only one variable, but an essential one, in evaluating reactions to interpretation, the significance of memories, and, more broadly, understanding the infinite vagaries of human behavior. It cannot stand alone, but without taking it into account, all our other findings become devoid of meaning.

In the ordinary course of events I should have been an internist or pediatrician. My father had died of tuberculosis when I was six, resulting in a good deal of maternal anxiety and some excellent medical supervision. My mother took me to be seen by a distinguished pulmonologist with a discreetly fashionable office on the Upper East Side of Manhattan. He struck me as wise, kind, and reassuring. It was he who served as my first model of the ideal physician. Why then did I become a psychoanalyst? And why so interested in levels of consciousness?

In childhood I had some vivid dreams that I never forgot and that I recall from time to time. Even before I was analyzed, I sensed that they had to do with my father's death and my sense of guilt. They were so clear that it required no great sophistication to perceive that much. My father had been a dentist and I, not being satisfied with my fatal conquest, would outdo him professionally by becoming an M.D. (Am I merely filling cavities in the human psyche, after all?)

In the course of my youth and medical training, I discovered, first, that I was interested in the human psyche; second, that I had an intuitive sense of psychiatric diagnosis; and, third, that some people, like Freud and various friends of mine, seemed to have some pretty interesting ideas about personality. Finally, since I myself was not a paragon of normality (whatever that might mean), I hoped a personal analysis would help.

Following the lead of an admired friend, I applied to the New York Psychoanalytic Institute. I began my career, first as a wild and eventually not quite a tame but rather, I hope, a disciplined analyst enjoying my work and learning all the time. I found the systematic analysis of dreams especially fascinating. And as so often happens, in spite of my attempts to keep this aspect of analysis in perspective, my patients dreamed a lot and I did nothing to discourage them.

I could in those days make a reasonable living, spending my days in work with, for the most part, intelligent and interesting if troubled men and women. Now, at the twilight of my professional career, I remain grateful for the privilege.

1

Premonition as a Defense

This fragment of an analysis is presented because it demonstrates a dramatic type of defense against guilt. The experience of premonition has been of interest to analysts ever since Freud described the relationship between telepathic experiences and unconscious wishes.[1] There is no attempt here to study the phenomenon of telepathy, the experience in question having occurred some two years before the analytic session to be reported, but in this case the patient's belief that he had had a real premonition was of the greatest significance in his life because it averted a serious depression.

A twenty-two-year-old man began his analysis three months before the session I am reporting. He was intelligent and highly educated without, however, much knowledge of analytic process or theory. He had spent his life in another city and came to New York ostensibly to continue his academic education but actually to seek analytic help. His most disturbing symptom was vomiting which had been present throughout his life. This became much worse after his father's death two years before. It occurred whenever he was excited in any way, particularly in anticipation of any sort of pleasure; for example, going to the theater or to a party. He was able to tolerate only very bland foods, eggs and milk making up a large part of his diet. In addition, he had for many years sexual fantasies having to do with kissing the ears of partners, most often males. There had been no overt homosexual or heterosexual activity. He had had considerable experience in the theater and radio. In the ordinary sense, he was not at all superstitious or credulous; quite the reverse.

He began his analysis in mid-June. The first few weeks dealt with anamnestic material, and in addition there were a number of dreams revealing thinly disguised oedipal fantasies, in elaborate dramatic settings derived from his experience in the theater. One dream demonstrated clearly his castration fantasy and its reversal by oral incorporation of a professor's (my) penis in the form of a dinner at my home.

---

[1]Freud: *Dreams and Telepathy* (1922). *Coll. Papers*, IV.

Eight weeks before the dream, which is the subject of this paper, I began a three-week vacation. He showed little overt reaction to this interruption, maintaining that it offered him a needed opportunity to visit his home and settle some affairs.

Two weeks before this session he began to feel rather depressed and he wept without apparent cause on several occasions while alone in his room at night. On October 15th he reported the following dream.

> I was walking along a road with a friend and I saw many scorpions which threatened us. I noticed their ribs and their big tails. I was afraid of them. In a second scene, I was going through the private papers of my sister-in-law. I felt very guilty about it and was afraid to be caught. It was in my father's den. Scene three: I was coming to your office for an appointment. It was very late at night, an unusual hour. You were meeting me because of some difficulties at radio station WQXR, which was somehow combined with WNEW. I arrived, and I lay on what looked like an operating table, or something of the sort. I was nude. You looked at a rash I had on my skin and scraped a little bit of it with a small measuring spoon. You said to me, "You are too thin; you need a Martini cocktail and two Scotches to help cure you." I went downstairs where there were ambulances and fire engines going back and forth. My brother Robert was somehow involved. Robert was going somewhere because our uncle's mother-in-law died.

His companion in the dream was a man whose father had been lost when the Athenia had been torpedoed early in the war. The son had been saved and my patient's comment at this time was, "He must somehow have felt responsible." The patient's sister-in-law, Helen, the wife of an older brother, had revealed a grasping character in dealing with his father's estate. My office, which was also the radio station, had been illuminated in the dream by curious flashing lights. The unusual hour of our appointment, not long before dawn, reminded him of a movie he had seen, *Dead of Night*, a film which told the story of a man who experienced a complicated three-part dream. At the end of the film the protagonist, on awakening, begins to experience in reality what he had dreamed the night before. In one episode a young man had a vision of a hearse and was thus forewarned of an accident which could have caused his own death had he not heeded the premonition. One of the characters in the movie was a psychiatrist.

At this point the patient remembered the significance of the date, October 15th, the day of the session I report. It was the anniversary of the date on which, two years earlier, his father had the cerebral accident which led to his death. Early that morning my patient had had a dream in which he saw his mother riding in a black ambulance. He awoke and thinks he noted the time:

five a.m. A few hours later he received a telephone call from his mother, informing him that his father had indeed fallen ill during the night and had been sent to the hospital at about five a.m. He believed this dream to be a premonition of his father's illness and death.

Some months after his father's death, a friend, in a casual conversation, mentioned the theory that all dreams somehow express wishes. The patient remembered thinking to himself: "This was not true of my dream. That was really a premonition—not a wish."

Some other aspects of the analytic dream now became clear. The radio station was not only my office, but that of his father, who had been a radiologist. WNEW referred to the "new" father, myself, as WQXR was the old. The Martini cocktail referred to my name, as the Scotch referred to his father's ancestry. Both involved an attempt at oral incorporation as a defense against overwhelming castration fears.

The scorpions have a special interest. They have a poisonous tail, which fact refers to his own unconscious fantasies of being poisoned through incorporation of his father's penis. Their ribs reminded him of the only way in which he had mourned his father. He had never wept for him nor experienced very much grief. He was kept very busy dealing with the estate. Three weeks after the death, however, he had a severe attack of shingles, causing him excruciating pain in the thorax, accompanied by a rash.

The relationship of the analytic dream to the one he had had two years before now becomes clear. The analytic dream says: "My first dream was the appointment with death in the *Dead of Night* and must have been truly premonitory. It was transmitted to my perceptions by the actual event of my father's illness, as a radio broadcast is transmitted from WQXR to my receiving set. If this is so, then I can deny successfully that I wish for and brought about my father's death. Therefore, I need not suffer death myself."

Following this interpretation of the dream, he recalled the day residue which had preceded the original dream of his father's death. The evening before, he had taken leave of his father at a railroad station as the latter was returning to his home in a suburb. He had noticed that his father's speech was awkward, a symptom which had not impressed him consciously but which he must have linked to the cerebral thrombosis. Eight weeks before his father had suffered an illness marked by transient aphasia. This was indicated in the dream by "difficulties at radio station WQXR." During the few months before his father's death he had, for the first time, established some degree of intimacy with him and they had had long talks together.

For two years he had avoided depression and averted mourning, and had been able to deny both his hostile wishes and his guilt. This precarious situation had been maintained by a projective mechanism which allowed him to assert, "I did not produce my father's death through a wish in my dream; rather, the dream was communicated to me by that event, or by my father himself out of love for me."

Subsequent analysis emphasized his castration fantasies and his powerful need to incorporate his father's penis, to be the "grasping one" referred to in his dream. In turn, for fear of being swallowed up and destroyed, he had to reject the wish for his father's penis and vomit what he had obtained. We have some idea of the reasons why he was led to solve his problem in this very primitive way. At the time he was born, his mother suffered from one of a series of severe depressions, and the child had suffered real oral deprivation and malnutrition in his early infancy. It is not surprising that his father's death resulted in a conflict which forced him to make the choice between denying his death wishes and his guilt, or facing the suicidal fantasies which would result. Being swallowed represented, on the one hand, punishment for his destructive oral wishes; on the other, the most regressive wish of all—well-fed sleep in the arms of his mother.

The most interesting question here is: Why did the defense mechanism begin to crumble at this time? What allowed the patient to face, although in a disguised way, his original death wishes toward his father? This is only partially explained by the increased intensity of the memory due to the approach of the anniversary. This was, moreover, the second, not the first, such anniversary; but in any case it would account only for the immediate timing of the dream—not altogether for its appearance now. How did the events in the analysis contribute to the emergence of the dangerous wish at this point?

The vacation I had taken so early in his analysis had occurred eight weeks before the patient's dream. This corresponded *exactly* to the interval between his father's first illness and the second, fatal stroke. It seems likely that it was this interruption which started the process culminating in the dream. Here a father surrogate was leaving on a journey, accompanied by incorporative and destructive wishes similar to those he had sent along with his real father. I not only returned but failed to become ill, indeed remained quite the same. His intimate talks with his father occurred only during the last few months of the latter's life. Would the talking, the sign of a similar intimacy with me, result in my death too? Material obtained later in the analysis demonstrated that seduction through speech was extremely important for this man but, if successful, destroyed the object through incorporation.

The fact that this did not occur in reality shook his inner belief in his own magic power to kill. It was with great apprehension that he awaited the significant date, October 15th. Evidently he was able with the more critical portion of his ego to allow the conflict to reach the surface in this dream.

Although all this took place at the beginning of an analysis, before many interpretations could be made, it might nevertheless be considered the patient's first approach to a primitive kind of working through. The process of mourning was instituted only after a kind of reality testing which could be done within the analytic situation.[2] This resulted not from the interpretation of transference, but rather from the experience of transference. Only through the transference could he test the omnipotence of his wishes and become conscious of the nature of his defense. He discovered that he could wish for his father's death, yet find him still alive in me. The dream was an attempt to deny that the projective defense previously effective in averting depression was beginning to break down. This defense had, however, served its purpose by protecting him from depression during a period when such reality testing was impossible. Now, in the transference, he could begin the struggle to discard it. The later course of his analysis made it clear that this had, in fact, occurred, for the recurrence of such anniversaries and interruptions was met far more successfully with relatively little depression.

SUMMARY

A man, who is unable to face wishes for his father's death without intolerable guilt, uses a premonitory experience to deny their existence. Two years later a separation from his analyst, in conjunction with the anniversary of his father's death, precipitates the delayed work of mourning and a dream which illustrates the nature of the defense—a graphic portrayal of projection. The close relationship of the analytic process (working through) to mourning is emphasized.

---

[2]Lewin, Bertram D. *The Psychoanalysis of Elation*. New York: W. W. Norton & Co., 1950.

2

The Cliché: A Phenomenon of Resistance

INTRODUCTION BY MILTON HOROWITZ

Once again, as in the body of his analytic work, Stein touches upon and explains aspects of normality as well as psychopathology. Cliché and jargon in the analytic work divest utterances of precise and personal meaning by presenting both truth and partial denial. The hackneyed phrase or locution can be shared with a wide public, with the analyst, or simply be the patient's private stereotypy which uses words but dismisses meaning. The patient may respond to interpretations as if they were hackneyed concepts that didn't apply to him but were cribbed from a textbook. Stein draws a contrast between such stereotypes used to rob meaning and the reiterations in the process of "working through," which may be rich in affect, giving access to new meaning by the careful retracing of old steps. The relation of cliché to aggressive and sadistic impulse may be seen in mimicry and mockery expressed in the hackneyed. On the other hand, Stein opens a door to viewing the cliché as having the reassuring quality of ritual, suggesting to this reader the possibility of deeper exploration of religious ritual and its clichéd repetitions. This touches upon the use of words for magic. The extraordinary stability and efficiency of certain clichés and their structural qualities may be explored through the concept of the organizing, integrating, and synthetic functions of the ego.

Professor Anton Zijderveld (a sociologist in the path of Durkheim, Weber, and Mannheim) in 1979 published a cultural analysis of *Cliché* subtitled *The Supersedure of Meaning by Function in Modernity*. Zijderveld sees modern society as "cliché-genic" in which the cliché becomes as indispensable to everyday communication as other traditional institutions. We should also remember in reading this paper Hartmann's concept of the energy-sparing qualities of habit and repetition. The cliché can be viewed then as a shorthand leading to *expression* rather than *communication*, that is, asking for affective rather than ideational response, head-nodding in agreement rather than new thought. This aspect of cliché when used by the analyst is an invitation to discipleship, a not inconsiderable problem in the history of psychoanalysis. When this use of cliché for affect-charged head-nodding is introduced in political speech it has the potential for menace.

The cliché[1] is best illustrated by the patient who early in her analysis uses the phrase, "mother-figure." She may be referring to a teacher, a supervisor, or, best of all, to her own mother. The analyst is tempted to exclaim, perhaps with irritation, "For heaven's sake, if you are talking about your mother, why don't you come out and say so?" A good question, the answer to which is the intent of this paper.

For the purposes of this discussion, the concept of the cliché will be expanded to include not only stereotyped words or word groups, but also somewhat broader verbal responses. This borders inevitably on a related phenomenon, the use of jargon by patients in analysis. Jargon in this context may be defined as "the cliché use of technical language."[2] This paper will deal with both cliché in the ordinary sense and jargon, as they appear in the service of resistance.

A usually inhibited young man described in everyday terms a round of sexual pleasures which he had achieved the night before. He continued, "But I was brought up in a referential system, designed toward the assimilation of a Christ pattern." He was referring to an intense sense of sin derived from his religious upbringing. The use of mathematical circumlocutions was an attempt to relieve the sharpness of his guilt. At the same time, as part of his usual analytic behavior, it represented his effort to be intelligent, to compete with me, and to avoid a sense of being inferior or degraded. It also communicated less of his intense emotional conflict than a direct statement.

A specialized, and even more instructive example is that of the expression which *becomes* a cliché in the context of the analytic situation itself. Such a phrase by becoming stereotyped loses the meaning it once had and becomes employed as resistance. It may be based on an early, perhaps premature, interpretation by the analyst,[3] or, as in this case, on some pre-existing knowledge of analysis by the patient.

---

[1]Cliché—"A trite phrase that has lost its precise meaning by iteration; a hackneyed or stereotyped expression" (*Webster International Dictionary*, 2nd Edition, Unabridged). The word is derived from the French *clicher*, to stereotype, and in turn, from the German *klitsch*, a clump or claylike mass, hence, originally to pattern in clay (*Webster's New World Dictionary*, 1955).

[2]A suggestion for which I am indebted to Lionel Trilling.

[3]See below for a discussion of this point.

A young woman, following a year of analysis, had a dream in which she found herself in a compromising situation with an unknown man. Certain features of the setting suggested my office. After her own associations suggested to her that the unknown man was myself, she said, "That man must be you. I guess it means I wanted to sleep with my father." Apparently this was an effective self-interpretation by this intelligent patient.

Yet was it? There were several things wrong. First, the words she used, their phrasing and tone, had occurred and were to occur again dozens of times during a rather long analysis. The expression therefore satisfied the first criterion of the analytic cliché, in that it had become stereotyped *in the context of her analysis*. Second, it was divested of precise meaning as an interpretation. Evidence for this was that it contributed nothing to the immediate progress of the analysis; effective insight was manifested neither by opening up of new material, significant change in the level of anxiety, nor ability to deal with related problems outside the analysis. Nor did it represent a real working through of difficult material. It was as if this dream and her interpretation of it had never occurred. Third, after presenting this stereotyped expression, the patient acted as if she had neatly wrapped up and disposed of the garbage. She left the subject with relief and talked of other things, comfortably, but not very clearly or usefully.

Her ability to do this suggested that, although the cliché had been entirely without value as an interpretation or idea, it had accomplished *something*. Like all analytic maneuvers, it attempted to fulfill a purpose for the patient.

Returning to the example itself, it is not very difficult to deduce the essential meaning of the dream. It represented a thinly-disguised, erotic transference wish. Behind this, again not too deeply concealed, was the infantile wish referring to her father. It is of special interest that during what should have been her latency years, this girl did in fact sleep with her father. She remained rigidly on her side of the double bed and controlled her thoughts strictly to avoid any appearance of sexual excitement. This situation, combined with other external factors, leading to enormous sexual stimulation, must have been overwhelming in its impact on the child. It did produce intractable guilt and a lifelong habit of severe inhibition of fantasy.

When she entered analysis, her greatest fear was that she might fall in love with her physician. The analytic situation represented a repetition of going to bed with her father, a procedure which demanded the highest degree of thought control to avoid overwhelming sexual fantasies which seemed to threaten sanity itself. Unconsciously, there was a good deal of gratification in re-creating through the daily visit to me the exciting and triumphant sensation of being her father's companion in bed.

For this young woman to allow herself to face, early in the analysis, her feelings about her father and to reawaken these feelings in the transference would have been experienced as a catastrophe. In her fantasies, pregnancy, disgrace, illness, insanity, and her own and her mother's death were only a few of the consequences of losing control of herself.

The conflict was intense enough so that the infantile wish and the analytic situation had sufficient force to produce such dreams repeatedly and often obviously. I pass rather briefly over the functions of such dream presentation as seduction, both sexual and intellectual, and will focus instead on her method of dealing with this problem through the device of the cliché.

First, she jumped over the transference to the infantile wish. She said in effect, "It is not you I wish to sleep with; it was my father." Ironically enough, this was perfectly true. The truth *can* be used, in a sense, to conceal itself. Yet there is no question that her understanding of herself, the analytic purpose, would have been served far more effectively had she been able to recognize directly her fear of the erotic transference wish.

This was dangerous precisely because it seemed to her that it was occurring in the present and might really go further. Therefore, she displaced the fantasy to the ultimately more dangerous, but more distant, infantile situation, at the same time isolating the idea from the associated excitement. Her expression of it appeared as the cliché.

It was said and even dreamed the same way many times. What is the further purpose of this reiteration? I suggest that it has a specific purpose in terms of communication, in this special case, in the transference. For this patient it was a way of expressing and being gratified by a very important wish and, at the same time, yielding a minimum of information about it. It is no news to an analyst that his patient wanted to sleep with father and now expresses this in the transference. The verbal interpretation she gave, therefore, contained no new information. It was entirely expected by both of us. Moreover, it prevented me for a long time from giving an effective interpretation of the content, that is, a statement which would be "new" to her, in a sense of increasing the preconscious cathexis of the idea, and which might lead to the release of other thoughts and feelings.

The cliché had the effect of denying *useful* information about content by isolation of its emotional components, and was an example of analytic resistance in the classical sense, "everything that prevents the patient from producing understandable associations derived from the unconscious."[4] It is true resistance, as well, in a more strictly defined sense,[5] as a manifestation of de-

[4]This is Fenichel's definition, slightly modified.
[5]I am indebted to Ernst Kris for this definition.

fense pattern characteristic of the individual and occurring as part of the analytic situation.

Beyond its function of denying information, the cliché had a number of other important functions, both defensive and otherwise. It helped the patient feel that she had successfully warded off both me and her father, at the same time preserving her control of her emotions. She was able, moreover, to prolong her analysis and her exciting "half-sleep"—in Glover's (1955) phrase, she made "the attempt to snatch real libidinal gain, as it were, on the run."

I have deliberately chosen this made-to-order cliché for discussion, rather than one which was ready-made or familiar, as both its development and its resolution could be observed within the analysis. It became a cliché only within the analytic context, and it eventually ceased to be one, after its functions and its relation to ego process had been analyzed. Understandably, the obvious content, even the transference content, was the last to be resolved.

A second example is the following, noteworthy, because of the almost too neat way in which the infantile origin of the cliché became manifest. This patient would interrupt very productive analytic periods with querulous and repetitive harangues on science and philosophy, expressed in the most pedantic jargon, and characterized by glaring logical fallacies. This was quite unlike his usual mode of thought, and was repeated in the most stereotyped fashion over long periods.

Transference interpretations of his hostility and its probable defensive functions were of no avail. Finally I told him, quite bluntly, that he couldn't possibly believe what he was saying, that he knew it was nonsense. In spite of his protests, he was not really thinking out an important decision with which he was faced. This, I insisted, was not thought, but brooding, not communication, but rather, ranting.

He said nothing at the time, but the next day recalled the following incident. At about five years of age, he used to visit his maternal grandmother, an elderly lady whose chief interest in him, so far as he could tell, lay in an enormous and critical interest in his stools. He resented this invasion of his privacy, and being an enterprising and mischievous little boy, evolved a clever scheme. He had discovered some brownish putty in the garage. He took a quantity of it, molded it into the proper shape and deposited it in the toilet bowl for grandmother's inspection. She was readily deceived, and he experienced a real sense of triumph.

After he finished the story, I did not hesitate to point out that he had prepared numerous false stools for me. He replied, with appropriate humor, "It's time I gave you the *straight* shit, instead!" Not every determinant of the cliché can be so neatly described, nor do we always find so elegant a correspondence in etymology, namely, the derivation of the word "cliché" from the original German *klitsch*, to pattern in clay.

Some patients are particularly adept at turning the analyst's remarks into clichés. A typical example is the following response to a transference interpretation: "You analysts always say the same old thing, that your patients want to fall in love with you!" This device frequently appears as parody or sarcasm, and may be employed to ward off an anticipated interpretation, as, "You are about to tell me that I'm in love with my mother." This is often the result of premature or naïve interpretation, but need not always be so. It may be a way for a very frightened patient to assert, "You cannot affect me by your remarks, they are trite and meaningless." My own interest in the cliché as resistance was stimulated by a very clever patient, who during a long process of working through, referred to my observations as clichés. They had been repeated many times and were, in fact, becoming stereotyped. He had made a good point; at the same time, he revealed this most powerful device employed in his own defense: the interpretation, demanding repetition, had been turned by him into a cliché, with some unsuspecting help from me.

Not every repetition constitutes a cliché, nor does every use of technical language deserve to be called jargon.[6] Only those repetitive and stereotyped phrases which have begun to lose their exact meaning should be so considered. For example, there are many repeated expressions which yield highly com-

---

[6]Theodor Reik (1948) attacks the tendency of other analysts to write in jargon. There is much to be said for his argument, but he fails to distinguish carefully enough between the cliché-ridden jargon which is the armor of the pedant, and the necessarily specialized language which is the most concise form of communication between two students of an art or a science. It is no more true (as Reik implies) that research in emotional processes could be expressed concisely and with adequate precision, without the use of technical words, than a scientific understanding of these processes could be attained without systematic study.

Reik is correct in his claim that many technical words could be eliminated without loss of meaning, and even with a gain of precision and clarity; but to try to express the whole complex knowledge of psychoanalysis in everyday language exposes one to the risk of transforming very extraordinary ideas into something very commonplace indeed. It is quite possible to hamper the development of a science by limiting it to "common-sense" concepts, reflected by an inadequate vocabulary.

Freud employed new terms for ideas which were original and complex, and which, in ordinary language would have required elaborate and repeated expository notes—e.g., *id, ego, superego, Ucs, Cs, Pcs.* To write meaningfully of the human personality now requires either using such technical terms, or less satisfactory substitutes, or else by using ordinary language, oversimplifying and blurring the whole field. The last solution may be justified when writing for an unsophisticated audience, but it should not be regarded as a means of scientific communication. A study of writings in mathematics and physics, for example, reveals that the same restrictions are present—psychoanalysis is by no means unique. In getting rid of useless jargon, therefore we must be careful not to go too far and (cliché) *throw the baby out with the bathwater,* dispensing with science altogether for the sake of simplicity.

The avoidance of technical words during the actual conduct of an analysis is accepted so generally that it needs nothing more than mention here.

pressed information, an excellent example being the technical term "id." In scientific discussion, it contains a great deal of meaning, and is a shorthand way of saying something quite complicated. When, on the other hand, a patient talks about his "id," we almost always assume that he is employing it as a cliché in the service of resistance.[7]

Some patients use formula expressions as signals which are not necessarily clichés. Ernst Kris furnished me with the example of a patient who began certain sessions with, "I had a fine time," to indicate that he had had a particularly boring evening. This began as a cliché, but when understood became something analogous to a family joke, a code expression known to a small group of people. It emphasized intimacy and had become an ironic abbreviation rather than a cliché.

During the process of working through as well as early in analysis, a good deal of reiteration is a necessary part of the process. This differs from the cliché in that it is not stereotyped, being expressed in different situations, different words, and with different emotions, although the underlying idea may be the same. Whether or not a particular expression should be considered a cliché, therefore, depends very much on the context.

Evans (1953), in discussing several types of evasive speech in analysis, emphasized the cliché as a means of expressing disbelief, as well as a masochistic device for evoking ridicule. He observed that such devices were often expressions of unconscious mimicry of one of the parents, a finding suggesting its relation to problems of identification.

For the most part, I have confined this discussion to a consideration of clichés directed from patient to analyst, or perhaps even from the patient to a critical portion of his own ego. I have mentioned only briefly the cliché directed from analyst to patient. Greenson (1955) gave an excellent example a few years ago, and Glover (1955) has a few penetrating things to say in his discussion of counterresistance, particularly the analyst's remark, "You are resisting," which readily becomes a cliché. A frank search of our memories will, I am sure, reveal our own lapses, the expression we use, not as stimuli or signals, but rather to conceal from ourselves an anxious and baffled state of mind in the face of some analytic difficulty.[8]

Our understanding of the function of the cliché as resistance is broadened considerably by a study of contributions from fields other than clinical analysis, for example, literary criticism, English usage, humor, anthropology,

---

[7]See Kris (1956): "The deep interpretation should not supply the patient with an empty 'id vernacular' which can easily be used for resistance and thus help to maintain repression."

[8]George Devereux (1950) emphasized the defensive use of technical terms by analysts themselves, "to desexualize the therapeutic relationship by means of an intellectual defense." He noted their value as "esoteric badges of status and (magical) 'power'."

logic, and not least, cybernetics. When information from these varied sources is correlated, it furnishes a reasonably consistent account of the cliché as a device for withholding information, concealing ignorance, and avoiding anxiety.

Lionel Trilling (1953) writes,

> A specter haunts our culture—it is that people will eventually be unable to say, "They fell in love and married," let alone understand the language of Romeo and Juliet, but will, as a matter of course, say, "Their libidinal impulses being reciprocal, they activated their individual erotic drives and integrated them within the same frame of reference." Now this is not the language of abstract thought, or any kind of thought. It is the language of non-thought, but it is the language which is developing from the peculiar status which we in our culture have given to abstract thought. There can be no doubt whatever that it constitutes a threat to the emotions and thus to life itself. [He says further,] . . . But to call ourselves the people of the idea is to flatter ourselves. We are rather the people of ideology, which is a very different thing. Ideology is not the product of thought; it is the habit or ritual of showing respect for certain formulas to which, for various reasons having to do with emotional safety, we have very strong ties of whose meaning, and consequence in actuality we have no clear understanding. The nature of ideology may in part be understood from its tendency to develop the sort of language I parodied, and scarcely parodied a moment ago.

George Orwell (1954) continues with this aspect of the cliché.

> But you are not obliged to go to all this trouble (of writing with precision). You can shirk it by simply throwing your mind open and letting the ready-made phrases come crowding in. They will construct your sentences for you—even think your thoughts for you, to a certain extent—and at need, they will perform the important service of partially concealing your meaning, even from yourself. . . . When one watches some tired hack on a platform mechanically repeating the familiar phrases . . . "free peoples of the world stand shoulder to shoulder . . ., etc." one often has the curious feeling that one is not watching a live human being, but some kind of dummy: a feeling which suddenly becomes stronger at moments when the light catches the speaker's spectacles and turns them into blank disks that seem to have no eyes behind them. And this is not altogether fanciful. A speaker who uses this kind of phraseology has gone some distance towards turning himself into a machine. The appropriate noises are coming out of his larynx, but his brain is not involved as it would be if he were choosing his words for himself. If the speech he is making is one that he is accustomed to making over and over again, he may be almost unconscious of what he is saying, as one is when one utters the responses

> in church. . . . When there is a gap between one's real and one's declared aims, one turns, as it were, instinctively to long words and exhausted idioms, like a cuttle fish squirting out ink.

Frank Sullivan's (1948) cliché expert, Mr. Arbuthnot, is a self-confident fellow who answers any questions with the greatest readiness. In testifying on the drama, when asked, "What kind of plays are there?" he answers, "Oh, their number is legion—there are dramas of frustration and dramas of extra-marital love, or the eternal triangle—there are plays that are penetrating studies and plays that are valuable human documents—there are pageants which ought to be glittering, if possible—tragedies should, of course, be stark, and melodramas lurid, and spectacles to be *de rigeur* should be lavish, colorful and handsome. But lampoons must be merry, farces must be rollicking, and comedies must be either of ancient vintage or sophisticated." The ignorance and smugness of the "expert" are clearly revealed, along with his skillful use of the cliché to conceal these defects and to defend his self-esteem. This process, although largely conscious, is analogous to the unconscious purpose of the cliché in analysis.

James Thurber (1955) in a delightfully titled article, "The Psychosemanticist Will See You Now, Mr. Thurber," attacks the use of the cliché term "security," among others, from a slightly different point of view, emphasizing not only the ignorance and anxiety behind it, but the hostility with which it may be employed—as it is often enough in analysis.

George Devereux (1956) gives an excellent example of the cliché in one of his anthropological papers. "The psychiatrist turns to the anthropologist more and more often for help with diagnosing patients whose cultural background is atypical or marginal. Far too often the anthropologist contents himself with the plaintive reiteration that, 'Among the Bonga Bonga, this type of behavior is normal, this kind of belief is culturally standardized, and this sort of personality is well adjusted.' " In terms of modern anthropology, the statement says nothing useful, whatever value it may have in supporting the self-esteem of the speaker and his vain hope that his hearer will be satisfied.

An illuminating discussion of the meaning of words in terms of formal logic is found in a paper by Kris and Kaplan (1952). One of their illustrations of ambiguity of meaning is the following: "Diplomatic language professionally exploits additive ambiguity; the commitment to 'support' a given policy lends itself to multiple interpretations ranging from sending troops to formal expressions of sympathy."

Here the word "support" is used as a cliché and is both stereotyped and imprecise. It is certainly intended to deny exact information, and to allay anxiety in some quarters. That it may arouse more anxiety in others is merely an ironic circumstance.

A most interesting contribution, useful at least by analogy, and perhaps more fundamentally, is that of Norbert Wiener (1954) in "Cybernetics and Society." He states,

> Messages are themselves a form of pattern and organization. Indeed, it is possible to treat sets of messages as having an entropy like sets of states of the external world. Just as entropy is a measure of disorganization, the information carried by a set of messages is a measure of organization. In fact, it is possible to interpret the information carried by a message as essentially the negative of its entropy, and the negative logarithm of its probability. That is, the more probable the message, the less information it gives. Clichés, for example, are less illuminating than great poems.

This highly condensed statement gives us still another useful way of expressing what we have already observed about the cliché. Resistance, in the strictest sense, is a disturbance of the communication between patient and analyst. (That it may be a source of communication as well is pertinent in another context.) The cliché is "meaningless" to the analyst in terms of content, given a particular analytic situation. When a patient says something we do not entirely expect, we are interested and stimulated. This is especially so if it is a response we had *hoped* for, but did not entirely expect at the time. If the session begins in the same old way with the same old words, however, we are disappointed and feel as if we and the patient have been learning nothing. The same might be said about our own remarks to the patient, if they are stereotyped and trite. The useful message in either direction must contain some degree of improbability or "surprise."[9]

What then of the habitual users of the cliché? These are commonly regarded as intolerably dull people, if not actual social menaces. An illuminating, but rather disturbing, recording of a song by Danny Kaye, "The Babbitt and the Bromide," makes clear the essential isolation of such people and their profound loneliness. We are reminded of the stereotyped nonsense of the advanced hebephrenic who "uses speech as a means of expression, not as a means of communication."[10] It is tempting and perhaps justified to regard this psychotic symptom as a markedly deteriorated form of cliché speech.

Neither its function as the protector of self-esteem nor its value in concealing dangerous ideas or feelings encompasses the total value of the cliché.

---

[9] I use the term "surprise" here in a sense more general than that of Theodor Reik (1937), who employs it to emphasize the spontaneous and intuitive character of his own insights, as well as the emotional responses of himself and his patient to interpretation. Here "surprise" is used as a synonym of "information" or "news," to emphasize the relative lack of probability of a message. (See Wiener 1954.)

[10] See Devereux (1956).

It seems often that the repeated use of the words themselves has a reassuring effect. This may be analogous on the one hand to the ritual of prayer (as suggested by Orwell), and on the other, to the incantations of those who attempt by meaningless syllables to protect themselves from occult dangers. Such magic spells are characteristically composed of nonsense words or syllables, impressive in sound, but meaningless to the ordinary man, and we expect, to the magician himself. It is necessary, moreover, to say them in the correct order without changes. In the "Tale of Ali Baba and the Forty Thieves," for example, the magic spell consisted of the words, "Open, Sesame!" When Ali's greedy brother-in-law forgot the spell and said, "Open, Barley!" instead, the door of the cave would not open. The stereotyped phrases of the schizophrenic have some of this quality. Perhaps the ordinary cliché as well has a kind of magic for the patient who employs it, feeding his hope that by saying the words in their proper order, he will somehow be relieved. When we offer a stereotyped interpretation in an attempt to solve a difficult analytic problem, we too are using magic, rather than analysis.

It does not seem possible, no matter how tempting, to classify the cliché as a manifestation of any single ego function or instinctual derivative. Most obvious is its role in support of identification. The cliché is never original, at least by the time it has become one. Its introjective functions and its derivation from the child's mimicry of adult speech appear to be common to all clichés. The process of stereotyping and cheapening the introjected words or concepts has such suggestive analogies to the manufacture of feces out of food, that it is difficult to omit anality and the defenses associated with it.

In fulfilling its regular purpose as a barrier to communication, however, the cliché shows considerable variation in its emphasis. Sometimes it serves repression in the strictest sense, by preventing the expression of an instinctual derivative. In other cases, for example in the tendency to minimize the seriousness of illness ("I'm sure it's all psychosomatic") or of other fear-inducing situations, it serves the purpose of denial. Isolation, too, may be involved.

What is most striking about the cliché, however, is its extraordinary stability and efficiency. It is ego syntonic to the point of smugness, and it may (as in Dickens' Mr. Podsnap) assist in reducing all of the turmoil of life to a series of simple formulas. If the synthetic function of the ego may ever be considered to be operating in the service of defense, this is the time. It is a synthetic function applied to unworthy purposes, it is true, to ego restriction rather than to ego development; but that this function contributes to the maintenance of illness as well as health has been familiar since its earliest descriptions (Nunberg 1955).[11]

---

[11]In a discussion of this paper, L. Loomie suggested that the concept of "organizing function of the ego" would add precision to this section.

Clichés may be used in certain cases to bar communication, not between two elements of the psychic structure, nor between the individual and his perception of the environment, but rather between man and man. Sometimes they are consciously produced, and are directly evasive, for the purpose of hiding an unpleasant truth from another person, or perhaps, saving the energy required for a meaningful answer. These may occur in analysis as expressions of resistance, but we are more likely to be interested in the intrapsychic conflicts which produce them.

Finally, there are clichés which have an emotional impact on groups, a result which appears to be linked to their very emptiness of idea in the intellectual sense. These we classify as slogans, and find ourselves outside the scope of resistance as a clinical phenomenon.

Technically, the cliché has great importance, increasing yearly as analytic expressions become more widely distributed in educated common speech. The patient who talks habitually in clichés, in and out of analysis, I should suppose would be a poor candidate for any analytic approach. Such activity is an indication of disturbed object relations, isolation and hostility, as well as the use of words for magic, rather than information. While the cliché discussed as resistance is a phenomenon based largely on certain ego functions, in these other cases, one gets the impression that it is ultimately a manifestation of the most rigid kind of defensive system, intractable, and a necessary protection against inner chaos and turmoil.

When the cliché appears as an incident in a specific analytic situation, however, its import is very different. Paradoxically, the *use* of a cliché during the analysis of a patient who ordinarily avoids this device, is anything but a cliché. In this setting, its *use* has a large element of improbability and is in itself rich in information, however trite the words and manifest content may be. In the case of my first patient, for example, it was by no means completely predictable that she would employ such a cliché in a significant way. That she did so was striking.

The words of the cliché could be disregarded, for the time, as having lost their meaning. Nevertheless, the phenomenon was capable of analysis and yielded invaluable information about transference and specific defenses, which could be fused ultimately with the hidden content of the words themselves.

REFERENCES

Devereux, G. (1950). Some unconscious determinants of the use of technical terms in psychoanalytic writing. *Bull. Menninger Clin.*, 14:202–206.

——— (1956). Normal and abnormal. In *Some Uses of Anthropology: Theoretical and Applied.* Washington: Anthropological Society.

Evans, W. N. (1953). Evasive speech as a form of resistance. *Psychoanal. Quart.*, 22:548–560.

Fenichel, O. (1945). *The Psychoanalytic Theory of Neurosis.* New York: W.W. Norton.

Fowler, H. W. (1954). *A Dictionary of Modern English Usage.* London: Oxford University Press.

Glover, E. (1955). *The Technique of Psychoanalysis.* New York: International Universities Press, pp. 53, 55, 56, 99, 105.

Gowers, E. (1955). *Plain Words, Their A, B, C's.* New York: Knopf, pp. 157–159, 116–122.

Greenson, R. R. (1955). On empathy and sublimation. Abstracted in *JAPA* 3:525.

Kris, E. (1956). Recovery of childhood memories. *Psychoanalytic Study of the Child,* 11:54–88. New York: International Universities Press.

Kris, E., and Kaplan, A. (1948). Aesthetic ambiguity. In *Psychoanalytic Explorations in Art.* New York: International Universities Press, 1952.

Nunberg, H. (1930). The synthetic function of the ego. In *Practice and Theory of Psychoanalysis.* New York: International Universities Press, pp. 120–136, 1955.

Orwell, G. (1954). Politics and the English language. In *A Collection of Essays.* Garden City, N. Y.: Doubleday.

Partridge, E. (1954). *A Dictionary of Cliches.* London: Routledge and Kegan Paul.

——— (1954). *The Concise Usage and Abusage.* New York: Philosophical Library.

Reik, T. (1937). *Surprise and the Psychoanalyst.* New York: E. P. Dutton.

——— (1948). *Listening with the Third Ear.* New York: Farrar Straus.

Sullivan, F. (1948). The cliché expert testifies on the drama. In *The Night the Old Nostalgia Burned Down.* Boston: Little, Brown.

Thurber, J. (1955). The psychosemanticist will see you now, Mr. Thurber. *The New Yorker,* May 28.

Trilling, L. (1953). The meaning of the literary idea. In *The Liberal Imagination.* Garden City, N. Y.: Doubleday.

Wiener, N. (1954). *The Human Use of Human Beings.* Garden City, N. Y.: Doubleday.

3

States of Consciousness in the Analytic Situation

Including a Note on the Traumatic Dream

"Consciousness is in general a highly fugitive condition" (Freud 1940). It has always been recognized to be so, yet even now we have great difficulty in deciding what it means to be "aware." Whether states of consciousness may be represented by a true continuum or by a discontinuous model is still a matter of argument, reminiscent of some of the matter-energy arguments among physicists some time ago. Our own problem is at a stage of development far less sophisticated.

The model of the continuum was postulated by Breuer (1893–1895) and greatly elaborated by Freud. The latter, however, used both the continuous and discontinuous models at various times in his career, and used them for different purposes. Recently there have been attempts to investigate consciousness systematically and even experimentally, by dreams and other methods (Fisher and Paul 1959, Klein 1959). Here I shall attempt to describe some clinically observed phenomena which may be of some value in approaching this problem, still relatively neglected and thoroughly baffling in many essential aspects.

During the last century, before systematic investigation of consciousness was well begun, people may have been more obviously subject to its vicissitudes. At least they seem to have been freer in experiencing the variable and fugitive quality to which Freud refers, and they appear to have reacted more frequently by gross changes of awareness without surprising anyone very much. It was quite common for healthy and courageous people to lose consciousness entirely in the face of sudden object loss or great mental pain from other sources. Dumas allowed his virile and picaresque hero d'Artagnan to faint at

Note: An earlier version of this paper was presented under the title "Trauma and Dream" at a meeting of the New York Psychoanalytic Society on February 28, 1961.

the death of his mistress. An even more courageous man, an intellectual hero and scientist, himself fainted on two occasions in the presence of his closest colleagues (Jones 1953). No one seems to have considered it very remarkable at the time.

It was natural, and not merely for clinical reasons, that psychoanalysis should have begun with studies of consciousness, and have found its origins in experiments with hypnosis. The novelists of a generation earlier, such as Dickens, were generally quite interested in changes in consciousness, and in dreams. They used them as literary devices, and revealed now and then, as in some of Dickens's letters (Dupee 1960), an uncanny gift for penetrating observation, alternating with sentimental naïveté.

Psychoanalysis began with the dream, as well as the symptom, and there was an all-absorbing, perhaps too exclusive interest in the phase of psychology dealing with consciousness, which lasted for a few decades in the case of Freud himself and somewhat longer in the case of more conservative colleagues.

Meanwhile, the novel itself had shifted its emphasis a good deal, to include conflict within the individual, and the development and disintegration of character, especially in the works of Tolstoy and Dostoyevsky. Dreams and fugue states were no longer simple literary devices, but when used at all became vehicles for exploring complex emotional states, as older novelists had used digressive chapters. Protagonists no longer fainted or developed the convenient "brain fever" of the earlier writers; they died, became psychotic, or were, so to speak, cured by having achieved a new integration of personality, as in the case of Nekhindoff in Tolstoy's *Resurrection*.

Freud gave due credit to his artistic predecessors, particularly to Dostoyevsky, although his own steps forward into the mysteries of character were foreshadowed in his very earliest papers. This broadening of the field was achieved at the cost, at least for a time, of major advances in the theory of consciousness, since the publication of *The Interpretation of Dreams*. This is all the more striking since the study of consciousness was for Freud himself one essential basis on which the essence of psychoanalysis was to be built.

With the development of interest in the study of character, we were inevitably faced with the need to develop a hypothesis that would take into account the groups of functions which were being described. These functions (defenses, for example) could be seen to change and develop, but only very slowly, not at all like the massive sudden changes of consciousness (or of symptom, or mood) which were the focus of attention of analysts in the early days.

These slowly changing functional groups required the development of a hypothesis which would take "structures" into account and which would allow, moreover, for the finding that normal and abnormal, health or illness, could not be correlated with conscious and unconscious in any simple way. As the original topographic hypothesis was found to be limited in its capacity to include the new range of data, it fell into some degree of disuse in theoretical discussion, although it has clung stubbornly to life in the thinking of clinicians. It may remain even now, if not the master of the house, nevertheless a quite lively corpse in the closet of structural metapsychology.

Apparently, we cannot think of everything, and advances have been few in the aspects of the science having to do with matters of awareness. During the past few years, things have changed, however. Investigators such as Rapaport, Fisher, Klein, among others, have explored the field once again and discovered buried cities, with evidence of still others to be uncovered. Fisher's (1954, 1956) confirmation of Pötzl's original work, and his successful effort to bring it into psychoanalytic theory, has led to a rash of similar experiments, a number of them already fruitful.

Certainly attempts to explore some of the factors which control awareness are as much in order at present as they were in the first years of psychoanalysis. It seems likely that in the analytic situation itself we miss many covert changes in states of consciousness, which we are not always well equipped to observe, much less to measure and describe. It is my thesis that such subtle changes occur often, that they are important, and that they may be correlated with symptom formation (a very old idea), with resistance and the dream, and further that they may be traced genetically.

My attention was drawn to these questions by events which were observed during the analyses of a special group of patients. They were not prone to fainting, to obvious trances or fugues, or to episodes of depersonalization or derealization. Their analytic behavior was marked rather by powerful tendencies to forget the material of the analysis itself, to be subject to periods of pseudo-stupidity, and in one case, by a special type of acting out. It would seem that all of these phenomena have something in common with the dream, and with one another, and that they represent circumscribed variations in the field of consciousness. In certain of the cases, one could trace the origins of these phenomena to attempts to adapt to special traumatic experiences during childhood.

We are generally familiar with the observation that those who have completed an analysis some years before may have forgotten a good deal of what actually occurred during the procedure. This does not in itself imply any lack of success, but it does raise some important questions about the significance of such amnesia.[1]

I had the opportunity, some years ago, to study such an amnesia in some detail. A patient, whose analysis I had conducted, returned to consult me ten

[1]Ernst Kris (1956) suggested that accurate recall of their own analyses was probably important for analysts, but not necessarily for those who had undergone personal analysis for purely theraupeutic reasons.

years later. The original result had been satisfactory, in that the symptoms had not recurred and he had functioned very well in the interval, through some trying episodes. A new symptom had appeared in response to a particularly distressing event, quite out of his control.

Beginning analysis for the second time, we were able to observe the foundations upon which the original good result had been built. The relief of symptoms and the achievement of well-integrated and reality-oriented personal behavior had been genuine enough, but had been maintained by some curious methods. The patient had used a number of verbal and written talismanic devices which revealed clearly enough not only the persistence of a residue of magical thinking, but also a massive unresolved block of transference. These devices included, for example, a written note which recorded an interpretation I had given originally. This version of it was hardly recognizable, for it was grossly oversimplified and expressed in clichéd language—but it was an echo.

This was particularly disconcerting because the transference had been extensively interpreted and reinterpreted. One could hardly say, in the light of the circumstances, that it had been worked through and analyzed, but it had been impossible ten years before to tell that it had not been dealt with quite adequately.

Further investigation revealed another striking phenomenon. Almost all of the content of the first analysis—trends, dreams, interpretations—had been forgotten. What few bits of content had been remembered, had been subjected to such gross distortion that they were hardly recognizable. They had been used magically, rather than otherwise.

In the face of this it was impossible to avoid questioning the procedure itself. It was not enough to fall back on Freud's classical example in "Analysis Terminable and Interminable" (1937), and maintain that the original analysis had gone as far as it could, while the vicissitudes of life had created a new situation and a new symptom. This was true as far as it went, but here we were faced with evidence that an important bit of work had been left undone at the time, and what is worse, the indication for it had been unsuspected. There must have been a gap in understanding and technique, which now required us to find a psychoanalytic explanation.

Continued work revealed that this gross amnesia and its correlates were only the most obvious manifestations of other more subtle and circumscribed disturbances of memory. These could be observed *in statunascendi* during the analysis of this patient and, when looked for, in other patients as well.

I imagine we have all had the following experience. One day, we offer our patient an interpretation which we consider to be appropriate, soundly conceived, and rather important. He responds with understanding and emotion, after bringing forth confirmatory associations. A day or two later we discover with disappointment that the interpretation has been completely forgotten.

Sometimes the patient is aware of the amnesia, and is troubled; he is then likely to request that the interpretation be repeated. Even worse, he may have retained a highly simplified, distorted caricature of it, which sounds as if he were mocking our original words. Resistance it is, and hostile, very often, but why does it take this form?

This amnestic process may at times be observed during the course of a single analytic session. At one point we are discussing some content, perhaps offering an interpretation. A few minutes later, the patient, who has responded to our remarks, suddenly announces that he has forgotten them: would we repeat them?[2]

The last seems a bit peculiar, not readily fitted into the course of ordinary mental life. How is it possible to forget so rapidly a group of quite important, endogenously derived expressions and concepts? The phenomenon bears only a limited resemblance to the usual parapraxes, such as blocking out an important name or number. Such rapid massive amnesia of emotionally significant content occurs typically, and even routinely, in connection with reveries and, above all, the dream.

There is something remarkable in the forgetting of dreams. A very common experience will serve as an illustration. We wake one morning and recall a vivid and interesting dream. A few minutes later we become aware that the dream has slipped away and cannot be recalled. It may, now and then, be felt as if it were a little object loss, accompanied by a trace of sadness.

It requires no radical theoretical step to encompass the finding that the manifest content of the analytic situation and that of the dream are treated alike in certain respects. Lewin (1955) has made the analogy very clear, using both historical and metapsychological arguments. It may be anticipated, therefore, that the forgetting of analytic content may be regulated by some of the same laws as those which govern the forgetting of the manifest dream.[3]

Many authors have commented on the forgetting of dreams, not nearly so many on the forgetting of analytic content (Kris 1956). The latter is likely

---

[2] I am indebted to Dr. Joseph Weiss for the suggestion that such requests for repetition of content reveal that the patient here uses the analysts as an accessory memory. This interpretation fits very well with the habit of some of these patients to take notes after the analytic session. It is also a way of asking, "What happened while I was asleep?"—which could be traced in one case to a history of long periods of febrile stupor while hospitalized with mastoiditis.

[3] It seems hardly necessary to add that the thesis that similar laws operate for two disparate phenomena does not imply that they are treated alike by the ego in all respects. But they are dealt with alike in certain ways, and we have much to learn about the analytic situation by applying the laws of dream psychology, and the converse. In a sense, a similar task was undertaken by Beres (1957) in establishing analogies between the analytic situation and the creative imagination. This treatment of concepts is neither exclusive nor reductive in its effects. It is reminiscent, ultimately, of Freud's treatment of symptom and dream in the Dora case.

to be regarded as a resistance, as a rejection of the disagreeable, manifesting the operation of the pleasure principle. And so it is, ultimately, but it must be much more.

The phenomenon of posthypnotic amnesia would seem to yield some useful clues to the process. In spite of studies of such authors as Schilder (1921, 1927), Rapaport (1951), and Gill and Brenman (1959), those leads have not been exploited extensively in this context. Lewin's reminder that the analytic session is an outgrowth, historically, of the hypnotic trance, contains a truth most of us would rather ignore.

It is to be regretted that excellent follow-up studies, such as Pfeffer's (1959, 1961, 1963), have so far not taken into account the analogies with posthypnotic phenomena. Originally it seems to have been necessary to prove that analytic results were not merely the effect of suggestion. Freud answered this many years ago, but perhaps even then was uncomfortable about this not entirely respectable ancestor. He did not, for example, make much of it in "Analysis Terminable and Interminable," which is a pity. It would be important to learn what we could of the similarities between posthypnotic amnesia and the forgetting of analytic content.

A clinical study, on the other hand, can exploit more fruitfully the analogies between the forgetting of analytic content and that of the dream, since both may be observed from day to day as part of the analysis itself. We are in a position, too, to examine the derivation of these phenomena from childhood experience, and to trace with some care the role of traumatization.

The half dozen patients included in this study demonstrated not only a very marked degree of amnesia for analytic content, but other related symptoms. They were prone to vivid daydreaming which was subject to rapid and complete automatic erasure. To a remarkable extent, they demonstrated the tendency to experience periods of gross naïveté, or pseudo-stupidity, during analytic sessions. In one case, this was correlated with a peculiar form of acting out.

This intermittent "naïveté" involved not only sexual matters, but even more characteristically affected the capacity to hold on to and express even the simplest analytic concepts. This was all the more striking because these were not emotionally dull people. On the contrary, they were generally extraordinarily perceptive, and as a rule were capable of keen and accurate introspection. One or two at times demonstrated such sharp self-observation that they made it possible to study with great care variations in their states of consciousness. It was this paradox, in fact, which led to the other observations and hypotheses to be described below. It is of little value to us to observe the dull man being dull, but our curiosity is whetted and likely to be gratified by the errors of the intelligent.

An example of this paradox may be described as follows. The patient mentioned above, who re-entered analysis after an interval of years, formulated the lessons of the first analysis in the most simplified and naïve terms, far less accurate and sophisticated than one would read in a popular, and somewhat hostile, article on psychoanalysis. It was this same patient who achieved, and contributed, the greatest depth of understanding of sleeping and waking; who was, in short, the most acute observer of the function of reality operating within himself. Once, for example, the patient reported this dream: "I seemed to be under water, at the bottom of the sea, held fast there in some way. Suddenly it was as if an anchor chain had been broken; I shot up to the air like a submarine surfacing. As I did, I awoke." It was, as may be inferred, a dream not only of birth, but of sleeping and waking, and of analysis. It was brilliantly interpreted by the patient. It was later forgotten, naturally, but I am glad to say the amnesia could be analyzed and the dream recalled and used.

The pseudo-stupidity with which interpretations were treated was worthy of special attention, since it could be quite exasperating if not recognized and analyzed. The patients would not only forget the point of an interpretation. They would distort it, misquote it, become naïve and ignorant without warning. Sometimes I was led to a suspicion of paranoid thinking, only to be forced to revise my opinion in favor of what could only be called "pseudo-paranoia," analogous to pseudo-stupidity itself. Even though my interpretation might be echoed back with implications of accusation and insult which were never even hinted in the original, I was compelled to recognize that there was something not quite paranoid in the process—just as we are "paranoid" in our dreams, or, especially, on waking from them. Again, these patients were not suspicious by nature, or even especially argumentative, and their capacity for establishing transference was unusually great—although the latter had moments of apparent fragility. They were not difficult to work with, in spite of the occasional strain of trying to understand and cope with these circumscribed regressive phenomena.

All these patients employed a form of resistance which was unusually highly developed, if not at all unique. They had the capacity to think, feel, and act so differently in and out of the analytic session that one could readily imagine oneself to be seeing different people. One young woman, for example, after sessions spent in furious silence (on her part) and great discomfort (mutual), would, as she left the room, turn to me and say good-by with the most charming friendliness. The next day saw a repetition of the same procedure, and so on for many months until it could be analyzed. Its mechanism involved the maintenance of an alteration of consciousness, not so obvious or severe as that of Breuer's Anna O., but not altogether dissimilar.

Another patient was often capable of participating with active interest and keen intelligence in an extensive analysis of his perverse impulses, including their origin and defensive functions. Upon leaving my office he would, as if in a dream, act out his fantasies in the most stupid and dangerous fashion. This stereotyped pattern of behavior may be considered, quite properly, to exemplify the combination of acting out in the transference and the negative therapeutic reaction as well as giving dramatic evidence of the repetition compulsion. But this constitutes an incomplete description if we omit the strange state of mind in which the behavior took place. It required a suspension of the sense of reality which had been so acute a short time before. It was also, in a sense, thought-less, characteristic of "true" acting out—and also of sleepwalking. True somnambulism is rarely subject to analysis, at least these days. But perhaps we miss variants of it more frequently than we suspect.

Several of these patients were quite gifted in music, creative writing, or painting. Sometimes such creative work was done in a state of mind which could be described only as trancelike—not an uncommon experience for artists. One patient, after working hard for several days in a tense sitting position, found that he had worn a hole in the side of the leg of his trousers. This, we discovered, was the result of an automatic rubbing movement of one patella against the tibia of the other leg, an activity of which he was entirely unaware. Another patient began to paint one Saturday at the exact hour of her weekday analytic session. During this hour she produced, while in a dreamy or trancelike state, an oil sketch which contained the material of a forgotten dream (later recalled) and a representation of an object in my office which she was not aware of having seen, although it was in her line of vision. This striking confirmation of Fisher's work was studied in detail and reported elsewhere (Stein 1958b).

The analytic situation, then, was not the only one in which such phenomena occurred. They characterize the "creative situation" as well, and make one think that such ready variations in the degree and type of awareness may be correlated, in turn, with the "flexibility of regression" which Freud ascribed to the artist.

Such variations of awareness have also been attributed to the psychotic. In the latter we see instability and uncertainty of repression, with very ready regression to dreamlike thoughts and dreamlike states. The major differences in the psychotic, however, are the lack of adaptive control by the executive ego and the all-encompassing scope of the regressive process. He lacks both the discipline and the capacity for appropriate reversal manifested by the artist, and by such patients as those discussed here.

The illnesses of the patients in this group were generally not too severe, with symptoms ranging from transient if very distressing obsessional phenomena to moderate and fairly persistent neurotic depressive reactions. The one patient who acted out a good deal was quite ill, but certainly not psychotic.

These patients demonstrated, after all, phenomena which can be found to some degree in all analyses. These phenomena occurred, however, to an extent not at all typical. This was the source of the most persistent and stubborn resistances, the ultimate field in which working through had to be conducted. The occurrence of amnesias of this special type, the proclivity to daydreaming, the startling and paradoxical pseudo-stupidity combined with the capacity for profound self-observation, all set them apart from the general run of analytic patients.

We are naturally curious to find an explanation for this hypertrophied development and pathological use of a specialized group of ego processes. It would be useful to be able to establish a convincing prototype from which we could trace the development of this behavior with some degree of continuity.

A *general* prototype for ready fluctuations of awareness is to be found in the universal experience of oral gratification and sleep. Consciousness in newborn babies varies all the way from deep sleep to something like being alert (see Gifford 1960).

A later, and related, general experience is that of the reverie of infantile and adolescent masturbation. Here alteration of consciousness plays an important role, especially at the point of orgasm. This is also true in coitus, in which something like complete loss of consciousness may occur momentarily. Freud placed considerable importance on this point as a link in his theory of symptom formation. I shall return to its theoretical importance later.

In any case, this is a general experience, so that we can hardly use it as a special prototype. Constitutional factors aside, we are correct, I think, in seeking a history of special experience, which might contribute to an explanation of a special phenomenon.

The common historical factor which emerged in these cases was that of severe childhood illness, of a type which itself affected consciousness. In several cases, specific types of perception were affected. One patient had suffered a severe cerebral concussion during the oedipal phase, several others had a history of recurrent severe otitis media followed by mastoidectomy. In one of the latter, there had been a transient but very dangerous episode of meningitis.

This patient demonstrated the symptom complex most clearly, with frequent reversible amnesias and paramnesias for analytic content, pseudo-stupidity, and unusual capacity for self-observation. It was here that changing states of awareness and the resistance were most firmly linked, and most convincingly analyzed, and it was here also that one could trace the path from childhood traumatization to adult symptom with the fewest gaps and uncertainties.

It would have been gratifying to be able to report that such a history could be obtained in all six patients. This was not the case. Nevertheless, the symptoms were most typical in those who gave a history of severe childhood illness of this type, and it was possible to establish genetic determinants with remarkable continuity. The other patients were included because they showed those symptoms to some degree and because the lessons learned from the others could be applied with profit (for example, in the case of the patient who acted out). In these cases the search for evidence of different states of consciousness was often rewarding in understanding particular resistances.

The most typical cases, on the other hand, were those with a history of severe otitis media. These could be most carefully traced and had the most to teach.

One may reconstruct readily enough some elements in the history of any young child with severe, confining illness. His experience with external reality is severely modified during a very crucial phase—in these cases between the early oedipal and latency phases. Not only do the high fever and toxicity produce changes of the state of awareness; further interference is produced by sedative drugs and anesthesia.

In several, very severe pain plays a role. Lancing the ear drum without an analgesic is an excruciating process, which can produce a period of "fuzziness," at least, in adults who have suffered it. What must it do to the child who can hardly understand its function, whose sense of helplessness is much greater, and who may have to be forcibly restrained? Some children become "courageous," and learn to accept such procedures without struggling—but at what cost?

We must consider as well the effects of another concomitant of such illness: confinement. Not only is the child kept in bed or indoors for long periods, with the inevitable stimulation of daydreaming and introspection. Added to this is interference with opportunities for outward expressions of aggression by active play. These children, whose aggressive drives had been severely stimulated by pain and the need for submission to it, had at the same time been deprived of the chance to express even the usual aggressive needs of the healthy child.[4]

If we take the experience of severe pain itself as a focal point, we may trace the relation between such traumatization and dream states as follows:

The child is exposed to a series of extremely painful stimuli which allow of no relief by motor activity, and are too intense to permit adaptation by devices short of massive withdrawal of cathexis; they must therefore be met by changes of consciousness ranging from mild feelings of unreality, or depersonalization, to full loss of consciousness (Freud 1926, Rosen 1955). This process is facilitated by the clouding which accompanies high fever, and by drugs.[5]

---

[4]I omit for several reasons a discussion of the effects of such illnesses on the relation between parent and child. We may take it that such effects are profound and important, but it would require a separate paper to do them justice.

[5]See Isakower (1938). The first case he cites is one in which the sensations experienced during fever are similar to those of the hypnagogic state—viz., the "Isakower phenomenon."

In any case, a memory is imprinted, of *both* the original painful perception and the adaptive device itself, i.e., the complete or partial loss of consciousness (Freud 1925a). Loss of consciousness, for whatever reason, is itself frightening. Even though adaptive, this acts as an additional trauma, constituting a threat to self representation and to assurances of self-control.

While the type, intensity, and surrounding circumstances of the trauma will to a great extent determine the nature of the "imprinting," a good deal more occurs than simply the recording and ultimate repression of an unpleasant memory (Greenacre 1960).

The second category of effects of the trauma may be classified within the concepts of fixation and ego distortion. (These, necessarily, depend far more on the phase of development—both libidinal and in terms of ego functions—than on the specific type of trauma; so that, e.g., a tonsillectomy "imprints" memories having to do with the oral zone, but any symptomatic manifestations resulting from it may have more to do with anal or phallic influences, if the operation is performed at such a point in the child's development. This is very familiar; I repeat it only to clarify a line of argument.)

Whatever the phase of development, from childhood to adult life, overwhelming pain or terrifying external danger—especially if the ego is unprepared, or weakened by fever or fatigue—may result in massive shifts of cathexis bringing about loss of consciousness, partial or complete.

We are generally familiar with the after effects of a sudden painful experience or emotional blow in adult life. Most people describe themselves as "dazed," "overcome by fatigue," even "unreal." Perception of external stimuli may be dulled or otherwise changed, while one may become much more aware of fantasy. In many respects these are states of modified consciousness, and we find in them very close ties to sleep and the dream.

Ordinarily the disturbance of consciousness is temporary, although exceptionally it may persist. Recovering awareness, one must then deal with the *memory* of pain, itself painful.

It becomes desirable then to push the memory away from the forefront or *fovea* of attention, to ignore it. (In economic terms, we postulate the development of a countercathexis.) It is too recent and too vivid for repression, particularly in a child. Moreover, being the memory of an externally produced sensory perception, it is in all respects suitable to be treated first by denial. Jacobson (1957) has described a mechanism which may apply here, as follows: "denial presupposes an infantile concretization of psychic reality, which permits persons who employ this defense to treat their psychic strivings as if they were concrete objects perceived" (p. 80). May not *memories* of pain be similarly treated, under special circumstances, that is, be concretized and denied?

Freud (1920) makes a pertinent statement in discussing the traumatic neuroses of adults: "I am not aware . . . that [such] patients . . . are much occupied in their waking lives with memories of their accident. Perhaps they are more concerned with *not* thinking of it" (p. 13). This phenomenon of suppression is closer to denial than to mechanisms such as repression or isolation, for it has to do with reinforcing the countercathectic barriers between preconscious and conscious ideation, to paraphrase from Jacobson (1957).

Such processes, partaking of denial, powerfully reinforce tendencies to fantasy formation. In this instance, fantasies of a masochistic nature would be facilitated. These in turn not only favor further denial of the unpleasant stimulus (the painful memory), but add a desirable fillip of pleasurable excitement as a consolation.

We now have an ideal concentration of forces for dream formation. "The unconscious prefers to weave its connections around preconscious impressions and ideas which are either indifferent and have thus had no attention paid to them, or *have been rejected* and have thus had attention promptly withdrawn from them" (Freud 1900, p. 563; my italics). So goes Chapter VII. The fresh memory is available as a day residue, for it has been rejected and suppressed by the ego—we may say it has been subjected to denial—during the waking hours. Such stimuli have been banished to the periphery of the attentive sphere which Fisher (1954, 1956) and Klein (1959) have demonstrated to be, at least with regard to "indifferent" stimuli, the richest source of day residues for dream formation. (It seems that a similar spatial analogy may be applied to rejected as well as indifferent stimuli.) In any case the memory is treated as if it were an "external" stimulus.

In addition to the day residue, the other essential ingredient for dream formation is also present: a repressed, highly charged fantasy, in this case, a masturbation fantasy with a masochistic content.[6] This now becomes not only an intermediary for the expression of a traumatic memory (Freud 1916–1917), but also carries the instinctual charge necessary for dream work and libidinal gratification (Freud 1900, 1917).

The dream has therefore an essential function in the adaptation to trauma and to the recent or distant memory of trauma. Not only does it allow the ego to attain at least an illusion of mastery, but it permits the terror and pain of the memory to be transferred and fused with libidinal gratification, often

---

[6]Children who have been subjected to repeated and very painful procedures will tend to experience the Oedipus complex as a sadomasochistic affair. It undoubtedly helps, when the child must submit to a painful experience, to turn this into a sexual assault, and thus derive not only pleasure, but a fantasy of control over the stimulus.

The parents are not the only ones involved. There are also the figures of physicians whose capacity to cause and relieve pain makes them objects of great significance. Inevitably, they are woven into masturbation fantasies. These are likely to be severely repressed, and are detectable usually only by their effects on the transference, which are profound and which require painstaking analysis. It is here that an interpretation readily becomes an assault!

masochistic. The dream may very well be a necessity for mental life, therefore, and deprivation of it a severe hardship, as Dement and Fisher (1960) have recently attempted to demonstrate experimentally.

It is possible that life could not go on without some access to denial of its terrors: the dream may, by its very nature, permit more adaptive denial in waking life. The traumatic dream is a peculiarly suitable vehicle for this process; moreover, it may be more effective than we generally recognize in dealing with acute severe trauma in adult life. We have observed that the memory occurs at first almost intact in the traumatic dream; the sleeper wakes in terror, to experience then the relief of being able to say: "It was only a dream—it's all imagination." If we may accept as the representative of a dream wish, "It's not real, it's only fantasy," it becomes possible to recognize the deepest instinctual component of the dream as the wish to restore omnipotence by the incorporation of the frightening event, to make it endogenous and therefore "unreal." In the very act of waking in terror, we reaffirm that same infantile omnipotence which is ordinarily represented in the wish to sleep. If this be granted, we may place the "traumatic" dream back in the category of wish-fulfilling mental operation from which Freud (1920) removed it.

Perhaps only after the memory of the traumatic experience has been thus relegated to the unreal, to the "It may never have happened," can effective forgetting be allowed to occur. Much of this was presaged, of course, in Freud's (1900) statement that "the currently active sensation is woven into a dream *in order to rob it of reality*" (p. 234).[7] Denial thus precedes and may even be a necessary step in the repression of affectively charged memories.[8] That this process can occur in the reverse direction is implied by Freud (1925b): "Thus the content of a repressed image or idea can make its way into consciousness, on condition that it is *negated*" (p. 235). Perhaps denial is after all a more inclusive process than it is generally considered. I have used the term broadly.[9]

If the fantasy and the night dream do have a useful function in dealing with the deprivations of daily life, and even more in coping with the massive and intolerable discomforts we call traumata, we may postulate this function not only for the dream itself and the reverie, but also for the varying states of

---

[7]A point more recently illustrated by Rubinfine (1952).

[8]A hypothesis I have borrowed from Jacobson (1957, pp. 83–84).

[9]Although the dreams of young childern are by no means as simple as they were once thought to be (Lewin, personal communication), there is little question that many early dreamy states are attempts to cope with the elementary frustrations of loss of the mother and the nipple. Certainly the thumb or pacifier seem to be indices of early prototypes of denial and of consolation. These states in the baby (see Gifford 1960) vary all the way from deep sleep through a kind of half sleep to about as complete awareness as the new baby ever seems to achieve. The fluctuation of consciousness is more marked in the newborn than it ever is later—except in the dying, and perhaps during the induction of general anesthesia and the awakening from it.

consciousness which facilitate such mental activity: from that degree of sleep which permits dreaming to occur (see Dement and Fisher 1960), up to that ideal state of "laboratory alertness" in which maximum attention is being paid to a deliberately limited area of conscious observation.

Such "laboratory alertness" had formerly been treated in psychological experiments as if it were a fixed variable. More recently a number of investigators (Gardner et al. 1959) have recognized that it should, instead, be considered a fluctuating variable, and they have conducted studies to determine the laws of such fluctuation of awareness. These studies are not always easy to follow in detail by one trained in a different though related field, but George S. Klein has done an invaluable service in communicating to us some of his own and his co-workers' findings.

Klein (1959) describes an increased responsiveness to subliminal stimuli during reverie states, and after developing this theme he writes: " . . . a proper evaluation of the incursion of motives in the cognitive act *must take into account the organization of the particular state of consciousness in which it occurs*, and the types of controls which characterize it. . . . there is good reason to suspect by now that perception in 'waking states' is not altogether free of characteristics seen more commonly in dreams" (pp. 26, 28). Although this statement was anticipated by Breuer, Freud, Lewin (1955), and by Aristotle,[10] Klein's formulation of it is a very important one, the entire value of which can hardly be communicated in this brief reference.

The experimental psychologists use the term "deployment of attention" to denote the degree to which certain stimuli, external or otherwise, are brought to awareness. I prefer the term "scanning" (electronic rather than military in its immediate ancestry) to denote this process of distribution of cathexis.[11]

"Scanning" might be said to include all continuously or intermittently mobile perception or awareness of the outer world, the body, ideational activity, memory, affects, and the connections among them. We might conceive of this ego function as if it involved a structure analogous to a very complicated and sensitive radar apparatus which is capable of rotating in all directions from time to time and is also capable of responding to itself. Its responses are based on the return of emitted impulses which themselves vary in frequency, intensity, direction, and quality. This model describes the continuum of conscious-

---

[10]"For it is quite possible that, of waking or sleeping, while the one is present in the ordinary sense, the other should be present in a certain way" (De Somnis, *The Works of Aristotle*, Vol. III, p. 462a, Oxford, 1931).

[11]They limit the term "scanning" to observation of phenomena, e.g., ideas. This leads to some difficulties. In asserting that isolation broadens awareness, for example, there is a tendency to gloss over the fact that it also narrows it by reducing the awareness of *connnections* between ideas, affects, and the like.

ness, not as a series of points on a straight line, but rather as a complex, multidimensional variable. This may seem far-fetched, but it is certainly not so in the light of some modern automatic machinery of communication.

I did not dream up this idea, of course. It was pretty well outlined by Freud (1925a). In discussing "the flickering-up and passing-away of consciousness in the process of perception," he continued:

> This agrees with a notion which I have long had about the method by which the perceptual apparatus of our mind functions, but which I have hitherto kept to myself. My theory was that cathectic innervations are sent out and withdrawn in rapid periodic impulses from within into the completely pervious system *Pcpt.-Cs.* So long as that system is cathected in this manner, it receives perceptions (which are accompanied by consciousness) and passes the excitation on to the unconscious mnemic systems; but as soon as the cathexis is withdrawn, consciousness is extinguished and the functioning of the system comes to a standstill. It is as though the unconscious [ego] stretches out feelers, through the medium of the system *Pcpt.-Cs.*, towards the external world and hastily withdraws them as soon as they have sampled the excitations coming from it. Thus the interruptions . . . were attributed by my hypothesis to the discontinuity in the current of innervation; and the . . . breaking of contact . . . [was accounted for] by the periodic nonexcitability of the perceptual system. [p. 231]

The cybernetic implications of this statement seem fairly obvious, particularly in its consideration of quantitative, qualitative, and directional controls, feedback, and innate periodicity. These are, like the radar, analogies, and possibly Freud has been of more use to Norbert Wiener than the latter has been to us, but I am not so sure. Electrical models, and now electronic-cybernetic ones, have been of considerable heuristic value to psychoanalysis from Breuer on, and may well continue to be.

Dreaming and reverie may, for example, be conceived of as states in which the bulk of emitted impulses or cathexes is being directed toward the fantasy life, memory, the body, while laboratory alertness implies more intense scanning of the world outside the body. (This is, it is true, little more than a paraphrase of a section of Chapter VII of *The Interpretation of Dreams.*) It is the relativistic and quantitative elements which are important, since the predominant direction of scanning, and its thoroughness and intensity, could probably be correlated with other ego functions, such as the relative proportion of primary and secondary processes—a matter discussed extensively by Arlow and Brenner (1964).

Most of this, both from a clinical and theoretical point of view, is not especially new. The tendency to treat one's analysis as if it were a dream was anticipated and described in the first psychoanalytic case report by Breuer, that of Anna O. His pioneer observation makes confusing reading these days, but we should ask ourselves whether some of this confusion may not be inherent in the phenomenology itself, dominated by varying, more or less dissociated levels of awareness. Reading the case as if it were all a dream does not explain everything in it, but it does give it a new coherence. It may even make possible the resolution of some of the diagnostic contradictions of such early case reports.

At the same time Breuer made a number of worthwhile suggestions about trauma and the onset of the neurotic symptom. He hypothesized the existence of a "hypnoid state," essentially a transient change in the ego brought on by fatigue or other stress, in which alertness and reality testing were markedly reduced while reverie was facilitated. During such states quite ordinary events, perhaps otherwise merely frightening or shocking, would enter the dissociated state and, "lacking access to the conscious portion of the mind," could lead to a persistent hysterical symptom (see Breuer and Freud 1893–1895).[12]

This was not so abortive a suggestion as it seemed; for while Freud rejected the concept of the hypnoid state, the idea stimulated his interest in dreams and dreamlike states, including the reverie. Other major papers aside, the very brief "Some General Remarks on Hysterical Attacks" (1909) establishes the connections between symptom and dream and the orgastic experience. Freud was well aware of the reverie states associated with masturbation. This proved to be one of the keys to the puzzle of the "hypnoid state," which led to the discovery of the significance of childhood sexuality—that the reveries must be sexual in origin.

Freud discusses specifically the alteration of consciousness which accompanies orgasm, whether in masturbation or coitus. He had been deeply impressed by the phenomenon of the epileptic seizure, and its resemblance to a violent orgasm. The concept was expanded very fruitfully later in Chapter XXIII of the *Introductory Lectures*, in which he worked out the role of fantasies as carriers of the original erotic charge, as middlemen, so to speak, between infantile sexuality and adult symptom.

We need not, any more than Freud, accept the hypnoid state as the crucial element in the onset of the neurotic symptom. Nevertheless, that there is a modification of consciousness, a closer approach to dreaming involved in the formation of a symptom, has been a most valuable idea. In this paper I have attempted to develop the converse of Breuer's thesis, namely, that trau-

[12]Kardiner (1932, 1941) exploited this theme in his book on the war neuroses as well as in one of his early papers.

matization itself favors the development of such a clouded state of consciousness, which in turn acts as a contributory factor and perhaps even a necessary one for the onset of certain types of neurotic reactions: it is sometimes at least a link in the chain of causality.[13]

It is worthwhile to return for a moment to clinical observation based on the analyses of patients with a history of otitis media and mastoid disease. Here occurred not only the interference with consciousness due to fever, drugs, and severe pain, but further, an intermittent but very significant interference with perception. Not only hearing but the sense of balance could be affected. One patient, in fact, revealed even now the late effects of damage to both sensory organs, demonstrating not only hearing loss but intermittent vertigo.

In his paper "On the Exceptional Position of the Auditory Sphere" (1939) and in personal communications, Isakower has clarified the profound influence on the developing structure of the personality of those aspects of perception which affect reality testing in a crucial fashion. The central question for this reality function may be most simply expressed in its earliest form as, "Is it from within or from the outside?" and in its later version, "Am I awake or am I dreaming?"

There is no doubt that this aspect of the reality function was impaired, in significant but circumscribed ways, in this group of patients. The all-too-ready shift from one state of awareness to another, often without the patient's knowledge and largely independent of conscious volition, was good evidence of interference with such controls.

Some patients demonstrated another aspect of the impairment of the reality function in persistent tendencies to blur "correct or incorrect" with "right or wrong" in the analytic situation and elsewhere.

One such patient, for example, discussing the fantasied commission of a horrifying crime, said it would be wrong because it was immoral, wicked. It proved impossible for the patient to entertain, at the same time, the recognition that the "crime" itself would have led to the most painful results for himself, involving loss of those dearest to him. That the crime would be not only immoral but highly unfortunate could not be adequately conceptualized. I need hardly add that the patient was of the most impeccable moral character.

Another such patient, who had also suffered mastoidectomy, still betrayed in his adult dreams traces of early birth fantasies which were influenced by the experience of the operation. These dreams portrayed his birth from his mother's ear. In addition, his birth fantasy was fused with the story of the Christ Child, Virgin Mary, Three Kings, and all. His moral principles were

[13]See Breuer and Freud (1893–1895): " . . . it also seems to be true that in many people a psychical trauma *produces* one of these abnormal states [of consciousness], which, in turn, makes reaction impossible" (p. 11).

highly idealized, Christlike in some respects, and very difficult to correlate with the *advisability* of certain acts.

Such dichotomy is characteristic of the neurotic, but rarely has it been so highly developed and marked by such splits and confusion in otherwise fairly effective people.

There existed, in effect, a very marked lack of integration in the double concepts of right (morally) and right (sensibly). It is as if "right" for the superego and "right" for the ego failed to fuse even to the extent they do for most adults. This phenomenon gives added weight to Isakower's (1939) suggestion that in the early development of the personality structure, the reality function cannot be totally included among the ego functions, but must have to do with the superego as well.

All in all, there is excellent evidence that early traumatization involving the auditory sphere may have a specific effect on ego and superego development. That it has been manifested in these patients in more or less benign, even rather interesting ways, speaks for the presence of extraordinary and still obscure compensatory factors in the ego and superego, which have effectively guarded these patients from psychosis. But this does not detract from the importance of the central impairment of what might be called, somewhat figuratively, orientation in consciousness.[14]

Hypnagogic and other dreamlike states, such as the reverie, have been studied quite extensively and their genesis has been linked closely with early oral experience (Isakower 1938, 1939, 1954; Lewin 1950, 1953, and others). In addition to these well-recognized dreamlike states, we might take notice of another group, a step further removed from the dream, which consists of such symptomatic manifestations as depersonalization, feelings of unreality, *déjà vu*, and the like. It is pertinent that in most of these conditions, sensations of vertigo or falling are very commonly experienced: all variants of falling asleep, and all containing elements of spatial disorientation. Among the many descriptions of these conditions are several which bring out very clearly their relation to traumatization and denial (Arlow 1959, Jacobson 1959, Linn, Rosen 1955, Stamm 1962). Federn's (1932) work is also relevant in this connection. Especially pertinent is Stone's (1947) description of transference sleep in a man with peptic ulcer, a case which had many features in common with some of mine.[15]

By far the most inclusive discussion of variations in awareness during analysis itself is to be found in Lewin's (1955) "Dream Psychology and the

---

[14]I have recently asked myself whether one common symptom in these patients, a recurrent fear of psychosis, may not be derived in part from fear of becoming "unbalanced," so to speak.

[15]His patient was much sicker and the symptoms of change of awareness were more obvious. The patient demostrated pseudo-stupidity of a particularly exasperating type. He had suffered from pneumonia and mastoiditis in early childhood.

Analytic Situation." He makes clear to what extent the analytic setting derives from and must be explained in terms of dream psychology. This work has been perhaps inadequately appreciated as a contribution to the theory of technique. Lewin brings to our attention that above all in the analytic situation we may study a variable which is under the partial control of, and may be observed by, the analyst: namely, the degree to which the patient approaches or withdraws from dreaming, while the analyst fulfills his role in soothing or waking the dreamer.[16]

Lewin's statement forces us to consider to what extent some ego processes are brought into play in the analysis as the dreaming state is approached, while others become active as it is abandoned. More attention might well be paid to this problem. For example, beginning with Isakower's (1954) notable observation on the spoken word in dreams as the representative of the superego, we might postulate that the extent to which the analyst's interpretations may be "registered" by the patient's superego rather than his ego may be to some degree a function of the patient's closeness to the dream state. At least, it ought to be considered among other determinants when an interpretation is met with guilt rather than knowledge.

This latter resistance is very common, and was very conspicuous in this group of patients. I wonder how often our interpretations are distorted and misunderstood, and we are disappointed, because unknowingly we have failed to consider to what degree we have been addressing our remarks to a relatively dreaming or waking patient. All ego functions, including the defenses and therefore the resistance, must necessarily vary not only with the degree of regression, but more particularly and in less global fashion, with the extent to which something analogous to the dream work takes place in the apparently wide-awake patient—or in the apparently wide-awake analyst.

All this is expressed most concisely in Lewin's own words: "As the surgeon cannot always ignore or completely forget the basic situation of anesthesia, so we cannot always ignore the ratio between sleep and waking in the analytic patient" (1955, p. 198). For my part, I should be inclined to make the statement more inclusive, asserting that we can *never* afford to ignore such a ratio, and that it must be observed not only in the laboratory of analysis, but wherever human behavior is studied.[17] It may be a large order; but to ignore such an important variable is to incur massive risks of error.

---

[16]Much of the inherent unpopularity of psychoanalysis may result from its function as a waking process. No one likes the alarm clock, although he may admit the need for it. To be a bit fanciful, we might imagine that the sound of the alarm acts again as a superego stimulus, while the face of the clock, the visual stimulus, is more readily accepted by the ego.

[17]For example, in studies of automobile accidents, and certain other phenomena in which we must deal not only with the incursion of primary process, but also with variations in attention and other ego phenomena which may be understood by *analogy* with dream phenomena.

I should like to emphasize, in a more logical order than has been followed heretofore, some of the principles and questions inherent in the relationship of varying states of consciousness in the analytic situation to a history of specific traumatic experience.

1. The extensive forgetting of analytic content in certain patients follows laws similar to those regulating the forgetting of dreams.
2. This may be correlated clinically with episodic pseudo-stupidity and certain secondary distortions of analytic content, which also suggest a parallel with the dream.
3. Such tendencies may often be traced genetically to the effects of childhood illness involving pain, clouding of consciousness, or both. This occurs most typically in patients with a history of severe otitis media and mastoidectomy in the preoedipal or oedipal phases of childhood.
4. Severe traumatic experience may be met with a response consisting in part of a modification of awareness in the direction of dream and sleep. This may vary from entire loss of awareness, such as fainting, to minor changes, such as sleepiness or reverie, reflecting the extent and direction of the cathectic shift. Illness which impairs the auditory and vestibular functions during crucial periods of development is likely to have specific effects on this aspect of the reality function.
5. Such modifications of awareness, especially in childhood, may act as the prototype for later changes in ego states. These will tend to recur with the reactivation of conflict due to new traumata, as in the neurotic symptom.
6. Modifications of awareness may come to be enlisted in the service of autonomous ego elements, as in the various creative processes, or they may serve the needs of sexuality in contributing to orgasm.
7. These latter processes (creativity and orgasm) may be severely blocked if excessive anxiety accompanies changes of awareness, particularly if regressive oral elements predominate, enhancing fears of being devoured.
8. Such modifications of consciousness are reproduced, often covertly, in the analytic situation. Understanding of such states may be increased by application of the psychology of the dream to the analytic session itself. The forgetting of the analytic experience, often so striking, is analogous to and partakes of the mechanisms regulating the forgetting of dreams.
9. Shifts in waking states occur probably at least as often and less predictably than corresponding changes in depth of sleep.
   It is ironic that in the EEG we have at least a crude method to estimate the depth of sleep. We have, so far as I know, no such quantita-

tive method for the waking state, but the work of Fisher, Klein, and others gives us hope that this may some day be accomplished.

10. Consciousness may for heuristic purposes be considered as a process of scanning the total environment, including the external world, the self representations, the body, ideation, memory, affect, their interconnections and barriers, including processes as well as objects.
11. Denial may be considered a sharply defined involvement of the scanning process, consisting of a cathectic change which affects a perception or a group of perceptions or ideas. The dreamlike state is a more general involvement of the scanning process, including significant qualitative, quantitative, and directional changes.
12. Changes occurring from time to time in the ego functions which control awareness and closeness to the dream must also affect secondarily the varying use of other ego functions, including the defense mechanisms and autonomous functions.
    One must include the superego in a consideration of such controls, particularly when impaired or regressive states of the ego are in evidence. Does the superego have a direct role in the reality function under normal conditions or does it operate only through its influence on the ego? This is a question not to be answered here, but one which needs further and intensive investigation.
13. It is suggested that the typical recurrent dream of the traumatic neurosis may be restored to the class of wish-fulfilling dreams without doing violence to current dream theory. It is proposed that the wish fulfillment is here concentrated in the waking process, in which the wish is concentrated: "It was unreal, it did not really happen, it was my imagination."[18]
14. It should be possible to carry out a more thorough correlation of variations in awareness with metapsychological concepts, e.g., of egoid fusion, of free and bound energy (and correspondingly of primary and secondary process), of defensive versus autonomous ego function. Much has been done to correlate sleep and the dream with orality, but other phase-specific elements are still largely to be worked out.

---

[18]Max Schur (1965) has arrived at a similar conclusion within a different context, namely, that recurrent dreams of the traumatic neuroses are not "beyond the pleasure principle."

REFERENCES

Arlow, J. A. (1959). The Structure of the *Déjà Vu* Experience. *J. Amer. Psychoanal. Assn.* 7:611–631.

Arlow, J. A., & Brenner, C. (1964). *Psychoanalytic Concepts and the Structural Theory.* New York: Int. Univ. Press.

Beres, D. (1957). Communication in Psychoanalysis and in the Creative Process: A Parallel. *J. Amer. Psychoanal. Assn.* 5:408–423.

Breuer, J. & Freud, S. (1893–1895). Studies on Hysteria. *Standard Edition* 2.

Dement, W. C. & Fisher, C. (1960). The Effect of Dream Deprivation and Excess: An Experimental Demonstration of the Necessity for Dreaming. Abstract: *Psychoanal. Quart.* 29:607–608.

Dupee, F. W. (1960). *Selected Letters of Charles Dickens.* New York: Farrar, Straus & Cudahy.

Eisenstein, V. W. (1949). Dreams after Intercourse. *Psychoanal. Quart.* 18:154–172.

Federn, P. (1932). Ego Feeling in Dreams. *Psychoanal. Quart.* 1:511–542.

Fisher, C. (1954). Dreams and Perception: The Role of Preconscious and Primary Modes of Perception in Dream Formation. *J. Amer. Psychoanal. Assn.* 2:389–445.

——— (1956). Dreams, Images and Perception: A Study of Unconscious-Preconscious Relationships. *J. Amer. Psychoanal. Assn.* 4:5–48.

Fisher, C. & Paul, I. H. (1959). The Effect of Subliminal Visual Stimulation in Images and Dreams: A Validation Study. *J. Amer Psychoanal. Assn.* 7:35–83.

Freud, S. (1900). The Interpretation of Dreams. *Standard Edition* 4 & 5.

——— (1909). Some General Remarks on Hysterical Attacks. *Standard Edition* 9:229–234.

——— (1915). The Unconscious. *Standard Edition* 14:166–215.

——— (1916–1917). Introductory Lectures on Psycho-Analysis. *Standard Edition* 15 & 16.

——— (1917). A Metapsychological Supplement to the Theory of Dreams. *Standard Edition* 14:222–235.

——— (1920). Beyond the Pleasure Principle. *Standard Edition* 18:7–64.

——— (1925a). A Note upon the "Mystic Writing-Pad." *Standard Edition* 19:227–232.

——— (1925b). Negation. *Standard Edition* 19:235–239.

——— (1926). Inhibitions, Symptoms and Anxiety. *Standard Edition* 20:87–174.

——— (1937). Analysis Terminable and Interminable. *Collected Papers* 5:316–357.

——— (1940 [1938]). *An Outline of Psychoanalysis.* New York: Norton, 1949.

Gardner, R., Holzman, P., Klein, G. S., et al. (1959). *Cognitive Control [Psychological Issues,* Monogr. 1]. New York: Int. Univ. Press.

Gifford, S. (1960). Sleep, Time and the Early Ego: Comments on the Development of the 24-Hour Sleep-Wakefulness Pattern as a Precursor of Ego Functioning. *J. Amer. Psychoanal. Assn.* 8:5–42.

Gill, M. M. & Brenman, M. (1959). *Hypnosis and Related States: Psychoanalytic Studies in Regression.* New York: Int. Univ. Press.

Greenacre, P. (1960). Regression and Fixation: Considerations Concerning the Development of the Ego. *J. Amer. Psychoanal. Assn.* 8:703–723.

Hartmann, H. (1939). *Ego Psychology and the Problem of Adaptation.* New York: Int. Univ. Press, 1958.

Isakower, O. (1938). A Contribution to the Patho-Psychology of Phenomena Associated with Falling Asleep. *Int J. Psycho-Anal.* 19:331–345.
——— (1939). On the Exceptional Position of the Auditory Sphere. *Int. J. Psycho-Anal.* 20:340–348.
——— (1954). Spoken Words in Dreams. A Preliminary Communication. *Psycho-anal. Quart.*, 23:1–6.
Jacobson, E. (1957). Denial and Repression. *J. Amer. Psychoanal. Assn.* 5:61–92.
——— (1959). Depersonalization. *J. Amer. Psychoanal. Assn.* 7:581–610.
Jones, E. (1953). *The Life and Work of Sigmund Freud*, 1. New York: Basic Books.
Kardiner, A. (1932). The Bioanalysis of the Epileptic Reaction. *Psychoanal. Quart.* 1:375–483.
——— (1941). *The Traumatic Neuroses of War.* New York: Hoeber.
Klein, G. S. (1959). Consciousness in Psychoanalytic Theory: Some Implications for Current Research in Perception. *J. Amer. Psychoanal. Assn.* 7:5–34.
Kris, E. (1956). The Recovery of Childhood Memories in Psychoanalysis. *Psychoanalytic Study of the Child* 11:54–88. New York: Int. Univ. Press.
Lewin, B. D. (1946). Sleep, the Mouth and the Dream Screen. *Psychoanal. Quart.* 15:419–434.
——— (1950). *The Psychoanalysis of Elation.* New York: Norton.
——— (1953). Reconsideration of the Dream Screen. *Psychoanal. Quart.* 22:174–199.
——— (1955). Dream Psychology and the Analytic Situation. *Psychoanal. Quart.* 24:169–199.
Linn, L. Personal communication about combat soldiers approaching the front.
Pfeffer, A. Z. (1959). A Procedure for Evaluating the Results of Psychoanalysis: A Preliminary Report. *J. Amer. Psychoanal. Assn.* 7:418–444.
——— (1961). Follow-up Study of a Satisfactory Analysis. *J. Amer. Psychoanal. Assn.* 9:698–719.
——— (1963). The Meaning of the Analyst After Analysis: A Contribution to the Theory of Therapeutic Results. *J. Amer. Psychoanal. Assn.* 11:229–244.
Rapaport, D. (1951). Consciousness: A Psychopathological and Psychodynamic View. In *Problems of Consciousness, Transactions of the Second Conference*, pp. 18–57. New York: Josiah Macy, Jr. Foundation.
Rosen, V. H. (1955). The Reconstruction of a Traumatic Childhood Event in a Case of Decrealization. *J. Amer. Psychoanal. Assn.* 3:211–221.
Rubinfine, D. L. (1952). On Denial of Objective Sources of Anxiety and "Pain." *Psychoanal. Quart.* 21:543–544.
Schilder, P. (1921, 1927). *The Nature of Hypnosis.* New York: Int. Univ. Press, 1956.
Schur, M. (1965). Comments on the Regulatory Principles of Mental Functioning (in press).
Stamm, J. L. (1962). Altered Ego States Allied to Depersonalization. *J. Amer. Psychoanal. Assn.* 10:762–783.
Stein, M. H. (1958a). The Cliché: A Phenomenon of Resistance. *J. Amer. Psychoanal. Assn.* 6:263–277.
——— (1958b). Reconstruction and Fantasy. Unpublished paper, presented to the New York Psychoanalytic Society, September 16, 1958.
Stone, L. (1947). Transference Sleep in a Neurosis with Duodenal Ulcer. *Int. J. Psycho-Anal.* 28:18–33.

4

Self Observation, Reality, and the Superego

My thesis is the following. First: self observation is an essential element in the process of reality testing. Second: self observation and self evaluation are inextricably linked, and are intimately involved with superego functions. Therefore, the superego functions play an essential, if indirect, role in reality testing and reality adaptation.

I

I should prefer to distinguish between the terms "reality testing" and "reality function," using the former as a special case of the latter, generic term. Thus reality testing, as used here, would consist of the examination of whether a sense impression is a genuine perception of objective reality, a distorted perception, or a hallucination.

Freud's simplest description of reality testing is to be found in "A Metapsychological Supplement to the Theory of Dreams" (1917), defining it as the "function of orientating the individual in the world by discrimination between what is internal and what is external . . . [via that] which determines whether the perception can be made to disappear or whether it proves resistant. Reality-testing need be nothing more than this contrivance." He ascribed it to "the system *Cs. (Pcpt.)* alone" (p. 233). Later, this should have placed it clearly in the ego, but it underwent a number of vicissitudes before and since in Freud's writings, and for good reasons.

The above definition did not quite cover the ground, for it failed to account sufficiently for the very "reality" in which Freud was interested, namely, that which is determined by the inspection of one's own mental processes. In his later writings he recognized this inadequacy, as well as the complications which accompanied a more inclusive definition. The latter was most clearly expressed by Hartmann (1956): "In a broader sense, reality testing also refers to the ability to discern subjective and objective elements in our judgments on reality" (p. 256).

It is reasonable to assume that reality testing as applied to the outer world, and that which is directed toward one's own mental processes, are interdependent. I am of the opinion that self observation plays a ubiquitous role in reality testing. The latter would be subject to serious limitations or impairment were there not a constant flow of stimuli from the inner world and were the capacity lacking to perceive and evaluate these inner stimuli.

This is, after all, one of the basic assumptions underlying the theory of psychoanalytic therapy. We do expect, at least implicitly, that as a result of analysis our patients will see the world more clearly and deal with it more efficiently. Our approach differs from other psychotherapies in that we explicitly *avoid* reality testing—at least in the usual sense. We need not tell our patients that they have misjudged a life situation, nor do we as a rule give in to the temptation to correct a misapprehension of some analytic event. Instead, we attempt to correct, by analysis, those distortions of self observation which become evident in the analytic situation. By attaining a clearer vision of his own mental processes, by unsparing honesty with himself, we hope that our patient's distortions of perception of the outer world will be reduced to a minimum.

Defects in self observation are not solely responsible for the misinterpretation of perceptions; lack of adequate data, unfamiliarity, disturbances of the perceptive apparatus, defective intellectual capacity may all impair reality testing. But I would maintain that self observation is a *necessary*, although not a sufficient or sole determining factor in the adequate evaluation of reality.

Not only does defective capacity for self observation result in impairment of reality testing; reciprocally, assaults from outside may impair the accuracy of perception of one's inner world. Sensory deprivation experiments and solitary confinement often result in serious disturbances of the capacity to distinguish inner from outer stimuli. So-called brainwashing, in which a mass of incongruous stimuli is supplied, may again lead to distortions of one's self image. Overwhelming external stimuli (such as exposure to prolonged combat conditions, or intractable pain) may produce similar disturbances. It is evident that some flow of more or less familiar perceptual stimuli readily capable of integration into one's past experience is necessary for the maintenance of adequate self observation and evaluation.

Ordinarily in the healthy adult we see the most marked shifts in the function of reality testing in connection with sleep and dreaming. The waking process, in fact, constitutes a crisis with respect to one's attitude toward the outer world. The chief task of one who wakes from sleep is to determine that he is *awake*; that what occupied him before, the thoughts, perceptions, and affects of his dreams, were indeed part of the dream; that they came from within and from the past, not from the outside and the immediate present.

This process of waking has been described most vividly by Marcel Proust (1920), who seems to have spent much of his life making observations for which the rest of us have neither the introspective capacity nor the leisure:

> That kind of sleep is called "sleeping like lead," and it seems as though one has become, oneself, and remains for a few moments after such a sleep is ended, simply a leaden image. *One is no longer a person.* How then, seeking for one's mind, one's personality, as one seeks for a thing that is lost, does one recover one's own self rather than any other? Why, when one begins again to think, is it not another personality than yesterday's that is incarnate in one? One fails to see what can dictate the choice, or why, among the millions of human beings any one of whom one might be, it is on him who one was overnight that unerringly one lays one's hand? What is it that guides us, when there has been an actual interruption—whether it be that our unconsciousness has been complete or our dreams entirely different from ourself? There has indeed been death, as when the heart has ceased to beat and a rhythmical friction of the tongue revives us. No doubt the room, even if we have seen it only once before, awakens memories to which other, older memories cling. Or were some memories also asleep in us of which we now become conscious? The resurrection at our awakening—*after that healing attack of mental alienation which is sleep*—must after all be similar to what occurs when we recapture a name, a line, a refrain that we had forgotten. And perhaps the resurrection of the soul after death is to be conceived as a phenomenon of memory. [my italics]

To the child who awakens from a nightmare, we say (after turning on the light): "There was no tiger, you are safe, it was only a dream." In effect we advise him to test reality by looking about him, to recognize that his experience was not based on external perception.

In urging him to admit: "It was only a dream," we hope to start another important mental operation. Now he is to inspect his own psychic processes, and to decide that what he experienced came from *within* and does not have the same significance as that which might have come from outside. This need not always be so. If we had said, "The tiger is gone now," we should have reassured him perhaps, but discouraged investigation of the internal source of the tiger in his room. But if we say, "There was no tiger, it was only a dream," we are urging him to look for the sources of the tiger within himself; inviting him, so to speak, to do a little bit of introspection. Here we urge more active self observation in order to strengthen the function of reality testing.

This experience is not confined to children. Many of us may remember episodes of awakening from a vivid dream and for a few interminable moments being unsure that the dream had really been only that, and not a part of the world's reality.

II

To what extent is the superego involved in this process? There has never been widespread agreement on this question, and Freud does not seem to have been altogether sure of the answer.

In 1921, he stated: "The fact that the ego experiences in a *dreamlike* way whatever he [the hypnotist] may request or assert reminds us that we omitted to mention among the functions of the *ego ideal* the business of testing the reality of things" (p. 114, my italics). The "omission" was a significant one, for reality testing was definitely attributed to the ego two years later (1923).

This shift inevitably followed the formulation of the structural hypothesis, since the ego was granted exclusive jurisdiction over transactions with the "external" world. Nevertheless, this did not settle the problem entirely for Freud (see 1933). He was not at all certain which structures, ego or superego or both, were responsible for the evaluation of the psychic processes themselves, and it seems likely that he was never satisfied with the answer.

Over thirty years ago, Waelder (1934) declared, "This function of the superego, self observation, with its perception of inner events, makes a contribution to the distinction between inner and outer world, between fantasy and reality. . . . The intactness of the superego function is therefore a necessary condition of proper reality testing."

A similar attitude is implicit in Isakower's (1939, 1954) work, and he is in general agreement with the point of view that the superego must play an important role in self observation (personal communication).

Gitelson (1964), in his last major statement, described reality testing as "not simply a solipsistic ego function, but . . . also a manifestation of social validations internalized in the superego" (p. 452).

With the progress of ego psychology, however, more and more functions have been ascribed to the ego portion of the mental apparatus. This has led to the development of a consistent and workable body of theory, thanks especially to Hartmann and to his collaborators, Kris and Loewenstein. It has reached a point of development which allows us to direct to it a great number of questions, with the expectation that it will be more or less successful in answering them.

In general, the implications of Hartmann's closely reasoned work are that self observation becomes, with progress toward maturity, more and more an ego rather than a superego function.

There is agreement, at any rate, that regardless of how it operates, reality testing is *influenced* by the superego. Hartmann's (1956) statement may be taken as representative: the superego "among other and partly opposite results . . . [may bring about] some degree of narrowing or distortion of the child's knowledge of inner reality . . . it may occasionally influence even the testing of outer reality" (p. 256).

Generally, it is stated that the superego's role in reality testing need not be a negative one, that it does not *necessarily* interfere with the efficient operation of this function. Nevertheless, it is often cast in the role of a nuisance, if not an actual obstacle to reality testing. Freud (1933) had suggested that the ego ought to become "more independent" of the superego, a puzzling statement in the context of some of his other ideas, and especially so in the light of his own character structure. Hartmann's (1960) suggestion that what is needed is "autonomy" of ego and superego functions is undoubtedly an improvement, emphasizing as it does the integration of functions.

Jacobson (1964), regarding self perception as an ego function exclusively, believes self evaluation to be shared by both ego and superego (p. 130). At the same time she concludes that "the superego introduces a safety device of the highest order, which protects the self from dangerous internal instinctual stimuli, *from dangerous external stimuli,* and hence from narcissistic harm" (p. 133, my italics).

Hartmann and Loewenstein (1962), while assigning perception of one's own mental processes to the superego as well as to the ego, are inclined to emphasize the "negative" influence of the former, its capacity to distort the ego's function of reality testing. But this argument by no means rules out the possibility that the superego, under certain conditions, may have an adaptive function.

But to relegate self observation exclusively to the ego makes it very difficult to describe with any precision the role of the superego, if any, in adaptation to external reality, nor can we be very clear how "self evaluation" occurs.

In deciding where we wish to place self observation in the psychic apparatus, we are faced with an uncomfortable dilemma. The ego must include the apparatus which regulates the drives, as well as that which is responsible for interchanges with the outside world. The power to regulate implies, of necessity, the power to register, to observe and discriminate. On the other hand, to the superego has been assigned the task of "keeping a watch over the actions and intentions of the ego and judging them, in exercising a censorship" (Freud 1930, p. 136). In contemporary language, it is the self, or part of the self, which is observed, and therefore we may describe this superego function as self observation. If the superego is responsible for at least some vital aspects of self evaluation, but not for self observation, how is the latter function performed? If the superego portion of the mental apparatus is fed information about the self by the ego (a reasonable assumption), should it then be thought of as evaluating without *observing* that information about the self? This would not make sense.

III

Reality testing and the other reality functions (those functions of the psychic apparatus having to do with direct adaptation to external reality) should be relatively easy to observe, and we ought to be able to postulate whether, and to what extent, superego functions are related to them.

An attempt to bring forward clinical and other observations which would allow us to trace more precisely the role of the superego in this field is by no means an easy task. While one can cite numerous adaptive aspects of superego function, of a general nature (Hartmann 1960, Schafer 1960, Waelder 1960, Jacobson 1964), to do so in the field of reality testing is another matter. Yet we must first try to answer the question whether the superego, like an ideal policeman (as it is so often represented in dreams), ever "prompts" the ego in the direction of *more* adequate reality testing, as well as the reverse.

But let us begin with a familiar example from clinical practice, in which the superego function is if anything an apparent nuisance. A patient is presented with an interpretation dealing with a bit of behavior. For example, he is told that a certain action of his seems to be determined, at least partly, by his need to express some aspect of an unconscious fantasy and to induce a particular reaction (not necessarily aggressive) in me.

The patient responds immediately, or a bit later, with the assertion that he has been *accused* by me, and that he now recognizes how much I disapprove of his behavior. Actually, I may not have disapproved in the slightest. The behavior itself may have consisted of something so overtly benign as coming to the session a bit early, or removing his wet shoes to avoid soiling the couch. We may assume, therefore, that the disapproval experienced by the patient is a projection of his own guilt.

But why the guilt? Current theory presents us with two available explanations, neither excluding the other. First, the interpretation has facilitated (in a way still obscure to us) the emergence of a drive manifestation, since it has interfered, at least temporarily, with some relatively stable defense. The superego responds to a threatened defiance of its prohibitions, by the id, or id and ego combined, and tension is produced between superego and ego, resulting guilt. This in turn is projected onto the analyst.

Second, the patient may be thought of as defending himself against the interpretation by distorting it, turning it into a hostile attack which must be met by a counterattack. Thus he obscures the clarifying function of the interpretation, and protects himself from the anxiety or guilt which might have been aroused by it. Which of these we would favor might depend on whether or not we could detect very much evidence of guilt in his response.

Other layers of meaning could be adduced. For example, the patient may have the desire to be an object of attack as a passive victim, but this is less pertinent in the context which interests us here.

In general such a reaction as the one described is most common when one interprets behavior, as opposed to a dream, for example, and when the interpretation is pertinent ("correct") if not necessarily ideal in its timing.

In any case we are dealing with a manifestation of resistance, a hindrance to communication between patient and analyst and (implicitly) between the self-observing functions of the patient's psyche and his other mental processes. As such, it interferes with that portion of the reality function which is at the heart of the analytic process, namely, the capacity for useful observation and evaluation of one's inner life.

Beyond that, the resistance also affects the accuracy of the patient's judgment of the "external" world—at least so far as he tries to determine for himself what really went on between him and his analyst. We do know that a premature attempt by the latter to deny the punitive role the patient assigns to him may result in quite absurd arguments, which serve only to fix the patient's belief in his analyst's disapproval of him.

On the other hand, it is not at all uncommon for the patient, on leaving the office at the end of the session, to recognize that his analyst was not at all disapproving. If this happens, it is generally possible to continue on the original path of analysis which began with the interpretation, including the resistance to it.

But let us try to go beyond this and to explain to our own satisfaction why he experienced manifestations of guilt, and how this was accompanied by distortions of his perceptions of both inner and outer world, the latter represented by the analytic situation. This is not so easily demonstrated in conventional structural language.[1]

There are fortunately other sets of observations which raise questions about the role of the superego in reality testing. Isakower's (1939, 1954) writings, previously cited, treat problems of consciousness as central, and have much

---

[1]Would things have gone more smoothly if guilt (and the superego) had not entered the picture? At first glance, we should say yes, but when we remember that such resistances may lead to very useful bits of analytic work, we are not so sure that even here, in the long run, reality testing may not have been "prompted" by superego function. But I fear that this presents us with a paradox which cannot be resolved in these terms and had better be left in a footnote for the present.

to do with my interest in the subject, but recent studies on superego function have placed little emphasis on sleep and the dream.

It seems very odd that phenomena which have been matters of common belief for centuries, and which are part of the personal experiences of most people, should have received so little attention from us. Who would deny that much insomnia is stimulated by the conscience? Why did Lady Macbeth pace the halls of her castle, if not out of guilt? And why do some of us awaken all too early in the morning with a vague discomfort which prevents our returning to sleep? Is it not often a sense of guilt, not anxiety alone, over an incomplete task? (Such as a scientific paper still unwritten!)

John Keats expressed most eloquently the plea of the insomniac: he addresses his words to Sleep, "soft embalmer of the still midnight . . . ":

> Then save me, save me, or the passed day will shine
> Upon my pillow, breeding many woes,
> Save me, save me from curious
> Conscience that still lords
> Its strength for darkness, burrowing like a mole,
> Turn the key deftly in the oiled wards,
> And seal the hushed Casket of my Soul.

We need not rely on poetic evidence alone, and can bolster our argument by citing clinical observations. Here the evidence is overwhelming that guilt, the conscience, the functions of the superego, have a pronounced effect on sleep.

In clinical depressions and often in milder transitory depressive states, in which the superego plays a crucial role, sleep disturbances are extremely common. Insomnia, particularly early waking, is typical. And while we need not doubt the accompanying ego disturbance, one could not describe such phenomena adequately without reference to the superego and its hyperactivity, relative or absolute.

This implies no oversimplification. But the regression, which overtakes the superego as well as the ego in sleep, results in phenomena which may well make sleep intolerable and waken the sleeper. An "internal" danger may be experienced as if it were an external one, whether that internal danger be a bodily sensation or a more truly "internal" drive manifestation. What is it here which rouses the sleeper? Is it the result of ego or of superego function? Or is it rather derived from a phase in which these apparatuses were poorly, if at all, differentiated? The danger signal is often marked by a good deal of guilty affect—a reliable sign of superego involvement.

We may return now to our analytic patient who felt accused. What is the central task of the treatment itself, if it is not to help the patient to distinguish "inside" from "outside," "fantasy" from "reality"? To do this, we must help him to recognize, to understand, and to evaluate his own mental processes. In this instance, we help him to see that his idea of the analyst's disapproval is fantasy, not fact, and we do this not by the usual kind of reality testing, which might degenerate into persuasion, but rather by allowing him to understand that he has confused "inner" and "outer" (the "reality ego" [Freud 1915]).

The analogy may be made closer and more pertinent by applying Lewin's (1955) concept of the analytic situation. Lewin demonstrated to what extent analysis retains its links with the hypnotic state out of which it developed, and how usefully it may be formulated in the language of sleep and dream psychology. The analyst "soothes" the patient into some state of awareness which has dreamlike characteristics, then acts to wake the "dreamer" by a confrontation or an interpretation, or merely by ending the session. I have suggested elsewhere (1965) that this approach may be useful in explaining why interpretations are often treated by the patient as if they had a "superego tinge." (See Isakower 1939, 1954.)

In states of consciousness generally considered "regressive" (e.g., the analytic session, sleep, psychopathological states such as the psychoses) the differentiation between ego and superego functions becomes blurred, if not entirely lost (Freud 1933). It is interesting that when Freud (1921) originally placed reality testing in the ego ideal, it was in the context of the "dreamlike" hypnotic trance.

But the problem is still not solved, for "intrusions" of superego functions do not seem to be limited to regressive states, or even to parapraxes, such as Freud's (1936) on the Acropolis. I refer to the everyday conflict over telling the truth, an activity generally recognized as having close connections with conscience and moral values, and thereby necessarily with the superego as well as the ego.

As analysts we are impressed with the very clear dependence of "truth telling" on "truth knowing," and therefore on reality testing—the need to know what is fantasy and what is fact, or what is "inner" and what is "outer."

Ordinarily if one tells an untruth out of ignorance, there should be no moral taint attached. Yet for young children this is not so. They feel a lie is a lie and should be punished, whether one has access to the facts or not. What becomes clear to the older child and adult had not been evident to the prelatency child (Piaget 1932).

When we proceed from the problem of telling the truth to other people to that of telling it to ourselves, we come closer to the child's point of view.

Many of us willy-nilly regard self deception as highly undesirable, not only in a utilitarian, but even more strongly, in a moral sense, and we are likely to react with guilt whenever we catch ourselves in a serious lapse. As analysts we possess, and attempt to inculcate in our patients, an attitude of telling oneself "the truth" which has the qualities of a moral imperative. We are anything but neutral on this subject!

Hartmann's (1960) discussion of this problem in *Psychoanalysis and Moral Values* is one of the best, for he demonstrates with the greatest skill both the elegance and the depth of ego psychology, along with its inevitable limitations. He comments on Freud's "self-control and discipline that had taught him to face reality at all costs" (p. 16), and on the moral factor implied by such intellectual integrity. For Hartmann, the ego "tests" moral values, interprets them and decides on their "genuineness" or "authenticity" (p. 50f.).

But can truth telling, especially to oneself, be explained adequately in terms of ego–superego tension? In terms of the structural hypothesis, it appears to be the best available brief statement. Yet if we attempt to apply it on the level of clinical observation and theory, we experience some serious difficulties. For example, if we examine the way people learn to tell the truth, we get the impression that the moral and punitive factors (those which will enter into superego) play a leading role in this area of childhood training. Moral teaching and reality testing are hardly to be distinguished by the young child. It takes a long time for him to be impressed with the unfortunate results of self deception and lying to others, if he ever is.

He is taught that lies are bad and forbidden, and only later that they are likely to carry penalties other than parental disapproval. While the first such lessons are interpreted morally (and generally so presented explicitly by the parents), the final stabilization of a well-structured rejection of self deception will depend on an advanced phase of ego development as well. But would the latter, alone, be a sufficient condition?

In the adult, while both ego and superego functions are involved in "telling the truth," it seems reasonable to suppose that the *first* automatic control of the tendency to lie is a well-internalized response in which superego function is dominant. It may be considered relatively archaic, although developmentally it would be traced chiefly to the oedipal or postoedipal period—that is, the phases in which superego precursors are being organized into an integrated structure.

Usually it is only after a fraction of a second has passed that one reacts to the (ego) assertion, "Honesty is the best policy." And so often, how weak is this voice compared with the earlier ringing commandment, "Thou shalt not lie." Here the first automatic superego-impelled response is more often than not adaptive in its effects, if not entirely rational in its sources. While it may not involve reality testing directly, it has much to do with its efficiency.[2] Are we therefore justified in regarding it now exclusively or nearly exclusively as an ego function?

We may go further, and examine how a child learns a piece of reality testing which is not ordinarily associated with ethical standards. Every city child must be taught quite early how to cross a street, as a matter of safety, not morals.

When he makes his first impulsive dash for the curb (often at 18 months, or earlier), he is restrained physically, and generally told "no" very firmly. With further attempts, he will be talked to rather sharply. If he has to be snatched from under the wheels of cars very often, he may even experience his parents' anger, by scolding or physical restraint which may go beyond what legal authorities call "necessary force."

He can hardly ignore the fact that his parents are prohibiting, and perhaps angry. No matter what words they use, their tone and gestures will carry *that* message more readily than the knowledge that the action must be inhibited for other reasons (Spitz 1958). Only later does he know that one avoids running into the roadway because the *cars* are dangerous to life. For in this period of the child's life (his reality testing being poorly developed), the primary danger is experienced as coming from the parents—idealized as they are.

Let us now try to trace the future of this bit of childhood experience. It depends for a time on the parents' real or imagined presence. Eventually, it may be internalized, and to the extent that it retains a morally tinged impera-

---

[2]Hartmann (1956) suggests a reason why many adults (some philosophers among them) cannot accept the logical difference between a moral imperative and a factual statement. He says "The child is constantly confronted with value judgements which cannot be validated objectively but which are presented to him as statements of fact. 'This is good' and 'that is bad' are often presented to him in the same way as 'this is red' and 'that is green.' Such presentations also become part of 'socialized reality'" (p. 258). Such a childhood experience is certainly dependent on the early stage of ego development at which the experience occurs. I should like to modify Hartmann's statement in only one respect, to admit that we are by no means sure that we can do better than the philosophers in this respect—and that perhaps most of the difficulty we encounter in differentiating superego and ego function arises from having been exposed to this experience as children, and never having recovered from it entirely.

Piaget's (1932) work on *The Moral Judgement of the Child* does nothing to encourage making sharp distinctions between moral judgement and other types, even in children of six or seven. He states, aphoristically, "Everyone is aware of the kinship between moral and ethical norms. Logic is the morality of thought, just as morality is the logic of action."

Isakower (1939) has pointed out that in a number of languages including English the terms "right" and "wrong" may be applied both to moral questions and to those of fact.

The logical differentiation between moral imperative and factual statement can be approached only asymptotically—ever coming closer to the line but destined never to reach it.

tive (that it is *bad* to run into the street) it becomes a nucleus[3] within the developing superego. It may therefore run parallel to another bit of learning (that it is *physically* dangerous to run into the street) which may be thought of as a nuclear element within the ego.

If today we approach a crossing, and are faced by a red light, which psychic agencies are involved in our behavior? Very often, if we have been well trained in childhood, we experience a quick hesitation, after which we pause to consider whether or not the signal may be safely disobeyed. The second, less automatic reaction, in which the risks are calculated and action is taken accordingly, is one in which ego function dominates, and we need not consider it further here.

The initial response of hesitation is not so simply explained. If it is derived, as I maintain, from the original prohibitions of the parents, and if it may be expressed by an internal voice, "Thou shalt not run into the street!" it would be directly related to those early parental prohibitions described above. As such, it would be related genetically to the experiences which we regard as destined to enter into the function of the superego.

We may infer that the superego, even in adult life, has "prompted" the ego in a situation in which there is no longer a true moral issue, but in which such an issue had been raised in childhood. While archaic in origin, this operation appears to have become "reality syntonic" or adaptive.

Hartmann (1955) has very properly pointed out that genesis and function are not identical, that in essence what may be derived in a superego fashion, so to speak, need not become or remain a part of the superego. The residues of an experience, however derived, may ultimately be incorporated into the ego in such a way as to ensure certain automatic responses. But the question remains, how often and how completely do such responses lose the marks of their origin? How often do they depend more or less permanently on relatively archaic mechanisms in which ego and superego functions are inextricably joined?[4]

In his paper "A Tribute to Heinz Hartmann," Solnit (1964) emphasizes Hartmann's contribution to the idea that the pleasure principle is related to reality testing, via the approval of the love object;

> if the child is not capable of coöperating with the love object or the love object with the child, early learning mechanisms may be jeopardized. These would include those mechanisms through which the ego's functions become experienced as pleasurable when they are harmonious with the directions and influences of the parental figure. A paucity of such early learn-

[3]Or a "microstructure" (Gill 1963).
[4]See Reich (1954).

> ing mechanisms interferes with the ego's ability to develop unpleasure in the face of danger and the child is then less well protected from the necessary—and desirable—risks of the average expectable environment. [p. 480]

To how great an extent this interference with learning to avoid danger enters into and becomes part of a superego as well as an ego disturbance is the kernel of the problem which we are trying to solve.

Another set of data is pertinent in this regard.

Greenacre's (1948) work on sexual differences in superego development, based on empirical observation and clinical theory, has not yet been adequately incorporated into the body of superego theory on a metapsychological level.

This was based on Freud's (1925) discussion of the effects of anatomical differences on the resolution of the Oedipus complex. He stated that "for women the level of what is ethically normal is different from what it is in men. Their super-ego is never so inexorable, so impersonal, so independent of its emotional origins as we require it to be in men" (p. 257).

Greenacre, accepting this point of view, goes further, and establishes even more direct and earlier links between body sensations and superego development. About the formation of ideals she says, "the boy has a more intact body image in which all his senses concur, while the girl has a mysterious, partly silent, unseen, and not directly palpable area of which she is dimly but not clearly aware and which stimulates her imagination without much chance for reality testing" (p. 164).

She ascribes to girls, on the basis of information from the most diverse sources, "less readiness to submit to the necessities of life . . . more bias . . . an unreliability as to facts; i.e., a tendency to lie" (p. 158f.). (This is not a value judgment by the author. I have chosen, out of context, those elements which have the closest relation to reality testing and superego function.)

The importance of her findings does not lie solely in the demonstration that men and women treat certain kinds of reality differently because of superego differences; rather it is significant on genetic grounds, since it furnishes us with an aspect of the superego concept which is rooted directly in perceptive experience, and which may be susceptible to being traced through later developmental phases. While the chief effects of the perceptions of different body parts will be in the formation of the ego, there will also be more or less direct influences on the development of the superego. Genetically, at least, the latter is close to external reality. Again, to what extent will genesis permanently influence function?

Nunberg's (1951) observation, "conscious perceptions of the ego must be sanctioned by the superego in order to acquire qualities of full, uncontested reality" (p. 8) is pertinent to the analytic situation (see above), and deals with still another aspect of the superego's relation to reality. It has a broad application to problems of derealization, depersonalization, and the like, in which the superego appears to play an important part (Oberndorf 1934, 1939, Jacobson 1959).[5]

The superego not only affects the sense of reality; it plays an essential role in giving permission to *know*.[6] When curiosity and the acquisition of knowledge are impaired, we generally look for a superego element in the disturbance. When, on the contrary, investigation and learning are active and efficient, we tend to ignore the role of the superego, as if it were operative only in a negative direction, forgetting both the permissive elements of the conscience and the positive influence of the ego ideals.[7]

The following clinical example illustrates the point. A patient had troublesome problems in study, particularly in case of reading. Any attempt to learn matters connected with his work, or even to read for pleasure, required undue effort and time, and was often accompanied by feelings of guilt. This could be traced to his childhood experience in attempting to investigate the circumstances of his own very traumatic birth. His efforts had been met with silence, evasion, or frank disapproval.

Once after a particularly successful day in which he had learned a good deal from a skillful teacher, he expressed the fantasy that I would show him that he was deceiving himself, that he had not really been so successful in learning. He was aware that his guilt was projected—but why the guilt? Then he said, "You know, I've noticed that I can read the magazines in your waiting room with great pleasure, and I never feel guilty about that!" It was because the magazines carried my sanction, implicit in their location.

In the analysis, my permission was necessary to allow him to investigate the circumstances of his birth and childhood. In a previous analysis, he had never done so, in spite of the obvious importance of the issue in the genesis of his neurosis; he never felt permission had been given, and such investigation

---

[5]The superego's relation to problems of identity may be illustrated briefly by a case described by M. H. Horowitz (personal communication). His patient, who suffered from a profound identity disturbance, was capable in an elated state of working rapidly and well. "He was in consonance with his aggrandized ego ideal. The *external* reality was *clear*; the cost was to the *internal* reality of his identity." When he felt differently about himself (ugly and inferior), "everything was fuzzy and work was impossible . . . visual perceptions were distorted."

Here, with the ego-superego fusion of the elated state (Lewin 1950), "external" reality testing was more acute than usual. In addition, the superego sanction seems to have given an increased conviction to the patient's sense of the reality of his experience, even though distortions of "internal" reality persisted. When depressed, however, all reality testing suffered and he experienced something akin to derealization.

[6]I am grateful to Eli Marcovitz and Robert Waelder, who highlighted some of this material in their discussion of an earlier draft of this paper.

[7]Nor do I see any substantial justification for considering the ego ideal to be separate from the superego—a concept which adds more difficulties than it resolves.

was therefore still forbidden. In this case the superego first *forbade*, and later *permitted*, the ego to be curious and to know a vital piece of reality.

The role of such superego sanction in the investigation of forbidden secrets is well known, although it has been insufficiently stressed. Everything of importance in science, from Freud's investigation of childhood sexuality to the astronomers' search for the secrets of the universe, has had a forbidden quality and often enough has been met with savage reprisals by the elders of society. Innately we place the "integrity" of the scientist, a character trait heavily dependent on the intactness of the superego, in a position even higher than his intelligence. Freud was of course the model of the scientist, who employed self observation (and self criticism) most explicitly, although the example of Darwin should also be cited.

I cannot omit one last example of the superego's connection with reality—humor. Freud's (1927) paper on the subject deals primarily with irony, that variety which depends above all on the capacity to observe oneself and one's own psychic processes. The superego, Freud says, repudiates reality and serves an illusion. Yet we may join him in regarding such humor as "a rare and precious gift."

This superego influence on reality testing again appeared at first sight to be a negative, interfering one. Yet irony implies a capacity for detachment, for sharpened recognition of the psychic processes, and for an evaluation of the latter which bespeaks not only the persistence of the parents' influence, but even more, the employment of that influence for the most highly developed uses. Irony is generally held to be a sign of maturity, and appears later in children than puns and other jokes.

Here the evaluation of "external" reality suffers only apparently. The evaluation of "internal" reality benefits, if anything; while on balance, the capacity to recognize and deal with all spheres of reality gains by this dynamic event (see also Waelder 1934, Rosen 1963).

The use of irony is not so very different from what happens in the "ideal" analytic situation, in which a temporary inhibition of attention to external reality is accepted as a condition for increased acuity of self observation (Stein 1965).

IV

If we deny the superego a clear role in self observation and relegate this function entirely to the ego (an extreme view), we acquire the merit of internal consistency, so long as we confine our considerations to the ego. But this reduces the superego, after all, to the status of a very tenuous structure, without clear connections with either ego or drives.

This is no easy dilemma. As noted previously, Freud (1933) gave as one of the primary objects of analysis the achievement of independence of the ego from the superego. Yet in the same lecture he had included among the superego's functions those of self observation, conscience and the holding up of ideals (p. 66). Unless we assume a deliberate paradox, which we have no right to do, we must assume that "independence" was meant in a very limited sense.

Among the attempts to solve this problem, the most prominent and probably the most systematic and consistent is Hartmann's, which has been described in a series of papers, most of which were written in collaboration with Kris and Loewenstein. His concept of the developed superego is narrower than Freud's (1933) description, although it has close logical connections with *The Ego and the Id* (1923) and other Freud papers.

Hartmann regards the superego as a structure formed under ego and drive influence, whose adaptive functions, at least, are taken over more and more by the ego during the individual's progress toward maturity. The mature conscience, "healthy" ideals, depend on ego functions, on which the superego exerts some influence, often silent. Mental health, particularly with regard to ethical problems, is a function of adequate integration of ego and superego function.

It would be inappropriate to describe Hartmann's conceptual system in detail; it is widely accepted as the most highly developed point of view in contemporary metapsychology, and most authors regard it as the standard by which alternative hypotheses must be measured. As a theoretical structure it has the virtues of great sophistication, elegance, and consistency.[8]

Even so, Hartmann's work leaves some questions unanswered, and there are still serious gaps in our theory. Rapaport (1960b), in one of his last works, attempted to deal with the "perplexities" which have plagued our attempts to achieve an adequate working definition of the superego, especially in terms of ego–superego differentiation. "The differentiation of the ego and the id is not sharp but progressive. It reaches a definitive crystallization with those defense identifications which arise as a solution of the oedipal conflicts. This point is a separating line between the integrates passive and those active in relation to the drive-tension. The former attain a dominant integration by the superego,

[8]Schafer (1960), in a discussion of the superego in energic terms (see also Beres 1958, Jacobson 1964), establishes a link between the use of aggressive energy by the superego and its adaptive function. One is reminded here that aggressive energy, in the early days before *Beyond the Pleasure Principle* (1920), was self-preservative. To some extent the dual instinct theory may have led to a situation in which the superego, being associated largely with aggressive energy, became more and more identified with punitive and even maladaptive functions—a situation which could be reversed only by assuming the neutralization of such energies, and leaving energic hypotheses of superego function in a quite uncertain state.

the latter a dominant integration by the ego, though these dominances and this separating line are, however, relative."

Rapaport's explicit attempt to clarify the relative and incomplete differentiation between superego and ego is analogous to Gill's (1963) treatment of ego and id differentiation (see also Rapaport 1960a). It is in accord with Freud's (1933) statement:

> We cannot do justice to the characteristics of the mind by linear outlines like those in a drawing or in primitive painting, but rather by areas of colour melting into one another as they are presented by modern artists. After making the separation we must allow what we have separated to merge together once more. You must not judge too harshly a first attempt at giving a pictorial representation of something so intangible as psychical processes. It is highly probable that the development of these divisions is subject to great variations in different individuals; it is possible that in the course of actual functioning they may change and go through a temporary phase of involution. Particularly in the case of what is phylogenetically the last and most delicate of these divisions—the differentiation between the ego and the super-ego—something of the sort seems to be true. [p. 79]

Rapaport himself lists the adaptive aspect of superego theory as one of those which are still to be clarified. Yet it is this, along with the genetic, which is closest to clinical observation and therefore should be most capable of being tested in the light of clinical theory.

Clinical observations do generally support that aspect of superego theory which allows for a blurred and readily permeable border between superego and ego. This is most evident in such regressive states as sleep and the analytic situation, in which superego–ego differentiation is reversed, a process similar to but not identical with that which occurs in mania.

The metapsychological concept of the superego's "closeness" to the drives, and its "passivity" with respect to them (Rapaport 1960b), offers greater difficulties in terms of clinical theory. The same is true to some extent of its investment with aggressive energy. These aspects of the theory cannot be replaced or dispensed with readily, for historical and other reasons. Moreover, they account quite adequately for some genetic observations, and are readily applicable to pathological conditions in which the punitive aspects of the conscience play a destructive, even catastrophic, role.

But it would seem that we have not yet been able to state clearly enough the role of the superego functions, such as the conscience, in "normal" adaptive behavior, and we are in a scarcely better situation with regard to such considerations as the maintenance of ideals and standards, and the upholding of traditions. Even such brittle reeds as "good manners," the inculcation of *noblesse oblige*, the doctrines of chivalrous behavior, all heavily dependent on superego function, have had an important, if somewhat unreliable, role in dealing with reality problems as well as with the drives.[9] We must find some way of accounting for remnants of moral teaching which persist in everyday life, for humor, for superego functions in waking, and for sexual differences in ideals.

If we were to relegate self observation to the ego, excluding the role of the superego, it would be difficult to avoid treating self evaluation similarly as an ego function. It is far too difficult to separate these two mental operations with any precision. Logically, excluding both self observation and self evaluation from the superego would lead to a concept of the latter as a vestigial structure, whose functions are to be taken over by the maturing ego. In the healthy adult, the superego would be active only under abnormal conditions; its persistent operations could be regarded as evidence of imperfect ego function, of psychopathology, or immaturity at least.

On the other hand, we might choose to regard the superego as a permanent and integral part of the psychic apparatus of the adult. A concept of the superego which includes self observation as a functional component, and which allows it some role, however indirect, in the handling of reality, would appear to be much more useful in accounting for our clinical and developmental data. And it might even reverse the trend toward what Sandler (1960) has called "conceptual dissolution" of the superego.

To consider reality testing as the manifest resultant of several components, namely, ego and superego (and the drives as well), is ultimately only an application of the principle of multiple function (Waelder 1936). It is not too much to expect that other manifest operations, which are observable or can be inferred at levels of clinical generalizations or clinical theory (Waelder 1962), may be treated similarly: as resultants of components representing all the major structures of the personality, rather than being treated as if they were a function of one alone—usually, although not invariably, the ego. We might speak then of "structural" rather than "ego" psychology.

It should not be a matter for surprise, or even for regret, that our theory on the highest level of abstraction does not correspond precisely to that which is closest to clinical observation. Metapsychology and clinical theory employ somewhat different methods of approach; and while they may use the same terms, we should not expect these terms to bear exactly the same meanings in different contexts. True, we must strive for unity and consistency which will

[9] Horowitz (personal communication) reminded me that it is the psychopath who is often most concerned with "politeness," as if he needed this superficial code to hide the absence of an efficient inner mechanism.

apply to all levels of abstraction. But we should be under no illusion that such a state of affairs can be attained without major changes in our theory—which will in turn bring about new and difficult inconsistencies. We should welcome such disturbances as signs of the continued growth of a major scientific discipline.

REFERENCES

Beres, D. (1958). Vicissitudes of Superego Functions and Superego Precursors in Childhood. *Psa. Study Ch.* 13:324–351.

Freud, S. (1914). On Narcissism. *Standard Edition* 14:73–102.

—— (1915). Instincts and Their Vicissitudes. *Standard Edition* 14:117–140.

—— (1917). A Metapsychological Supplement to the Theory of Dreams. *Standard Edition* 14:222–235.

—— (1920). Beyond the Pleasure Principle. *Standard Edition* 18:7–64.

—— (1921). Group Psychology and the Analysis of Ego. *Standard Edition* 18:69–143.

—— (1923). The Ego and the Id. *Standard Edition* 19:12–59.

—— (1925). Some Psychical Consequences of the Anatomical Distinction between the Sexes. *Standard Edition* 19:248–258.

—— (1927). Humour. *Standard Edition* 21:159–166.

—— (1930). Civilization and Its Discontents. *Standard Edition* 21:64–145.

—— (1933). New Introductory Lectures on Psycho-Analysis. *Standard Edition* 22:3–82.

—— (1936). A Disturbance of Memory on the Acropolis. *Standard Edition* 22:239–248.

Gill, M. M. (1963). *Topography and Systems in Psychoanalytic Theory. Psychological Issues*, 10.

Gitelson, M. (1964). On the Identity Crisis in American Psychoanalysis. *J. Am. Psa. Assn.* 12:451–476.

Greenacre, P. (1948). Anatomical Structure and Superego Development. *In Trauma, Growth and Personality*, pp. 149–164. NY: Norton, 1952.

Hartmann, H. (1955). Notes on the Theory of Sublimation. *Essays* 215–240.

—— (1956). Notes on the Reality Principle. *Essays* 241–267.

—— (1960). *Psychoanalysis and Moral Values*. NY: IUP.

Hartmann, H., & Loewenstein, R. M. (1962). Notes on the Superego. *Psa. Study Ch.* 17:42–81.

Isakower, O. (1939). On the Exceptional Position of the Auditory Sphere. *Int. J. Psa.* 20:340–348.

—— (1954). Spoken Words in Dreams. *Psa. Q.* 23:1–6.

Jacobson, E. (1954). The Self and the Object World. *Psa. Study Ch.* 9:75–127.

—— (1959). Depersonalization. *J. Am. Psa. Assn.* 7:581–610.

—— (1964). *The Self and the Object World.* NY: IUP.

Lampl-de Groot, J. (1962). Ego Ideal and Superego. *Psa. Study Ch.* 17:94–106.

Lewin, B. D. (1950). *The Psychoanalysis of Elation.* NY: Norton.

—— (1955). Dream Psychology and the Analytic Situation. *Psa. Q.* 24:169–199.
Loewald, H. W. (1951). Ego and Reality. *Int. J. Psa.* 32:10–18.
Nunberg, H. (1951). Transference and Reality. *Int. J. Psa.* 32:1–9.
Oberndorf, C. P. (1934). Depersonalization in Relation to Erotization of Thought. *Int. J. Psa.* 15:271–295.
—— (1939). On Retaining the Sense of Reality in States of Depersonalization. *Int. J. Psa.* 20:137–147.
Piaget, J. (1932). *The Moral Judgement of the Child.* NY: Collier, 1962.
Proust, M. (1920). The Guermantes Way, I. *Remembrance of Things Past.* London: Chatto & Windus, 1960.
Rapaport, D. (1960a). *The Structure of Psychoanalytic Theory, Psychol. Issues,* 6.
—— (1960b). A Theoretical Analysis of the Superego Concept (third version). Unpublished manuscript.
Reich, A. (1954). Early Identifications as Archaic Elements in the Superego. *J. Am. Psa. Assn.* 2:218–238.
Rosen, V. H. (1963). Variants of Comic Caricature and Their Relationship to Obsessive-Compulsive Phenomena. *J. Am. Psa. Assn.* 11:704–724.
Sandler, J. (1960). On the Concept of the Superego. *Psa. Study Ch.* 15:128–162.
Sandler, J., & Rosenblatt, B. (1962). The Concept of the Representational World. *Psa. Study Ch.* 17:128–145.
Schafer, R. (1960). The Loving and Beloved Superego in Freud's Structural Theory. *Psa. Study Ch.* 15:163–188.
Solnit, A. J. (1964). A Tribute to Heinz Hartmann. *Psa. Q.* 33:475–484.
Spitz, R. A. (1958). On the Genesis of Superego Components. *Psa. Study Ch.* 13:375–404.
Stein, M. (1965). States of Consciousness in the Analytic Situation. *Drives, Affects, Behavior,* ed. M. Schur, 2:60–86. NY: IUP.
Waelder, R. (1934). Ätiologie and Verlauf der Massenpsychosen. *Imago* 21:67–91, 1935.
—— (1936). The Principle of Multiple Function. *Psa. Q.* 5:45–62.
—— (1960). *Basic Theory of Psychoanalysis.* NY: IUP.
—— (1962). Psychoanalysis, Scientific Method and Philosophy. *J. Am. Psa. Assn.* 10:617–637.

5

Acting Out as a Character Trait: Its Relation to the Transference

INTRODUCTION BY MARIANNE GOLDBERGER

This paper made an enormous impact on me when it was published just a few years after I completed my formal analytic training and it has remained with me as a cornerstone of my continuing efforts to develop a secure analytic attitude. Aside from my supervision with Paul Gray, this was the first time I had known an analyst to approach acting out from a consistently analytic point of view with no pejorative connotations.

Because of its extraordinary clarity, Martin Stein's paper helped me to gain a more balanced idea of the clinical and theoretical issues that had previously been confused for me. He made a distinction between the wide range of behavior sometimes included under the heading of acting out, and what he called a distinct character trait—that is, the tendency to act out. He described adult neurotic patients who had manifested this character trait before they began analysis. They had a history of repetitive, complexly patterned behavior, most often precipitated by frustration, which was clearly at variance with their more usual way of behaving. Once in analysis, these patients' repetitive behavior patterns might intensify as a transference neurosis developed.

With this last observation, it was not hard to keep an analytic attitude of interested attention to important information about the patient. Thus, these complex, repetitive actions were taken as "stories" to be understood. Stein pointed out that the episodes often were related to a particular kind of frustration and that the disturbance of reality testing and considerable magical thinking were temporary and limited to the area of each patient's particular fantasy. He also pointed to the element of drama usually present in the repetitive acts. He acknowledged that the dramatic element had already been described by Anna Freud and Greenacre, but he believed that its dynamic and genetic significance was often not sufficiently explored. He also emphasized the implications of this point of view for technique: far from being tempted to inhibit the patient's actions, an analyst would now be interested in obtaining as rich and detailed a picture of the behavior and its accompanying feelings as possible.

Stein's perspective made me feel free to just pay attention to analyzing a patient's tendency to express himself in action. It was liberating to know that I was doing my analytic job, leaving no need to attempt to influence my patients' actions. During my analytic training, various course instructors and some supervisors had a different attitude toward acting out. In general they thought that it was always preferable that patients put their thoughts into words and that repeated episodes of acting out should be interpreted. Conveying an interpretation of the action was expected to make the action stop. In fact, there were some older analysts who believed that an analysis was threatened if acting out was permitted to continue too long. For example, a patient usually seen on the couch should not be allowed to sit up; if such a patient did indeed sit up, the first order of business was to get the patient to lie down again.

Finally, this paper is remarkable in foreshadowing the enormous interest in the last fifteen years in the phenomena now variously subsumed under the headings "enactment" and "actualization." Martin Stein touched on many elements described in these more recent papers. For instance, he said that while the repetitive behavior was often related to one predominant fantasy, it carried a large group of meanings when fully developed. He pointed to the frequency with which one or more traumatic experiences engendered the conflicts that were eventually expressed in dramatic action. He also said that "the specific acting out sooner or later makes clear the patient's attachment to a past object. . . ." (p. 63). He linked increased occurrences of acting out to the development of an intense transference neurosis, and stressed that complex and stormy analytic situations ensue that reflect patients' intense ambivalence toward their parents.

Stein's prediction and then elaboration of the various stormy transference interactions that are seen were extremely helpful for me as a young analyst. While he was dryly realistic about the fact that "some patients with well-developed tendencies to acting out are simply not analyzable. . . ." (p. 69), he was in favor of not dispensing with the usual psychoanalytic method too readily in the face of acting out in the transference. Stein quoted Glover (1926) regarding this temptation: "we can say definitely concerning the treatment of neurotic character that the ultimate success of any treatment depends on classical psycho-analytic methods which do not shrink from subjecting the seemingly banal routine of everyday life to detailed scrutiny" (p. 68). By saying that Glover's statement still stands he strengthened my motivation to keep examining—to keep trying to understand—the details of the various enactments of my patients. He helped me become both more relaxed and more persistent in my analytic attitude.

Few terms in our field of inquiry have been subjected to more abuse than has the expression "acting out." For the most part it has been interpreted so broadly as to include any behavior which is assumed to be irrational. As a reaction to this trend, there has been a move to confine it narrowly to the status of a transference phenomenon.

Even analysts are by no means unanimous about what acting out is, in whom it occurs, and how it should be treated. Some have suggested that we do away with the term altogether, but I am inclined to agree with those (e.g., Greenacre 1968) who feel that we should be in no hurry to do so. It is my thesis that acting out, adequately defined, is the prototype of complex human behavior and that a thorough study of the phenomenon can teach us a good deal about the nature of human activity on a wide scale, including something about the nature of social and political forces.

One attempt to resolve the confusion which has beset the term was that of Anna Freud (1968). At the 1967 Copenhagen symposium she advanced the thesis that in the neurotic patient, acting out occurred only in the analytic situation, thus: "Unlike the neurotic, the delinquent, the addict, and the psychotic act out habitually, i.e., also without the releasing benefits of the analytic technique" (p. 168).

This idea, which is held by others as well (e.g., Rangell 1968, Vanggaard 1968), is based on the proposition that the adult neurotic acts out to a significant degree *only* in connection with the analytic situation, while in a state of resistance stimulated by the transference.

Such a thesis was perhaps necessary to reduce the intolerable diffusion of the term which had overtaken Freud's original definition in "Remembering, Repeating and Working-Through" (1914): "we may say that the patient does not *remember* anything of what he has forgotten and repressed, but *acts* it out. He reproduces it not as a memory but as an action; he *repeats* it, without, of course, knowing that he is repeating it" (p. 150).[1]

We could indeed adhere to Anna Freud's use of the term "acting out," so long as we confined ourselves to the analysis of the "ideal neurotic," i.e., that elusive patient whose analysis consists only of the resolution of neurotic

---

An earlier version of this paper was presented at the Regional Psychoanalytic Meeting, Mohonk Mountain House, June 3, 1972.

[1] In the preface to this work the Editor of the *Standard Edition* stated: "This paper is noteworthy, apart from its technical interest, for containing the first appearance of the concepts of the 'compulsion to repeat' (p. 150) and of 'working-through' (p. 155)" (p. 146).

symptoms—obsessional thoughts, phobias, and the like. With such patients we might treat the analytic situation as if it were a closed system, with due regard for the other 23 hours and 10 minutes of the patient's life, and view that residue of the day as a period during which the patient undergoes a set of experiences for the sake of his 50-minute analytic sessions.

This is of course a caricature, as Freud learned when he attempted the analysis of Dora. His patient's character structure and the vicissitudes of daily life made the analysis a highly complex and fluid situation, although—this cannot be repeated too often—it need not threaten the essential intactness of the analytic method for analysts and patients who are willing and able to use it. I have discussed this at length in a previous paper (1969).

I propose that Freud's relatively restricted definition, as restated by Anna Freud, be made more broadly applicable, without at the same time encouraging the overuse to which it has been subjected. It is regrettable that the term "acting out" has been applied to a very wide range of behavior, including the impulsive behavior of delinquents and criminals, the actions of political extremists, sexual promiscuity, extended even to defiant or merely mischievous behavior by which patients succeed in provoking their analysts.

This has created a clinical and theoretical confusion which needs to be resolved, as Anna Freud suggested, but not, I propose, at the cost of leaving out of our description a highly interesting series of characteristics manifested by adult neurotic patients, not only during, but *before* analysis has begun. These are best denoted as a distinct character trait: "the tendency to act out." Such patients give a history marked by repetitive, complexly patterned behavior, generally precipitated by frustration. This pattern offers a contrast to their usual mode of life; it has certain features distinctly at variance with what appear to be the dominant modes of the personality.

When such patients enter analysis, the acting-out pattern continues as before and it may, for a time, become more flamboyant, a development which is likely to be disconcerting even to the most unflappable of analysts. Nevertheless, in the more favorable cases, this situation changes with the development of a transference neurosis. We are likely to see an increasing control of the repetitive behavior pattern outside the analysis, followed sooner or later by the occurrence of some equivalent behavior within or in clear relation to the analytic situation. In other words, acting out in life is replaced by acting out in the transference.[2]

This is analogous to the classical development of the transference neurosis in the predominantly "symptomatic" patient, whose character problems are

---

[2]This is reminiscent of Aichhorn, but we are not dealing with delinquents, nor are we departing from the usual analytic technique.

less prominent in the pathological structure, and in whom symptom formation rather than "acting-out" behavior recurs in a transference setting.

"Acting out in the transference" would be defined now very much as Freud defined it in 1914. But the *tendency* to act out, regarded as a character trait, implies that the patient has been "acting out" for much of his adult life; and, further, that the acting out in the transference which occurs during analysis is a secondary development—and, as I shall try to demonstrate, a crucial one for the success of the analytic method.[3]

I am in agreement with those authors who maintain that the character trait, "the tendency to act out," need not be considered pathognomonic of delinquency, addiction, or psychosis.[4] On the contrary, it may be seen in its purest form in a group of neurotic patients, otherwise fairly well-integrated, sometimes talented and distinguished people, who may have achieved considerable personal success and even prominence in fields in which a dramatic way of life has some advantages.

It is true that we observe in delinquency, addiction, and psychosis, as well as in adolescence, a great deal of impulsive, grossly irrational, even violent behavior which is likely to be chaotic and unpredictable. I maintain that such chaotic behavior, often referred to, all too loosely, as "acting out," should not be so classified, for it is in essence quite different.

"Acting out," whether in preanalytic daily life or during analysis, is irrational and may indeed be impulsive and violent. It is, however, neither chaotic nor unpredictable. On the contrary, it is highly organized, requiring a well-structured ego, though it may not be fully adequate in some important respects. The phenomenon of acting out includes a number of constant features, which allow us to establish a distinct category and in turn to describe a recognizable character trait. None of this is new to the literature of acting out, yet it is worth summarizing here (cf. Bird 1957, Fenichel 1945, Greenacre 1950, 1963, 1968, Spiegel 1954).

The term should be restricted to actions which are complex and are repeatedly carried out over extended periods of time—not merely a series of symptomatic acts which are in themselves trivial and relatively simple.

Acting out is repetitive in the strict sense, not merely recurrent, and it is often predictable by the individual's friends and family and, ultimately, his analyst. When such an action has occurred, there are plenty of people ready to say, "He (or she) has done it again." Only the patient is likely to be surprised—

---

[3]In a discussion of an early version of this paper Burness E. Moore emphasized the usefulness of the distinctions between "acting in," "acting out," and "living out." Although these are useful distinctions descriptively, I wish in this paper to emphasize the continuity of these various phenomena and therefore employed the rubric "the tendency to act out" as a character trait.

[4]See "Reports of Discussions of Acting Out" (Klauber 1968, Calef 1968, Gonzalez 1968, Heilbrun 1968, Laplanche 1968).

or, more often, chagrined. Distinct episodes are related to a particular type of frustration to which the individual responds in a characteristic way.

A constant feature is the disturbance of reality testing, which is temporary and confined to the area that is under control of the dominant fantasy. Judgment, otherwise excellent, is ignored, impaired, or largely suspended. In this respect it differs from the disturbances in reality functions which characterize the psychotic and delinquent, in whom these defects are likely to be widespread and fixed. Although not immediately evident, the progress of the analysis reveals the extent of magical thinking. Here again its prominence is temporary, and is confined to the area controlled by the fantasy.

At the time the action occurs, it is usually completely rationalized. It is, so to speak, ego-syntonic, so that it is carried on free of criticism, and generally is not immediately subjected to moral disapproval.

A really well-developed piece of acting out will soon reveal a distinct element of drama in the act itself. It occurs most often and most distinctly in individuals with some ambition or flair for drama—or melodrama. Prominent narcissistic and exhibitionistic features are observed or readily inferred.

The state of mind in which acting out occurs is comparable to the person's normal alert wakefulness. In a few cases, often associated with perverse activity, or alcohol, rather complex acts may be carried out in a dissociated, almost fuguelike state. Not typical of the neurotic acting out, such a state occurs now and then in this group of patients.

The tendency to act out is in my experience more likely to be associated with so-called "hysterical" characters—at least it seems to be less frequent in obsessional and phobic patients. When it occurs in borderline and psychotic patients, or addicts, it is less well defined, more chaotic and impulsive—and more likely to be associated with disturbances of consciousness—and must be understood and treated rather differently.

When acting out is subjected to analysis, it *may* take only a few weeks or months to give some idea of the unconscious fantasy which underlies the phenomenon, and which is being quite literally "acted out." Very often, the patient's behavior may best be described as a dramatic performance in a play which he has written, and in which he plays the chief role and often others as well. The play is acted over and over again. Except for the (usually tragic) hero or heroine, the cast changes from time to time, but the script remains the same, and the ending is anticipated by the audience—but not by the author-director-actor, who each time looks for a happy ending which is never to occur. And so it goes, again and again. This dramatic element has been described by Anna Freud (1949) and Greenacre (1963), yet even now its dynamic and genetic significance and implications for technique are not sufficiently explored.

Usually late in the analysis we discover that the underlying fantasy is highly organized and condensed, and that it represents both the direct derivatives of, and the defense against, the conflicts engendered by an early traumatic experience or set of experiences. While such fantasies are highly charged with erotic elements, they do not lack aggressive features, often of a castrating type, but which may be even more primitive, e.g., cannibalistic.

The acting out, although related often to one predominant fantasy and one traumatic experience or a series, nevertheless carries when fully developed a large group of meanings. It constitutes an ideal illustration for the principle of multiple function, as I have discussed it elsewhere (Stein 1969).

Greenacre has suggested that the significant traumatic experiences are likely to date from that special period during which speech development is particularly rapid, viz., the age of 2 or 3 or so. While such a speculation is difficult to establish as a general rule, it makes very good sense theoretically, accounting for the predilection for action rather than thought and verbalization. Now and then one comes across some striking clinical evidence which tends to support it.

For some months a young woman patient, well advanced in analysis, had been voicing the most intense admiration for me, my skill as an analyst, my standing in the profession, and the like, a phenomenon akin to if not identical with the "idealizing transference" described by Kohut (1971), of which more below. Meanwhile, her pronounced tendencies to act out seemed to have disappeared entirely. She became, for the time, a "perfect" analysand.

When, after some thought, I indicated, as gently as I might, the need to subject this development to analytic scrutiny, she reacted with intense anger and threatened to resume her formerly well-established pattern of behavior.

These threats were not carried out, but a few days later, she told me at the beginning of a session that she would refuse to leave my office at the end of the session. Perhaps she would stay all day! If I wanted her out, I should have to remove her forcibly. At the appropriate time, I indicated the end of the session. She stood up, gave me a somewhat wry smile, and left without further incident.

The following session revealed this episode to have been a reenactment, in the transference, of a distinctive childhood experience. At the age of 2, she had been sent off to a nursery school, but she cried so uncontrollably that she had to be removed, and the attempt abandoned for the time. Two years later a sibling was born, and she was again sent to school.

Now she tried to remain home by complaining of illness, but after being pronounced fit on several occasions by the family pediatrician, she was carried out of the house and to the nearby school, kicking and screaming. It may have been the doctor himself who took her on several occasions. Once at school, she was transformed into a model student, a bright and well-behaved little girl. But each morning, for some time, the "act" would be repeated, until it finally disappeared.

The little girl had in fact been neglected by her elegant and narcissistic parents, who, professing the highest ideals of child rearing (according to Freud and other authorities), flouted these ideals in practice and ignored the child, except when they could show her off to advantage.

This young woman demonstrated discrepancies between verbalized thought and behavior to an extent which permitted self-destructive acting out to occur in an atmosphere of apparent rationality—or rationalization. Throughout life, she provoked rejections and desertions, each time being disappointed when the inevitable occurred. It was a pattern entirely predictable by close friends and regarded with chagrin by the patient when the episode was over.

Interestingly and not at all atypically (for this type of patient), the acting out affected her personal life most severely. In contrast to a long series of self-induced setbacks in her attempts to establish a gratifying home life, her very complicated professional career remained virtually free of the tendency to reenact the traumatically determined fantasy, thus permitting considerable occupational success and gratification.

In another patient, acting out in the transference was persistent, taking the form of breaking away from the analysis psychologically, while remaining in it physically. This behavior seemed to have been influenced by a period of physical restraint in childhood, a situation in which only the mind could roam freely while the body was literally bound. The resistance to analysis reenacted what must have been an early acceptance of physical restraint, while rejecting any psychic bonds.

The adult life of this patient was marked by a pattern of repetitive responses to stress which consisted of complex and futile attempts at solution of conflicts that appeared to be current, but which represented on a deeper level the process of being restrained and trying to escape. Highly articulate, he used speech for manipulation and, as is so often the case, quite successfully, but its employment to advance thought, particularly in the quest of self-understanding, was far less successful.

Originally, the capacity for expressing, for enthusiasm, for charm, even for a certain degree of impulsivity, had provided crucially valuable techniques for preserving individuality and effectiveness. Now they had become grossly inadequate to deal with important aspects of adult life.

A convincing memory of traumatic experience in early childhood may be recovered and worked through, but this is a development that occurs late in the analysis. Usually the memory is screened by massive conflicts dating from the oedipal phase and relived in adolescence. While episodes of "acting-out" behavior may occur in adolescence as an effective mode of reality testing (Blos 1963), the drama in the group I am describing continues to be reenacted throughout adult life, while little effective reality testing occurs and nothing is resolved.

The specific acting out sooner or later makes clear the patient's attachment to a past object, usually a parent or parent surrogate. The lovers who are chosen, for example, may look quite different at first, but we soon discover that they are all the same and that they represent a highly idealized infantile object—idealized negatively, very often, under a cover of worshipful admiration of the parent's remembered image. These and other related narcissistic phenomena are very much part of the clinical picture.

Ultimately, the intense ambivalence of attitudes toward the parents appears in the transference, creating a complicated and stormy analytic situation which places enormous demands on the analyst's understanding, self-discipline, and technical skill (see Bird 1957). The analyst is particularly subject to attempts at seduction by the most subtle means—and not necessarily at all in the conventional erotic mode. Much more often he is idealized as being beyond such unworthy feelings, and is regarded as truly godlike in his wisdom and self-control. By some patients, he is treated as if he were a powerful protector against destructive impulses, and a totally perfect and benign parent—in complete contrast to the all-too-imperfect parents in reality.

During this phase of the analysis, patients who previously acted out a good deal may become model analysands, entirely happy with their analyses, and behave as if they were totally and miraculously cured. At this point their love for the analyst seems entirely desexualized, and they appear to be in love with analysis itself, as in one of the patients described above.

While this phenomenon bears a close resemblance to what Kohut (1971) has termed "the idealizing transference," I am not sure that the patients I have considered would warrant classification as "narcissistic personality disorders." Narcissistic problems are evident enough, but the essential structure of the personality is not very different from that originally described as "transference neurosis," and there is every reason to adhere to standard psychoanalytic technique.

Kohut's emphasis on special consideration, tact, and careful timing is of course altogether warranted and should be part of any analysis. But in these cases we find little justification for long delays in confronting the analysand with the need to subject his transference attitudes and fantasies to analytic scrutiny.

This does not at all imply an early *interpretation* of transference, but it does assume that the analysand is capable of a degree of critical self-scrutiny, including an awareness of his narcissistic conflicts and their role in distorting his views of reality (see Greenacre 1950), including the image of the analyst.

Failing to convey this until late in analysis exposes the analyst to the risk of being cast in a role as the sharer or even the accomplice of the most regressive elements in the personality of the analysand, a tricky if not untenable (i.e., unanalyzable) transference position. In patients like these, with a fair capacity for reality testing and high perceptivity, such modifications are rarely necessary and generally undesirable, however indicated they may be in the narcissistic disorders described by Kohut.

It is too bad to introduce trouble into paradise, but it is a task which cannot be too long delayed in the quest for understanding. The patient may, of course, react to such confrontation rather violently, threatening resumption of the more distressing features of old behavior patterns. But this is often followed by a flood of new memories and associations, revealing a history of attempts to be an ideal child who, in the act of overcoming the more violent erotism of the oedipal phase, seduced his parents by his delightful behavior and intellectual accomplishments.

Seductive attempts by these complex and often very intelligent people may therefore consist of playing on the analyst's therapeutic zeal and his narcissistic investment in his work. It is so easy to be off one's guard with a patient who seems to be (and perhaps really is) working very hard at analysis and showing important signs of improvement, and fail to realize the erotism and violence which are so carefully concealed.

More familiar, of course, are hostile attempts to provoke the analyst into activity, to induce him to intervene in such a way as to make further analysis complicated or frankly impossible. Anxiety in the analyst may induce him to prohibit, to warn, or to interpret unnecessarily and prematurely. He may even be impelled to intervene in more massive ways, making ultimate analysis of the transference futile. Rather than destroying the analysis themselves, these patients are more likely to manipulate the analyst into doing so—a victory of sorts, which preserves the self-esteem of the patient and convinces him of the uselessness of analysis. It may convince the analyst, too, but that is another matter.

In these patients, therefore, the hostile transference is most likely to take the form of an attack on the analyst by destroying his work, a self-destructive phenomenon which is sometimes regarded as a manifestation of the negative therapeutic reaction. Whether or not it is so classified, it offers a difficult technical problem (see also Bird 1972).

Fortunately, in this group, reality testing is reasonably intact in most areas, and the problem can usually be brought within the scope of analysis, although by no means is it easy to recognize, understand, and interpret. Nevertheless, the capacity to bring the acting-out pattern into the analytic situation in the form of a transference resistance is a great step forward, if it is accompanied by some degree of self-imposed control of behavior outside the analysis. It is only then, probably, that the patient can understand it in the immediate and vivid (i.e., the "analytic") sense with the analyst as object.

Difficult as this procedure is for the analyst, it is incomparably more distressing for the patient, who must tolerate frustration and anxiety to an extent previously unfamiliar to him. Not only is this extraordinarily painful, but the memories which are invoked and reexperienced are likely to be even more distressing. The situation described in the brief vignettes I presented included extreme suffering, requiring all the resources of the patient to tolerate analysis without resuming self-destructive behavior. Self-control and attempts at renunciation often gave rise to panicky feelings of identity confusion, and even to brief attacks of depersonalization, as if to say, "If I do not act, who am I? Do I exist?"—phenomena which in these patients are generally no more severe than they are in reasonably healthy adolescents in time of stress.

These people are often articulate and may even have chosen careers in which speech plays a crucial role. Their use of words presents us with a fascinating and often exasperating problem. They are experts at what might be called "pseudocommunication" in analysis, using speech to charm, to attack, to confuse, and much less often to reveal, explore, and inform. The analyst's "best" interpretations (i.e., those of which he is most proud) are taken by the patient and related back as proofs of good behavior, as magical incantations, as intellectual resistances, all without being allowed to touch the core of conflict and memory (Greenacre 1950, 1963, 1968, Loewenstein 1956).

In some patients, the memories evoked are those of serious and prolonged illness during the very early years. Sometimes only the later period of an illness is remembered, its earliest symptoms having developed during the first year or two of life. Part of the history consists of the tales told by the parents, especially of their sacrifices for the sick child. The illness also leaves its traces in the form of somatic patterns, in both voluntary and involuntary muscular systems.

Psychically, the experience of forced inactivity during childhood may leave its mark in the need to resist any constraints, including those imposed by the analysis. The analytic principle of thought before action, implied if not spelled out, the regularity of sessions, the use of the couch and the like, may all be treated as if they were revivals of the discipline of the sickroom, with the analyst cast as the oversolicitous or neglectful parent. What more natural than that the child should want to go out and play with his friends, regardless of his illness? And the patient to act, regardless of his neurosis? And to be forbidden and protected?

Here, analysis of the acting out is more difficult, and sometimes limited in scope. But with some adequate structure, it may be possible for the patient to accomplish a good deal, in the way of substituting more for less appropriate defenses, and to derive the substantial benefits of a more efficient reality testing function. Some material may remain intellectualized, partly out of the need to hypothesize early events, rather than reconstruct them; sometimes the memories of infantile disease or neglect are simply too painful to allow extensive reconstruction and recall. Even so, much of the self-destructive quality of the acting out comes under control, and the need for fantasy-bound action is less urgent. The life pattern may follow the same general outline as before, but on a more gratifying, less destructive level.

All of this group demonstrate what might be called "neurotic character," in that their conflicts are expressed in the form of fantasy-bound complex actions, rather than primarily in the form of phobias, conversion symptoms, or obsessions. Aside from the important predilection for repetitive dramatic and maladaptive action in response to special stresses, they do not differ so much in other respects from the symptom neurotics.

Many of our patients who begin analysis as phobic or obsessional lose their symptoms within a few months, leaving us with the task of analyzing the underlying character structure; in a number of cases this contains the tendency to act out as a prominent trait, a fact which may be clearly recognized only after some months or even years of analysis. It is this problem of character which furnishes the essential indication for analysis, even though it may never have appeared as an original complaint.

We know little about those constitutional factors which predispose to acting out, but it would be wise to postulate the existence of early, perhaps biologically classifiable determinants, e.g., the presence of hyperactivity at birth, as well as very early experiential factors, such as those noted by Greenacre (1941). Sociocultural factors are also of the greatest importance in facilitating certain modes of action which are more or less acceptable to the particular society in which one lives, furnishing what Hartmann, Kris, and Loewenstein (1951) called "pathways of discharge." The latter may not predispose to acting out, but they do make one or another form of it more likely (for examples, see Gans 1962, Becker 1964). This, however, deserves a separate discussion beyond the scope of this paper.

The ego functions which control action are unstable, and there are serious, if temporary lapses in reality testing and judgment. But the disturbance of function is limited in scope and duration, and occurs generally only during the course of the performance, so to speak. Defects there may be, but they are fluid and subject to attempts at repair, often successful.

This group does not correspond precisely to what Helene Deutsch (1930) described as "fate neurosis," a term with overtones of Wagnerian doom. Her cases occupy a place at the lower end of the scale, with the more severely masochistic, self-destructive character disorders. A similar qualification applies to Greenacre's classic descriptions of "the predisposition to anxiety" (1941), a group of cases which occupy perhaps the lowest level of what might still be called neurotic.

There is some overlapping as well with the borderline and "narcissistic" patients described in some detail by Kohut (1968, 1971) and Kernberg (1970). It is particularly difficult to fit the group I am concentrating on precisely into one or another of Kernberg's categories, which may be too restrictive for the purpose. Generally, my patients would be considered under his "Higher Level of Organization of Character Pathology"—yet the predilection for impelled action would place them in an "Intermediate Level," as would the evidence of pregenitally determined conflicts. At the same time their general level of functioning in many aspects of life gives one the impression of a relatively highly structured and efficient ego and superego functioning—with qualifications.

Such categories as Kernberg's and Kohut's are valuable in allowing us to communicate more freely with others who are investigating the same general questions. But there is the danger that even applying the terms "narcissistic" or "pregenitally determined" may influence the analyst to decide too readily to dispense with the usual psychoanalytic method. As long ago as 1926, Glover concerned himself with this temptation, citing the efforts of Ferenczi, Wilhelm Reich, Waelder, and Aichhorn. He concluded: "we can say definitely concerning the treatment of neurotic character that the ultimate success of any treatment depends on classical psycho-analytic methods which do not shrink from subjecting the seemingly banal routine of everyday life to detailed scrutiny" (p. 30).

His statement still stands. If the patient is analyzable at all, major therapeutic modifications are generally undesirable in that they consist of maneuvers which render the subsequent analysis of transference impossible—or, at the very least, hellishly difficult.

In this group of patients, the development of the transference neurosis is signaled by episodes of acting out in relation to the analyst. If these constitute vital threats to the analysis itself and cannot be dealt with by analytic methods, it becomes obvious sooner or later that the analyst will be forced to break off the analysis and recommend another approach. It should be a reluctant decision, but openly recognized by analyst and patient alike. It may require terminating the treatment, perhaps a transfer to another analyst, in order to avoid stalemates, those analyses which are neither psychoanalysis nor good psychotherapy, but which may go on for years with no benefit to anyone. Some patients with well-developed tendencies to acting out are simply not analyzable, and the sooner this is recognized the better (Bak 1970), so that other means may be employed for their benefit.

Ideally, however, and fairly often, the acting out in the transference, which has replaced the acting-out pattern in life, need not bring about modification or destruction of the analysis. Given a patient who has the capacity to control action sufficiently to continue the analysis, and an analyst who can tolerate and understand the threats of destructive action, the analysis can maintain its course.

The neurotic character disorders are particularly suited to analytic study and treatment, whether they appear as character problems from the start or are screened by one or another of the classical symptoms of neurosis (e.g., "Dora"). Even though analysis is not invariably effective, it remains the procedure of choice. I do have the impression that it is not given an adequate trial nearly often enough, with an open understanding by both analyst and patient of the goals and limitations of the method and the need for periodic evaluation of its effectiveness.

The importance of the tendency to act out one's fantasies in a recurrent and compelled fashion extends far beyond the small group of cases discussed here. In other neurotic patients, perhaps the majority who request analysis, acting out does not play a prominent role in preanalytic life, but some form of it appears sooner or later with the development of the transference neurosis. Such "acting out in the transference" differs only in degree from the "characteristic" acting out I have described. It is likely to occur later in the analysis, to be less flagrant in its appearance and less threatening to the analytic situation.

In its fundamental quality and genesis, however, it is much the same as in our prototypical group. All the criteria are there, although more difficult to find, including evidence of a previously established repetitive pattern of behavior. At first sight, this would seem to have been well integrated and adaptive, quite unlike "characteristic" acting out. Yet when such an episode of acting out in the transference is carefully analyzed, we find that it and the previously established pattern may be traced to unconscious fantasies and their infantile sources.

Unless this behavior plays a major role in the personality, it is not justified to describe it as a character trait. But the wide occurrence and reenactment of romantic fantasies, of rashly conceived rescues, are the stuff of everyday life. They serve on the one hand to make it tolerable in the face of crushing burdens, but they also act as carriers of anachronistic and irrational elements. We may even postulate such manifestations in the lives of so-called normal individuals, in whom they appear as regressive phenomena without frank symptom formation. They are like the lunatic fringes in stable societies, active and dangerous during periods of severe stress, but fading out of sight with the return of stability.

We may therefore hypothesize a continuum of individual tendencies to act out, from those in whom such patterned behavior becomes evident only under unusual circumstances, such as serious object loss, to those whose lives are dominated by the need to reenact the same pattern of destructive behavior over and over again.

Returning to my central argument, the tendency to act out may be regarded as a universal human characteristic, which in some individuals is sufficiently marked to be considered a character trait of some pathological significance, in that it affects seriously and adversely the course of the individual's life, while in other individuals it is of only minor significance.

In neurotic patients of the type described here, acting out in the transference does not develop *de novo*; it occurs rather as an irresistible shift into the analytic situation, of a previously well-established and clearly outlined pattern of pathological behavior, evoked by the pressure and opportunity offered by the transference. It is in these patients a signal of the development of a transference neurosis and a development essential to the advance of the analytic process.

REFERENCES

Bak, R. C. (1970). Psychoanalysis Today. *J. Amer. Psychoanal. Assn.* 18:3–21.

Becker, H. S. (1964). *The Other Side.* New York: Free Press.

Bird, B. (1957). A Specific Peculiarity of Acting Out. *J. Amer. Psychoanal. Assn.* 5:630–647.

—— (1972). Notes on Transference: Universal Phenomenon and Hardest Part of Analysis. *J. Amer. Psychoanal. Assn.* 20:267–301.

Blos, P. (1963). The Concept of Acting Out in Relation to the Adolescent Process. *J. Amer. Acad. Child Psychiat.* 2:118–143.

Calef, V. (1968). Reports of Discussions of Acting Out. *Int. J. Psycho-Anal.* 49:225–227.

Deutsch, H. (1930). Hysterical Fate Neurosis. In *Neuroses and Character Types*, pp. 14–28. New York: International Universities Press, 1965.

Fenichel, O. (1945). Neurotic Acting Out. *Collected Papers* 2:296–304. New York: Norton, 1954.

Freud, A. (1949). Certain Types and Stages of Social Maladjustment. In *Searchlights on Delinquency*, ed. K. R. Eissler, pp. 193–204. New York: International Universities Press.

—— (1968). Acting Out. *Int. J. Psycho-Anal.* 49:165–170.

Freud, S. (1914). Remembering, Repeating and Working-Through. *Standard Edition* 12:145–156.

Gans, H. J. (1962). *The Urban Villagers.* New York: Free Press.

Glover, E. (1926). The Neurotic Character. *Int. J. Psycho-Anal.* 7:11–30.

Gonzalez, A. (1968). Reports of Discussions of Acting Out. *Int. J. Psycho-Anal.* 49:227–228.

Greenacre, P. (1941). The Predisposition to Anxiety. In *Trauma, Growth and Personality*, pp. 17–82. New York: International Universities Press, 1969.

—— (1950). General Problems of Acting Out. *Psychoanal Quart.* 19:455–467.

—— (1963). Problems of Acting Out in the Transference Relationship. In *Emotional Growth*, pp. 695–712. New York: International Universities Press, 1971.

—— (1968). The Psychoanalytic Process, Transference, and Acting Out. *Int. J. Psycho-Anal.* 49:211–218.

Hartmann, H., Kris, E., & Loewenstein, R. M. (1951). Some Psychoanalytic Comments on "Culture and Personality." In *Psychoanalysis and Culture*, ed. G. B. Wilbur & W. Muensterberger, pp. 3–31. New York: International Universities Press.

Heilbrun, E. (1968). Reports of Discussions of Acting Out. *Int. J. Psycho-Anal.* 49:228.

Kernberg, O. F. (1970). A Psychoanalytic Classification of Character Pathology. *J. Amer. Psychoanal. Assn.* 18:800–822.

Klauber, J. (1968). Reports of Discussions of Acting Out. *Int. J. Psycho-Anal.* 49:224–225.

Kohut, H. (1968). The Psychoanalytic Treatment of Narcissistic Personality Disorders: Outline of a Symptomatic Approach. *Psychoanalytic Study of the Child* 23:86–113.

——— (1971). *The Analysis of the Self.* New York: International Universities Press.

Laplanche, J. (1968). Reports of Discussions of Acting Out. *Int. J. Psychoanl.* 49:228–230.

Loewenstein, R. M. (1956). Some Remarks on the Role of Speech in Psycho-Analytic Technique. *Int. J. Psycho-Anal.* 37:460–468.

Rangell, L. (1968). A Point of View on Acting Out. *Int. J. Psycho-Anal.* 49:195–201.

Spiegel, L. A. (1954). Acting Out and Instinctual Gratification. *J. Amer. Psychoanal. Assn.* 2:107–119.

Stein, M. H. (1969). The Problem of Character Theory. *J. Amer. Psychoanal. Assn.* 17:675–701.

Vanggaard, T. (1968). Contribution to Symposium on Acting Out. *Int. J. Psycho-Anal.* 49:206–210.

6

A Psychoanalytic View of Mental Health: Samuel Pepys and His Diary

INTRODUCTION BY MILTON HOROWITZ

Written with his usual sense of perspective and balance, Martin Stein's essay on mental health as illustrated by Samuel Pepys's diary is an outgrowth of a long psychoanalytic tradition. With historical roots in the work of Abraham, Freud, and most specially Heinz Hartmann, he attempts a panoramic view of mental health not as a mythical "ideal" but as the consequence of development, ubiquitous conflict and its resolution, and the formation of psychic structure in the "approximation of an ideal."

Pepys provides the reader of his diaries with a complex picture of a man capable of work and love, with varying standards of morality and very much a product of his turbulent era in those fluctuating standards. Sticking closely to the evidence provided by the diaries (which contain little information about Pepys's early life experiences), Stein completely avoids a commonplace psychoanalytic hazard: speculating upon origins of current traits from past history. He thus avoids the pitfall of "genetic fallacy."

Taking a page out of Hartmann, Stein focuses upon Pepys's capacity for adaptation in the midst of the conflicts and anxieties of everyday life and a fluctuant but ongoing ability to achieve mastery. Stein emphasizes Pepys's insatiable curiosity about the world *and* himself linked to unsparing introspection and an obvious desire to avoid self-deception. Central to the diary is Pepys's esthetic sense, whether about music or sexuality, and the link to wanting pleasure when he was still young enough to enjoy it. Stein shows us that the diary allows us to explore the inner life of a real person without the constraints of confidentiality that hinder us from reporting about our patients. With this, we are reminded that our patients, as well as the rest of humankind, are complex mosaics of health and pathology and not easily pigeonholed into pathological categories as now seems popular in conventional psychiatric nosology. In this paper, the emphasis is upon Pepys's health with some mention of brief lapses into greater conflict and symptoms. Pepys's remarkable attention to his dreams also took Dr. Stein's special interest in that it places within the realm of everyday life dreaming as an aspect of "thoughts while asleep."

A careful reading of this paper asks the reader to reconsider his prior predilections and prejudices about what constitutes mental health and put it into a much broader historical and functional perspective. It asks the reader to avoid static concepts of health and to recognize the essential and necessary fallibilities and vulnerabilities of real people. The essential content of Dr. Stein's paper is that there are some aspects of character and of mental health that serve as an internal gyroscope that keeps our day-to-day fluctuations of inevitable conflict, mood, symptom-potential, and our capacities for the acting out of inner life on a relatively steady course. We are alerted to differentiate between culturally determined and variable morality and rigid moralizing. We are asked to smile upon our humanness and not to sneer at our imperfections.

It has been difficult to illustrate specific criteria for mental health, largely because of the lack of adequately documented examples. The Diary of Samuel Pepys *is a unique source of data about a man who was not only exceptionally interesting, but was relatively healthy as well.*

It has come to be asserted almost as a matter of course that everyone in Western society is "sick," that all of us suffer from neurotic illness, if not some more serious psychopathology. This assumption bears an uncanny resemblance to what may well have been its ancestor: the Christian doctrine of original sin. That too was a matter of faith and was about as useful in eliminating evil as the doctrine of universal psychopathology has been in eliminating neurotic illness.

Although such a point of view is by no means accepted by most analysts, we do bear some measure of responsibility for its propagation. While we speak with authority of what went wrong and how, and are experts in describing and giving examples of psychopathological disturbances, our conceptions of mental health are all too often based on negative and vague criteria. Is mental health simply the absence of neurotic illness? That would make it a distinctly boring condition, which would be a pity.

This difficulty cannot be ascribed to the pioneers of psychoanalysis. While their interests were first and naturally aroused by patients with complaints that could best be understood in terms of psychopathology, they were impelled to make a number of contributions to the subject of mental health. These have been admired and occasionally quoted but have failed to exert the impact we might have anticipated on the basis of their intrinsic value as scientific hypotheses. The first influential work was that of Karl Abraham (1925) who, in "Character Formation on the Genital Level of the Libido," described an ideal of mental health in terms of psychosexual development. This ideal was linked to the dominance of genital libido and the development of object relations as determining factors in the individual's capacity to deal with the world at large in a healthy fashion. Abraham's statement was carefully phrased and is worth quoting at length.

> The final stage of character-formation shows traces everywhere of its association with the preceding stages. It borrows from them whatever conduces to a favorable relation between the individual and his objects. From the early oral stage it takes over enterprise and energy; from the anal stage, endurance, perseverance, and various other characteristics; from sadistic sources, the necessary power to carry on the struggle for existence. If the development of his character has been successful the individual is able to avoid falling into pathological exaggerations of those characteristics, whether in a positive or a negative direction. [p. 415]

He emphasized that it was possible to "steer a middle course" between the pathological extremes of one or another type of behavior, and that such exquisite control might be taken as an index of genital dominance or, in other terms, the achievement of maturity and mental health. Such a brief summary of Abraham's ideas may suggest that he has accomplished no more than a banal rewriting of the Greek ideal of the golden mean, but this hardly does him justice, for his theoretical analysis, expressed in terms of the dominance of the latest phase of psychosexual development, is by no means obsolete or lacking in value.[1]

Freud (1931), writing some eight years after his formulation of structural psychology, continued to support the view that "the libidinal situation will have a first claim to serve as a basis for our classification [of psychological types]" (p. 217). He indicated that the erotic, obsessional, narcissistic and various mixed psychological types "must comprehend all the variations which according to

---

[1]Abraham's (1925) work contained another concept for which he has not often been given credit: " . . . we consider the character of a person to be the sum of his instinctive reactions towards his social environment" (p. 408) and, "We should be inclined to consider as normal in the social sense a person who is not prevented by any too great eccentricity in his character from adapting himself to the interests of the community" (p. 413). To do Abraham justice, I doubt that he was thinking of *passive* adaptation to the "community" which would have been as inappropriate in Weimar Germany as in the world today.

our practical judgement fall within the limits of the normal" (p. 217), suggesting as an "ideal" a perfect mixture, an erotic-obsessional-narcissistic type, "no longer . . . a type at all; it would be the absolute norm, the ideal harmony" (p. 219).[2]

Further contributions to the subject were made by Fenichel (1945), Glover (1939), Jones (1931), and Waelder (1936). Their work, while constituting valuable extensions and elaborations of Freud and Abraham, were overshadowed by the more sweeping and original contributions of Heinz Hartmann in a group of papers published between 1939 and 1960. These were part of his attempt to establish psychoanalysis as a general psychology to encompass all of the adaptive, nonpathological operations of the personality, as well as those pathological disturbances which had been included in the past.

Hartmann emphasized several points, which can be reviewed only briefly. He made it clear that "conflicts are part and parcel of human development, for which they provide the necessary stimulus" (1939b, p. 315). Further, he insisted that "a healthy ego should be able to make use of the system of rational control and at the same time take into account the fact of the irrational nature of other mental activities. . . . The rational must incorporate the irrational as an element in its design" (1939a, pp. 313–314). This echoed Freud's (1932) aphorism concerning the goal of psychoanalysis: "Where id was, there ego shall be" (p. 80)—taking into account the desirability of the dominance of secondary over primary process thinking, without implying at all the elimination of the latter. A cold, controlled intellectuality was for Hartmann and Freud by no means an indication of mental health.

Accordingly, Hartmann emphasized that successful adaptation may be achieved not only by progressive development, but by regression as well, a process described by Ernst Kris (1934) as "regression in the service of the ego," a phrase which has suffered the undeserved fate of becoming a cliché. One of Hartmann's warnings strikes us as especially relevant today. "By skilful conjuring with these kinds of standards [ethical, aesthetic, and political], it becomes easy enough to prove that those who do not share our political or general outlook on life are neurotic or psychotic" (1939b, p. 317).

A notable contribution was Hartmann's emphasis on the multiple role of defense. He wrote, "the same process of defense quite commonly serves the twofold purpose of acquiring mastery over the instincts and of reaching an accommodation with the external world" (1939b, p. 320). In some sense this was an echo of Waelder's "Principle of Multiple Function" (1936), but Hartmann went further to describe in developmental terms the phenomena of secondary autonomy, according to which a defense, previously employed to master in-

[2]Somewhat paradoxically, Freud added, " . . . we might expect that mixed types would provide a more favourable soil for conditions leading to a neurosis" (p. 219).

stinctual drives, becomes less and less bound to its origins, taking on a less conflictual, more adaptive function (1939a, 1950, 1955).[3]

Returning to the subject in 1960, Hartmann, again without relinquishing his primary emphasis on intrapersonal dynamics discussed the vital role of the individual's experience within his sociocultural milieu and its effects on superego development. He referred to "the integrative function of the moral codes" which have been derived, at least in part, from society at large. Here Hartmann brought together two of the senses of the term "character," first as a mosaic of stable modes of thought and behavior and second as possession of an effective set of ethical standards.

But even Hartmann, who was so comfortable with abstract concepts, felt the lack of a specific clinical instance to illustrate his theoretical discussion of mental health. "It is clearly essential to proceed on purely empirical lines, i.e., to examine from the point of view of their structure and development the personalities of those who are actually considered healthy instead of allowing our theoretical speculations to dictate to us what we 'ought' to regard as healthy" (1939b, p. 312).

That psychoanalytic concepts of mental health, such as Freud's, Abraham's, and Hartmann's, have not achieved the influence they deserve is to a great extent the result of the lack of the kind of specificity and vividness which can be afforded only by well-documented clinical examples. For psychopathology, we have such cases as Dora, the Wolf-man, and others to illustrate the author's ideas and to lend a sense of conviction about their usefulness. For the state of mental health, we have up to now no such example.

The reasons for this deficiency are obvious. Our richest source of clinical material is derived from the analyses of patients and colleagues, as well as our own. Such information is generally unsuitable for the purpose of establishing criteria for mental health. For one thing, people who engage themselves in a serious effort at analysis are not likely to be free of substantial neurotic conflict and suffering. This is also essentially true of those who engage in training to become analysts. Beyond this, the requirements of discretion are so demanding that full case presentation outside the limits of a clinical conference becomes virtually impossible, especially when publication is considered. It is no longer acceptable, for example, to consider a case presentation complete

[3]This was part of Hartmann's attack on what he termed the "genetic fallacy." Most simply expressed, this was equivalent to an assumption that psychic processes could be regarded as pathological, purely on the basis of their origins in primitive conflict, e.g., that a personality trait could be traced to sources in the oral or anal phase or to an archaic stage of ego development, which would constitute sufficient justification for labeling it pathological. This has become a myth *about* psychoanalysis, rather than part of psychoanalytic theory, having been disavowed by virtually every major figure in psychoanalysis from Freud and Abraham to the present, perhaps most effectively by Hartmann.

when matters of class, religion, and especially occupation are omitted. Vignettes may of course be employed for demonstration, but even these must be limited in their coverage and are often disguised, i.e., distorted, to prevent identification of the subject. We have been criticized, often scornfully, for our failure to present "scientific" evidence of our clinical results, e.g., detailed case reports. To this, our answer must rest on humanistic and moral considerations.[4]

The latter objection—the requirements of discretion—need not apply to the use of biographical sources, at least with regard to historical figures, but the subjects are rarely if ever notable for mental health, often the contrary. This is especially true of the group of very useful studies by such analysts as P. Greenacre, K. R. Eissler, B. C. Meyer, W. Niederland, and others. Autobiographies, memoirs, and diaries, especially the latter, constitute another potential source. They vary enormously in quality and it is rare to find one which satisfies our requirements.

Just recently we have gained access to a work which is ideal for our purpose: *The Diary of Samuel Pepys, Vols. I–VIII*, edited by R. C. Latham and W. Matthews (1970–1976). The editors claim that "No one else has composed so brilliant and full an account of an actual man as he actually was" (Vol. I, p. cxiii). In the course of reading the first seven volumes and with access to proofs of Volumes VIII and IX (by courtesy of Mr. Robert C. Latham), it appeared to me that we might at last have discovered a full and thoroughly documented account of a man who could be described as relatively healthy for a large portion of his adult life, and an individual of great interest in his own right.

Pepys began his *Diary* on New Year's Day, 1660, during a period of intense political upheaval. For nine and a half years he recorded entries for virtually every day, often but not always before retiring for the night (Latham and Matthews 1970–1976). He wrote chiefly in shorthand, employing a system which had been published in 1626. By no means a secret code, it ensured some degree of privacy since few people, least of all his wife and his colleagues at the Navy Office, possessed sufficient knowledge or application to read it.[5]

Much of the text consists of factual observations dealing with every aspect of his life and work; these are so closely interwoven with personal experiences, opinions, thoughts, and feeling as to suggest from time to time the

[4]For the long term effects of being a "famous case" see F. Deutsch's (1957) follow-up of the Dora case and M. Gardiner's (1971) of the Wolf-man. Freud's contributions to knowledge more than justified his publications. But it is noteworthy that he wrote no detailed case reports after 1918. And most analysts, including those who have made massive contributions to clinical theory, have confined themselves largely to unidentifiable excerpts and vignettes.

[5]One friend, Sir William Coventry, was told of its existence, but was given no details (*Diary*, March 9, 1669).

kind of associative data we are accustomed to obtain in an analysis. As a result, it is often possible to make inferences based not only on the content of the text, but also on the order in which details are presented.[6] Some entries have the characteristics of "night thoughts," less guarded and more loosely organized than the rest. Quite a few dreams are reported, some at length. Several such entries include the day residue, the dreamer's reaction to his dream, the nature of his sleep, and the content of his waking thoughts.

All this gives the *Diary* the quality of immediacy which makes it a fascinating study for the psychoanalyst and the student of character as well as for the historian and critic, not to mention the general reader. While we must be cautious in interpreting the text as if it were the record of an analysis, it does furnish us with one of the richest sources of psychological data we are likely to find, at least before the advent of Freud and the great novelists of the nineteenth century. And the portrait presented is very much that of a healthy man.

Pepys discontinued his *Diary* in May, 1669, stating that his vision had become too poor to allow him to make entries without severe discomfort, nor could this kind of material be entrusted to a secretary. It is possible that he suffered from astigmatism with increasing presbyopia, which could not be corrected by lenses then available.

There has naturally been much speculation about why Pepys wrote the *Diary* and preserved it. Did he have an imaginary reader in mind? Himself perhaps? Posterity? By nature and endowment an excellent recorder and collector, possessed of a keen historical sense, he may well have anticipated that he was to make an important contribution to the history of his time. He had witnessed a destructive civil war, the decapitation of Charles I, the establishment and subsequent collapse of the Puritan Commonwealth and the chaos which followed. He was soon to take part in the restoration of the monarchy and to live through the Plague and the Great Fire. He was to become an integral part of a rapidly changing social and economic structure, still small enough to retain a considerable degree of intimacy.

But the *Diary* must have had more than a historical meaning for him. He was a man in conflict, especially with respect to moral issues, having been profoundly influenced by the puritan value system of the Commonwealth under Cromwell, and exposed now to the extreme permissiveness of the Restoration under Charles II. His awareness of intrapsychic conflict was sufficiently acute to justify the editors' description of him as "both the observer and the observed, the penitent and the priest, the patient on the couch and the psychiatrist, the man on the street and the behavioral sociologist" (Latham and Matthews 1970–1976, p. cix). Perhaps the very transcribing of his days' thoughts

[6]The new edition is especially valuable in that it supplements the text with records of Pepys's own errors and corrections.

helped him to deal with his conflicts and the anxiety which accompanied them. If so, it was remarkably effective.[7]

Pepys was naturally unwilling to have his *Diary* read by his contemporaries, for it would have been both embarrassing and dangerous. He was evidently not disinclined to have it studied by posterity, however, for he had it bound in leather, the six volumes being placed among the three thousand books and manuscripts which made up his excellent library. He left this collection to Magdalene College, Cambridge, with meticulous directions for its intact preservation. It was not until 1825 that the *Diary* was brought to light and a small fraction of it published. Only now for the first time, is it being brought out in an uncut, faithful, and properly edited version. Most of the material omitted from the earlier editions consisted of exactly those details which are essential for a full knowledge of Pepys's personality.

Among his many virtues as a diarist was his remarkable capacity to listen, in which he rivaled Boswell himself. But his range was broader in terms of social interests, for he enjoyed the confidence of a great variety of people, including actresses, musicians, lace-sellers, shipwrights, scientists, politicians, contractors, naval commanders, and a host of others, from innkeepers to royalty. He enjoyed them all, one way or another. His contacts with these people are recorded fully and with considerable accuracy, allowing for the writer's personal biases, which could be strong but generally not entirely unfair. When his statements are checked against other contemporary sources, serious distortions of fact and interpretation are found to be relatively uncommon (Latham and Matthews 1970–1976). His skill in perceiving and evaluating external reality must have been highly developed and closely related to his capacity to observe, discriminate, and record the workings of his own mind (see Stein 1966, 1972).

To acquire an adequate impression of the *Diary* as a source of information about Pepys's character, it is advisable to read it in its entirety, rather than to skim it. It is never dull, even when it deals with the details of Pepys's personal life and thoughts, including conversations, meals, walks, sexual adventures, marital disputes, gossip, political news and events, parties, music, dreams, and internal conflicts—all that made up the daily life of an active, competent, and pleasure-loving man, who was at the same time a person of increasing importance in his own milieu. Aside from its value as a personal document, the *Diary* is generally accepted as a literary and historical document of the first rank.

Samuel Pepys was born in London in 1663. His father was a not very successful tailor. The fifth child of eleven, he was to be the oldest of the four who reached maturity. He may have been the best loved son—at any rate, he

---

[7]For a discussion of Pepys and other diarists, see Fothergill (1974).

was to be by far the most successful. He was fortunate enough to have a number of well-placed relatives on his father's side, including a distant cousin, Edward Montagu, who as Earl of Sandwich and naval commander became his patron. Pepys received a degree at Magdalene College, Cambridge, without having achieved any special honors; there was one recorded reprimand for being drunk and disorderly.[8]

After leaving Cambridge, he was employed by his cousin Montagu to take care of the latter's properties in London. Soon afterwards, although still in very modest circumstances, he fell in love and married the fifteen-year-old daughter of an improvident Huguenot refugee, Elizabeth St. Michel. A year later, through his cousin's influence, he obtained a minor position in government service.

In 1658, when he was twenty-five, he became seriously ill with a bladder stone "which was as big as a tennis ball" (Evelyn June 10, 1669 [see Francis 1963]). This was removed surgically, probably by a perineal approach, a procedure which must have been both painful and extremely hazardous under seventeenth century conditions, but it was evidently entirely successful. For years afterwards, Pepys celebrated the anniversary of this event by giving a dinner party for friends, very much as if it had been a birthday. His surgery was recalled nine years later in a dream (June 29, 1667).

In 1660 Charles Stuart, then in exile in Holland, was recalled to England to assume the crown as Charles II. Pepys was invited by his cousin who commanded the naval convoy to accompany him as his secretary, thus being afforded a precious opportunity to meet the King and the Duke of York, and to see much else that was new and exciting aboard ship and in Holland. It was then that he remarked about himself that he was "with child to see any strange thing" (May 14, 1660), a fair description of his insatiable curiosity, one of his more conspicuous character traits.

A few months later, through the influence of his cousin, now an influential member of the Court, Pepys received an appointment as Clerk of the Acts to the Navy Board, to be in effect an executive secretary and a member of the Board, although he was much the junior in terms of age, experience, and rank. Instead of confining himself to purely clerical duties, he set about learning everything he could about the Navy. He became an expert, probably the only one of his time, not only on naval history but on every aspect of naval administration. Within a short time he was by far the best informed, and soon to be recognized as the most effective member of the Navy Board.

For two decades (1660–1679) his rise was virtually uninterrupted, due to

[8]We know very little about his early life, and the *Diary* refers to his childhood on only a few occasions (May 12, 1667; January 1, 1668). Genetic inferences, so far as they can be made at all, will be at best highly speculative.

a fortunate combination of lively intelligence, administrative skill, a fine political sense, and an extraordinary capacity for hard work. The last would have been conspicuous in any age, but was especially so in the government of Charles II. He received a setback in 1679, but five years later he was restored and promoted to Secretary for Admiralty Affairs, becoming the effective administrative head of the Navy (comparable to Secretary of the Navy in the United States). He held this post for five years when another political upheaval occurred. Pepys, identified with the previous administration and by this time well into middle age, resigned to enter into a characteristically active private life.

Having amassed an important collection of books, prints, and manuscripts, of which the most precious of all was his *Diary*, he lived quietly until his last illness at the age of seventy.

Surveying his life and career, we may regard him as a successful and happy man, a judgment supported by his contemporaries, by nearly all those who have written about him since, and by Pepys himself. Not only was he highly respected and at least moderately prosperous, he was also a loyal and beloved friend of many people of talent and distinction, including John Evelyn, the other great diarist of the period. Highly regarded by both Charles II and James II, he was rewarded by some material considerations, praise, and whatever moral support they were capable of giving.

As a public servant, Pepys had a distinct and positive influence on the future course of British history. The records of the seventeenth century Navy are studded with references to him, and he has been credited with the transformation of that service from a most haphazard collection of ships and seamen into a well organized and effective fighting force. His administrative innovations remained in use until well into the nineteenth century (see Aiken 1960, Bryant 1933, Lloyd 1968, Ogg 1934, Ollard 1974). He may also be considered the first of a long line of British civil servants derived from the middle classes, rather than the aristocracy.

In this brief sketch, I have given some of the reasons why Pepys should be regarded as not merely an entertaining writer but as an effective and important individual as well. We have, moreover, not only the extensive information derived from the *Diary*, but access to a mass of documents, including letters, official records, and other sources which, while less vivid and immediate, confirm and supplement the *Diary* and extend our knowledge into the years after Pepys discontinued his daily entries.

Having met the need for adequate documentation, we are now obliged to satisfy our second essential requirement—that our evidence is sufficient to indicate that we are dealing with a reasonably healthy man. I shall try to demonstrate this by presenting a small fraction of the available evidence which tends to support the thesis that Pepys was relatively free of serious neurotic symptoms and defects of character and that he qualifies in positive respects as well. This view has been held generally by his biographers and by historians[9] who are virtually unanimous, even though some have been highly critical of his sexual behavior[10] and inclined as well to look askance at his ethical standards in the conduct of his official duties.

To begin with the simplest criterion of mental health, Pepys had few neurotic symptoms, and these were generally mild and self-limited. During the ten years of the *Diary*, distinct phobias, obsessions, compulsions, and conversion reactions were insignificant or absent. His level of anxiety varied a good deal, but it never interfered with his working or with his search for pleasure, and only rarely did it disturb his sleep (e.g., *Diary*, February 23, 1668). The same may be said with reference to his concerns over physical illness, in an era in which conditions such as smallpox, typhus, and typhoid were endemic and very often fatal, and medical care largely ineffective, although perhaps not so detrimental as it was to become during the next century. Even in good years, when there was no epidemic, the mortality rate was appalling, especially among children.[11] And most adults died young, including both of Pepys's brothers who had reached adult life.

At the age of forty-four, well into middle age by seventeenth century standards, he composed a document which he called *The Present Ill State of My Health* (see Bryant 1933, Vol. II, pp. 406–413). He listed a group of symptoms which must have been quite familiar in England at the time; many of them still are. He noted recurrent colds and chronic catarrh, symptoms of urinary stone, some mild arthritic pain, indigestion, and "wind." It has been suggested that he may have suffered from nervous indigestion of the type supposed to be common in high-pressured executives today, but my reading of the *Diary* does not support this. These abdominal symptoms may have been largely the result of his diet, composed for the most part of meat, often in a doubtful state of preservation, with relatively little in the way of fruit, vegetables, and cereal. The taking of "physic" was in any case a regular practice among Pepys's contemporaries. All this yields little evidence of neurotic ill health, or of those somatic illnesses usually associated with chronic anxiety.

Finally, neither documentary evidence nor the opinions of contemporaries gives us the least reason to suspect any degree of thought disorder. Pepys was, if anything, noted for his fine grasp of reality and his ability to deal with highly charged and complex situations.

---

[9]See Bryant (1935), Emden (1963), Heath (1955), Latham and Matthews (1970–1976), Ogg (1934), Ollard (1974), Tanner (1924), Wilson (1959).

[10]See Braybrooke (1825), Ponsonby (1928), Wilson (1959).

[11]" . . . I was mightily taken with a little girl [Betty Gysby], the daughter of the maister of the house which, if she lives, will make a great beauty" (*Diary*, August 19, 1665).

When we turn to a detailed evaluation of Pepys's character structure, the picture appears more complex, but again there is little to contradict our overall impression of an essentially healthy man by any of the psychoanalytic criteria we employ (e.g., Abraham 1925, Fenichel 1945, Freud 1931, Glover 1939, Hartmann 1939a,b, 1950, 1955, 1960, Jones 1931, Kernberg 1970, Stein 1969, Waelder 1936). For the sake of organization, I shall employ the structural model of the psyche, since it is the most familiar and perhaps the most readily adaptable to the analysis of character traits. I shall not resist entirely the temptation to draw inferences about Pepys's unconscious mental life; too much caution would be as little in the spirit of Samuel Pepys as would a tendency to rash conclusions.

His physical and mental energy were phenomenal. He worked a long day, often rising at daybreak (which might be 4 a.m. in summer) and getting to bed at midnight. Thus, in spite of his devotion to a wide variety of other activities, he was able to complete his official duties without too much pressure. Both energetic and efficient, he was very soon recognized to be an outstanding administrator and executive, many of whose accomplishments may be fairly regarded as innovative, if not actually creative.

Pepys's achievement occurred during a period in which government administration was characterized by bureaucratic inefficiency and corruption, in which hardworking officials were rare, and during which the financial affairs of the government were chaotic, to say the least (see p. 103). His success required not only high intelligence and zeal, but also considerable understanding of and ability to deal with individuals and political groups. In terms of character, therefore, we may infer a very highly developed capacity to understand and to deal actively with the external forces which impinged upon him. Not only was his perception of reality excellent, but he was aggressive enough to influence events without lapsing into impulsive behavior or grandiose attitudes.

Nor was his work impaired by those traits which partook of the obsessional, e.g., his tendency to record and classify; rather, the latter became subordinated to and was an essential component of his administrative skill. His interest in amassing and counting his personal funds was similarly transformed into a successful effort to establish sound methods for raising and administrating funds for the Navy. These changes may be traced in his *Diary* entries between 1660 and 1669, and confirmed by the evidence to be found in later official records.

A man who understood and valued power, he managed ultimately to acquire a good deal. It would appear that he used it well, again subordinating a source of narcissistic gratification to the needs of the Navy and the nation.

Pepys was insatiably curious as well as ambitious. He explored a great many fields of learning, becoming a well qualified amateur in several and an expert in a few. Beginning with the multiplication tables (apparently not part of the curriculum at Cambridge), he mastered the elements of shipbuilding, the measurement of lumber, and the testing of cordage for ships' rigging. He was an expert, possibly the only one of his day, on naval history, financing, and personnel policy. Fascinated by science, he became a member (an amateur, it is true) and eventually President of the Royal Society, his name appearing on the title page of Isaac Newton's *Principia.*

But work and learning were not to be entirely subordinated to the search for less puritan pleasures. His addiction to the theater, for example, was so extreme that he feared it would threaten his official career. His attempts to control his impulse by self-enforced contributions to the poor-box appear to have benefited the poor but only intermittently interfered with his attendance at every play on the boards, often more than once.

The most important influence in his search for pleasure was related to what he described as his "strange slavery to beauty" (September 6, 1664). Although he was a connoisseur of the graphic arts, it was the beauty of music and of women that affected him most deeply. On one occasion he wrote: "Here was the best company for Musique I ever was in in my life, and wish I could live and die in it, both for music and the face of Mrs. Pierce and my wife and Knipp, who is pretty enough . . . " (December 6, 1665).

After attending a performance of a play, he made the following entry:

> . . . but that which did please me beyond anything in the whole world was the wind *musique* when the *Angell* comes down, which is so sweet that it ravished me; and indeed, in a word, did wrap up my soul so that it made me really sick, just as I have formerly been when in love with my wife; that neither then, nor all the evening going home or at home, I was able to think of anything but remained all night transported, so as I could not believe that ever music hath that real command over the soul of a man as this did upon me; and makes me resolve to practise wind-music and to make my wife do the like." [February 27, 1668]

Expressing so vividly the association between the ecstasy of musical experience and that of sex evinces a remarkable freedom of thought and affect. Nor was it confined to these spheres, for he was capable of deriving the keenest enjoyment from activities as diverse as observing a scientific experiment at the Royal Society or walking in the country.

We may ask to what extent he was capable of genuine object love, of developing attachments to individuals for their own sake. About his regard for himself, we need have no doubt at all. His persistent self-criticism did not seriously impair his good opinion of his own abilities; he was aided further by numerous signs of respect by others, including superiors and employees. In view of such efficient regulation of self-esteem and an almost entire absence of either grandiosity or depression, it is difficult to regard his "narcissistic" features as signs of pathology.

Toward his parents and other close relatives, he was benign and often generous, although by no means lavish or sentimental. He was especially fond of his father; toward his mother, who had become senile and querulous, he was at least tolerant and when she died his experienced genuine grief.[12] His rather difficult siblings he treated with considerable forbearance, and he took a good deal of responsibility in seeing them established in the world. By the age of thirty, he had already become the supporting figure and the leader of the family, having been at least, to paraphrase Winnicott, a "good enough" son and brother.

It is sufficient to note that as a husband he was appreciative, loyal, and loving, very much after his own fashion; but this is a complicated question which I shall enlarge upon later.

To others, he was a faithful friend or, if an enemy, not usually an implacable one. To show open support for his friends when they were in disgrace took considerable courage, but he did so openly, all the while recording privately his fears of risking career and livelihood. While some commentators have regarded him as a physical coward, based on expressions of anxiety confided to his *Diary*, the record of his actual behavior offers the best evidence to the contrary. London was noted for the violence and unpredictability of its mobs, especially during periods of political unrest; assault and robbery were fairly common, and traveling was especially risky, whether by foot, on horseback, or by water. But the greatest peril and the most difficult to avert was that of epidemic infection.

In 1665, London suffered a terrifying outbreak of bubonic plague. The Court and the Navy Office were moved to Greenwich, but Pepys's duties often required him to be in London. The atmosphere was a grisly one, the city largely deserted except for the carts full of corpses and the lonely quarantined houses. Whole families might be wiped out in the space of a week. Pepys was a member of a committee to rule on matters of quarantine, a task he found heartrending. One entry reads:

> Among other stories, one was very passionate methought—of a complaint brought against a man in town for taking a child from London from an infected house. Alderman Hooker told us it was the child of a very able citizen in Gracious-street, a saddler, who had buried all the rest of his children of the plague; and himself and his wife now being shut up; and in despair of escaping, did desire only to save the life of this little child; and so prevailed to have it received stark-naked into the arms of a friend,

[12]His dreams of March 25 and June 29, 1667, are of special interest in this connection.

> who brought it (having put it into new fresh clothes) to Greenwich; where, upon hearing the story, we did agree it should be [permitted to be] received and kept in the town. [September 3, 1665]

Yet he often managed to be "merry" in the company of friends; sometimes he found a young woman willing to console him in bed (August 8, 22, 23, September 2, October 5, 1665, etc.).

On August 14, he ended his entry for the day: "Great fears we have that the plague will be a great Bill this week." The entry for the next day begins:

> Up by 4 a-clock and walked to Greenwich,[13] where called at Captain Cockes and to his chamber, he being in bed—where something put my last night's dream into my head, which I think is the best that ever was dreamed—which was, that I had my lady Castlemayne in my arms and was admitted to use all the dalliance I desired with her, and then dreamed that this could not be awake but that it was only a dream. But that since it was a dream and that I took so much pleasure in it, what a happy thing it would be, if when we are in our graves (As Shakespeare resembles it), we could dream, and dream such dreams as this—that then we should not be so fearful of death as we are in this plague-time. [August 15, 1665]

It was not accidental that Pepys should have recalled his dream at the moment of seeing Captain Cockes in bed, for the word "cock" had already, in 1665, taken on the meaning of penis. It is reasonable to assume that the dreamer had experienced an erection during the course of such an erotic dream, and thus the associative connection took place.

Lady Barbara Castlemaine, whom the dreamer had embraced with such rapture, was at the time the favorite mistress of the King, the mother of five of his children. While Pepys did not admire her character, he was entranced by her beauty, taking every available opportunity to gaze at her. Almost certainly this was accompanied by sexual arousal to some degree. For him she was that most exciting of women, combining ultimate desire with absolute prohibition, and as such a likely surrogate for the expression of deeply repressed oedipal fantasies.[14]

The reference to Shakespeare is doubly relevant. Pepys, the ardent playgoer, was very familiar with *Hamlet*, the most frankly oedipal of all the plays.

---

[13]From Woolwich, the town to which he had moved his wife and the maids to protect them from the plague.

[14]Oedipal fantasies appeared in other dreams which occurred during periods of stress (e.g., March 25, June 29, 1667). His other dreams are to be discussed in a future study of Pepys's character structure.

Here he refers to the soliloquy in which Hamlet thinks upon sleep and death, a passage which Pepys had committed to memory:

> . . . ; 'tis a consummation
> Devoutly to be wish'd, to die, to sleep;
> To sleep; perchance to dream; ay, there's the rub;
> For in that sleep of death what dreams may come,
> When we have shuffled off this mortal coil,
> Must give us pause; . . . (III, i).

Hamlet, impelled toward suicide, fears that death would be no solution for it might lead only to a perpetual sleep disturbed by terrifying dreams. Pepys, on the contrary, is not in the least suicidal, nor does he have much belief in an afterlife. He plays with the idea that death may indeed be only a dream, but no nightmare, rather an exciting, sexually gratifying, ultimately oedipal dream. The plague need no longer be so terrifying, for the death it brings may be embraced with joy. Most remarkable is that this seventeenth century dreamer interpreted his dream so skillfully as to recognize its function in protecting sleep by alleviating anxiety. It was the dream of a highly imaginative rationalist.

A year later, the plague having abated, the City of London was virtually destroyed by a fire which raged for five days and came within yards of engulfing the Navy Office and Pepys's dwelling. This second brief but terrifying event brought out all of his capacity for effective action in an emergency. He moved swiftly to protect both his personal possessions and the Navy Office (September 2, 1966). His entries for each of the five days of the Great Fire are the most accurate and vivid accounts we possess. It says much for his ability to deal with anxiety that he could act to protect himself, his family, and his community, and at the same time produce a moving literary and historical account of a major event.

Pepys's capacity for aggressive behavior in the service of self-protection again became evident in the face of two major political threats. During the Second Dutch War, in 1667, Admiral de Ruyter attacked and largely destroyed the English fleet as it lay at anchor in the Medway. It was not long before Parliament sought scapegoats in the persons of the Commissioners of the Navy. Although a junior member and an inexperienced speaker, it was Pepys who was chosen to defend the Navy Board. At the cost of some sleepless nights, he prepared a detailed and masterfully organized defense of his colleagues and himself, averting further attacks on their administration, enhancing his own reputation considerably in the process.

In 1678, he was exposed to an even more dangerous threat when, in the course of a thoroughly nasty political battle, Pepys was accused of high treason. The evidence against him was clearly perjured, but even so it took him years to clear himself of the charges. He established his innocence by amassing volumes of evidence proving that his accusers were notorious criminals and professional perjurers. Charges were dropped before trial, but we may suspect that Pepys would have enjoyed his day in court, had his enemies been rash enough to take the risk. He capped this episode in a very Pepysian fashion, collecting all the documents in the case, having them bound and incorporated in his library, where they are now to be seen.

So far, Pepys seems to have met most of our requirements. But two aspects of his life in particular call for more searching consideration. These are, first, whether his conduct in office revealed a serious defect in his moral character, and, second, whether his sexual behavior should be considered a sign of serious psychopathology.

The first question is easier to dispose of. Pepys did accept gifts from job seekers and contractors, and once nearly got into trouble over the irregular disposition of a naval prize. Some earlier writers were inclined to regard him as corrupt, and on this basis expressed serious reservations about his moral character, which they felt fitted in all too well with the reprehensible quality of his sexual habits.

Pepys gives a number of candid examples in his *Diary*. One of the more diverting is an early entry:

> I met Captain Grove, who did give me a letter directed to myself; I discovered money to be in it and took it, knowing, as I found it to be, the proceed of the place I have got him, to have the taking up of vessels for Tanger. But I did not open it till I came home to my office; and there I broke it open, not looking into it till all the money was out, that I might say I saw no money in the paper if ever I should be questioned about it. There was a piece in gold and 4 l. [pounds] in silver. [April 3, 1663]

Any attempt to evaluate the psychological significance of an individual's ethical standards must take into account the cultural milieu in which the latter are developed and applied. Pepys spent his youth in a country rent by civil war and violent social change, with all the uncertainty and shifting of values inevitable at such times. Virtually all of his official career coincided with the Stuart restoration, which was marked by a pronounced reaction against the moral rigidity and self-righteousness of the Commonwealth.

Government financing was in a state of chaos, making it difficult for us today to understand how the state survived at all. Public employees, such as Pepys, were paid on a scale which was based on the assumption that they would find other sources of income. It was taken for granted that expediting a contract, arranging for official payment, finding some individual a job, would be rewarded by a fee or a gift of value appropriate to the service rendered. Most official positions were openly bought and sold, as were Army commissions, a usage which lasted well into the nineteenth century. Practices which would today be classified as extortion and bribery were generally accepted as proper, so long as they remained within "reasonable" limits.

Pepys's behavior must also be viewed against the background of the Court of Charles II and its ideal images, such as they were. The King himself accepted substantial subsidies from Louis XIV of France, a monarch and a nation profoundly distrusted and feared by the English. John Churchill, the rising young military leader and future Duke of Marlborough, acquired a small fortune by his services as a lover to one of the King's mistresses, a fact widely known at Court and almost certainly by the King himself. This made for juicy gossip, but it was not universally condemned at the time.[15]

Historical evidence supports the thesis that Pepys's progression was not, as in the case of so many other public officials, from minor to major peculation, but rather toward increasing personal integrity. This development was accompanied by his largely effective efforts to set up more adequate fiscal procedures for the Navy. Having started as a thievish puppy, he grew to become a reliable watchdog. This gives us little reason to infer a major defect of character in this area.

More complex are the questions which have been raised concerning Pepys's sexual behavior. Earlier editors of the *Diary* felt obliged to censor portions of the text they regarded as unprintable (e.g., Wheatley 1893). Even Bryant (1933), who was very fond of Pepys, found this aspect of his behavior offensive enough to write: "like a dog, he returned to his vomit" (p. 295).

A more complete understanding of his sexual behavior requires some picture of his marriage. When he met Elizabeth, he was an ambitious but impecunious young man of twenty-two. She was fifteen, the pretty daughter of a penniless Huguenot family. It was beyond doubt a marriage for love, since they had little else to offer one another.

Very much a child bride, Elizabeth was never able to match her husband's intellectual growth. Pepys was always inclined to seek out other women for their conversation as well as for sexual diversion, while she reacted by becoming querulous and provocative. She was constantly having trouble with her housemaids, who were generally close to her own age; she would accuse them of lying or stealing, often on evidence her husband found unconvincing.

---

[15]Winston Churchill (1933) in his biography of Marlborough commented with ironic emphasis: "Securely established upon the rock of purity and virtue, ceaselessly cleansed by the strong tide of universal suffrage, we can afford to show tolerance and even indulgence toward the weaknesses and vices of those vanished generations without in any way compromising our own integrity" (p. 13).

Pepys was undoubtedly "houseproud," and Elizabeth, while she worked very hard by modern standards, was not often able to meet his exacting requirements. One entry in 1660 describes a typical dispute:

> At night to bed; and my wife and I did fall out about the dog's being put down into the Sellar, which I have a mind to have done because of his fouling the house; and I would have my will. And so went to bed and lay all night in a Quarrel. This night I was troubled all night with a dream that my wife was dead, which made me that I slept ill all night. [November 6, 1660]

It is easy to sympathize with both parties. This brief quarrel was typical of the marriage which, being fundamentally stable, survived a good many storms. In spite of Elizabeth's frequent disabilities—painful menses, a genital abscess, possibly even a perineal fistula—they seem to have had a reasonably gratifying sexual life together. In 1664, after a busy day at the office, they spent a merry evening watching a friend's dog trying to mount their own. He wrote:

> going home, I found the little dog so little that of himself he could not reach our bitch; which I am sorry for—for it is the finest dog that ever I saw in my life—as if he were painted, the colours are so finely mixed and shaded. God forgive me, it went against me to have my wife and servants look upon the while they endeavored to do something, and yet it provoked me to pleasure with my wife more than usual tonight. [March 22, 1664]

Theirs was a close, interesting, and complex relationship, unmarked by persistent dislike, hatred, or desperation; they were fundamentally loyal to one another.

When in turmoil over the approaching parliamentary investigation in 1668, it was to Elizabeth that he confided his anxieties, and she who comforted him in this as well as other crises. That year he remarked to his friend Coventry: "[I] thanked God I have enough of my own to buy me a good book and a good fiddle, and I have a good wife" (February 18, 1668). His friend could not say the same for himself.

It was nevertheless impossible for him to resist the temptation to engage in extramarital adventures, which were frequent throughout the period covered by the *Diary*. They were recorded in a curious mixture of Spanish and French, with occasional phrases in other languages, including Greek. Generally however, they are not difficult to follow. One example—after a day of conversation and a dinner party:

> Thence home, and there comes my Lady Pen, Pegg and Mrs. Turner, and played at cards and supped with us, and were pretty merry—and Pegg with me in my closet a good while, and did suffer me a la besar mucho et tocar ses cosas upon her breast—wherein I had great pleasure, and so spent the evening; and then broke up, and I to bed, my mind mightily pleased with this day's entertainment. [November 28, 1666]

At first, he confined his efforts to kissing various young women, but he soon became more daring and successful, fondling their breasts and inducing them to handle his penis. Increasingly often he was able to achieve "all" he wished. Some of these opportunities arose when applicants for positions in the Navy brought their wives to meet him. He was ready enough to accept what was so freely proffered, usually a few kisses and some fondling. Once or twice, however, such meetings resulted in lasting intrigues.

Nevertheless he showed few of the traits we associate with the typical Don Juan character. While he nearly always explored the ultimate possibilities of a sexual encounter, he had a true admiration for women and enjoyed their company and conversation, whether or not they yielded. There is little evidence of sadism in his treatment of women, nor does he seem to have used them for advancement, which was common enough in Court circles.[16]

Most of his sexual adventures occurred while on the way to or from work. He seemed most concerned about his reputation as a hardworking civil servant, and in spite of his puritan upbringing, he does not appear to have undergone any profound moral conflicts. His anxieties, in any case, interfered with his pleasures only rarely.

These adventures remained casual for the most part until the period 1665–1668, when he experienced a progressive increase in the intensity and frequency of his sexual impulses. By 1668, the *Diary* entries suggest a driven, almost desperate quality. He would seek out more than one woman during the same day (e.g., February 1, 1668) and sometimes managed two or three sexual adventures with different women in one week (February 16, March 20, 1668).

In October, Pepys became even more impulsive and careless, having become infatuated with Deb Willett, a young girl employed as a companion to his wife. One of Deb's regular duties consisted of combing her master's hair as he prepared for bed. He was unable to resist the temptation to make advances, and one evening as he was fondling her breasts and genitals, his wife discovered them in the act (October 25, 1668). Elizabeth understandably refused to accept his assertion that he had done no more than hug the girl. Having induced Deb to confess that matters had indeed gone much further, she pro-

---

[16]There is relatively little evidence of concern about homosexuality, latent or otherwise.

ceeded to revenge herself first by claiming (to Pepys's horror) that she had secretly embraced Roman Catholicism and then by insisting that his secretary accompany him everywhere out of her sight.

On another occasion, her behavior became more extreme. He had gone to bed after a quarrel. He writes:

> At last, about one o'clock, she came to my side of the bed, and drew my curtains open, and with the tongs red hot at the ends, made as if she did design to pinch me with them, at which, in dismay, I rose up, and with a few words she laid them down . . . and about two . . . came to bed, and there lay well all night, and long in bed talking together, with much pleasure, being I knew, nothing but her doubt of my going out yesterday, without telling her of my going, which did vex her, poor wretch! last night, and I cannot blame her jealousy, though it do vex me to the heart. [January 12, 1669]

Pepys had already begun the process of reconciliation with Elizabeth by consoling her sexually, on one occasion writing: "and there je did hazer con ell to her content" (November 19, 1668).[17] His wife's jealousy was never completely resolved, nor did she cease to have some justification. He did become less driven and more careful, and he had learned his lesson: that he could comfort Elizabeth by sexual attentions. He could be most artful, as we observe in the following passage:

> . . . and so home, where my wife mightily dogged, and I vexed to see it, being mightily troubled, of late at her being out of humor, for fear of her discovering any new matter of offense against me, though I am conscious of none; but do hate to be unquiet at home. So, late up, silent, and not supping, but hearing her utter some words of discontent to me with silence, and so to bed, weeping to myself for grief, which she discerning, come to bed, and mighty kind, and so with great joy on both sides to sleep. [January 21, 1669]

By May of 1669, when increasing difficulty in reading forced Pepys to end his *Diary*, he writes that there "cannot be much" which requires such privacy, for "my amours to Deb are past" (May 31, 1669). After Elizabeth's death of an acute fever (possibly typhoid) the following year, he seems to have led a quiet personal life. He established a liaison with a young woman of good family, who became his housekeeper and almost certainly his mistress, living with

[17]His use of the *lingua franca* to describe marital intercourse was not usual: for the most part it was employed to record his extramarital adventures.

and caring for him until his death in 1703. Her family seem to have accepted the situation, and Pepys left her a generous bequest in his will. Whether he ever sought out Deb Willett again, we do not know. There is no evidence that he did.

We may agree in general with one evaluation of Pepys as "a normal, reasonably healthy male animal, ruled, as all men are by passions and appetites. He gave way to lechery because of his innate love of beauty and pleasure, because of the temptations of an easy-going, loose-moraled society dominated by a libertine King and Court, and because of tensions which developed between him and his wife" (Wilson 1959, p. 4).

The statement is correct as far as it goes, but it fails to give sufficient weight to the character and intensity of Pepys's sexual behavior during the years 1665–1668. The latter must be regarded as symptomatic, even though self-limited. For a time, he was quite out of control, not at all his usual self. He nearly wrecked his marriage to Elizabeth whom, notwithstanding his intermittent neglect and complaints, he loved dearly, and he incurred the risk of causing irreparable injury (as he saw it) to a young, probably virginal girl. The *Diary* reveals intense conflict and some remorse, but even so, it took months before he could overcome his yearnings for the girl and acquire a reasonable degree of control over his own behavior.

Such a dramatic outbreak of irrational behavior is perhaps to be classified as an episode of acting out, although it occurred in an individual not ordinarily characterized by any such tendency.[18] We are faced with a single, well-defined incident during which his ordinarily excellent integration of pleasure seeking and reality perception broke down, so that he acted "out of character," impulsively and carelessly, a significant phenomenon, even though limited to only one area of his life and to a relatively brief period.

It is likely that this was a response to a series of threats to his psychic integrity, of which the most important was a progressive deterioration of his vision, which gave him every reason to fear that he was becoming blind. To him, who was "a slave to beauty," a playgoer, a voracious reader, a superb writer and keeper of records, such a prospect was appalling, threatening the total loss of his career and most of his pleasures.

Other factors exerted considerable influence; for instance, the plague, the death of his mother, and the parliamentary investigation. It seems likely that the threat of blindness played an important role in exacerbating castration anxieties which had been stimulated originally by the surgeon's invasion of his genital area ten years before. His intense anxiety over his vision could very well have resulted in limiting the range of adaptive devices ordinarily avail-

[18]In this connection, see Stein (1973).

able to him, thus facilitating this outbreak of uncharacteristically irrational behavior in the late 1660s. Aside from his work, the most effective device remaining readily available was indulgence in sexual fantasy and activity. Sexuality then became not only a source of pleasure but a means of defending himself against castration anxiety and fear of death. This was brilliantly demonstrated during the plague, in his dream of Lady Castlemaine.

It would be easy to choose illustrations to prove that Pepys possessed a number of distinctly undesirable, even pathological traits of character, that he could be lecherous, venal, acquisitive, hypocritical, self-righteous, vain, and petty. No doubt the list could be extended. We could, if we wished, emphasize the oral and anal elements in his personality structure and thus establish a more or less plausible psychopathological diagnosis.

This would be, in my eyes, far too narrow an approach, and a potentially misleading one as well. A more thorough study of the *Diary* itself, correlating it with the many other sources available, justifies a different conclusion, based upon recognition of larger patterns of thought and behavior and seen in the light of sociocultural data. By this means, we become aware of Pepys's progressive development over the years, during which traits such as those listed above were controlled and modified, their component elements now directed toward productive rather than primarily defensive or frankly narcissistic ends. And we begin to see him more clearly in the context of his own society, subject to its influences, and eventually himself becoming one of those who exerted a significant influence upon that very society.

We can make a case, therefore, that the Pepys we know from the *Diary* and other sources satisfies nearly all the criteria formulated by Abraham, Freud, Hartmann, and other psychoanalytic writers (e.g., Fenichel, Glover, Jones, Waelder). At least, he does so more convincingly than any other well-documented historical figure.

It is not necessary to go on with a recital of details, function by function, although such a study might well be feasible. It is sufficient for the purpose to point out that Pepys's capacity to love, to be loved, and to maintain a wide range of stable object relations would have satisfied Abraham's criteria for the establishment of genital dominance; that he approaches very closely Freud's fantasy of the ideal character type, combining the erotic, obsessional, and narcissistic in more or less equal proportions; and that he seems to have fulfilled most of Hartmann's requirements, based upon the orderly development and integration of ego and superego functions and the quality of adaptation.

The latter may be summarized very briefly as they apply here. Pepys's capacity for reality testing and rational control of behavior was combined with a ready ability to employ such regressive phenomena as the dream, fantasy, and direct sensual pleasure for adaptive purposes. His ability to work, and for that matter to love, was relatively invulnerable to stress—a reliable index of well-established autonomy of ego functions and evidence of a strong libidinal organization.

With increasing maturity, he demonstrated remarkable proficiency in transforming or replacing maladaptive and inefficient processes by more suitable ones, for instance, by sublimation. As for superego functioning, his ethical standards, conscience, and ideals developed in parallel with the maturing of his ego processes, achieving about as complete an integration as we are likely to find in healthy, if imperfect, human beings. Finally, the aggressive components of his personality appear to have been put to good use, neither severely inhibited, turned against the self, nor expressed in violence.

Citing Pepys as an instance not of neurosis but of mental health implies that our concept of the latter is necessarily an approximation to an ideal, not the ideal itself. We have seen that Pepys did develop occasional neurotic symptoms and on one occasion at least behaved inappropriately under stress. But such clearly pathological manifestations were self-limited in scope and duration, and they were not followed by constrictions of character but quite the contrary. As for the moral aspects of his personality, while he never became, nor aspired to be, a paragon of virtue, civic or private, he did demonstrate a lifelong tendency toward increasing integrity and consistency of behavior without the lash of remorse.

A number of questions inevitably remain. First, why should a presumably healthy man have recorded his daily activities in such intimate detail? Does this in itself not constitute evidence of some distortion of personality? We may see in this phenomenon signs of Pepys's notable passion for order, a good deal of exhibitionism, a need for confession, the wish to achieve immortality, and so on, but none of these necessarily constitute evidence of psychopathology. With more justification, if may be claimed that the *Diary* was the result of a largely successful attempt to resolve a series of internal conflicts; thus it was the very opposite of a neurotic solution. In this respect, Pepys differed sharply from such major geniuses as Goethe, whose productivity was closely related and even dependent upon his psychopathology (Eissler 1963).

A second question is raised by an almost complete lack of knowledge of Pepys's childhood experiences. A few facts are available, e.g., the dates of birth and death of his many siblings, but there are only a few innocuous references in the *Diary* itself. This is indeed a serious limitation of our ability to understand his development in a psychoanalytic sense. Yet we are not limited to a static picture. We possess an exceptionally complete and vivid picture of his development over ten crucial years of early adult life and a good deal of information about his middle and later years. His life after age fifty-five was one of forced retirement from public responsibility due to political disfavor. He was plagued by ill health, including a urinary fistula. Nevertheless he remained cheerful and active. His extensive correspondence reveals intense mental activity and wide-ranging curiosity almost to the day of his death. His interest in people—for instance, Mrs. Skinner, his housekeeper-mistress-nurse, his nephew and heir, John Jackson, and his old friends—remained unimpaired.

A final question is more difficult, especially in these days of shifting cultural values. Is it possible to establish criteria for determining the state of mental health apart from social considerations? Obviously not. Yet we can conceive of certain standards which may be broadly applied, at least to cultures with which we are reasonably familiar. These would correspond generally to what Hartmann (1960) has called "health values." They include such traits, already cited, as the capacity "to face reality at all costs"; the predominance of rational thought processes and control over behavior; ready access to fantasy, dreams, and imagination; the capacity for pleasure and comfort in sexuality and object relations; a feasible combination of ethical standards with a life-preserving code of conduct. It is difficult to conceive of cultures in which these would not be useful if not altogether necessary, although they would take very different forms, depending upon the time, place, and sociocultural circumstances. From this point of view, Pepys represented the ideal product of a fusion of Puritan and Restoration influences, deriving from the former his devotion to hard work, self-improvement, and introspection, and from the latter, his love of pleasure, tolerance, and saving humor.

We cannot say with any confidence how he would have managed today, although the stable character traits he possessed would have stood him in good stead. The lively, bawdy, corrupt, and dangerous London of his day strikes some chords which echo down to us. But it was a more intimate world; men in public life, even if thorough villains, were at least a more colorful lot than we are faced with today. Perhaps there was more scope for the expression of the individual character in the world of Pepys.

We may leave Mr. Pepys on this philosophical note:

> The truth is, I do indulge myself a little the more pleasure, knowing that this is the proper age of my life to do it, and out of my observation that most men that do thrive in the world do forget to take pleasure during the time that they are getting their estate but reserve that till they have got one, and then it is too late for them to enjoy it with any pleasure. [March 10, 1666]

REFERENCES

Abraham, K. (1925). Character-Formation on the Genital Level of the Libido. In *Selected Papers on Psycho-Analysis*. New York: Basic Books, Inc., 1927, pp. 407–417.

Aiken, W. A. (1960). The Admiralty in Conflict and Commission. In *Conflict in Stuart England*, edited by W. A. Aiken and B. D. Henning. London: Jonathan Cape, Ltd., pp. 203–225.
Braybrooke, R., editor. (1825). *Memoirs of Samuel Pepys. Volumes I and II.* London: Everyman, 1950.
Bryant, A. (1933). *Samuel Pepys. The Man in the Making.* New York: MacMillan.
——— (1935). *Samuel Pepys. The Years of Peril.* New York: MacMillan.
Churchill, W. S. (1933). *Marlborough: His Life and Times*, abridged by H. S. Commager. New York: Charles Scribner's Sons, 1968.
Deutsch, F. (1957). *A Footnote to Freud's "Fragment of an Analysis of a Case of Hysteria." Psychoanalytic Quarterly*, XXVI: 159–167.
Eissler, K. R. (1963). *Goethe: A Psychoanalytic Study 1775–1786.* Detroit: Wayne State University Press.
Emden, C. S. (1963). *Pepys Himself.* London: Oxford University Press.
Fenichel, O. (1945). *The Psychoanalytic Theory of Neurosis.* New York: Norton.
Fothergill, R. A. (1974). *Private Chronicles: A Study of English Diaries.* London: Oxford University Press.
Francis, P. (1963). *John Evelyn's Diary: A Selection from the Diary.* London: The Folio Society.
Freud, S. (1931). Libidinal Types. *Standard Edition* 21:215–220.
——— (1932). New Introductory Lectures on Psycho-Analysis. *Standard Edition* 22:3–182.
Gardiner, M., editor. (1971). *The Wolf-Man.* New York: Basic Books, Inc.
Glover, E. (1939). *Psychoanalysis.* Second Edition. London and New York: Staples Press, 1949.
Hartmann, H. (1939a). *Ego Psychology and the Problem of Adaptation.* New York: International Universities Press, 1958.
——— (1939b). Psychoanalysis and the Concept of Health. In *Essays on Ego Psychology. Selected Problems in Psychoanalytic Theory.* New York: International Universities Press, Inc., 1964, pp. 1–18.
——— (1950). Psychoanalysis and Developmental Psychology. In *Ibid*, pp. 99–112.
——— (1955). Notes on the Theory of Sublimation. In *Ibid*, pp. 215–240.
——— (1960). *Psychoanalytic and Moral Values.* New York: International Universities Press.
Heath, H. T. (1955). *The Letters of Samuel Pepys and His Family Circle.* Oxford: Clarendon Press.
Jones, E. (1931). The Concept of a Normal Mind. In *Papers on Psychoanalysis.* Fifth Edition. Baltimore: Williams and Wilkins, 1948, pp. 201–216.
Kernberg, O. F. (1970). A Psychoanalytic Classification of Character Pathology. *J. Amer. Psa. Assn.*, XVIII, pp. 800–822.
Kris, E. (1934). The Psychology of Caricature. In *Psychoanalytic Explorations in Art.* New York: International Universities Press, 1952, pp. 177–188.
Latham, R. C., and Matthews, W., eds. (1970–1976). *The Diary of Samuel Pepys, Vols. I–IX.* London: G. Bell & Sons.
Lloyd, C. (1968). *The British Seaman, 1200–1860.* London: Collins.
Ogg, D. (1934). *England in the Reign of Charles II.* London: Oxford University Press.

Ollard, R. (1974). *Pepys: A Biography*. London: Hodder & Stoughton.

Ponsonby, A. (1928). *Samuel Pepys*. New York: MacMillan.

Stein, M. H. (1966). Self Observation, Reality, and the Superego. In *Psychoanalysis—A General Psychology. Essays in Honor of Heinz Hartmann*. Edited by R. M. Loewenstein, L. M. Newman, M. Schur, and A. J. Solnit. New York: International Universities Press, pp. 275-297.

——— (1969). The Problem of Character Theory. *J. Amer. Psa. Assn.*, XVII, pp. 675–701.

——— (1972). A Clinical Illustration of a "Moral" Problem in Psychoanalysis. In *Moral Values and the Superego Concept in Psychoanalysis*. Edited by S. C. Post. New York: International Universities Press, pp. 226–239.

——— (1973). Acting Out as a Character Trait: Its Relation to the Transference. In *Psychoanalytic Study of the Child*, Vol. XXVIII. New Haven and London: Yale University Press, pp. 347–364.

Tanner, J. R. (1924). *Mr. Pepys: An Introduction to the Diary Together with a Sketch of His Later Life*. New York: Harcourt Brace.

Waelder, R. (1936). The Principle of Multiple Function: Observations on Over-Determination. *Psychoanalytic Quarterly*, V, pp. 45–62.

Wheatley, H. B., ed. (1893). *The Diary of Samuel Pepys. Volumes I and II*. New York: Random House.

Wilson, J. H. (1959). *The Private Life of Mrs. Pepys*. New York: Farrar, Straus & Cudahy.

7

Kohut's *Restoration of the Self*: A Book Review

Interest in the self is very much with us. We are to live life to the fullest as individuals, a doctrine popularly expressed as "doing our thing," which includes not only loving oneself, being creative and joyful; it often encompasses activities that are disconcerting, at least to other, nonself, entities. Thought, delayed gratification, attempts to resolve inner conflict in reasonable ways tend rather to be de-emphasized as part of the relegation of secondary process to a subordinate position in the hierarchy of desirable developments in human psychic life. This trend has been associated with adverse criticisms of the methods and principles of modern ("Western") science, with its emphasis on neutrality and objectivity, and its rejection of much historical study.

Concern with the self has not been entirely neglected in psychoanalytic writings: Edith Jacobson's *The Self and the Object World* is a significant attempt to deal with problems of narcissism in the context of object relations theory; Otto Kernberg has published a series of papers dealing with the same theme, with even more emphasis on the importance of extremely early object relations. In the works of Kohut, however, we find the "self" dealt with as an entity separate and central in human development, its formation and growth perhaps even more important than later or parallel evolvement of relations to objects; and we are presented with a new term: self-object. His first volume, *The Analysis of the Self* (1971), had a profound effect on many psychoanalysts, shifting the focus of some toward an interest in "the psychology of the self," which was viewed as a fundamental, perhaps the basic element, in an understanding of the human psyche. Without accepting Kohut's premises and formulations, many, including myself, found a number of sections interesting and provocative. His observations of transference phenomena, e.g., idealization and "mirroring," were perceptive and described in a detailed and vivid fashion. The account of analysts' reactions to these manifestations was clever and sometimes correct in its assumption that analysts may react to intense transference impressions with embarrassment, anxiety, and guilt, and thus be provoked into premature and often unwise interpretive efforts. To the extent that Kohut's earlier monograph led us to examine more critically our own reactions to such intense transference manifestations, it was of considerable value.

His positive prescriptions for dealing with transference were, however, much less enlightening. Emphasis on the need for patience in interpreting was well taken but gratuitous, since such advice has been for many years an explicit element in the teaching of technique by such writers on ego psychology as Rudolph Loewenstein, Ernst Kris, and others in the United States and elsewhere.

One might sum up the impact of *The Analysis of the Self* by remarking that even for those who regarded the theory as confusing and regressive, Kohut's clinical observations and some of his personal digressions in later chapters were worthwhile for their effort in stimulating the reader, even though he might reach conclusions quite opposite to those advanced. We may also appreciate his emphasis on the use of introspection and empathy, about which he had written a good deal in the past. While these have been recognized elements in the armamentarium of every psychoanalyst, the profession has been exposed to powerful influences from within and without which have tended to relegate these essential functions to a secondary role in favor of the collection of "objective" data, statistical or otherwise, and to have overemphasized, perhaps, the role of cognitive functions, without regard to the nature of the instrument we employ. Allowing that Kohut went much too far, he at least attempted to reverse a potentially destructive trend. It is to be regretted, however, that he did so by presenting us with a view so one-sided as to introduce its own very serious problems, which have, if anything, been compounded by the publication of the book under review.

The Restoration of the Self goes even further in its elaboration of the ideas outlined or merely hinted at in the previous work. It raises questions about the present relevance of Freud's work and that of others (Heinz Hartmann's, for example) in the mainstream of psychoanalytic thought. For that reason alone, it is certain to arouse controversy, which should, we hope, constitute ultimately a healthy development in our field.

The psychoanalytic community has often been accused of failing to keep up with the demand for progress, to move with the times, to remain "relevant." Putting aside the regrettable fact that moving with the times may not always constitute progress (all too often the reverse), there is some basis to those charges, at least sufficient to yield us no ground for complacency. A substantial breakthrough in our understanding of psychosis, for example, or of those severe character disorders which do not respond regularly to the treatment methods currently employed would be of enormous value. In this respect we have not always obeyed our own dicta, which demand of us an unceasing search for more refined and inclusive models and systems, and we have failed to explore to the full the kind of data that can be obtained by the psychoanalytic method. Correspondingly, these new hypotheses must also be subject to a lively scrutiny and their validity tested, step by step. Those who hypothesize should be the most active, if not the most severe, critics of their own ideas.

Kohut's work does indeed reflect a search for new ways of understanding the human psyche, in terms of both normal and pathological manifestations. Constructing a model of the development of the "self," he has erected around this a broadly applicable system of approaching and understanding human behavior. For that reason alone, his work should be taken seriously and read carefully. The central questions, as with most newly presented systems, concern not only the appeal of what claims to be innovative and all-inconclusive, but the soundness of a theory based in observable data, the precision of its step-by-step reasoning, and its capacity for correlation with other sciences—not always an easy matter in our field. It is in these respects that *The Restoration of the Self* must be evaluated.

The author presents his theory of the personality as more inclusive, elegant, and explanatory than what he refers to as "traditional" psychoanalytic theory, his system superseding, in effect, the whole of metapsychology and clinical theory. The thrust of the argument is most eloquently stated in the author's preface, in which he traces the development of his ideas:

> . . . the present work expresses more explicitly my reliance on the empathic-introspective stance, which has been defining my conceptual-theoretical outlook ever since 1959. This step—the full acceptance of the consequences of the fact that the psychological field is defined by the observer's commitment to the introspective-empathic approach—led to a number of conceptual refinements, indicated by terminological changes, as exemplified by my use of the term "self-object transference" instead of the formerly used termed [sic] "narcissistic transference." I do not regard these changes in terminology as lying in the forefront of the contributions offered by the present work: still, they are the expression of a move toward a clearly defined psychology of the self—or rather, as I shall state more explicitly shortly, of a move toward two self psychologies that complement each other. [pp. xiii–xiv]

A bit later, he writes:

> Still, I have come to recognize the limits of the applicability of some of the basic analytic formulations. And with regard to the classical psychoanalytic conceptualization of the nature of man, too—however powerful and beautiful it might be—I have become convinced that it does not do justice to a broad band in the spectrum of human psychopathology and

> to a great number of other psychological phenomena we encounter outside the clinical situation. [p. xviii]

Anticipating some of the objections to his theory, he asserts "the necessity for an expansion of the psychoanalytic outlook, for a complementary theory of the self which both enriches our conception of the neuroses and is indispensable for an explanation of the disorders of the self—with the hope that the empirical evidence I shall be adducing and the rationality of the arguments I shall be advancing will prove persuasive" (pp. xviii–xix). These passages, brief as they are, serve to convey the tone of the entire volume, a tone which reflects, in a remarkable fashion, the subject matter itself.

In evaluating Kohut's empirical evidence, it is most interesting to examine the presentation of clinical data, which brings into sharp focus both the power and the weakness of his argument. It is upon such data, as he points out, that his theoretical structure must rest.

The text begins with a chapter on "The Termination of the Analysis of Narcissistic Personality Disorders," an ingenious and effective method of demonstrating the author's understanding of clinical situations, in many respects quite different from the understanding that would be arrived at by what he calls "a psychoanalytically tutored mind" (p. 43). Mr. M. suffered from the manifestations of "his primary structural defect—chronic enfeeblement of his self with some tendency toward the temporary fragmentation of this structure" (pp. 6–7). This defect Kohut ascribes largely to lack of maternal empathy during the patient's early years which was not compensated by the father's inadequate efforts.

Somewhat later, however, we discover that the "mother" referred to on p. 8 was not the biological mother but an adoptive one. The biological mother had abandoned the baby, who remained in an orphanage until he was three months old (p. 25). The author refers to this "primordial trauma" and acknowledges that the situation would have created empathic difficulties for the adoptive parent. But we are not provided with data that would be essential to allow us to judge the cogency of his central argument. For example, he fails to describe how and when Mr. M. discovered that he had been adopted, what it meant to him, what if any fantasies it generated, how it was reflected in adolescent development (a phase to which the author pays little attention), and, finally, how, in more than general terms, it was reflected in the transference.

This analysis offers difficulties for the reader who has not yet been convinced. The account is one-sided, emphasizing a few of the patient's memories and the analyst's inferences, based on a minimum of impressionistic data. At the same time, it plays down what might be considered somewhat "harder" historical data, the interpretation of which requires fewer inferential steps, e.g., the significance to the patient, throughout life, of having been abandoned by his biological mother, the death of his adoptive mother during the crucial period of his puberty, whether he was guilty over these events, and so on. Fairly or not, one gets the impression that defects in maternal empathy constitute *the* overriding factor, at the expense of a number of alternative etiological hypotheses which may strike the psychoanalytically experienced reader as at least equally plausible. In a presentation covering 48 pages, more or less, such omissions seriously impair the author's case.

His formulation as proposed in the case of Mr. M. is uncannily reminiscent of Freud's original acceptance of the major role of actual parental seduction in the etiology of neurosis. Kohut, however, has been less inclined to question the literal accuracy of his sources, and thus undergoes the danger of basing his subsequent formulations on a defective mode of inference, which takes no account of unconscious sources of distortions of memory.

Describing Mr. M.'s "unaccountably joyful" response to an adolescent boy, he writes:

> What he experienced with regard to the boy was not the repetition of a passive erotic relation to his father, was not the repetition of an old jealousy vis-à-vis his father's new wife (in a reactivated negative Oedipus complex). It was a portrayal of the manifestations of a mature development level, with the boy as principal actor, and with himself playing both the supporting role and the audience. [p. 44]

The reductive nature of this argument foreshadows the author's treatment of other psychoanalytic formulations and appears to ignore such concepts as overdetermination and Waelder's concept of multiple function. This is striking in the light of the author's remarks about Freud's "absolute determinism" (p. 244).

Elsewhere Kohut makes the point: "It is not the interpretation that cures the patient. And while it is correct to say that the work of analysis consists in making conscious what had been unconscious, this statement is only an appropriate metaphor about one aspect of the gross psychological transformations that do indeed occur during the analytic process." He goes on: "I believe we are describing the curative process more accurately and cogently if we focus on the changes in the psychological 'microstructures' " (p. 31). To this paragraph is appended a footnote:

> I will add here that the parallelisms between the development of physics from Newtonian theory to quantum theory (Bohr, Heisenberg) and the development of psychoanalysis from Freudian metapsychology to the psychology of the self go beyond the facts that the physicist's attention shifted from the investigation of large masses and their interactions to the inves-

> tigation of minute units of matter and that the psychoanalyst's attention shifted from the investigation of macrostructures (the agencies of the mind) and macrorelationships with objects (the Oedipus complex) to the investigation of molecular units of psychic structure. . . . And there is finally the fundamental claim of modern physics that the means of observation and the target of observation constitute a unit that, in certain respects, is in principle indivisible. This claim finds its counterpart in the equally fundamental claim of the psychology of the self that the presence of an empathic or introspective observer defines, in principle, the psychological field.

The citation of this parallelism is more bold than apposite. Bohr and Heisenberg presented collections of data, readily replicated, to support their conclusions. Kohut, on the contrary, is cavalier in his attitude toward those who value the role of observable data in judging the value of a new hypothesis. In our field, moreover, it is hardly a new finding that the presence of the observer has a profound and readily observable effect on the phenomena to be studied. It dates, in fact, to Freud's earliest descriptions of the transference neurosis, and has been elaborated in writing by Robert Waelder and Brian Bird, along with a host of others. Indeed, it is so familiar a finding that it is difficult to understand exactly what Kohut has added, aside from a new and if anything less felicitous formulation. The implication of priority is therefore most surprising.

Elsewhere Kohut emphasizes that one need not deal with all aspects of the personality once "the maintenance of the self is assured." In another footnote he writes (with regard to "patients suffering from self pathology"):

> . . . it is the better part of wisdom in a particular case not to try to promote further the transference reactivation of unmodified archaic drive-wishes—a reactivation that might lead to dangerous acting out or to other states of ego-insufficiency—if a point in the analysis has been reached in which the patient's defenses appear to operate reliably, and sufficient ego-autonomy in conflict areas has been achieved. While our decision to end the analysis in some such instances is fully justified on the basis of the realistic attitude of letting sleeping dogs lie (Freud 1937), we will nevertheless have to admit that the analysis was *in principle* incomplete. [p. 183]

This would appear to be the reverse of Freud's meaning. In "Analysis Terminable and Interminable" (1937) we find:

> If an instinctual conflict is not a currently active one, is not manifesting itself, we cannot influence it even by analysis. The warning that we should

> let sleeping dogs lie, which we have so often heard in connection with our efforts to explore the psychical underworld, is particularly *inapposite* [my italics] when applied to the conditions of mental life. For if the instincts are causing disturbances, it is a proof that the dogs are not sleeping; and if they seem really to be sleeping, it is not in our power to awaken them. [p. 231]

Further, in the same paragraph: "Analytic experience has taught us that the better is always the enemy of the good and that in every phase of the patient's recovery we have to fight against his inertia, which is ready to be content with an incomplete solution." Freud was clear enough about it.

It does not follow that Kohut is incorrect in maintaining that some conflicts, even though available, are better left alone in cases in which the resources of the ego (as we would put it) are inadequate to deal with the overwhelming anxiety that might result. (To put it succinctly, not everyone can be analyzed!)

Kohut emphasizes that it is necessary to go beyond Freud's limitations in order to understand disorders of the self. Again we do best to employ the author's words.

> But, however pertinent Freud's theoretical conceptualizations remain with regard to the structural neuroses and to other similarly constructed psychological phenomena, they are not, as the present work will attempt to demonstrate, sufficiently relevant with regard to the disorders of the self and other psychological phenomena that lie within the domain of self psychology—phenomena that require for their observation and explanation a more broadly based scientific objectivity than that of the nineteenth-century scientist—an objectivity that includes the introspective-empathic observation and theoretical conceptualization of the participating self. [p. 68]

Kohut's theories about Freud's commitment to truth are interesting and provocative; he suggests that it constituted not only an admirable trait of character, but also a limitation, the product of his culture, and that perhaps "his nuclear self was threatened more by the danger that knowledge was withheld from him than by the danger of physical destruction" (p. 65). While Kohut is on firm ground in emphasizing Freud's unflinching search for truth, the impression he gives that this "truth" had the quality of an objectively perceived absolute is misleading, especially when Freud's later works are considered.

The latter's early clinical results, Kohut suggests, stemmed from "the pressure of his personality, his charismatic certainty that, via suggestion, brought about a behavioral alteration which he took to be a manifestation of a structural change achieved via interpretation" (p. 36n), although he admits that Freud's later results may have been more soundly based.

Later, in a discussion of the Oedipus complex, the role of which in human development, he maintains, has been greatly overrated, he makes the following statement.

> Let us now move for a moment beyond clinical issues and examine, in the light of self psychology, a problem I confronted many years ago and found unmanageable. It gives me some satisfaction to see that the pieces of a puzzle that had stumped me then, now fall into place. Being at that time fully committed to the traditional acceptance of the fact that the domain where the authority of absolute determinism holds sway was unlimited, and clinging to Freud's model of the mind depicted as an apparatus that processes forces within a hypothetical space, I could find no place for the psychological activities that go by the name of choice, decision, and free will—even though I knew that these were empirically observable phenomena. [pp. 243–244]

This leaves us with an imperfect and, in important respects, inaccurate impression of Freud's intellectual stance. To describe him as fully committed to "the authority of absolute determinism" fails to do justice to the complexity of Freud's intellectual roots, which were to be found not only in the mechanistic aspects of nineteenth-century science, but in the more romantic and teleological influences of the same period (for some of the implications of psychoanalytic theory with respect to determinism, see Waelder 1962, 1963).[1] The import of Kohut's work is, paradoxically, far more literally deterministic than that of Freud, since it tends to ascribe an extremely complex set of disturbances and developments to what is essentially a single etiological factor: defects of maternal empathy. By implication it can be effectively replaced by the experience with an empathic analyst. It is to be regretted that readers of this book will receive a severely biased and often inaccurate impression of Freud's ideas. I have cited only a few examples.

Sooner or later, all of what most analysts have thought of as psychoanalytic theory comes under fire: drive theory; the focal importance and the universality of infantile sexuality, and the Oedipus complex; the ubiquitous role of conflict, defense, and resistance; the need for insight, for working through (as we understand it), and for most of the principles of psychoanalytic technique, especially the "benign neutrality" or striving for objectivity of the analyst, the search for something as close to the "truth" as we can get.

Kohut's view of dream interpretation is widely at variance with that established by Freud in 1900 and elaborated by analysts since then. He writes

[1]Waelder, R. (1962). Psychoanalysis, scientific method, and philosophy (1963). Psychic determinism and the possibilities of predictions. In *Psychoanalysis: Observation, Theory, Application*. New York: International Universities Press, 1976, pp. 248–274; 283–307.

that there are basically "two types of dreams": the type (described by Freud) "expressing verbalizable latent contents (drive wishes, conflicts, and attempted conflict solutions), and those attempting, with the aid of verbalizable dream imagery, to bind the nonverbal tensions of traumatic state . . ." (pp. 108–109).

The first type he regards as analyzable in the usual way, via free associations and exploration of

> the formerly unconscious meaning. . . . In the second type of dream, however, free associations do not lead to unconscious hidden layers of the mind; at best they provide us with further imagery which remains on the same level as the manifest content of the dream. The scrutiny of the manifest content of the dream and of the associative elaborations of the manifest content will then allow us to recognize that the healthy sectors of the patient's psyche are reacting with anxiety to a disturbing change in the condition of the self—manic overstimulation or a serious depressive drop in self-esteem—or to the threat of dissolution of the self. I call these dreams *"self-state dreams"*: they are in certain respects similar to dreams of children, to the dreams of traumatic neuroses, and to the hallucinatory dreams occurring with toxic states or high fever. . . . Associations to these dreams did not lead to any deeper understanding, did not uncover any deeper hidden meaning, but tended to focus increasingly on the diffuse anxiety that had been part and parcel of the dream in the first place. And the correct interpretation—not a supportive, psychotherapeutic maneuver—explains the dream on the basis of the analyst's knowledge of the vulnerabilities of his patient in general, including the knowledge of the particular situation that, by dovetailing with a specific vulnerability, had brought about the intrusion of the hardly disguised archaic material. . . . [In these dreams] archaic self-states are presented in an undisguised (or only minimally disguised) form. [pp. 108–110]

In the author's view, this second type of dream (dreamed, as is implied, by modern, "Tragic" man, as he later puts it) should therefore be interpreted with reference to the manifest rather than the latent content. This discussion is in many respects most characteristic of the author's view and style of presentation. There is no reference, here or in the index, to such champions of manifest-content interpretation as Thomas French, or to nonpsychoanalytic sources, e.g., current dream research, which might have some bearing on the author's views—either to support or to refute them.

The analogy with children's dreams is potentially misleading, exposing the argument to the same sort of error made by anthropologists who regarded primitive cultures as infantile, and the psychiatrists who viewed psychoses as more or less direct outgrowths of the child's psychic structure. There is no evidence that patients suffering from narcissistic personality disorders are any less complicated than other individuals—perhaps the reverse. The claim that they have different kinds of dreams, frequently if not invariably, is difficult to substantiate. Is it not possible that the resistances of the dreamer make it far more difficult to discover the latent content? This is even more likely if the analyst himself lacks a firm conviction of the importance of conflict and of the analysis of resistance.

One example does much to make clear Kohut's view. His analysis of the daydream of Mr. X (pp. 203–211) relies chiefly on symbolic imagery and the patient's wish for cure. It is a type of dream analysis very familiar to us, as it was to Freud (1923),[2] who rejected it. The dream wish is presented as abstract, inspirational, and without relation to unconscious conflict, in essence ego-syntonic. This example is, of course, a daydream, but it is treated at greater length than the night dreams—which are interpreted in similar fashion both in this and Kohut's previous book.

In short, he has presented us with anagogic interpretation, without reference to Silberer or to Freud's several discussions of the subject. Kohut has revived an old view of dreaming, far more plausible in the nineteenth century than it was to become after Freud seemed to have disposed of it at the turn of the twentieth. It is a method that allows analyst and patient to put aside the marvelous complexity and arduous work of psychoanalytic dream interpretation. It is doubtful, even, whether the author's resort to Freud's older discussions of children's dreams or traumatic dreams will stand up in the light of more recent work on the interpretation of these phenomena, which appear to be far more complex than at first suspected (see, among others, Stein 1965).[3] It is a more comfortable method of interpreting dreams—Kohut's technique often suggests a rather cozy atmosphere—but is it useful in any respect other than maintaining that pleasant state of affairs? It may be feasible to modify, even reject much of Freud's dream theory, but it is hard to justify doing so without much more evidence and weightier arguments than those the author advances.

I have chosen to deal primarily with the author's approach to clinical problems, for it is on this that his metapsychology will stand or fall. The latter is also widely different from what he describes as the "classical dynamic-structural" view. An excellent discussion of this aspect of his theory may be found in reviews of this book by Levine and by Schwartz.[4] Kohut presents his self-psychology as basic theory, in effect relegating the psychology of conflict, of consciousness, of drive and defense to a special case, applicable perhaps to

---

[2]Remarks on the theory and practice of dream-interpretation. *Standard Edition* 19:108–121.

[3]States of consciousness in the analytic situation. In *Drives, Affects, Behavior*, vol. 2, ed. M. Schur. New York: International Universities Press, pp. 60–86.

[4]Levine, F. J. (1978). *J. Phila, Assn. Psychoanal.* 4:238–247. Schwartz, L. (1978). *Psychoanal. Quart.* 47:436–443.

the "Guilty Man" of the nineteenth century, but no longer relevant to "Tragic Man" of the twentieth. This view carries with it the implication that conscience is no longer so important an issue as it may once have been. Is there, after all, some folk wisdom in the view that even "transformed" narcissism reduces the capacity to care for and respect others? I am sure the author would argue against this naïve belief, but it is easy to get such an impression from the dominant importance which he places on the development of the self, as compared with object relations. Kohut spends very little time on those phases during which the superego undergoes marked spurts of development (and sometimes regression), e.g., oedipal conflict and resolution in later childhood, adolescence, and early adult life.

His categorization of disorders of the self has a distinctly engulfing quality, tending to swallow up all neurosis, at least, and a good deal else. Most of us have regarded narcissistic problems as very much part of any neurosis and have been inclined to regard psychoanalytic theory, if not invariably psychoanalytic treatment, as relevant and applicable. His categorization is not much help in establishing useful criteria for those who could benefit from "traditional" (his term) psychoanalysis, as against the presumably far greater number who require the application of his method. This has tended to favor the use of his basically reductionist and, one suspects, rather comfortable approach, as against the relatively austere and demanding discipline of psychoanalytic practice. The apparent complexity of his theory seems to be based ultimately on the simple principle that disorders of the self are the result of lack of parental empathy; cures are brought about by the (kindly) efforts of an empathic analyst who understands and employs this method, even perhaps innocently unaware that he is doing so.

It is regrettable that we find ourselves once again presented with an apparently easy solution for the extraordinarily complex problems of the origin of psychopathology: defects in maternal (or parental) empathy. Blaming one's parents, whether they deserve it or not, is simple and satisfying; it reflects, at best, only part of the truth of the origins of human character. The accidents of fate—from the meeting of ovum and sperm, the physiological condition of the mother (empathic or not) that affects the fetus and the newborn, access to nutrition, literal or cultural, the presence of siblings, early death of parents, and others—none of these factors is given sufficient weight in Kohut's world of etiology or (if we must put aside so deterministic a term) of empathic and introspective understanding of the patient's past and present.

One's impression of his views as reductionist and solipsistic is reinforced by his failure to take into account the work of not only so many others who have presented contradictory evidence, but even those whom he might have cited to support his arguments. Other writers on the subject of narcissism are given short shrift in the preface; some, e.g., Jacobson, Kernberg, Erikson,

Mahler, Balint, are merely named; some, e.g., Greenacre (1956), Arlow (1966), Gitelson (1952), and so on, are merely named in the text. This would be perfectly excusable in a lecture, perhaps in a brief scientific article. It represents a serious, if conscious omission (see p. xx) in a volume that puts forward a radical revision of, even a departure from, psychoanalytic theory.

Kohut does mention two influential figures, Franz Alexander and Heinz Hartmann. The former is a curious choice as a representative of "classical drive theory," in view of his later drift away from "traditional" psychoanalytic thought, and more especially his therapeutic innovations, with some of which Kohut's own technical admonitions have been compared.

Hartmann's ideas are treated as severely limited in explanatory power and relevance. A thinker of great intellectual power and complexity, he is hardly done justice by Kohut's account. There is far too much of the straw-man method in the latter's attempts to deal with Hartmann's arguments, presented as they are in such a simplistic version. This approach is applied generally to all of psychoanalytic theory and practice as formulated by other contributors.

In the epilogue we find this statement: " . . . the true scientist—the playful scientist as I put it before—is able to tolerate the shortcomings of his achievements—the tentativeness of his formulations, the incompleteness of his concepts. Indeed, he treasures them as the spur for further joyful exertions" (pp. 311–312). Such joyful exertions have led the author to construct what he regards as a deeper and more comprehensively explanatory theory.

We may appreciate his intention to enlarge the scope of psychoanalytic theory to encompass groups of disorders that have proved stubborn in practice. It is possible that he has indeed developed a therapeutic approach which will be helpful to very ill patients who cannot tolerate the demands of a psychoanalytic procedure. His repeated emphasis on the importance of introspection and empathy is valuable, if rather overdone; and he has reminded us, if we need to be reminded, of the importance of patient listening and careful timing of interpretations. About all of this there should be little disagreement.

Beyond this, however, there is a great deal of question about the advantages of a body of theory and clinical admonition which is largely solipsistic. He rejects that part of scientific method which places a high value on accurate observation of all varieties (not merely empathic-introspective). He has little to do with reasonable skepticism and restraint with regard to his own conclusions. Nor is he satisfied with Freud's[5] modest and tragic statement of the goals of therapy, "that much will be gained if we succeed in transforming your hysterical misery into common unhappiness. With a mental life that has been restored to health you will be better armed against that unhappiness" (p. 305).

[5]Freud, S. (1893–1895). The psychotherapy of hysteria. *Standard Edition* 2:253–305.

Kohut emphasizes the achievement of "joy" (rather than pleasure) and of creativity. These are indeed worthwhile goals; whether they can be achieved by the method he describes remains to be seen.

Kohut's views have had a considerable appeal for many thoughtful colleagues, here and abroad, a circumstance not difficult to understand when we recognize that he has made a serious effort to solve problems inherent in the various psychoanalytic hypotheses dealing with narcissism and disorders of early development. If there is a theoretical vacuum, it demands to be filled; a serious attempt to do so is to be commended. I am not convinced that the models advanced by Freud, by Hartmann, and others are quite so empty as the author would lead us to believe, but it must be admitted that they are less satisfying theoretically and less readily applicable clinically than many other aspects of psychoanalytic theory.

But there are other important, if less intrinsic, reasons for the popularity of Kohut's recent books. Beneath the series of formulations and newly coined terms is a basically simple system, far less complex than psychoanalytic theory as we know it. It is indeed very appealing to minimize or even virtually to do away with the role of infantile sexuality and of aggression (as a fundamental characteristic of the human psyche, if not a primary drive). To put to the side, at the same time, ego and superego development, the central roles of the Oedipus complex, of castration anxiety and penis envy, of the intricacy of the dream work, would seem to satisfy many of the objections which have been directed toward psychoanalysis. Whether these objections (which date back to the early years of this century) should be met in this fashion is another matter, for Kohut's solution suggests a retreat, the necessity for which is far from clear; this, in spite of the author's arguments and those of others who find the core concepts of psychoanalysis irrelevant, unconvincing, or out of date.

From one point of view it might be argued that some of the appeal is the derogation of the role of defense, i.e., permission to support the resistances, always a tempting maneuver in conducting an analysis, but not as a rule productive of the more profound insight which we tend to value. Is the search for insight and recovery of unconscious material a mistaken, perhaps futile, goal in the treatment of so many of our patients? It is an arduous one, which may arouse a good deal of annoyance, if not worse, on the patient's part, and fatigue and discouragement on ours. Shall we therefore discard it, in favor of a more comfortable philosophy and technique?

Replacing pleasure-seeking by "joy" is likely also to have a popular, even inspirational, appeal. The two are not, in fact, on the same level of discourse. Pleasure-seeking was generally regarded by Freud as a highly abstract, almost physiological concept, and it was by no means his view that this was a goal of analysis or a characteristic of mental health, any more than was the avoidance of unpleasure. It is more difficult to achieve the capacity to love and to work, which require other individuals, than to experience "joy" which may in one form or another be achieved in an essentially solitary state (e.g., Mr. M.). Its appeal is not too difficult to understand.

There is another characteristic of this volume that caters to youth, modernity, and progress, namely, the doctrine that virtually all psychopathology in this large group of cases is due to the deficiencies of one's elders, especially mothers, who were so lacking in empathy. There is comfort to be found in ascribing one's personal deficiencies and misfortunes to a single first cause, especially when it corresponds to the young child's fantasy of the all-powerful and rejecting mother—the model for the goddesses who controlled the fates of pagan peoples.

We must nevertheless ask whether this is a sound piece of work, a true advance, a paradigm in Thomas Kuhn's sense. Throughout this volume, the author makes clear his conviction that he has made a forward leap, an advance of the greatest importance, in enhancing our ability to understand mental life and to treat a large proportion of otherwise inaccessible emotional disturbances.

This invites comparison with Freud, beyond whom Kohut claims to have advanced. We may contrast them: Freud made it clear that he learned by his errors, by painful struggle and suffering. His view of life was genuinely tragic, clear-eyed, constantly in search of new observations and elaborations and clarification of his theories, with all their brilliant insights and inevitable deficiencies. He was firm in his convictions, but neither rigid nor complacent.

Kohut's work appears to be the product, not so much of painstaking exploration, of trial and error, and of attempts to test the truth, as of a more purely subjective and inspirational process, largely confined to the empathic-introspective method and relatively independent of other sources of knowledge—more akin to revelation. While we cannot expect to use the methods and criteria of science to the extent possible in more readily quantifiable and experimentally verifiable fields of investigation, it would be a pity to move even further in the direction toward which he seems to be pointing. The problems he addresses are far from being completely solved; his work surely deserves the most careful consideration and discussion. But whatever its contribution, it is difficult to accept as a genuine addition to psychoanalytic theory and practice.

8

The Unobjectionable Part of the Transference

INTRODUCTION BY MANUEL FURER

In "The Unobjectionable Part of the Transference" (1981), it might appear that Dr. Stein has written about a problem of technique, namely Freud's recommendation in 1912 not to analyze the unobjectionable positive transference. However, one would be more correct in saying about this paper, as Strachey (Freud 1912) did about Freud's paper, "Although Freud included this paper in the series on technique, it is in fact more in the nature of a theoretical examination of the phenomenon of transference and the way it operates in analytic treatment" (p. 98).

At the time, Freud believed that this aspect of the relationship, although he called it transference, keeps the patient in analysis, motivates him to overcome the resistances to free association, and contains the influence of the analyst that leads both to cure and to the removal of the objectionable transference, erotic and hostile. The latter represents the new edition of the neurosis, particularly the attachment to unconscious sources of gratification.

Writing in 1981 in a contemporary vein, Stein explores the concept of the treatment alliance, as well as that of countertransference. This paper is a remarkable presentation of Martin Stein the person, the teacher, and the imaginative psychoanalytic thinker. Although written 17 years ago, this paper is also important in questioning recent technical innovations that seem to disregard the essential role of the analysis of the resistances in the patient and represent a return to ideas of cure by influence that Freud held in 1912. Stein makes the observation that we all assume there is a factor that allows the patient to cooperate in the analytic process, which bears some connection to the positive transference without being clearly based on repressed erotic impulses.[1]

---

[1]For an opposing point of view see E. Kris, "On Some Vicissitudes of Insight in Psychoanalysis," *International Journal of Psycho-Analysis* 37:445–455, 1956.

Stein's major point is that this factor, variously named suggestion, influence, therapeutic alliance, working alliance, basic trust, new object that fosters development, has not been subjected to the same degree of analytic scrutiny as the more obvious transference elements. The recognition of this phenomenon, Stein states, is far more ancient than Freud's technical paper, referring, I assume, to Hippocrates.

In psychoanalysis, the initial pitfall, as Stein goes on to say, is "if all goes swimmingly, we might congratulate ourselves on the maintenance of a good working alliance" (p. 124) and helping the patient. However, this conclusion will impede "our search for the nature of the [so-called] unobjectionable component" of the transference (p. 124).

Dr. Stein uses as his illustration a group of patients in whom the unobjectionable positive transference is integral to their psychic balance. He describes this group as "likable, attractive people, cultivated and often gifted" (p. 124), who find the analytic process interesting and gratifying and respond thoughtfully but with a healthy skepticism. These seemingly ideal patients, who are also in their cultivated way teasing and ironic, keep feelings of any intensity at bay. Passion, particularly sexual passion, is missing. Stein makes obvious to the reader that this transference is a compromise formation that includes hidden gratification of the more intense drive derivatives that in this form are acceptable to both the analyst and the patient; an "exciting, yet innocent, liaison" (p. 126), but delicious as it absorbs their sexuality. Upon interpreting the defensive purpose of the patient's good nature, distress and anger are expressed. "The analysis is no longer such an unalloyed pleasure, and one almost regrets having introduced the subject" (p. 126). Stein notes that what has been stimulated in the analyst prior to interpretation is what corresponds to the unobjectionable component of the transference, presumably for the same reasons of gratification and resistance, with the same innocent disguise; the analyst "Finds himself regarding the patient as if he or she were a favorite child" (p. 126).

The contradictions in Freud's writings in regard to the transference were pointed out most emphatically by Brian Bird (1972). In the postscript to the Dora case in 1905, Freud states that all of the neurosis is contained in the transference and can be analyzed therein. In 1912, as noted, he writes of a component that is useful and not analyzable. In "Analysis Terminable and Interminable" (1937), he conceives of a latent or inactive transference that the analyst cannot bring into the analysis. Stein's paper returns us to Freud's conviction in 1905.

To help us understand the psychology of both patient and analyst in the psychoanalytic endeavor, Stein turns to an admired figure, these days often neglected. Bertram Lewin, in a paper entitled "Dream Psychology and the Analytic Situation" (1955), points to the analogy of the patient in analysis to the sleeper and the dreamer, and to the analyst as the one who either soothes or awakens the patient by interpretation. In rousing the sleeping, dreaming patient, the analyst not only interferes with his wish to sleep, but with his wish fulfillments in general. On the other hand, the analyst also guides the process of self-observation, substituting the secondary process, or as some say today, substituting higher ego functions and integration for more archaic ones (Gray 1973, 1990, Loewald 1960).

Stein goes on to point out that inevitably the analyst in this role becomes "the . . . representative of that agency most often responsible for insomnia, the conscience" (p. 131). In that sense, the unobjectionable positive transference is directed toward the analyst, who presumably, like the good mother, soothes and induces sleep and is treated like a benign superego; this gratification in the analyst or in the patient is a formidable resistance. It is interesting to note that in the 1930s the incorporation of this soothing, benign conscience and its substitution for the patient's harsh superego was the primary goal and in fact the method of cure in psychoanalytic treatment—a continuation at that late date of the importance of the analyst's influence (Strachey 1934).

As an observant physician, Stein knows that in certain patients the understanding, protective analyst can bring improvement in the patient but not analytic change. He bluntly states that it is a mistake to put "too great an emphasis on an introspective-empathic response at the expense of thoughtful questioning and evaluation" (p. 136). In the same vein he is critical of the attribution to good mothering as the "only essential genetic factor in the capacity to develop this aspect of transference" (p. 137). If we accept manifest content without skepticism, the pernicious corollary follows that if the fundamental cause of the neurosis is the unempathic mother, the simplified cure is to provide a "new and more reliable object or 'selfobject' " (p. 137). He does not deny the importance of the early mother–child relationship as was emphasized in the 1940s by Hartmann, Kris, and Loewenstein. They cautioned, however, that there is a long chain of "historical events" that makes for the complexity of both human development and psychoanalysis. In the analysis of the here and now of the transference, in Stein's group of patients he demonstrates the inadequacy of this simplified myth. He also notes that although the patients may not complain during the unobjectionable positive transference, their lives in regard to work and love do not progress. On further analysis, an important source of this configuration is the disguised substitution and discharge of aggressive and erotic impulses. This character trait seems to me to be more like a symptom or inhibition that appeared during the course of the analysis. By being weak and innocent, the erotic and destructive impulses of the Oedipus complex are rendered seemingly harmless. As Stein notes, as in a dream, the "erotically excited vengeful child" (p. 134) finds discharge until she is awakened.

Characteristic of Dr. Stein's style is a subtle weaving together of the myriad elements in a clinical instance by a mind steeped in psychoanalytic knowledge and acute clinical perception of the patient and of his own personal responses. He shows convincingly that the unobjectionable positive transference is on the one hand a character symptom but also, in particular, a resistance in analysis and one that can capture the analyst by flattery. Interpretation, he observes, brings about a particularly charged negative response, which he almost always regrets, to explain his countertransference, shared by us all. In reminding us of dream psychology on the one hand and the importance of having the patient participate in the analysis of resistance on the other, he brings us back to the importance of the unconscious as well as to the value of contemporary technique derived from ego psychology.

REFERENCES

Bird, B. (1972). Transference: universal phenomenon, hardest part of analysis. *J. Amer. Psychoanal. Assn.* 20:267–301.

Freud, S. (1912). The dynamics of transference. *Standard Edition* 12.

——— (1937). Analysis terminable and interminable. *Standard Edition* 23.

Gray, P. (1973). Psychoanalytic technique: ego capacity to view intrapsychic activity. *J. Amer. Psychoanal. Assn.* 21:474–494.

——— (1990). The nature of therapeutic action in psychoanalysis. *J. Amer. Psychoanal. Assn.* 38:1083–1097.

——— (1991). On transferred permissive or approving superego fantasies: the analysis of the ego's superego activity. Part II. *Psychoanal. Q.* 60:1–21.

Hartmann, H., Kris, E., and Loewenstein, R. M. (1946). Comments on the formation of psychic structure. *Psychoanal. Study Child* 2: 11–38. New York: International Universities Press.

Lewin, B. (1955). Dream psychology and the analytic situation. *Psychoanal. Q.* 24:169–199.

Loewald, H. (1960). On the therapeutic action of psychoanalysis. *Int. J. Psychoanal.* 41:16–33.

Stein, M. (1981). The unobjectionable part of the transference. *J. Amer. Psychoanal. Assn* 29:869–891.

Strachey, J. (1934). The nature of therapeutic action of psychoanalysis. *Int. J. Psychoanal.* 15:127–157.

To introduce this subject I shall begin with Freud's (1912) statement about transference resistance:

> Thus the solution of the puzzle is that transference to the doctor is suitable for resistance to the treatment only in so far as it is a negative transference or a positive transference of repressed erotic impulses. If we "remove" the transference by making it conscious, we are detaching only those two components of the emotional act from the person of the doctor; the other component, which is admissible to consciousness and unobjectionable, persists and is the vehicle of success in psychoanalysis exactly as it is in other methods of treatment. [p. 105]

The "negative transference" and "positive transference of repressed erotic impulses" have generally been accepted as sources of resistance, although we have come to recognize that "removing" them by making them conscious is much more difficult than it sounds. But most of us have no doubts about the necessity of resolving them to a considerable extent, even if we are not so optimistic about being able to "remove" them. How often we do all we can in this respect is open to question.

I shall direct my attention here to what Freud called "the other component, which is admissible to consciousness and unobjectionable, persists and is the vehicle of success in psychoanalysis . . . " On the face of it, it is reasonable enough to assume that there is some factor that allows the patient to begin work and to continue to cooperate in the process of analysis, and that this factor bears some relation to the positive transference, without, however, being very clearly based on "repressed erotic impulses."

Inevitably, this brings us to question how we are first to cultivate this component, which is essential for the success of the analysis; what is to be done with it as the analysis draws to a close; and how we may recognize and understand the origins, development, and meanings of this useful, even essential component. The answer to the latter question, as we shall see, is by no means clear. This positive component has by no means been neglected in the literature and in clinical work, but we may question whether it has been subjected to the same degree of analytic scrutiny as have other elements of the transference. It has been exploited most obviously by those who developed the concept of the "alliance" between patient and analyst, for example, Greenson (1967, the working alliance) and Zetzel (1970, the therapeutic alliance). Greenson emphasized that the working alliance is indeed part of the transference, at the same time contrasting it with the full-blown transference neurosis (p. 209); he sees them as parallel antithetical forces in the analysis. Elsewhere, he refers to "transference reactions, a working alliance and [the] real relationship" (p. 223).

Greenson and Zetzel are by no means alone or even in a minority in considering some concept such as the working alliance integral to our understanding of the therapeutic process in analysis. There are many variants: Erikson's (1959) "basic trust," numerous references to "rapport," and the like. One way or another they all seem to be related to Freud's "unobjectionable" component, although we may conclude that their true sources are far more ancient.

For better or worse, the terms *working alliance* and *therapeutic alliance* have entered into the common parlance of psychoanalysis and perhaps even more intrusively into the variants of psychoanalysis classed as psychotherapy. It is generally stated that an adequate alliance is a necessary prerequisite for successful therapy, a claim which on the face of it might seem incontrovertible. Of course, the patient must be willing to do his best to conform to the behavioral demands of the treatment, to come to the analyst's office with some regularity, to talk as honestly as he can, to pay his bills, and generally to demonstrate that he and the analyst have some goals in common. If, on the other hand, he behaves in such a way as to make the analysis impossible, we could claim that an adequate alliance was never established or, if it were, not maintained. But if all goes swimmingly, we might congratulate ourselves on the maintenance of a good working alliance.

I share with Brenner (1979), Curtis (1979), and others a serious concern about the usefulness of the concept and, even more, about its capacity to be misleading by encouraging the blurring of important transference elements and impeding our search for the nature of the "unobjectionable" component to which Freud referred.

Let me illustrate this by reference to a special group of patients. These are typically young intelligent adults who enter analysis rather readily and take to the process with considerable skill and apparent ease. They tend to be highly articulate, and their lives are well organized, or at least not chaotic. They have varying degrees of anxiety, uncomfortable but not disorganizing, and there are generally a few neurotic symptoms with phobic and obsessional features, usually moderate in severity. They have decent, if not ideal, relations with their families, are capable of close friendship, and do work that is productive. They are generally self-supporting, if not quite on a level one would expect on the basis of their general intellectual level and training. They are, by and large, likable, attractive people, cultivated and often gifted.

Their reaction to the analytic process is quite characteristic. They find it interesting, even gratifying; they associate well, bring in dreams which are capable of being interpreted in a surprisingly large number of instances; they respond to most interpretations thoughtfully, often raising objections that reflect a healthy skepticism. They appear, above all, to be highly rational, demonstrating excellent judgment about most matters. Their friends regard them as not only normal, but as givers of good advice. In their manifest expressions and daily behavior, they are, if anything, a bit too reasonable. Acting out, when it occurs, is rarely impulsive or particularly destructive.

Their expressions of transference are again characteristic. Being knowledgeable, they accept the inevitability of attraction to their analysts, even the likelihood that it may take sexual forms, particularly when expressed in dreams. Very often they will reveal this attraction through clever teasing and a kind of innocent flirtation, all the while reminding themselves and the analyst that it can go no further. It is almost as if they were saying, "If only you were young and handsome or a woman instead of a man, etc., etc., I could fall in love with you! Even though sometimes you make the most appallingly stupid remarks, I do like and respect you." And so they go on expressing their transference feelings, predominantly positive, respectful, and sometimes affectionate, employing the very effective devices of teasing and irony. Flashes of anger do occur, but they seem as a rule to be self-limited and only rarely deeply disturbing, with one exception which I shall come to later.

Such patients often dispose of their neurotic symptoms within a few months of beginning analysis, and they go on analyzing just as eagerly as before. Resistance is expressed with silences, usually not very prolonged; by complaints, not very bitter; or by acting out, not particularly disruptive. One condition, however, does not change. These attractive people may be married or single, living with a lover or alone, but they are not in love and doubt the capacity for passionate sexuality. They may be affectionate, but sexual intensity seems strangely lacking in these otherwise sensitive and often loving individuals.

The issue is this: their most passionate feelings, previously inhibited, find their goal in the transference. They fall in love, after a fashion, with the older man or woman analyst, but do so in a way which can be readily concealed by what looks like the "unobjectionable" component of the transference and is manifested by their devotion to analysis or to what some would call "the working alliance." It seems a device for reliving and at the same time concealing the intense, infantile oedipal conflict. It is not expressed in obviously seductive forms. The analyst is indeed seduced, not into becoming a lover, but rather into a kind of pleasant appreciative parent surrogate, charmed by intelligence, warmth, and humor, concerned about his patient's welfare, and perhaps failing to notice and deal with the underlying sexuality and hatred that are so effectively disguised.

These are "good patients" who are cooperative, interesting, and very adept at the analytic process. They demonstrate very little evidence of severe pathology; their conflicts appear to be centered about the resolution of the oedipal phase; but they are not limited to these conflicts by any means, nor would we expect them to be. Ego and superego functions are highly developed, with perhaps a too skillful use of the synthetic function and too unsparing a tendency to self-criticism which, again, is expressed through irony rather than obvious self-flagellation. They have generally been healthy babies and attractive children, precocious above all. In adolescence they may have been troubled and rebellious, most often, however, giving the impression of unusual adaptability during that protean phase.

These do not, alas, constitute the majority of patients we see in practice, but they are by no means so rare as some would claim. Current emphasis on "narcissistic" and "borderline" character disorders has had the effect of diverting attention from just those patients who have the most to gain from analysis and from whom we have the most to learn.

In them, at any rate, the transference neurosis is very highly developed, taking on distinctly oedipal forms: it is powerfully defended by these patients, who demonstrate the characteristics of brilliant, charming, and precocious children, who on a superficial level appear very mature. The main current of their sexuality becomes directed into the analysis, turning the process into a kind of exciting, yet innocent, liaison. When this transference neurosis is brought to these patients' attention, that is, interpreted for what it is, the reaction is likely to be dramatic: most often they become anxious and depressed, experience great difficulty in associating, stop remembering dreams, and may be inclined to engage in acting out. This seems to be the one area of interpretation that produces a distinct reaction of anger and some distress. The analysis is no longer such an unalloyed pleasure, and one almost regrets having introduced the subject. After all, the machine had been running so smoothly!

In completing my somewhat idealized description of this group of patients, I must remind myself and you that there is considerable variation among them. Some have rather worse family histories, but seem to have been protected during childhood by one or more loving and admired adults; some appear to have been endowed, genetically or otherwise, to deal with traumatic situations better than most; and not all of them get on with their families quite so decently.

What they do have in common is their high intelligence combined with considerable cultural breadth, a highly developed ego and superego organization, the use of sophisticated and effective defenses, a history of having established a well-developed oedipal organization, and difficulty in achieving resolution of the conflicts arising out of that phase.

This type of transference neurosis is certain to evoke complicated reactions in the analyst, stimulating his own transference neurosis or, as it is more usually described, his countertransference. One has a tendency to fall into a comfortable situation dominated by mutual teasing, appreciation, and intellectual competition. It is likely, therefore, that such patients will evoke on the part of the analyst what corresponds to the "unobjectionable" component of the transference. He finds himself regarding the patient as if he or she were a favorite child, going out of his way to be kindly and protective, taking considerable pride in the patient's accomplishments, and so on.

Even though such attitudes are kept strictly within the bounds of analytic propriety (these patients, for one thing, are too sensible to allow otherwise), their subtle effects may nevertheless be hostile to the analytic process, perpetuating infantile patterns on the part of the analysand, and making it very difficult for both parties to bring about a proper termination. In this respect the analysis of the "good" patient offers difficulties which, while they are certainly less disturbing than those presented by other, more troublesome patients, are just as important to resolve by an unflagging attention to the transference resistance concealed by such attractive gifts.

The emphasis I place on the role in the resistance of such traits as rationality, intelligence, and the capacity for cooperative effort should not be construed as a denigration of their vital part in making analysis at all possible, and in advancing the process. It hardly needs to be said that they are integral components of any sort of mature, not to say civilized, behavior. Nevertheless, it may be necessary to remind ourselves from time to time that even the most essential and finely constructed instruments are double-edged; these aspects of character are no exceptions. We are simply less likely to recognize their function not only in resolving, but in maintaining neurosis; and they may operate by seducing the analyst into the self-satisfying belief that he has accomplished far more than is in fact the case. Sadly, therefore, we must confront and analyze unsparingly those traits we are most likely to admire.

I shall mention only briefly my view that the same principles and problems would apply if the structure of the neurosis had been more firmly rooted in preoedipal than in oedipal conflict. The difficulties would simply have been more severe for both analyst and patient.

Solving the problem of analyzing the transference neurosis, necessary for more than purely abstract reasons, would have been impossible, I should judge, had we adhered literally to Freud's (1912) principles. In that statement he had not only described this unobjectionable part of the transference, but went further: "*So long as the patient's communications and ideas run on without any obstruction, the theme of transference should be left untouched*" (p. 139). Once again, this dictum can be evoked to support the concept of a working alliance and, while not quoted by Kohut (1971), may well have contributed to his specific advice to delay interpreting positive, idealizing statements made by the narcissistic analysand.

If we examine Freud's statement more closely, we are struck by a number of difficulties. First, what is meant by "admissible to consciousness"? In 1912, it implied that this transference component was part of the system Pcs-Cs. Since during this same period interpretation consisted in essence of making conscious that which had been unconscious, it would in any case have been irrelevant, if not conceptually impossible, to do more than draw the patient's attention ("hypercathexis") to it; but there could be no question of unconscious elements playing an important role.

In the case of the patients I have described, many derivatives of oedipal fantasies may be largely within awareness. Non-erotic or de-erotized admiration and affection may be conscious from the first, and their role in the analytic process may be quite clear. What is generally obscure is the role of this positive, overtly nonerotic transference in maintaining a powerful resistance, not only to the resolution of inhibitions, but also to the analytic exploration of hidden springs of defiance and revenge. What looks accessible to consciousness may be so only in part; what seems free of suppressed erotic impulses may be by no means so in fact; and what seems altogether unobjectionable may after a time constitute the most difficult aspect of the transference neurosis. What appears on the surface to be so very positive may also be a screen for stubborn aggressive elements, in that respect a persistent obstacle to analytic resolution.

To return now to Freud's 1912 formulation, we need to be reminded that he never regarded consciousness as a simple matter, but always conceived of it as fluid and uncertain of definition. This is evident in Chapter VII of *The Interpretation of Dreams* and is elaborated in his brilliant little paper, "A Note upon the 'Mystic Writing-Pad' " (1925) in which he presents a view of consciousness as not simply a passive receptor, but rather as being dependent on an active function:

> This agrees with a notion which I have long had about the method by which the perceptual apparatus of our mind functions, but which I have hitherto kept to myself. My theory was that cathectic innervations are sent out and withdrawn in rapid periodic impulses from within into the completely pervious system *Pcpt.-Cs.* So long as that system is cathected in this manner, it receives perceptions (which are accompanied by consciousness) and passes the excitation on to the unconscious mnemic systems; but as soon as the cathexis is withdrawn, consciousness is extinguished and the functioning of the system comes to a standstill. It is as though the unconscious stretches out feelers, through the medium of the system *Pcpt.-Cs.* towards the external world and hastily withdraws them as soon as they have sampled the excitations coming from it.

He might have been describing a kind of psychic radar, an ingenious device by which the mind tests external reality.[1] In any case, a careful reading of his work from the *Project* (1895) to the *New Introductory Lectures* (1933) gives

[1]It is intriguing to note how many modern technological advances in the field of communication, for example, radar, sonar, digital computers, correspond to the images Freud used as models for the psychic apparatus in 1900.

no comfort to those who would see a simple definition of what was meant by "admissible to consciousness." How accessible, how fleeting, under what conditions, are all open questions, the answers to which are not determined in any simple way.

By 1937, when Freud published "Analysis Terminable and Interminable," it was evident how much his views had developed. He no longer insisted on the existence of a relatively simple nonerotic or de-erotized conscious positive transference which required no analysis. Now, with some regret, he emphasized the presence of conflictual elements which were inaccessible to analysis not because they were conscious and "unobjectionable," but because they were latent or inactive during the period of the treatment. They could, in fact, be very objectionable indeed. Not the least of these conflicts were those centered on the transference which, unanalyzed, could so often predispose to future difficulties.

These latent conflicts, he decided, could not be brought into the analysis by the analyst, either by verbal intrusions or by active manipulation, maneuvers he regarded as both ineffective and potentially damaging. Yet in the same paper he stated what appears to be a contradiction, in his disavowal of the principle of "letting sleeping dogs lie." He went further: "Analytic experience has taught us that the better is always the enemy of the good and that in every phase of the patient's recovery we have to fight against his inertia, which is ready to be content with an incomplete solution" (Freud 1937, p. 231).

It is difficult to define precisely what would justify us in regarding a conflict as inactive or latent and therefore inaccessible to analysis. Undoubtedly some conflicts are so heavily defended during the period of analysis that even as we suspect their presence, we are baffled in our efforts to uncover them, much less to analyze them. We may become aware of them only when the patient returns to us for further help or when he enters analysis with a colleague and lets us know of his decision. It is possible to achieve some comfort by convincing ourselves that conditions had not been propitious, for example, that the patient was a candidate in training, was caught in a difficult marriage or in some other situation that favored stubborn resistances. No doubt this is often the case—I have used the excuse myself—but still, was that the only reason? Could we and should we have done more?

The analyst, by his very presence and his willingness to listen, sets up a relationship described by Bird (1972) as a "false" transference, to become in effect "the worst enemy of the transference." I agree with his assessment of the complications inherent in this necessary early development of the analytic situation, but I am not inclined to consider it "false," but rather very much a part of the transference. For one thing, it is often manifested before the first visit, sometimes even in transparent dreams, and as such it reflects the wishes and fantasies of the patient rather than his recognition of the reality of the situation.

It would be wise, therefore, to question ourselves as to the nature of this response, to ask which conflicts are being expressed and concealed by it, and to what extent it is dependent on the reality of the analytic situation. The patient's conviction that the person he consults is benign, wise, and helpful is, we hope, justified by the reality. Yet we know well enough that a patient may experience extreme distrust of an analyst who is in fact perfectly trustworthy, and conversely he may place his implicit confidence in one who deserves it not at all. The personal successes of so many charlatans in the mental health field is evidence enough.

This positive response to the analyst corresponds in part at least to Freud's unobjectionable component, and in its more developed phases it may be called the working alliance. But in spite of the fact that it is necessary and useful for initiating and maintaining the analysis, we are hardly justified in concluding that it is altogether accessible to consciousness, or that it is by its nature unobjectionable. In fact, it carries a particularly heavy load of unconscious conflict, much of which has to be repressed in order for the treatment to begin, and its long-term effects are often highly objectionable. Eventually, therefore, we need to understand this phenomenon as thoroughly as any other we encounter in analysis. If we accept that sooner or later it must be interpreted, we accept also that we must study it in detail. But how?

It is instructive to listen carefully to a patient's first impressions of us. They may consist of apparently diverse observations about the furniture of the office, of personal idiosyncrasies, and the like. At the same time there appears to be a neglect of such matters as whether or not we are relaxed and confident, youthful or aged in appearance and manner, and other factors we regard as far more significant.

This is not to say that these latter details are not perceived and stored in memory, quite the contrary. But they are often repressed and subject to distortion, to appear later in the analysis in various forms. Often the patient will question, for example, whether I wear glasses, although he has seen me a hundred times or more, never without them, or he will be wildly wrong in estimating my age, or suddenly become aware of a picture that has been facing the couch for years. Such familiar phenomena may, with some effort, be understood and analyzed; it is my belief that they contain the clues that can help us solve the mystery of the unobjectionable element.

The patient's reactions to and impressions of the analyst are built up of many determinants. They are first and most profoundly the needs and desires he brings to the analysis, the unconscious wishes that seek to be gratified. Superimposed on these are his early impressions of the analyst, derived from a host of perceptions, for example, the mode of referral, the initial telephone call, early impressions of appearance and manner, discussions of indications and conditions for the analysis, including hours and fees. An entry into a new world, it often takes on an overwhelming quality—far too much to be dealt with in a few sessions. Inevitably its effects are manifested throughout the course of even a very long analysis, often in forms that make their sources difficult to detect. Yet here is the material of much of the transference, especially of the unobjectionable component.

This aspect is not so willingly scrutinized with the same intensity with which we approach other phenomena. The reasons are, upon examination, not so obscure. For one thing, the trusting, positive attitude of the analysand does allow the analysis to continue, and it is comfortable for both parties—unless the analyst forces himself to put aside that comfort. Second, it seems to be free of conflict. Third, it seems to make sense, to be entirely rational, that one person should admire and trust another who is so worthy of it. And finally, we are influenced by the dictum that we analyze the transference only when it serves the resistance, advice that would be easy to follow if we could always be sure when that took place. I suspect that such ready prescience is a very rare gift. If we resist the temptation to take the positive transference for granted, therefore, we must find some way of analyzing a component which on the surface looks unanalyzable.

In 1955 Lewin wrote "Dream Psychology and the Analytic Situation," a work which has been insufficiently recognized for its theoretical and technical importance. It described the analyst as fulfilling a double role, first as one who encourages the patient to allow himself to regress, to suspend criticism, to associate freely, to put himself into his past, to allow himself to feel relatively helpless, and to restrain his impulses toward physical movement, although not to speech. Lewin pointed out the analogy with hypnosis, with the analyst as inducer of quasi-sleep and dreaming states, in which the wish to analyze is substituted for the wish to sleep.

The encouragement of regression is fundamental to the analytic process, but it is by no means the analyst's only function, a fact that seems to be ignored in many therapeutic innovations. The analyst must also become the one who rouses the "dreaming" patient, who interprets, who encourages and guides the process of self-observation. By this token, he is the one who awakens, who insists on the substitution of secondary for primary process, of higher ego functions for more archaic ones. Inevitably he becomes the transference representative of that agency most often responsible for insomnia, the conscience.

I would venture that the loving, conscious, unobjectionable part of the transference is directed toward the analyst as the one who soothes, who induces sleep and allows the patient to feel less frightened, for he is "in good hands"; but not for a long time can this love be directed toward the one who accomplishes the awakening. It is possible, of course, to conduct a long treatment while maintaining one's role as the inducer of sleep and dreams, to accomplish a good deal in the way of symptom relief, and thus be rewarded by expressions of gratitude. Whether, without fulfilling one's role as awakener, one may be rewarded by having accomplished effective analysis is another matter. I would say not (Stein 1965, 1966, 1973).

To employ Lewin's striking metaphor, I suggest that we experiment in treating the patient's demands on the analyst as if these were derivative of unconscious wishes expressed in a dream, and that we consider the various perceptions which are stored and used from time to time as if they were the memories and day residue employed by the dream work. By this device we may treat the patient's overtly expressed attitudes as if they corresponded to a manifest dream. We make the assumption that there are unconscious wishes that seek gratification, that such wishes are subject to conflict and must attain expression in disguised forms. In order to achieve expression, memory traces of percepts, including day residues, are used both to afford a vehicle for the wish fulfillment and to disguise, so far as necessary, their true purpose. Thus these wishes are allowed to reach consciousness in some form in spite of disapproval by other agencies—e.g., by evading the (preconscious) censorship according to the model described in *The Interpretation of Dreams* (Freud 1900), or the (largely unconscious) repressive functions of the ego and superego according to the later structural model.

The patient's wishes and fantasies may be worked over further, brought into more rational, logical, organized form by a process analogous to secondary revision; in the topographic model this is a function of the preconscious system; in the structural model it would be considered a manifestation of the synthetic function of the ego. The description of secondary revision, described by Freud in 1900, may be regarded as one of the earliest precursors of the structural model of the ego.

Let us pursue further the analogies between this aspect of transference and the secondary revision of dreams. Freud (1900) wrote: "As a result of its efforts, the dream loses its appearance of absurdity and disconnectedness and approximates to the model of an intelligible experience" (p. 490). The connection of secondary revision with daydreams may also be extended to the transference; how much of the patient's attitudes are based on fantasies of what the ideal patient-analyst relationship should be? A respectful, filial attitude, an eager pupil–teacher reenactment, an innocent liaison with no threat of consummation? All of these are so appropriate, so sensible, so truly helpful to the analysis that we tend to forget how much of the wildly irrational, erotic, and hostile they may conceal. By this process certain aspects of this analysis are thus "molded" into kind of a daydream (p. 492).

In what is admittedly a highly simplified fashion, we might consider the case of these patients who treat their analysts as if they were kindly, intelligent, benign, well-trained and disciplined, very interested and even fond of them, but not a danger in any erotic sense. It seems a reasonable enough description of the actual situation so long as one does not examine its unconscious components.

Rather than taking this at face value as an intelligent patient's evaluation of the reality of the analytic situation, accepting gratefully a fine working alliance or an unobjectionable component, if instead we insist upon the arduous and possibly disagreeable task of analyzing beliefs and attitudes, we find something very different, far more conflicted, complex, and not altogether benign. The patient has been a model analysand, working hard, associating well, bringing gifts of associations and dreams. For example, she may be charming without being erotically seductive, and faithful to the point of causing concern on the part of both of us. It seems to be entirely rational, justified by the reality of the situation. It is, of course, much too good to be true, for it is not accompanied by progress in the most urgent therapeutic goals, for example, that of achieving a gratifying sexual life and an ultimately satisfying career. There are also likely to be curious distortions and self-deceptions displayed, for example when a patient talks of herself as obnoxious and without friends, statements that are manifestly false whatever their unconscious truth. And young women patients particularly complain of the usual distortions of body image so common in them, of being fat and ugly, all the while being quite aware of the contrary. They may be fishing for compliments, but that is not all. These analyses, smooth as they seem to be most of the time, do not altogether result in untroubled "sleep." Sometimes without understanding why, patients become frightened, agitated, and depressed, as if repressed impulses had broken through, rather like a bad dream.

We might now try the experiment of treating this material as if it were a manifest dream, consisting of a childlike, innocent, and highly educational liaison under the name of analysis. The underlying wishes that have emerged contain erotic fantasies about the parents, combined usually with violent impulses to destroy them both. Behind the well-behaved and rational person may be the image of a lustful, destroying angel, who would kill without mercy in a kind of oedipal rage. In order to allow these wishes to achieve any kind of expression, they must be made more acceptable for the patient by allowing her to assume the identity of a young child who is permitted to experience such desires without penalty and whose weakness is such that she need not fear actually destroying the beloved parents. Or they may be expressed more openly by an ironic stance, which allows them to be proclaimed, only to be disowned.

The use of memory traces may again be compared to how they are dealt with in the dream work. The patient may recall being a great favorite of many older people and always having been a teacher's pet at school, always loved;

these generally appear to be accurate. They often recall at least one and perhaps more screen memories which include some early sexual experience with a parent, fantasies which may have been related to horseplay with siblings and even more to medical procedures later in childhood. Most of the childhood memories reported in the analysis are generally quite plausible and subject to relatively little obvious distortion, except for the inevitable effects of the passage of time. There is little of the bizarre and strange about them, reflecting both the powerful reality sense of these patients and the fairly highly organized structure of their intelligent and well-disciplined families.

Whatever is observed in the analytic environment, the patient uses as a day residue, as material to carry fantasies. Yet the whole is likely to be so sensible, so rationalized, so free of manifest erotic or violent elements, that we may assume that a powerful synthesizing ego function is at work, rather like a very effective secondary revision of an otherwise bizarre and disturbing dream, with few breakthroughs of incongruous ideation and affect.

This process, again by analogy, "protects sleep," that is, it helps the ego to maintain a comfortable regressive state of affairs in analysis, in which the patient is apparently a sensible, conscious, and sophisticated adult and at the same time an erotically excited, vengeful child. To "awaken" her, that is, to interpret, would be to lead her to recognize her unconscious wishes for what they are, to help her deal with her repressive and ironic defenses which have allowed the neurosis to continue and the analysis to go on without much real impact on the most important problem. To continue in a sleeplike state, on the other hand, permits her to act both roles and to continue to play out the surprising contradictions in her personality.

So long as we suppose that interpretation "removes" the transference, as Freud suggested in 1912 (p. 105), we should be hesitant to bring it to consciousness before it has produced a resistance—assuming we are so prescient as to be able to detect the moment at which that latter event occurs. But we are not sure any more that transference is so easily "removed" by interpretation. It seems certain that Freud no longer believed this when he wrote "Analysis Terminable and Interminable."

How and when to interpret phenomena such as these constitutes a real enough dilemma. Kohut (1971), for example, approaching his patients with a theory which emphasizes a developmental view and puts aside conflictual considerations, would "accept," possibly for a long period, even the most highly idealized expressions of admiration for himself. And he warns against "premature interpretation" of such positive expressions, especially in the cases he classifies as narcissistic character disorders.

Many years earlier Phyllis Greenacre (1954), employing a somewhat different point of view, cautioned against early transference interpretations with narcissistic patients who are prone to acting out, since such interventions might well result in at least temporary impairment of certain defensive controls and result in episodes of destructive behavior. She made it clear that she was discussing a limited group of patients and her remarks were not confined to the "unobjectionable" component. She was at the same time very much concerned with the development of fixed over-idealizing attitudes toward the analyst and the problems engendered by these.

Without question it is rarely if ever advisable to interpret the patient's friendly, cooperative attitudes during the early part of analysis. It is not merely likely to be inadvisable; it is worse than that, because during the first few weeks or months we could not possibly understand the unconscious components of this phenomenon. Early interpretations might hit close to the mark, out of luck or intuition, but during the phase when we hardly know the patient it would be foolhardy to venture definite statements of meaning.

We need not interpret early, therefore, and could not if we would. But there is a vast difference in accepting a phenomenon as reality-based, conflict-free, representing only itself, and, on the other hand, treating it more properly as a surface manifestation of a complex set of opposing forces, most of which operate outside of conscious awareness, and which require explanation sooner or later in the course of analysis.

The questions we encounter are like those that are addressed to a particularly well-defended dream which has taken on a superficially reasonable form. A good example would be Freud's "Dream of the Botanical Monograph." It is brief enough to repeat: "I had written a monograph on a certain plant. The book lay before me and I was at the moment turning over a folded coloured plate. Bound up in each copy there was a dried specimen of the plant, as though it had been taken from a herbarium" (1900, p. 169). It would have been easy to jump to the conclusion, by no means incorrect, that the dream expressed the wish that the yet incomplete monograph which was intended to make his reputation was already published and on display. How reasonable and easy to understand! Freud was, fortunately, not so easily satisfied. He discovered, in his analysis of the dream, references to matters ranging from his experiments with cocaine back to infantile sexual investigations to which he understandably only alluded.

Similarly, if the patient imagines that his analyst is a fine and helpful person, he is expressing a wish, which on the face of it is perfectly reasonable. He is, we hope, correct in his expectations. We are certainly not obliged to contradict him, any more than we contradict the statements of a manifest dream. But we are obliged to ask ourselves questions, not only about the origins of this wish, which may impress us as both obvious and universal, but also about a complex of different wishes and defensive operations which may lie concealed beneath this understandable and benign phenomenon. To what extent is it seductive? To what degree masochistic and tricky? Is it possible that the patient harbors a deeply passive wish which says in effect, "You are so great, my fate lies in your hands; do your best and I shall yet defeat you"?

These inquiries need not be spoken out loud, but neither need they be entirely as secret from the patient. The latter, when deeply engaged in the analytic process, is likely to be especially sensitive to nuances in the analyst's state of mind, especially with respect to emotionally charged attitudes, a phenomenon commonly observed in children and present to a disconcerting degree in certain paranoid individuals. In the analysis of neurotic patients it varies with the state of regression encouraged by use of the couch and of free association.

Complex as it is, there is nothing necessarily mysterious about it. While the patient does not during the session itself see the analyst's facial expression, he is generally keenly aware of his minimal responses, his tone of voice, movements, and the like. Furthermore, he has the opportunity to pick up clues from the latter's expression at the beginning and end of the session. That he may draw some quite inaccurate conclusions is to be expected, and these misinterpretations themselves become material for the analysis. A patient senses pretty quickly and often accurately, for example, whether the analyst responds to expressions of appreciation by a warm glow of satisfaction or by a questioning attitude, the latter signifying a willingness to wait until the phenomenon can be understood in depth.

Whether the analyst reacts by "acceptance" or by questioning makes considerable difference in the future course of the treatment. What has often been taken for granted as an "empathic" approach tends to reduce emphasis on the importance of questioning, treating the patient's appreciation, for example, as if it were simply genuine, taking it at face value, justifying this by the need to establish the kind of transference situation that is believed essential for the progress of the treatment.

Such an approach has its own appeal; it appears to be humane, understanding, and protective; it is often regarded as a manifestation of a loving attitude on the part of the analyst, which is perfectly appropriate—a counterpart, it would seem, of the unobjectionable component on the part of the patient. Nevertheless, we must raise questions whether its usefulness may not ultimately be outweighed by its cost.

The failure to maintain a questioning attitude, an active curiosity about the unconscious dynamics and meaning of this type of response, is likely to favor the persistence of troublesome misunderstanding as to the true nature of the transference. This may in turn lead to serious errors in attempts to understand the sources of the patient's difficulties. It is a mistake, therefore, to place too great an emphasis on an introspective-empathic response at the expense of thoughtful questioning and evaluation of all types of data obtained by observation of the analytic situation. One of the risks of the former approach is that patient and analyst may find themselves existing in a state of mutual narcissistic regression, a kind of near-erotic mutual sleep. This can be a very gratifying experience for both; its prototype was the sleep therapy employed by the Greeks at Epidaurus and Pergamum, which provided symptomatic relief. We need not decry it, so long as it is recognized.

Analysis, however, requires regular "arousal" in Bertram Lewin's sense, accomplished by the analyst's activity, by questioning and interpretation, which may be explicit and verbalized or silent, expressed by less intrusive means, e.g., by gesture, look and tone. Only in this way are we likely to achieve some understanding of the function and the origins of the "unobjectionable" component as well as the other factors in the transference with which it is likely to be joined.

It would be desirable at this point to establish some hypotheses to account for the origins of this phenomenon of transference. This is not so easily accomplished, and must wait for further exploration. Up to now, our efforts have been partial at best, and for the most part have failed to take into account such factors as genetic endowment, at the one extreme, and late childhood, adolescent, and adult experiences at the other. Its genetic sources have been sought for largely in the experiences of early childhood, the neonatal and preverbal phases by choice, concentrating especially on mother–child exchanges. It would be rash to deny the importance of early mothering in this regard, but it is difficult to be persuaded by those who would make it the one crucial determinant, as if good mothering were not only the earliest, but also the only essential genetic factor in the capacity to develop this aspect of transference.

It is a too-simple if appealing explanation, and too dependent upon treating the manifest phenomenon as the whole article, as if the patient's trust and cooperation were a direct reflection of the trust and cooperation he learned at his mother's breast, and on the other hand, as if it reflected the need to replace a disappointing "unempathic" mother by a new and more reliable object—or "selfobject," to employ Kohut's (1971) term.

Primordial explanations are understandably popular. Those historical events which are most deeply buried in the distant past are the most difficult to evaluate and thus the more apt for myth-making. Even the most meticulous hypotheses about the psychic development of preverbal children require inferences based on giant steps which become even larger when we attempt to extend them into explanations of behavior and symptoms in adults. It is undeniable that very early experiences contribute significantly to the nature and severity of adult psychopathology, and the more we know about them the better. But to know them is not nearly enough. It is essential that we undertake the arduous task of tracing the effects of such experiences through later childhood, adolescence, and adult life, thus establishing the coherent chain of historical events which is indispensable for a soundly based sense of conviction. It is only by accomplishing this that we may be able to prevent psychological explanations from deteriorating into a series of appealing fantasies, a kind of pseudohistory based on presumed prehistoric events, which tends to operate as a defense against the discovery of something close to the genuine article.

Gill (1979) has described some of the difficulties in the tendency to interpret transference by a too-ready resort to early genetic factors rather than by recognizing the immediate context of the analytic situation. We need not go all the way with him in his emphasis on the "here and now" in the analysis of the transference, to recognize the relevance of his argument.

SUMMARY

Even those aspects of transference which initially favor the analytic process and seem to have the least connection with resistance do become integral parts of the transference neurosis and contribute massively to some of the most subtle difficulties in the process, especially in its resolution. These phenomena are, by their very appearance of rationality and cooperation, all the more difficult to bring under analytic scrutiny. They operate as resistances not only to the analysis of preoedipal conflicts, but even more effectively in the case of neurotic disorders centered on inadequate resolution of oedipal conflicts, i.e., in the so-called classical neurosis, "the case of the ideal analytic patient."

I suggest, therefore, that the appearance of the "unobjectionable component" be regarded not only as a welcome manifestation of certain conflict-free psychic elements, but also as the manifest resultant of a complex web of unconscious conflicts which must be, and are capable of being, sought for and described. Further, that their analysis may be facilitated by the use of a process analogous to that employed in the analysis of dreams, particularly with respect to secondary revision.

Finally, I have emphasized that these aspects of transference, which we are tempted to explain, and in effect dismiss, by reductionist references to early development, be regarded rather as the complex resultant of a prolonged historical experience, and that they be so interpreted.

REFERENCES

Bird, B. (1972). Notes on transference: universal phenomenon and hardest part of analysis. *J. Amer Psychoanal. Assn.* 20:267–301.

Brenner, C. (1979). Working alliance, therapeutic alliance, and transference. *J. Amer. Psychoanal. Assn.* 27:137–158.

Curtis, H. C. (1979). The concept of therapeutic alliance: implications for the "widening scope." *J. Amer. Psychoanal Assn.* 27:159–192.

Erikson, E. H. (1959). *Identify and the Life Cycle. Psychol. Issues*, Monogr. 1. New York: Int. Univ. Press.
Freud, S. (1895). Project for a scientific psychology. *Standard Edition* 1.
——— (1900). The interpretation of dreams. *Standard Edition* 4 & 5.
——— (1912). The dynamics of transference. *Standard Edition* 12.
——— (1925). A note upon the 'mystic writing-pad.' *Standard Edition* 19.
——— (1933). New introductory lectures on psychoanalysis. *Standard Edition* 22.
——— (1937). Analysis terminable and interminable. *Standard Edition* 23.
Gill, M. M. (1979). The analysis of the transference. *J. Amer. Psychoanal. Assn.* 27:263–288.
Greenacre, P. (1954). The role of transference. In *Emotional Growth*. New York: Int. Univ. Press, 1971, pp. 627–640.
Greenson, R. R. (1967). *The Technique and Practice of Psychoanalysis*. New York: Int. Univ. Press.
Kohut, H. (1971). *The Analysis of the Self*. New York: Int. Univ. Press.
——— (1977). *The Restoration of the Self*. New York: Int. Univ. Press.
Lewin, B. D. (1955). Dream psychology and the analytic situation. *Psychoanal. Q.* 24:169–199.
Stein, M. H. (1965). States of consciousness in the analytic situation. In *Drives, Affects, Behavior*, 2, ed. M. Schur. New York: Int. Univ. Press.
——— (1966). Self Observation, Reality and the Superego. *Psychoanalysis—A General Psychology: Essays in Honor of Heinz Hartmann*, ed. R. M. Loewenstein, L. M. Newman, M. Schur, and A. J. Solnit. New York: Int. Univ. Press.
——— (1973). Acting out as a character trait. *Psychoanal. Study Child* 28:347–364.
Zetzel, E. (1970). *The Capacity for Emotional Growth*. New York: Int. Univ. Press.

9

Rational versus Anagogic Interpretation: Xenophon's Dream and Others

INTRODUCTION BY MILTON HOROWITZ

Stein's point of departure in a study of rational versus anagogic interpretation of dreams is Xenophon's momentous dream as reported in his *Anabasis*. This was written circa 370–360 B.C. about his participation in an earlier Persian war where he served in a Spartan mercenary army. The book, which has thrilled its audiences since ancient times, is a product of the Greek thought of Socratic Athenian times; in fact Xenophon was a student of Socrates and wrote a brilliant memoir of him.

As Stein points out, in ancient times and in other cultures the dream was often the only path to understanding inner life and its relation to the universe: revelatory of supernatural forces, predictor of the future and of the causes and prognosis of illness. The Greeks placed unworthy desires outside themselves in the actions of the gods. By contrast Freud's view of the dream was as an indicator and record of desire within, wishes represented as having come true and anxieties portrayed pictorially. Recently some analysts have rejected the concept of biologically driven needs and the ubiquity of conflict, and the exploration of the dream and its associations has diminished based on the lesser importance placed upon the dream by some colleagues.

Since the early history of analysis, it was thought that dreams could be understood rationally, that is, as a part of the mental life filled with desires and conflicts and difficult of access. These views stand in opposition to anagogic interpretations (mystical, allegorical, and intellectual) which can be given by the dreamer without any difficulty.

Xenophon dreams of danger and for the first recorded "analytic event" associates to the dream in somewhat clichéd terms, but galvanizes himself and the Greek troops into action as a response to the perception of danger. He puts aside an anagogic interpretation and searches for a rational view in the "latent" content. This is an example of a dream "from above," all from left-over unfinished business of the day. However included in Xenophon's interpretation was the leftover business of the past: the need to replace the authority of fathers with his own authority as a self-declared general.

Stein also touches upon the fictional dreams of literature, the made-up, dream-like narratives used to advance future plot or present action. He comments that all dreams are, in some sense, fictions. The secondary revision, the need for intelligibility in narrating the dream to another, creates a fictional entity from the often disconnected bits of the dream as dreamed. For the practicing analyst, it is not possible to view the psychology of dreaming as related to, but distinct from, the physiology of dreaming. For the analyst studying conflict Stein's paper is indispensable.

> " . . . the interpretation of dreams is like a window through which we can get a glimpse of the interior of . . . the mental apparatus"
>
> (Freud 1900, p. 219)

Some years ago, I came across two accounts of dreaming which at first seemed to have nothing in common, yet which ultimately seemed to lead to the same question. The first I read in the course of preparing my notes for a course on Freud's (1900) *Interpretation of Dreams*. It was an account by two neurobiologists of experiments with dreaming in cats. The second, which I came across in the course of more idle reading, i.e., for pleasure and travel, was a vivid account of a dream by an Athenian aristocrat and soldier of the early fourth century B.C.

What could these two accounts, written some 2300 years apart, have in common? What questions do they bring up about the place of dreams in human life? In this paper I shall deal with this perennial question, and present the reasons for my belief that the innate understanding of the Athenian gentleman had more relevance to this question than the meticulous work of these sophisticated scientists. Do we once again have to demonstrate that Freud was correct? I am afraid we do.

Since the dawn of history, man has been asking questions about the role of dreams in human affairs. How these were answered depended, in each case, upon the culture, the circumstances under which the dreams were experienced, the character and beliefs of the dreamer and of the persons to whom he reported the dream—if he did.

We, who are members of a highly introspective cultural group, may remind ourselves that attitudes have been very different in other cultures, especially in the distant past, when dreams, visions, and myths were the chief, often the only access to the inner life of the individual as well as the group. In the ancient world, dream interpretation was most often used to detect supernatural forces, as if dreams were omens, for example, in the *Iliad;* or else dreams were interpreted in relatively mechanical ways to infer or predict developments in the life of the individual (as by Artemidorus) or to yield clues to the nature of illness (e.g., Hippocrates)[1].

In all of these views about the dream, there was no explicit place for the principle that we accept or try to accept that, in Freud's (1900) words: "*A dream is a (disguised) fulfilment of a (suppressed or repressed) wish*" (p. 160). Here he emphasized the ubiquity of the wish-fulfilling function of the dream work. He was later (1916) to admit that " . . . it is one of those [theoretical points] most exposed to attack in the whole theory of dreams, and that many contradictions and misunderstandings arise from it" (p. 221). He took the opportunity, once again, to repeat the arguments he had made in 1900, and to restate his conviction in characteristically Socratic style.

This principle, so positively stated, has for long been the keystone in the arch that makes up the psychoanalytic model of the mind. A careful reading of *The Interpretation of Dreams*, published at the turn of the century, reveals to what extent it laid the groundwork for such concepts as the central position of the unconscious components of the psychic apparatus, drive theory, symptom formation, conflict psychology, the mechanisms of defense, and eventually the structural model. Ultimately, our views of responsibility for our thoughts and actions are traceable to Freud's revolutionary discovery of the significance of concealed, even unsuspected, desires in human affairs as evidenced in parapraxes, symptoms, character traits, and perhaps most vividly in dreams.

Although he was the first to express this principle in scientific terms and to follow it to its logical conclusion, Freud (1900) recognized that some of the great minds of the past had shared this view. Perhaps the clearest statement from the classical world is to be found in Book IX of *The Republic*, in which Plato had Socrates say, "What we wish to recognize is the following: surely some terrible, savage and lawless form of desires is in every man, even in some of us who seem to be ever so measured. And surely this becomes plain in dreams" (572b).

Of the tyrant he says, " . . . what he had rarely been in dreams, he became continuously while awake. He will stick at no terrible murder, or food or deed" (574e, 575a). The worst man " . . . is awake, presumably, what we describe a dreaming man to be" (576b).

Socrates' view was by no means universally accepted. Rather, Greeks,

[1]I am indebted to S. Rabson for a discussion of this source.

like most people, preferred to place these unworthy desires outside themselves and thus evade moral responsibility for them. Most often, they were ascribed to the immortal gods, who sent dreams in order to give beneficent advice or commands, or to deceive and destroy the sleeper. Exception was made of some dreams by Hippocrates, for example, who regarded many dream experiences as capable of being interpreted and used by the physician as a clue to the area of somatic disturbance and the indicated treatment. The best-known writer on dreams in the ancient world, Artemidorus, emphasized the significance of dreams in bringing good or bad luck. He was inclined to find specific meanings in the dreamer's life according to the manifest symbolism of the dream. For the most part, the secret desires of the dreamer were not given great weight in the formation of dreams or in their interpretation. (See Brelich 1966, Dodds 1951, Edelstein 1967, Van Lieshout 1980.)

It would be a mistake to assume that even now Freud's dictum is universally accepted. Kohut, for example, is only the most prominent of a number of psychoanalysts who teach that some dreams may be adequately interpreted without including the unconscious dream wishes and the distortions wrought by the dream work. They present evidence which is largely clinical and is correlated with their rejection of the central importance of drive theory and the ubiquity of conflict (Kohut 1977).

Kuper and Stone (1982) also question Freud's emphasis on the distinction between manifest and latent dream, the central role of conflict, the use of free association, the nature and perhaps even the existence of "the unconscious." They base their inferences on a "structural analysis" of the dream of Irma's injection (Freud 1900), pointing to its "internal coherence and structured development" as an argument against the psychoanalytic understanding of dreams. Their comments do cast some light on the "Irma" dream, but their argument suffers from their neglect of the process of secondary revision, which Freud used to answer just such questions.

Another critical attack comes from a different discipline, neurobiology, based on the work of Hobson and McCarley (1977). These investigators demonstrated that stimulation of the brain stem of cats could produce dreams, as evidenced by electroencephalographic tracings and rapid eye movements, the same neurophysiological signs accompanying dreams in man. They employ these findings to dispute both of Freud's theses, that of the ubiquity of the wish-fulfilling function of dreams and of the conflictual elements in the dream work. While it is true that they are on firm ground in finding Freud's neurophysiology of 1895 obsolescent, they go too far in assuming that the major elements in Freud's theory of the interpretation of dreams were based on his early neurophysiological preoccupations and assumptions, as they were formulated in the "Project" (1895). He did attempt to fit these into his psychological theory, but a reading of *The Interpretation of Dreams* leads us to the conclusion that his theory was based to a much greater extent on his experience in analyzing his patient's dreams and his own. His conclusions were empirical and clinical, and he never succeeded in integrating them fully with his early neurophysiological concepts. For all practical purposes, he gave up the effort during and after the writing of Chapter VII, in 1900.

That dreams are neurophysiologically mediated is beyond question, but this tells us little about their significance in the life of the individual. We must still reckon with the kind of desires expressed therein, more or less directly or, more often, in complex disguise. Dreaming must therefore be understood as part of mental life, ranking in importance with waking thought and integrated with it. Freud insisted that although the logic of the dream work differed in important respects from that of the waking thought processes, nevertheless the underlying dream thoughts could be understood in rational terms. He therefore placed great importance on the need for "psychoanalytic" (ultimately, rational) interpretation of the dream, as opposed to the "anagogic." The latter term had referred originally to mystical or allegorical interpretation, but Freud, following Silberer (1914), enlarged its meaning to include the kind of abstract and highly intellectualized examples cited by the latter, interpretations "given by the dreamer without any difficulty" (Freud 1900, p. 524) which are likely to give the outside observer as well a less disturbing and therefore more acceptable view of human nature, certainly far more palliative in its implications than Socrates' harsh statement.

This is by no means an academic question. The view that dreams are generated outside the psychic apparatus, that they may have no important role in the expression of wish fulfillment, and that their frequent obscurity is unrelated to the dreamer's conflicts is misleading and potentially dangerous in that it deprives the dreamer of important clues to the sources of his own decisions. A case in point may be found in the writings of Herodotus *(The Histories)*: Xerxes, in planning his invasion of Greece in 480 B.C., was "troubled in mind by the speech Artabanus (his chief adviser) had made opposing the decision; and pondering it in the dead of night he became convinced that to make war on Greece was not worth the risk." He fell asleep, and dreamed "that the figure of a man, tall and of noble aspect, stood by his bed" and commanded him to adhere to his original intention to proceed (p. 449). His first reaction was to reject the command, but when the dream was repeated the following night he found himself in a state of doubt and anxiety.

He consulted Artabanus, who had argued against the expedition, and he commanded him to don his (the King's) clothes and sleep in his bed, to see whether he would have the same dream. Artabanus demurred, replying:

> Now you lean toward the better course; but you tell me that since you gave up your intention of attacking Greece you have been haunted by a

> dream that will not let you lay your purpose aside. You imagine, my son, that your dream was sent by some god or other; but dreams do not come from God. I, who am older than you by many years, will tell you what these visions are that float before your eyes in sleep: nearly always these drifting phantoms are the shadows of what we have been thinking about during the day; and during the days before your dream we were, you know, very much occupied with this campaign. Nevertheless it is possible that your dream cannot be explained as I have explained it—in which case what you have said sums up the matter completely: let it appear to me as well as to you, with its commands.

Hoping to prove that Xerxes was mistaken, Artabanus did as he was told, slept in the king's robes and in his bed.

> He dreamed that the very same figure which had twice visited the king stood over him. "Are you the man," said the phantom, "who in would-be concern for the king is trying to dissuade him from making war on Greece? You will not escape unpunished, either now or hereafter, for seeking to turn aside the course of destiny; and as for Xerxes, he has been told already what will happen to him if he disobeys me." The phantom after uttering these threats was at the point of burning out Artabanus' eyes with hot irons, when he leapt up with a shriek, and ran to find Xerxes.

Understandably, Artabanus withdrew his opposition to the invasion. To oppose the Great King was to risk the fate of Oedipus. The king, finally reassured, embarked on the campaign which, as we know, ended in disaster for the Persians (Book VII, pp. 12–18).

Herodotus presents us with two opposing hypotheses. Either Xerxes' dream came from a god, as the dreamer supposed, or it was a product of conflict within the mind of the dreamer, as Artabanus first suggested. The outcome of the story supports the second hypothesis, that it was an expression of the dreamer's attempt to overcome his doubts, which were in conflict with his grandiose wish for conquest. In order to sustain his desire, he was forced to disguise the command, the product of his own mind, by externalizing it, putting it into the mouth of a supernatural being.

Artabanus had a characteristic dream about an omnipotent father-ruler. The dream thoughts contained a message as well, which must have been in consciousness as Artabanus fell asleep, that his own safety depended on his ability to overcome, or at least conceal, his disagreement with the king, who had evidently already made up his mind to proceed. Xerxes was a ruler known to be both ruthless and impulsive. The god who appeared in Artabanus' dream was therefore invoked by him to gain permission to ignore his better judgment, to allow considerations of personal safety to outweigh his sense of duty to his nation.

Herodotus relates the tale as an object lesson, expressing his conviction of the importance of self-knowledge as opposed to self-deception. David Grene (1981, unpublished manuscript) summarizes Herodotus' point of view: "And the medium which is most fertile in showing the true nature of reality is the human mind, remembering, reflective, and most of all when its memory and reflection are put at the service of its dreaming and fantastic side" (see also Macan 1927).

A remarkable dream of even earlier date was that of Penelope in Book XIX of *The Odyssey*. She addresses Odysseus who has returned to Ithaca in the guise of a beggar:

> But come, listen to a dream of mine and interpret it for me. I have twenty geese here about the house, and they feed on grains of wheat from the water trough. I love to watch them. But a great eagle with crooked beak came down from the mountain, and broke the necks of them all and killed them. So the whole twenty lay dead about the house, but he soared high in the bright air. Then I began to weep—that was in my dream—and cried aloud, and around me gathered the fair-haired Achaian women as I cried out sorrowing for my geese killed by the eagle. But he came back again and perched on the jut of the gabled roof. He now had a human voice and spoke aloud to me: "Do not fear, O daughter of far-famed Ikarios. This is no dream, but a blessing real as day. You will see it done. The geese are the suitors, and I, the eagle, have been a bird of portent, but now I am your own husband, come home." So he spoke; and then the honey-sweet sleep released me, and I looked about and saw the geese in my palace, feeding on their grains of wheat from the water trough, just as they had been.
>
> Then resourceful Odysseus spoke in turn and answered her: "Lady, it is impossible to read this dream and avoid it by turning another way, since Odysseus himself has told you its meaning, how it will end. The suitors' doom is evident for one and all. Not one will avoid his death and destruction."
>
> Circumspect Penelope said to him in answer: "My friend, dreams are things hard to interpret, hopeless to puzzle out, and people find that not all of them end in anything. There are two gates through which the insubstantial dreams issue. One pair is made of horn, and one of ivory. Those of the dreams which issue through the gate of sawn ivory, these are deceptive dreams, their message is never accomplished. But those that come into the open through the gates of polished horn accomplish the truth for any mortal who sees them. I do not think that this strange dream that I had came to me through this gate. My son and I would be glad if it did so."

The dreamer herself, in the guise of Odysseus, interprets the dream while she is still dreaming: a dream within a dream. When after waking she tells the dream to the disguised Odysseus, he confirms the interpretations, making clear not only the prediction, but the wish to destroy the suitors. It is not too much to suppose that turning the greedy suitors into geese was the product of the dream work, which accomplished several purposes simultaneously. The destruction of the goose-suitors was rendered easy: they were no longer formidable, dangerous young warriors, but helpless barnyard fowls; and it was no crime to kill them. Penelope does, however, weep for the geese and is relieved to discover, upon awakening, that they are still alive. Her distress may well be a tribute to her femininity: as a woman, she might have abhorred such violence directed toward these young men in their prime; but it is reasonable to assume as well that after twenty years of Odysseus' absence at the war, and her enforced sexual abstinence, sexual desire and anger with her husband may have played a role (Devereux 1957). These interpretations are by no means mutually exclusive, as Finley (1978) suggests. Quite the contrary; they reinforce one another. Her understanding of the dream was followed by the decision to prepare the trial of Odysseus' great bow, leading eventually to the destruction of the suitors and the open recognition of her husband.

This is, of course, a poem, not a historical fact, much less a clinical one. We may consider it a poet's dream, a creative act, with the internal consistency and believability of a great work of art. We have little to add to Homer's explication.

These two dreams, Xerxes' and Penelope's, are poetic fiction or, at best, historical myths—the creations of the author and poet. They are in that respect in a different category from first-hand accounts of psychological experiences. An excellent example of the latter is to be found in Xenophon's "Anabasis." This account of a military expedition in the year 401 B.C. was written some thirty years later; nevertheless it conveys a remarkable impression of vividness and accuracy of observation. It is more personal memoir than objective history, and is all the better reading thereby. Whether it is based on a diary or on the author's highly developed memory is a matter of some speculation (see Cawkwell 1972, pp. 22–23).

Xenophon was an upper-class Athenian in his late twenties, who had become disaffected with the democratic rule which was responsible, as he saw it, for the loss of the Peloponnesian War. He was attracted to Sparta, finding it a more congenial society. Young, and at loose ends, he was strongly motivated to advance himself, financially and otherwise, by some military exploit. His opportunity came when Cyrus, brother of the King of Persia, recruited 10,000 Greek mercenary soldiers, ostensibly as part of a punitive expedition, but secretly with the intent of killing and taking over the throne of his brother Artaxerxes.

Xenophon was invited to join the Greek force. Having been a disciple of Socrates, he consulted his mentor, who advised him to seek guidance at the Oracle at Delphi. He did so, phrasing his question to Apollo as follows.

> "To what god shall I pray and sacrifice in order that I may best and most honorably go on the journey I have in mind, and return home safe and successful?" Apollo's reply was that he should sacrifice to the appropriate god, and when Xenophon got back to Athens he told Socrates the Oracle's answer. When Socrates heard it, he blamed him for not asking whether it was better to go on the expedition or stay at home; instead of that he had made his own decision that he ought to go and then inquired how he might best make the journey. . . . [p. 141]

Xenophon's piety was considered typical (Cawkwell 1972, p. 10); but the way his belief was subordinated to his intention in this instance is significant, in the light of later developments.

After he joined the Greek forces at Sardis, Xenophon was appointed a junior officer "neither a general, nor a captain, nor an ordinary soldier," the ancient equivalent, perhaps, of a volunteer lieutenant. All went well during a long march into the center of Babylonia. There, in September of 401, the combined force fought a battle near the town of Cunaxa, close to the junction of the Tigris and the Euphrates. The well organized and experienced force of Greek mercenaries was successful in defeating the troops opposed to them, but the rest of the battle went badly and at the last moment Cyrus himself was killed, leaving the Greeks locally victorious but with neither a leader nor a cause.

The Persian authorities offered the Greeks supplies and a safe conduct if they would cooperate and depart peacefully. Since their situation appeared desperate, they accepted. They were at least a thousand miles inside hostile territory without supplies, and more than two thousand miles from Greece, surrounded by an overwhelming number of Persian and satellite forces. In spite of their distrust of the Persians' intentions, they felt they had no choice.

Their doubts were soon justified. The five leading generals and two hundred troops were decoyed into the Persian camp and treacherously slaughtered; at least this was how Xenophon saw it. The remainder of the Greek force, deprived of their senior officers, short of cavalry and without adequate food, were largely demoralized and many were tempted even now to accept the Persian terms, including the demand to lay down their arms. In this state of mind they retired for the night.

> Xenophon [he wrote in the third person] was no different from the rest, and now in their difficult position he was as miserable as anyone else and

> could not get to sleep. However, he got a little sleep in the end and had a dream. He dreamed that there was a thunderstorm and that a thunderbolt fell on his father's house and then the whole house was on fire. He woke up immediately, feeling very frightened, and considered that in some respects the dream was a good one, because in the midst of his difficulties and dangers he had dreamed of a great light from Zeus.[2] [This optimistic interpretation did not satisfy him; he continued:] But in other respects he was alarmed by it, because the dream seemed to him to have come from Zeus in its character of the King and the fire had seemed to blaze all around him and this might mean that he would not be able to leave the King's country but would be shut in on all sides by one difficulty or another. *But what is really meant by having a dream like this can be seen from what happened after the dream.*
>
> [He went on with his waking thoughts:] This is what did happen. As soon as he woke up the first thing that came into his head was this: "What am I lying here for? The night is passing and at dawn the enemy will probably be here. If we fall into the King's hands, there is nothing to prevent us from seeing the most terrible things happening, from suffering all kinds of tortures and from being put to death in ignominy. Yet so far from anybody bothering to take any steps for our defence, we are lying here as though we had a chance of enjoying a quiet time. What city, then, do I expect will produce the general to take the right steps? Am I waiting until I become a little older? I shall never be any older at all if I hand myself over to the enemy today."

He aroused himself immediately and called his colleagues together in order to organize a plan that would allow them to return to their homeland, in spite of Persian treachery. He ended his speech to his fellow officers thus: " 'I am prepared to follow you, and if you appoint me to be your leader I am making no excuses about my age. Indeed I think I am already sufficiently grown up to act in my own defence' " (pp. 140–143, *passim*; italics added).

He was soon chosen to replace one of the murdered generals and to reorganize the demoralized troops in order to plan a return to their homeland, requiring a march across more than a thousand miles of hostile territory. Eventually, after suffering many hazards and hardships, the troops, still an organized force and relatively intact, reached the shores of the Black Sea and safety.

Following his dream, Xenophon's first waking thought (or was it part of the dream?) was that he had received reassurances from Zeus—a comforting

---

[2] W. T. MacCary (1982, personal communication) notes that the original Greek employs the word *lampesthai* whose literal meaning is "glow, shine," which suggests also the thought of greatness.

interpretation. In rejecting this it occurred to him that Zeus of the thunderbolts really stood for the Persian King, who had no reason to love him. He thus put aside his anagogic interpretation, and looked instead for the latent content of his dream. In this fashion he made the connection between the manifest dream and the day's residues, consisting of the terrible danger and the conflict of wishes that had obsessed him as he fell asleep: on the one hand, the wish to escape the imminent danger to his life; on the other, to seek solace in denial and sleep, exhausted as he was.

Then, as he had really come awake, he faced openly his immediate peril and the need for prompt action. He recounts the experience as if there had been two awakenings: the first accompanied by the anagogic, that is, the supernatural and comforting interpretation; the second by a more searching, rational, and disturbing recognition of the thoughts which had contributed to the creation of the dream. He overcame his denial, at the expense of his sleep, and took an action which would save his own life and that of his comrades. It was the expression of sound common sense.[3]

Understandably, Xenophon took the interpretation no further. His experience was a classic example of a "dream from above," the content of which is dominated by a powerful conflict left over from the day's residues, and very much unsolved at the time of falling asleep. There was no reason he should have been expected to explore more deeply; on the contrary, he had every reason to take action rather than engaging in further thought—just as well for him that he was not by nature an introspective individual.

Someone with the leisure and inclination, an analyst, for example, might ask why his father's house should have been destroyed by the thunderbolt. Considering his repeated references to his own youth, his presumption in wishing to take command over his elders, the fact that most of these elders had so recently been destroyed, it would be fair to speculate that the less accessible parts of the dream, the underside, so to speak, contained the unconscious, archaic wish to destroy the father—the fathers in the guise of the senior generals, Cyrus, also destroyed, Artaxerxes, even Zeus himself. This was going too far; it could invoke a thunderbolt.

I have been reminded that to a Greek of the classical period, "his father's house" represented not merely a structure, but the family line itself, his father *and* his descendants, including the dreamer and his own descendants. (P. Hartocollis 1982, personal communication). The parricidal wish, of infantile origin, reinforced the contemporary and far from buried wish to destroy the Persian king: the unconscious conflict was derived from the former, the preconscious from the immediate situation of danger.

[3]Some of the characteristics of this dream are shared with the dream of the "burning child" reported by Freud (1900, p. 509).

Xenophon was a very ambitious young man. He had ideas of using the Ten Thousand to form a colony somewhere in Asia Minor or Thrace, with himself as leader or perhaps even tyrant. In this he was unsuccessful, but he did in fact become, after his campaign, a man of some substance and an important figure in Greek political life.

The dream may therefore be considered to be like most or all dreams, multiply determined: by the need to sleep, by the opposing need to take action to save his own life, and, on a level less accessible to consciousness, the wish to replace his elders, all of them if necessary, to accomplish his life ambitions.

For us, the importance of the dream lies in his having reported it, along with the thoughts and actions preceding and following. He did not, so far as we can tell, use it as propaganda by reporting it to his colleagues. The reporting of dreams for this purpose was a common practice among military leaders of the classical world, and on one occasion, later in the campaign, was employed by Xenophon himself. But in this instance Xenophon interpreted for himself, in advance, the arguments that arose out of the dream thoughts as he understood them. He employed the dream for his own understanding, and later to explain to posterity the way he reached the crucial decision to awaken and take action. His arguments to the troops on this occasion were based on logic, not divine support. We may therefore accept his interpretation of his dream as being correct, if not exhaustive in a psychoanalytic sense.

Since his account was written so long after the event, we need not accept the details of the dream experience as literally true—a qualification we would have to make even if he had reported it on the following day. The dream would very likely have been subject to a good deal of secondary revision, perhaps years after the event. We simply do not know. Even so, the dream, the dreamer's understanding of it, its relation to the previous day's residues, and the actions Xenophon was impelled to take remain essentially convincing. This account has an internal consistency and conveys a sense of conviction which force us to regard it as an elegant piece of work.

How he managed to convey all this detail many years later raises some interesting questions. Cawkwell (1972) points out that no matter whether he kept a diary or not, Xenophon evidently shared with other ancient Greeks a highly developed memory. While not a totally reliable historian by any means, he was an excellent memoirist, whose retention of personal details was superior to his historical understanding. To suppose that he had not dreamed this dream, but deliberately invented it, would be to credit him with a knowledge of dream psychology we would not expect in a man of action—a fine writer, it is true, but not an outstanding intellect. To invent a dream of this sort out of whole cloth is an extraordinarily difficult task for anyone, impossible, I would judge, for Xenophon, who was no Homer and certainly no Freud. I prefer to believe that his memory was faithful in this instance. If not, it was a creative tour de force of the first order.

Simon (1978) cites a manifestly similar dream, that of Iphigenia in Euripides' *Iphigenia in Tauris*. In this instance, however, the dreamer misinterprets the dream, an error which Simon points out was necessary for the formal construction of the plot. The dreamer takes the dream to be a message that her brother Orestes has died, implying that the information is of supernatural origin. Her unconscious ambivalence is not acknowledged, i.e., that she might have harbored a wish for her brother's death. There is still another dream worth citing for its intrinsic interest. It is the incestuous dream of Julius Caesar, which Plutarch describes as having occurred on the fateful night Caesar was deciding whether to cross the Rubicon. He says no more about it. Suetonius, contemporary with Plutarch, gives a far more interesting account:

> . . . At Cadiz he saw a statue of Alexander the Great in the Temple of Hercules, and was overheard to sigh impatiently: vexed, it seems, that at an age when Alexander had already conquered the whole world, he himself had done nothing in the least epoch-making. Moreover, when on the following night, much to his dismay, he had a dream of raping his own mother, the soothsayers greatly encouraged him by their interpretation of it: namely, that he was destined to conquer the earth, our Universal Mother. [p. 13]

We can hope that they were handsomely rewarded for this apt, although incomplete, interpretation. We do not know whether they were aware that the dreamer, on the previous day, had seen and reacted to the statue of the great conqueror. Caesar was almost certainly aware of the stories and myths that had arisen about Alexander, among them the rumor that his father Philip had been murdered with the connivance of Olympias, his mother, and that Alexander himself may have been implicated in this successful attempt to achieve the throne prematurely. We might speculate, therefore, that Caesar's dream had a meaning in addition to the one conveyed by the soothsayers, correct as far as it went. Like Alexander, he would achieve conquest by overcoming his father, at least in archaic retrospective fantasy.

Of Julius Caesar's ambition we need have no doubts, nor that under stress it could have taken on a frankly incestuous form. The clever soothsayers looked beyond the manifest dream, with its archaic, forbidden wish; they brought him back to the meaning of the dream thought related to the day's residue. Because it was within the reach of his waking imagination and therefore dangerous, it was disguised by an image, which, though more shocking, was not remotely possible. They read him sensibly and correctly, saying in effect, "You might have once desired your mother; now you merely wish to emulate Alexander's military conquests." In his present situation this constituted a less forbidden but in reality a far more dangerous desire. His worldly ambition was ultimately fated to bring about his death.[4]

How far we may trust Suetonius' account, as to whether Caesar had the dream at all, it is impossible to say. Military leaders of the classical world cultivated the habit of having significant dreams before great events, and it is possible that this was a later invention. Still, it holds together, and if Caesar had been alive in Rome today, he might well have commented, *"Si e non vero, e ben trovato."*[5]

We might be impelled to make the same remark with regard to any of the interpretations, or for that matter, the records of dreams from antiquity, given the virtual inevitability of second-hand or more distant accounts, corrupted texts, the absence or at least the paucity of the dreamer's associations, and finally, our ignorance of his response to the interpretation. Xenophon's account was exceptional in that it was reported by the dreamer himself and was accompanied by a fair amount of associative and background material (given that thirty years allows for a good deal of secondary revision). We may be reminded that all dreams are in some sense fiction, and their value is that of fiction. The dreams cited here have the virtue of being good, rather than bad, fiction. They can cast some light on the degree and quality of the understanding, implicit or explicit, of dream psychology possessed by writers of the past, from Homer to Samuel Pepys (Stein 1977).

One of Freud's happier analogies is to be found in *The Interpretation of Dreams* (1900).

> A daytime thought may very well play the part of *entrepreneur* for a dream; but the *entrepreneur*, who, as people say, has the idea and the initiative to carry it out, can do nothing without capital; he needs a *capitalist* who can afford the outlay, and the capitalist who provides the psychical outlay for the dream is invariably and indisputably, whatever may be the thoughts of the previous day, *a wish from the unconscious.*
>
> Sometimes the capitalist is himself the *entrepreneur*, and indeed in the case of dreams this is the commoner event: an unconscious wish is stirred up by daytime activity and proceeds to construct a dream. So, too, the other possible variations in the economic situation that I have taken as an analogy have their parallel in dream-processes. The *entrepreneur* may himself make a small contribution to the capital; several *entrepreneurs* may apply to the same capitalist; several capitalists may combine to put up what is

[4]The interpretive tradition was a familiar one. According to Herodotus, a similar dream had been experienced by Hippias centuries before; it had been similarly interpreted.

[5]Italian, translated: "If it is not true, it is well found"—i.e., it is a good story!

> necessary for the *entrepreneur*. In the same way, we come across dreams that are supported by more than one dream-wish . . . [p. 561]

In clinical practice today, it is not uncommon to come across dreams in which like in Caesar's, an overt incestuous wish is brought to consciousness in the attempt to deal with a highly conflicted wish of another type. For example, a patient in analysis reported the following dream: "I was going to a brothel, accompanied by a minister of some sort, who was going to show me what to do. There were a number of women there. I looked at them and between their legs I saw things like seashells and coral, with sharp edges. I was disgusted and awoke with a sense of horror."

The brothel reminded him that he had never been able to bring himself to visit a prostitute, although he had often masturbated while daydreaming about a beautiful whore. He had hoped that the analysis would give him sufficient courage to live out this fantasy. The clergyman represented the analyst, myself, who would give him permission and guide him in realizing this desire, which revealed itself, ultimately, to be directed toward a childhood image of his mother. He was in fact a happily married and potent man, although afflicted by a sense of unsatisfied desire, and a curiously blocked attachment to his mother.

He went on to talk about an immediate source of concern, his business affairs. He was engaged in an ambitious project which, if he could bring it off, would lay the ground work for financial success. Meanwhile, however, he found himself risking all of his assets, working with partners who were greedy and dishonest; inexperienced as he was, he felt like a child among dangerous adults. What he wanted, in this context, was a father who would guide him through the dangers of his business affairs, giving him permission to take risks and guarding him against loss.

The shells and coral were associated not only with archaic fantasies about the dangerous genital of the woman, but were also a reference to the sharp tools and dirty mess incidental to his business project.

There were thus two chief wishes contributing to the dream: the more obvious and yet more distant was an infantile unconscious desire for his mother, to be carried out with his father's permission and guidance. The other wish, derived from the day's residue, was close to consciousness. "I am in a dangerous situation, having overreached myself out of ambition to become richer than my father. I wish my analyst could help me, as my father might have, even though my ambition is a hostile one."

To employ Freud's analogy: the wish for brilliant success in business was conscious, although certain elements in it were not, e.g., his drive for crushing oedipal conquest, including the ruin of his father by destroying his financial assets. The conscious wish was the entrepreneur who instigated the dream.

The capital was supplied by the unconscious oedipal wishes, playing the part of a primitive but powerful outlaw organization, like a Mafia, with capital to spare, but in need of a more respectable outlet for it, so that it might, in current parlance, be "laundered," and thus establish what looked like a legitimate position in business, i.e., be allowed exposure in consciousness.

But things went wrong. The illicit source of the capital revealed itself and the dreamer awoke in distress. It was no accident: at this point, the infantile desire constituted a less immediate danger than the apparently more innocent financial one, which was in fact associated with a real and imminent danger of bankruptcy. It is less threatening to dream of imagined incest than real failure.

All of these examples may be considered "dreams from above," as Freud (1923) defined them. They "correspond to thoughts or intentions of the day before which have contrived during the night to obtain reinforcement from repressed material that is debarred from the ego," as opposed to dreams from below, "provoked by the strength of an unconscious (repressed) wish which has found the means of being represented in some of the day's residues" (p. 111). But the distinction must not be made too sharply and is in any case quantitative rather than qualitative.

Dreams from above are likely to deal with more or less abstract thoughts, often of a complex nature.[6] In order to be represented in the dream, as we know, they must as a rule be rendered in graphic form. The imagery is likely to be crudely anatomical, as in the case of my patient's dream of the brothel.

Freud (1900) cites an excellent example from his own experience—the dream of the "open-air closet" (pp. 468–469). The gross imagery of the dream, which consists of washing away heaps of feces with a stream of urine, was used to express the grandiose wish (so it must have seemed at the time) that the dreamer would be able, through the influence of his work, to clean out the Augean Stables of human ignorance, especially in the field of sexuality. Clearly, it conveyed a wish that expressed the dreamer's overweening ambition and even a certain ruthlessness. He knew this and was in conflict about it, as evidenced by his disgusted reaction to being told, the afternoon before, that he was "a very great man." Here the gross imagery of the dream was employed to conceal his aggression; at the same time it was one of the experiences that gave him a clue to the psychosexual determinants of the very character traits that made him so uncomfortable. His interpretation dealt with a somewhat abstract idea; it was not anagogic, in that it dealt with an extremely important, even painful conflict of the dreamer's. It was certainly not a "noble" thought, in Silberer's (1914) sense.

[6]See Lewin (1958) for a fine example of a "dream from above."

When the day's residue is an "indifferent" one, we are more interested in the power of the archaic wish and dream thoughts derived from long-buried memories, oedipal for example, while we need pay less attention to the current context—although, when it is transferential, it may by no means be ignored. When, however, the day's residue is powerfully registered and productive of conflict, as in Xenophon's case, or as we observe in patients who have suffered a recent traumatic experience, we are inclined to pay more attention to the dreamer's ways of dealing with that conflict, and to interpret accordingly. Only later, often much later, do we interpret the archaic forces that were stimulated and that contributed both to the individual's reaction to the trauma and to the content of the dream.

Imperceptibly, I have been led from my original intention to discuss anagogic versus rational interpretation, into a related discussion of dreams "from above," which are most likely to tempt us into being satisfied with an anagogic interpretation. Most self-interpretations are likely to fall into the latter category, with some notable exceptions such as those reported here, and of course, the historic example of Freud's. For a truly inclusive interpretation we do, of course, need the patient in analysis. The best we can do with historically reported dreams is to form hypotheses, with some reasonable degree of probability, about how the dreamer has treated the day's residue and how his understanding of the dream affected his subsequent action; sometimes, with a lower degree of probability, we can speculate about the archaic sources of the dream, for example, the infantile wish (Freud 1929).

To return to the classical world, the same principles may be applied to Xenophon's dream and to Caesar's. Xenophon's wish to destroy his father was by now irrelevant in reality, and he had no actual intention of defying the gods. But these archaic desires supplied the capital, while the real and immediate need for action represented the entrepreneur. So also with Caesar: incest was the capital, ambition the entrepreneur. In each case, the incestuous desire broke through and concealed, for the moment, the danger of the entrepreneur's wish to conquer (the day's residue). In each of these examples, the dreamer was an ambitious young man, eager to outdo his elders.

It is instructive to compare Xerxes' treatment of his dream with that of Xenophon. Neither of them was immediately satisfied with the literal message conveyed by the manifest dream. Xerxes questioned it, even after he dreamed it again, each time awakening in a state of anxiety. He insisted that his skeptical advisor conduct the experiment of deceiving the god who must have sent the dream. Ultimately he rejected Artabanus' rational interpretation that the dream represented his own internal conflict over a very questionable strategic decision. At the same time he denied the role of his own grandiose desires in generating the dream, thus failing to recognize how these desires could have influenced his military judgment. The deceiving god was generated by his own unconscious desires.

Xenophon also arrived first at an anagogic, i.e., a higher, supernatural interpretation, that the message came from Zeus. But his rejection of this meaning was immediate. Instead he recognized the urgent conflict which had instigated the dream, and soon impelled himself to express the wish to be a leader, in command of his elders—most of whom were already out of action. The oedipally influenced wish to conquer the Great King of Persia was permissible; for one thing the latter was a barbarian, and for another, he represented an actual threat to the dreamer's life.

These days, our patients are not likely to look to supernatural powers for the sources of their dreams, although they occasionally become interested in the possibilities of telepathic influence. Freud (1922), although unwilling to reject this possibility, was not convinced that such experiences were in a category different from other latent dream thoughts. Telepathy was, in any case, not of supernatural origin. Such explanations do not therefore constitute much of a problem in interpretation in dealing with those Western educated individuals who make up the great majority of analytic patients today.

Anagogic interpretation in the "higher" sense does however represent an important issue in psychoanalytic practice today, as it always has. Freud did not deny that some dreams can convey "highly abstract thoughts from waking life which were incapable of being given any direct representation" (Freud 1900, p. 524). These thoughts are usually detected by the dreamer himself without any great difficulty; he may in fact be rather pleased with them. The dream thoughts which are subject to conflict are not nearly so easy to recover.

In clinical practice the more common examples of the deceptive nature of anagogic interpretation (in the latter sense) may be found in dreams of cure during the course of analysis. While such dreams may in fact be concurrent with symptomatic improvement, the wish for cure which is represented therein has been perfectly conscious and relatively conflict-free. The question we must ask is, "Why the dream?" If we accept it as simply conveying a clear and positive message, we miss the more important underlying dream thought, "If only I could escape from this disagreeable process of facing the reprehensible nature of my desires and the intensity of my conflicts over them, and no longer be forced to meet with this irritating person who forces me to look at them!" Accepting the anagogic interpretation as sufficient ("You wish to be cured") and ignoring the negative conflictual aspects may well lead to "a flight into health," a transitory relief of symptoms and a premature termination of the treatment.

An even more dramatic and potentially dangerous phenomenon is the optimistic recurring dream of cure experienced by patients suffering from serious depression. This, we have learned to our sorrow, often signals reunion with the archaic mother, the "cure," by suicide. Certainly, these dreams enter through the gate of carved ivory and need to be so regarded by us. Neglect of their disguised wish-fulfilling function and the intensity of the conflict by which they are generated may well have serious consequences. In Freud's (1923) statement, "it happens only too often that the compulsion to repeat . . . is not content with the return of the repressed merely in the form of dream-pictures" (p. 118)—the next step is an episode of acting out.

We are all inevitably tempted to assign elsewhere the responsibility for our dreams. This is easy enough to understand in the case of dreams that contain an obvious "expression of immoral, incestuous and perverse impulses or of murderous and sadistic lusts" (1923, p. 132). But the same temptation is strong even in the case of dreams "from above," in which such obviously forbidden wishes are not prominent at all, for example, in those of Xenophon and Xerxes. Xenophon's wishes to save his life and command his elders may strike us as ambitious, even arrogant, but they were not in themselves deserving of punishment. The underlying archaic wish, however, to destroy his father and take over his function, was of another order of magnitude altogether and had to be treated differently, by ego and superego.

Xenophon was well enough integrated, mentally healthy, as we might put it, to perceive the first wish, which was close to consciousness and reasonable in itself, even if disagreeable, and he was able to act upon it; but he was to remain unaware of the second, which had no immediate relevance for him. This latter element, however, may have supplied the extra push necessary to bring the dream itself into consciousness, as if he had said, "Under the circumstances it is justified and perhaps possible to defeat the Great King, even though, on some level, he might represent my fantasy, but not the real danger of passive defeat."

The ancients had their gods to act as external forces to account for dreams; we have neurobiology. To the modern mind the latter is far more appealing, and it is in fact of the greatest potential value in furthering our understanding of sleeping, dreaming, wakefulness, perhaps even thought processes. But like anagogic dream interpretation, our knowledge of neurobiology will be misused if it is employed to encourage the tendency to divest ourselves of responsibility for our dreams and our desires, to avoid discomfort about their nature. Confining our efforts to understanding the physiology of dreams at the expense of the elucidation of their meaning is like becoming fascinated by the optical glass of the dream window while ignoring what may be seen through it. For it is a window that reveals not only the forbidden desires of the dreamer, but also, through the dream work, conveys an understanding of the complex and largely unconscious ego and superego processes with which we try to express and conceal those very wishes.

Most of the classical world, like ours, evaded responsibility for unconscious wishes and conflicts, ascribing them instead to the gods who appeared in their dreams. It was no accident that these very same gods behaved in ways that revealed "immoral,incestuous and perverse impulses or murderous and sadistic lusts." Quarrels among the immortals were no bad picture internalized conflicts within our own psyches. The Socrates of *The Republic* was not taken in, for he knew these lusts were our own, that the gods who appeared in dreams represented warring forces within the dreamer or the waking tyrant. Like Freud he recognized that dream thoughts were intimately related to waking life, rather than being sent by the gods: it is no wonder he was accused of impiety.

As military leaders of the classical world who were about to embark on a campaign sought out the hidden intentions of the gods, we seek out the hidden intentions of the individual, where rewards of understanding may be great, and the penalty for self-deception, heavy: a plus for Xenophon, a minus for Xerxes.

SUMMARY

Freud's insistence that "a dream is a (disguised) fulfilment of a (suppressed or repressed) wish" has come under attack repeatedly. This principle, while never widely accepted, was nevertheless expressed, explicitly or otherwise, in the works of Homer, Herodotus, Plato, and other writers of the classical world. A detailed account of a dream of Xenophon's is employed to illustrate the capacity of a psychologically naïve Athenian writer to reject anagogic interpretation in favor of a more soundly based understanding of his own dreams. This is followed with a discussion of "dreams from above," which are most likely to raise this particular issue, one of considerable clinical and theoretical importance.

REFERENCES

Aristotle (384–322 B.C.). On dreams. On prophesying by dreams. On sleep and sleeplessness. In *Britannica: Great Books*, trans. R. M. Hutchins, 1952.

Artemidorus (1975). *The Interpretation of Dreams*, trans. R. J. White Park Ridge, N. J.: Noyes.

Brelich, A. (1966). The place of the dream in the religious world concept of the Greeks. In *The Dream and Human Societies*, ed. G. E. Van Grunebaum and R. Callois. Berkeley: Univ. Calif. Press, pp. 293–301.

Cawkwell, G. (1972). In Xenophon (435–354 B.C.).

Devereux, G. (1957). Penelope's character. *Psychoanal. Q.* 26:378–386.

Dodds, E. R. (1951). *The Greeks and the Irrational.* Berkeley: Univ. Calif. Press.

Edelstein, L. (1967). Greek medicine and its relation to religion and magic. In *Ancient Medicine: Selected Papers of Ludwig Edelstein*, ed. O. Temkin and C. L. Temkin. Baltimore: Johns Hopkins, pp. 205–246.

Finley, J. H., Jr. (1978). *Homer's Odyssey.* Cambridge & London: Harvard Univ. Press, pp. 1–24.

Finley, M. I. (1978) *The World of Odysseus.* New York: Viking.

Freud, S. (1895). A project for a scientific psychology. In *The Origins of Psychoanalysis.* New York: Basic Books, 1954, pp. 347–445.

——— (1900). The interpretation of dreams. *Standard Edition* 4 & 5.

——— (1916). Wish-fulfilment. *Standard Edition* 15.

——— (1922). Dreams and telepathy. *Standard Edition* 18.

——— (1923). Remarks on the theory and practice of dream interpretation. *Standard Edition* 19.

——— (1929). Some dreams of Descartes'. A letter to Maxime Leroy. *Standard Edition* 21.

Herodotus (485–425 B.C.). *The Histories,* trans. A. de Selincourt. New York: Penguin Books, 1972.

Hippocrates (460–377 B.C.). *Regimen I–IV,* trans. W. H. S. Jones. Cambridge: Cambridge Univ. Press, 1967.

Hobson, J. A., and McCarley, R. W. (1977). The brain as a dream state generator: an activation-synthesis hypothesis of the dream process. *Amer. J. Psychiat.* 134: 1335–1348.

Homer (c. 1900 B.C.). *The Odyssey of Homer,* trans. R. Lattimore. New York: Harper & Row.

Kohut, H. (1977). *The Restoration of the Self.* New York: Int. Univ. Press.

Kuper, A., and Stone, A. (1982). The dream of Irma's injection: a structural analysis. *Amer. J. Psychiat.* 139-1225–1234.

Lewin, B. D. (1958). *Dreams and the Uses of Regression.* New York: Int. Univ. Press.

Macan, R. (1927). Herodotus and Thucydides. In *Cambridge Ancient History* (Athens). Cambridge: Cambridge Univ. Press, 1958, vol. 4, pp. 398–419.

McCarley, R. W., and Hobson, J. A. (1977). The neurobiological origins of psychoanalytic dream theory. *Amer. J. Psychiat.* 134:1211–1221.

Plato (c. 427 B.C.–347 B.C.) *The Republic of Plato,* trans. A. Bloom. New York: Basic Books, 1968.

Plutarch (c. 46–120 A.D.). Caesar. In *The Fall of the Roman Republic,* trans. R. Warner. New York: Penguin Books, 1972, pp. 243–310.

Silberer, H. (1914). *Problems of Mysticism and Its Symbolism.* New York: Moffat, Yard, 1917.

Simon, B. (1978). *Mind and Madness in Ancient Greece.* Ithaca, N. Y.: Cornell Univ. Press.

Stein, M. H. (1977). A psychoanalytic view of mental health: Samuel Pepys and his diary. *Psychoanal. Q.* 46:82–115.

Suetonius (75–160 A.D.). *The Twelve Caesars,* trans. R. Graves. London: Folio Society, 1964.

Van Lieshout, R. G. A. (1980). *Greeks on Dreams.* Utrecht, The Netherlands: HES Publishers.

Xenophon (435–354 B.C.). *The Persian Expedition,* trans. R. Warner; introduction and notes by G. Cawkwell. New York: Penguin Books, 1972.

10

Irony in Psychoanalysis

INTRODUCTION BY MILTON HOROWITZ

Stein's paper on irony takes as a central premise the idea that conflict is an inherent feature of the human psyche and that conflicts of desires, of affects, and of beliefs make up the essence of irony. Irony postulates a double audience, one party hearing and not understanding, the other knowing that more is meant than meets the ear. We recall that in the dramatic irony of ancient Greek theatre, the initiated audience steeped in the myths of their society was the "initiated," and on stage Oedipus, Prometheus, Orestes et al. were operating in the dark, unaware of the inevitable fate that awaited them. In the analytic situation the roles of the initiated (the analyst) and the uninitiated (the patient) may be reversed or shared and utterances may convey two different, even opposing, meanings. The shared secret messages may have powerful drive-related meanings of erotic or aggressive import.

The paper is characteristic of Martin Stein's work: it is about ordinary human behavior, seen to have multiple functions and meanings through the powerful lens of analysis. Furthermore, it allows us to see into a depth behind the economy of expression and representation, a depth of multiple layers of meanings and functions, a depiction of worlds in grains of sand.

Stein places the concept of irony (one of the many forms of humor depicted since ancient times and including wit, satire, sarcasm, invective, cynicism, and the sardonic) in a developmental framework. He sees the origins of irony in childhood object relations, in the early awareness that ideas may be expressed by their opposites for witty effect in verbal interchange, and in behavior, both in dreams and in waking life. As in any aspect of compromise-formation (e.g., screen memory) aggressive and libidinal conflicts may be expressed with economy, through condensation.

Irony may be viewed as having both drive-related content and defensive functions, and in the analytic work has to be analyzed for both its expressive use and resistance functions. In this latter regard Stein also conceptualizes a character trait of irony that might lead to sterile coldness and intellectualized joking, which would be antithetical to analytic study if not dealt with as a resistance. The paper, similar in some aspects of tone to the paper on premonition as defense, is a simple observation that all aspects of the patient's communications, and ours as well, are the subject of analytic scrutiny. I would add that before the actual onset of the analysis while thinking of a patient's "analyzability," the presence of a self-observing irony has generally been, for me, an indicator of the patient's willingness to do analytic work.

> *Analyst*: "I have your bill ready."
> *Patient*: "Fantastic!"

Freud (1895) wrote in "The Psychotherapy of Hysteria":

> When I have promised my patients help or improvement by means of a cathartic treatment I have often been faced by this objection: "Why, you tell me yourself that my illness is probably connected with my circumstances and the events of my life. You cannot alter these in any way. How do you propose to help me, then?" And I have been able to make this reply: "No doubt fate would find it easier than I do to relieve you of your illness. But you will be able to convince yourself that much will be gained if we succeed in transforming your hysterical misery into common unhappiness. With a mental life that has been restored to health you will be better armed against that unhappiness." [p. 305]

The epigraph and Freud's statement are only two examples of the application of irony to an understanding of the psychoanalytic situation. The patient's response to the presentation of his bill is an illustration of verbal irony, in which a meaning is expressed by its opposite. Freud's (1895) statement describes the analytic situation as fundamentally ironic, based as it is on the principle that conflict is inevitable and inherent in the human psyche as it is in life itself.

Irony has not yet received its due as an important aspect of psychoanalysis. It has many implications for our understanding of transference and resistance; it employs a number of defenses, not necessarily in the service of pathology; its study leads us to further thoughts about sublimation; finally, it raises questions about its origins in early childhood.

Verbal irony, the witty response, is the simpler form. Freud regarded it as a subspecies of the comic, very close to joking. He had relatively little to say about it, which is a bit surprising in the man who, upon leaving Vienna, declared, "I can heartily recommend the Gestapo to anyone" (Jones 1959, p. 226).

The *Oxford English Dictionary* defines irony rather too narrowly for our purposes: "a figure of speech in which the intended meaning is the opposite of that expressed by the words used; usually taking the form of sarcasm or ridicule in which laudatory expressions are used to express condemnation or contempt." Fowler (1954) gives us a more comprehensive definition of verbal irony: ". . . the word *irony*, which in its more general sense may be defined as the use of words intended to convey one meaning to the uninitiated part of the audience and another to the initiated, the delight of it lying in the secret intimacy set up between the latter and the speaker; it should be added, however, that there are dealers in irony for whom the initiated circle is not of outside hearers, but is an *alter ego* dwelling in their own hearts" (p. 296).[1]

This variety of irony has been described at length by a number of literary critics, notably Muecke (1969, 1970, 1982), Knox (1961, 1972) and Booth (1974). The last lists a number of "marks" or criteria of irony which are particularly useful for our purposes: (1) It is "deliberately created by human beings to be heard or read and understood with some precision by other human beings . . . ," in other words, it is not a parapraxis. (2) It is nevertheless "intended to be reconstructed with meanings different from those on the surface . . . "—so far, so good. (3) It is "stable or fixed in the sense that once a reconstruction of meaning has been made the reader is not invited to undermine it with further demolitions or reconstructions." Presumably this applies to the listener as well. This last characteristic, as we shall see, must be put aside in our analytic world: we have no choice but to do our best to analyze the irony beyond its consciously intended meaning. (4) This variety of irony is finite in its application: it implies no general claim about the universe, a qualification that will lead us later to the larger subject of situational irony.

Let us see how the criteria of verbal irony apply to the exchange between me and my patient. My remark, "I have your bill ready," was literal and straightforward, allowing of no other meaning. My patient's reply, "Fantastic!" was clearly ironic, and would be so understood by any person familiar with analysis. The speaker did not imply that he was thrilled at being presented with a bill—quite the contrary; he intended that I should understand him in a sense opposite to the literal expression. The device could not be undermined, so far: it was bad news, and I was not immediately invited to see it in any other way.

---

[1]Ultimately, irony is meant to be understood by those who are prepared to understand. There are those who do not—a group to whom the term *alazony* has been applied. The alazon is the arrogant and literal-minded individual who fails to understand the ironic exchange, e.g., a reader who would have decided that Jonathan Swift was advocating genocide and cannibalism, and that Dickens admired the pious Mr. Pecksniff. I am indebted to D. C. Muecke (personal communication) for elucidating the concept of alazony. The Oxford English Dictionary lists it as an obsolete term meaning "arrogancy or pride."

And it was finite, for it did not imply total negation. There was no necessary implication that analysis was valueless, much less that all knowledge or existence was.

To return to Fowler's definition, we may ask what constituted the double audience, first the "uninitiated," who do not understand, and second, the "initiated," who do understand the ironic meaning. The analyst is both, the one (the "alazon") who thinks his patient is really pleased at receiving a bill and at the same time the one who appreciates the latter's witty expression of his displeasure.

The transference elements were obviously complex. On the one hand, the patient assumed my stupidity, that I might take his remark literally; on the other, he revealed his certain knowledge that I would understand and accept his irony. At the same time he took the opportunity to express his resentment over my fee, which represented a considerable sacrifice for him; yet he was deeply attached to his analysis and me. The one word "Fantastic!" exemplifies the economy of ironic wit.

On another occasion he expressed ironically a thought which is familiar enough. About to begin a long disquisition on an obsessional preoccupation with the style of his clothing, one of a series of many such, he said, "I know you'll be fascinated by this!" The ironic meaning was, "You will be intensely bored." This was obvious enough. But beneath this was the desperate desire to have the really distressing symptom analyzed well enough so that he could free himself of it; this would require great concentration on my part.

Another example, an even more complex one, from the same patient: Analyst: "Good morning." Patient: "May God bless you and keep you, Dr. Stein, and ensure your continuing good health—at least for the duration of my analysis!"

A few days earlier I had suffered an exacerbation of a respiratory infection and had to cancel my appointments for a day. It was unnecessary to tell the patient why I had canceled; the reason was obvious. Nevertheless, his anxiety was severe. This was understandable in that his first analysis had been terminated by the death of his analyst.

More recent events contributing to this exchange were as follows. A week or so earlier, the patient had made it evident how important it was for him to express in action his urgent sexual fantasies, predominantly anal and promiscuous. These were for him not only a source of intensely pleasurable excitement, but were important in warding off the inevitability of growing older toward maturity, dullness, castration, and death. Maturity he saw as constricting, a kind of gloomy imprisonment in conventional habits, sexual practices, and clothing. At an age long beyond adolescence, he valued his youthfulness as a way of gratifying himself without adult penalty—e.g., castration—meanwhile defying the authority of the grownups, including his analyst. Above all, if he could remain young, even infantile, he might some day regain the mother he had lost so long ago, and who appeared constantly in one or another form in his dreams. A few days earlier we had discussed the problems raised by his need to carry his sexual impulses into action so directly and immediately as to make analysis of them very difficult. It was not easy to remark on this without his seizing upon it as a moralizing statement. Treating it as preaching was a most effective resistance against analyzing. At any rate, he found it a good focus for his resentment.

His ironic counterattack was clever: he cast me as a moralizing authority like his father and mocked me by intoning a blessing such as that delivered at the conclusion of a sermon. Thus he expressed at least two wishes. The most obvious was the inverted ironic meaning of wishing me good health: that I should die and relieve him of my hated domination, not to mention my burdensome fees. He was aware of this, and no comment was necessary. But at the same time, the literal meaning was also to be taken seriously. He was worried about my health and concerned that he might lose me prematurely as he had lost his first analyst and, before that, his mother. I was invited to understand his ironic remark in both senses, not only the inverted hostile sense, but also the literal one, which carried the message "Do not leave me, I need you forever!"

This man was perfectly aware of his ironic stance. For a long period of his analysis he was habitually late for his sessions, by a few minutes at least. But after we began to discuss termination, he changed: he began to arrive very promptly. Once I kept him waiting two minutes or so, about which he complained, rather good-humoredly. At the end of this session he remarked: "It's funny, now that I'm leaving the analysis, I'm coming on time. It's one of the ironies of life."[2] Here he used the term irony in a sense broader than the merely rhetorical, which we have been discussing; he was hinting at a more general view.

That we are required to undermine the ironic device is one of the inevitable hardships of practicing analysis. Having understood the inverted meaning, we proceed to treat the literal statement as equally worthy of notice. Whether we like it or not, we must go beyond appreciating the joke to analyzing it, a reluctant reaffirmation of the dominance of the reality over the pleasure principle. It need not destroy our sense of humor altogether: we should have learned by now that understanding is not equivalent to destruction.

One of the most familiar examples of literary irony may be treated in this way, without destroying its point. Mark Antony in *Julius Caesar* (Act III,

[2]A reader has very acutely observed that the patient's ironic use of time was stimulated by the wording of my initial remark, "I have your bill *ready*," thus emphasizing my own promptness, as opposed to his procrastination.

scene 2) addressed the mob after Caesar's murder: "For Brutus is an honourable man, so are they all, all honourable men." His statement was intended to be understood by the mob only in its reverse sense, that Brutus was as much a scoundrel as the rest of the conspirators. It was a classic example of one of the commonest ironic devices, "blame by praise" (Knox 1961), a masterpiece of rabble-rousing.

Yet the artistry of the device is not independent of the fact that there was a good deal of literal truth in the ironic statement. Brutus was by reputation a man of the greatest integrity, who joined the conspirators out of sincere, if misguided motives of patriotism. Self-deceptive he may have been, but fundamentally dishonorable he was not, especially when compared with Antony. It was Brutus's very reputation, however undeserved, that made Antony's attack so effective. So Antony himself admitted after Brutus's death: "This was the noblest Roman of them all. . . . This was a man." This last statement was meant to be taken not ironically, but literally. We are reminded finally of Antony's internal conflicts, between envy and admiration of a much more appealing and popular character. Conflicts of desires, of affects, of beliefs make up the essence of irony.

The subtlety and effectiveness of Antony's funeral oration was heightened by the fact that the irony expressed more than one level of meaning; it depended also upon the timing, which was superb, and upon the context. The Roman mob was to accept only the reversed ironic implications of the statement that Brutus was an honorable man; the theatre audience was to recognize that the statement was true in both its literal and ironic senses. It was a classic example of "dramatic irony." Antony's was a risky device; mobs often fail to recognize the irony and may not react according to the wishes of the speaker, as some contemporary politicians have learned. This perhaps understandable fear of using irony in political speeches has no doubt contributed to their increasingly boring character.

But a patient should not have to fear that his irony will be misunderstood, at least not for long, unless his audience, that is, his analyst, really is stupid. If his analyst does miss it at first, the patient can and will attack him with it again. Patients may be as ironic as they wish.

Does this apply to the analyst as well? There is certainly a temptation to make ironic comments now and then in the course of an analysis. I have on occasion permitted myself ironic remarks in the service of interpretation. These are rarely misunderstood, but I cannot altogether put aside some reservations, even though they are not sufficiently weighty to stop me from indulging myself now and then. The danger is not that the patient will misunderstand, or experience hurt feelings: the use of irony may be a compliment to the hearer, who is expected to understand the joke; rather, it can become part of a clever game, a rivalry of wit. It may be fun for the analyst, but one must rely on other gratifications more consistent with the goal of the treatment.

It is noteworthy that ironic responses such as I have cited often call for no immediate response by the analyst, and none is demanded by the patient. The ironic patient regards the analyst as one of the "initiated" (in Fowler's sense). As a rule, he assumes an unspoken mutual understanding, although occasionally he is not sure and exclaims, "That's a joke!" Certainly some such compatibility is necessary for the analytic process. In this case, however, the ironic exchange may become the sign of a secret understanding, a kind of collusion between patient and analyst, which excludes the "uninitiated," a shared secret that may have important erotic implications, accompanied by excitement and perhaps some guilt.

To some patients irony comes naturally and is a useful defensive as well as a gratifying device. The patient may use it aggressively to express anger or contempt under the cover of wit; he may employ it as a vehicle for more or less sadistic mockery. Perhaps more importantly, it permits the patients to treat the analyst as an equal, a partner in joking. In addition to warding off feelings of helplessness it may, in the form of self-irony, give a sense of detachment in dealing with very intense affects, particularly related to moral conflicts. As such it allows the patient to verbalize fantasies in a joking way, thus warding off the embarrassment they might otherwise engender.

A fine example of self-irony is the following exchange, which took place during the analysis of a very clever young woman who, for a variety of reasons, experienced the process as a constant humiliation. She complained that, when she was in distress, I did nothing to advise nor specifically reassure her. I agreed that this was in fact characteristic of the analytic process. She then reminded me, in a tone of triumph, that on one occasion early in her analysis I had in effect done so, and in rather banal fashion at that. I had to admit she had a point. She responded, rather wryly, "I'm sure you'll benefit from my advice!"

The inverted meaning was clear enough. She had nothing to teach me, for she was the child and I the parent. I made the rules and she had to abide by them, even though she found it humiliating that I was always in the superior position. Yet the other, direct meaning of her remark was equally relevant. Adults had much to learn from their children, and I had much to learn from her, a point I was hardly prepared to refute.

In this highly condensed ironic remark she had therefore expressed a great deal. She felt constantly humiliated by the analysis, always in the position of the child, lacking respect and dignity, her high intelligence ignored. Her statement could have been an angry outburst; instead it became a wry, self-mocking remark, containing a view of herself as young and stupid. At the same time it constituted a rejection of this image, for she could make fun of me and herself. It implied a great deal about the relations of parents and children, teachers and students, men and women.

The examples of ironic remarks I have cited vary in their closeness to sarcasm. Irony need not be sarcastic. The aggressive elements, which are always present, may be directed toward the hearer, toward the third listener who fails to understand, or toward the self. It is in this sense always a mode of attack. Yet it is as well a way of expressing a kinship of understanding, by sharing a joke. In analysis, it is most often used as a vehicle for expressing transference, constituting a complex and often difficult mode of resistance which must be treated as such.

Certain types of behavior may remind us of verbal irony. These consist of literal obedience to a request or command, knowing all the while that it is not meant to be so interpreted. Some patients express very powerful resistance by caricaturing the process of free association. They say "everything" that comes to mind, so that the session consists of chaotic sentences or nonsense words, all of which are meant to confuse and upset the analyst. It is very like the angry child who, when asked to "drop everything and come here," lets go an armful of dishes. We may observe something similar in industrial disputes, in the action known as "working to rule." Workers perform their task mechanically, deliberately, with exaggerated care, following every regulation so carefully that very little gets done.

Such actions are never really funny, hostility being the most prominent component. While there is some resemblance to irony, the anger has overwhelmed the wit; the joke is lost; and the inner conflict so essential to irony has become external. The audience no longer shares the joke, but has instead become the victim.

SITUATIONAL IRONY

Situational irony[3] is altogether a larger and less well defined subject than the comparatively simple form we have been discussing up to now. Correspondingly, its application to psychoanalysis is both more complex and more difficult to clarify. We are faced with the question, "To what extent is the analyst an ironist in a sense broader than the rhetorical?" Socrates, arguably the most famous of ironists, is quoted as having said, "It isn't that, knowing the answer

[3]There is no universal or widely accepted classification of the various aspects of irony. I have found D. C. Muecke's (1970) nomenclature most useful for my purpose. He has suggested the terms "Verbal" and "Situational," which can be neatly applied to my own division of irony into the first, which includes the verbal exchanges between analysand and analyst, and the second, which can be used to describe important aspects of the analytic situation itself.

myself, I perplex other people. The truth is that rather I infect them also with the perplexity I feel myself" (in Plato, 80d). We are reminded of the situation in which we find ourselves trying to convey to our patients that the useful answers to questions about the mind do not as a rule make themselves easily available, and that our task is to try to inculcate a sense of perplexity and of curiosity, which we ourselves must share in order to do our work.

A familiar example is the situation created when a patient announces: "I hate you, I'm leaving!" Such a statement must be treated seriously, but this does not imply that it need be taken literally. It may contain any number of meanings, including the direct opposite: "I love you and I shall never leave!" Therefore, instead of saying goodbye or trying to persuade the patient to stay, we try to stimulate his curiosity in order to achieve some understanding of his outburst. We assume he is not completely aware of the psychological components of his statement, and neither are we.

We grant that the patient is really experiencing anger and is aware of an impulse to leave, but that usually his feelings are mixed and he has no immediate intention of breaking off the treatment—given that occasionally such an impulse may be too powerful to subject to analysis. Most often, in analyses that are running well, we may treat such an event as one which is to be understood. Neither the patient nor we are immediately privy to its constellation of meanings, and must do a good deal of work to discover them.

Often patients do in fact treat us as if we were feigning ignorance (as Socrates was often accused of doing, although this was not his point). We are accused of holding back the answers, of knowing the explanations but waiting (insincerely) for the patient to voice ideas we have been harboring all the time. It is difficult for our patients to accept that we really do not know the answers until they themselves reveal them to us. We are familiar with the principles of interpretation, but we must await the willingness and capacity of the patient, in order to obtain the information that makes the interpretation possible. The idea that the analyst presents himself as knowing more than he will admit is a projection by the patient, for whom it fulfills a number of transferential purposes. For one thing, it is reassuring to tell oneself, in the absence of an omniscient deity, that *someone* knows what is going on—if not the patient, then the analyst. Contrariwise, to what extent does the patient's insistence on the analyst's great wisdom represent an exercise of irony on the part of the patient?

Freud was candid in admitting what he did not know, but firm in maintaining the correctness of what he did believe. Some of his writing, for example the "Introductory Lectures" (1916–1917) might be regarded as Socratic in an important if limited sense. By raising questions, he was able to demonstrate how little we all knew about the origins and even the nature of our own psychic processes and contents.

Situational irony, as opposed to verbal irony, is a more recent concept and a far more complicated one. It was not recognized as such until the eighteenth century, although ironic attitudes are probably as old as organized thought (Knox 1961). It is inevitable that psychoanalysis should be capable of being seen as ironic, for it takes for granted that conflict is an inherent feature of the human psyche. It deals with problems that are not, and cannot be, resolved in an absolute sense. This was inherent in Freud's (1900) description of the dynamic tension between the first and second agencies of the mind, the systems Unconscious and Preconscious, while consciousness was relegated to the status of a sense organ. Later, in discussing the tension between ego and id, he used the metaphor of the not altogether assured rider attempting to control a spirited and somewhat unpredictable horse, burdened by the added feature of a highly judgmental riding master who introduces questions concerning the moral aspects of the struggle itself, not always reasonably or fairly (I have added a bit to Freud's original imagery). To complicate matters further, many instinctual strivings lead to perpetual struggles with the structure of society itself. When we add intrasystemic conflicts, those between instinctual derivatives and between incompatible ego forces, and the imperfections of compromise formations (which so often lead to neurotic symptoms), we are led to expect a state of variable but perpetual tension within the organism, a tension reflected in the operations of social groups. Such tensions may be alleviated, but never entirely resolved. Considering the role of irony in a more general sense, Muecke (1969) writes:

> . . . in those contradictions, apparently fundamental and irremediable, that confront men when they speculate upon such topics as the origin and purpose of the universe, free will and determinism, reason and instinct, the scientific and the imaginative, ends and means, society and the individual, art and life, knowing and being, self-consciousness (what is conscious of what?), the meaning of meaning and the value of value. It has to do with the world as men see or have seen it and not with the world as it is or may be [p. 121] . . . There is a vast potential for General Irony in the psychoanalysts's discovery of the unconscious processes of the mind. We are told of radical oppositions within the psyche, of self-submissive and self-assertive instincts, of the masculine Persona and the feminine Anima, of the death-wish, of the Super-ego and the Id. Our conscious life it seems is a facade behind which a very different "real" life goes on in secret; our hidden fears and desires evade the Censor and emerge disguised in symbolic form to betray us. The operations of the unconscious are described in much the same terms as we use in talking of irony: a man intends to say one thing but by a Freudian slip he says something quite different and so reveals his real preoccupation; artists through their unconscious "choice" of subjects, symbols, or motifs, reveal meanings they

> did not intend; the concept of "compensating" enables us to reverse the ostensible meaning of everything men say or do (the psychoanalysts, being aware of this, are obliged to psychoanalyze themselves and this resembles the obligation on ironists to practice self-irony). . . . Again, we can look upon the Ego as being in an ironic predicament, caught between the amoral, irresponsible, nonconforming Id and the moral, responsible conforming Superego, much like Prince Hal between Falstaff and the Lord Chief Justice, the former life-giving and dynamic, the latter life-denying and orderly—The irony lies in the contradictory opposition of values; we feel we must be for and against both sides. [p. 142; see also Muecke 1970]

Coles (1974) gives Freud credit as an ironist, implying at the same time, not altogether without justification, that not all analysts have been able to develop the kind of ironic stance that makes it possible to accept how much cannot be known and to recognize the necessity of tolerating some degree of ambiguity and contradiction.

One of the most useful discussions from within psychoanalysis is by Schafer (1970). His treatment anticipates many of my own views on both the clinical significance of irony as a mode of resistance and the relevance of the ironic stance to analytic thought.

This point of view was expressed very clearly by Freud in "Analysis Terminable and Interminable" (1937), one of the most powerful and disturbing of Freud's papers. His attacks on the belief in the inevitability of progress, and the possibility of certainty in human knowledge combined with the threat to narcissistic smugness, led many to wish that Freud had shared Socrates' hemlock.

It should be clear that an ironic stance carries no implication of cynicism. Great ironic writers, e.g., Shakespeare, Swift, Austen, Dickens, were anything but cynical; on the contrary, they gave evidence of the most serious, even passionate attachment to ideals. Their irony represented a perspective toward, not a rejection of, those ideals. Irony in its mature form is above all a means of dealing with the sadness inherent in the tragic aspects of life. It is not, however, part of depression, and it is to be questioned whether it operates habitually as a defense against it.

It is just as well for us to be aware of the irony of our own situation as analysts. Each patient is expected to develop a transference, one of the components of which will be an erotic attachment to the analyst, however it is manifested, heavily or less well disguised. The analyst accepts this development with the full knowledge first, that it is vital for the success of the analysis; second, that it really stands for something else, a displacement from figures of the past, the parents, for example; and third, that it must be analyzed, subjected to a painstaking process that will make it possible, ideally to renounce it, or at least put it into perspective, to be regarded as an artefact. As we have learned, this process is rarely if ever entirely successful in an absolute sense. There are other contradictions: the more intense and florid the erotic attachment, the more likely it is to be accompanied by, and even be a defense against, powerful elements of hostility. And useful as it is, the transference represents one of the greatest dangers to the success of the treatment (Bird 1972, Stein 1981).

The more intensely the analyst finds himself responding, the more energy he must expend in understanding and controlling his own responses. Yet patients are understandably upset by experiencing and being required to voice an attachment that is not reciprocated in kind. They would be vastly more distressed if they were to sense that their feelings were being responded to on the same level. The very idea that the patient sees us in the role of an omniscient, loving, perhaps now and then hating, parent is in sharp contrast to his recognition that we are charging him a substantial fee for allowing him to regard us as such (Socrates would have been sharply ironic about that!). All the while, our task remains that of making clear to the patient, and tolerable if possible, that we are not surrogate parents in fact and never intended to be, that he is, after all, alone. To accentuate the predicament, we conduct a procedure based on psychic determinism on the one hand, and the implicit assumption of purposeful choice, including moral choice, on the other. There are no ultimate solutions to these dilemmas. Psychoanalysis demands the development of a clear view of contradictory principles and a tolerance for the tension created by our attempts to accommodate them. This is in essence an ironic stance.

DEVELOPMENTAL ASPECTS OF IRONY

We are accustomed to think of irony as an adult phenomenon, a highly sophisticated form of wit. The finest types of irony are indeed exemplified by Gibbon, Jane Austen, and Dickens, not to mention such classic examples as Socrates, Chaucer, and Shakespeare among the big guns. Yet it is not too difficult to detect its roots in childhood, and early childhood at that, a finding that may itself be regarded as ironic.

Children between two and three, "the terrible twos," so-called because they are inclined to say no to whatever we suggest, may be prone or at least readily led into a very familiar game. We urge the child to eat his breakfast; he responds with a defiant "No!" and may make his point even clearer by dumping his cereal on the floor. The wily mother, or father as the case may be, changes the procedure. She says, with mock severity, "Don't you dare eat that cereal!" The child looks at her mischievously and immediately proceeds to wolf down his breakfast, as if in defiance. The mother portrays a kind of mock horror, perhaps even exclaiming, "You bad child!" Both laugh gleefully, enjoying the process. This is clearly ironic. The command, "Don't you dare eat that cereal!" and the scolding, "You bad child!" are understood by the child, correctly, as meaning the opposite. He is pleased by being treated not as a stupidly literal baby, but rather as an intelligent being who is capable of understanding a joke. At the same time, he is relieved at having to submit passively to orders from above. He returns the favor by obeying cheerfully and actively. He and his parents have become partners in joking.

This ironic exchange fulfills the criteria of stable irony (according to Booth), even though one of the participants is a child in the early phases of verbal and psychosexual development. The raw psychological material is, of course, present from the first in the inherent characteristics of unconscious thought processes: the capacity to express ideas and feelings by their opposites and in condensed forms, mechanisms of primary process which Freud described as typical of the dream work.[4]

Children of two or three, even the most obliging, are characterized by negativism, stubbornness, and defiance, at least some of the time. These traits are, if anything, emphasized by the internal and external struggles that occur under pressure from the parents. What may be more surprising is the development of an ego structure that enables the child not only to employ opposites, but to know when opposite meanings are intended, and to enjoy the joke.[5]

We need not assume that the capacity to appreciate verbal irony must develop in all children. It is not a pleasure shared by everyone. No doubt parental influence plays a considerable role in determining whether the individual child develops an appreciation of irony, for some families foster it, not only by the kinds of exchanges exemplified by the breakfast game, but in other ways as well. There are some mothers who will, in the most caressing tones, refer to their children as "dreadful little beasts" or "monsters," accompanied by a smile, the ironic meaning being conveyed by the evident incongruity between the words and the affective expressions accompanying them. Very young children respond to the affective tone; later, when they understand the words, they begin to appreciate the irony, perhaps referring to themselves as "dreadful little beasts." They have become ironists. That the mother may at the same time have vented some exasperation with the problem set by her little darling is not to be doubted, but the hostility is effectively warded off, if not altogether discharged, by the ironic joke.

---

[4]In the case of an "absurd" dream, Freud (1900) described the dream thoughts as speaking "ironically," i.e., by employing a reversal (p. 440).

[5]Studies of young children should leave us in no doubt that some capacity for joking, not very sophisticated, it is true, develops very early, perhaps before the first year. Two-year-olds are quite capable of verbal jokes, including teasing exchanges (Caplan 1973).

The capacity for ironic expression need not, however, be altogether limited to this kind of familial influence. There is much use of ironic expression, often sadistic, in street language and in criminal argot as well. It is enough to point out that verbal irony occurs in cultures not exposed to sophisticated ironic joking or to the reading of ironic literature.

But how do we account for those children who, other things being equal, do make ironic jokes and those who don't, and perhaps never will? It is not a question that admits of a ready answer, least of all that all ironic children were reared by ironic parents or in an ironic culture. In a sense, the capacity for irony may be thought of as inherent in the psychic capacity, which must be universal, to express ideas and affects by their opposites, as in the dream work. But the ability to understand and appreciate and to employ irony, while widespread, is not shared by all adults. I suspect that the inherent capacity for irony is analogous to that for artistic expression, i.e., well-nigh universal in young children. It is a well-known and distressing fact that most children lose their capacity for free artistic expression, usually in latency. Perhaps the same is true of irony—that the preservation of this capacity depends not only on intellectual and verbal development, but on the culture and traumatic influences as well.

An ironic stance is pathognomic of neither illness nor health. It is not necessarily inhibited by emotional illness; while some obsessional individuals, for example, are appallingly humorless and lack any capacity for ironic expression or understanding, others are capable of biting irony, generally in a sarcastic mode, having become ironists of the harsher variety, closer to Jonathan Swift than Jane Austen.

To return to my patient who made the joke about his bill: he was a man who most often gave the impression of being unkempt and actually dirty. In fact, he was preoccupied with cleanliness, sometimes arriving for his session with all his clothing just out of the washing machine and not completely dry. His sexual life was dominated by preoccupations with anal intercourse, and he soon lost interest in women not so inclined. He was painfully obsessional about time, money, and literal honesty, symptoms that were hardly controlled by his keen intelligence and some degree of understanding of their origins. In short, he seemed to meet the criteria for the diagnosis of obsessional neurosis in the setting of an "anal" character structure.

It was he who furnished me with an apt example of the connections between irony and negativism, and some hints of their relation to anality. Habitually he would delay paying his bill, all the while promising to do so "tomorrow," clearly as a form of teasing. When I brought this to his attention, he replied, "I resist paying you on time because I know you want me to; if you didn't care I would probably pay you a lot faster." It was not quite so simple of course; he was still teasing. Evidently he wanted me to play the breakfast game with him. His childhood had been characterized by a series of defiant moves against his parents, later against all authorities, as if only in this way could he achieve the love he craved without being entirely passive, helpless, and castrated. Irony was only one of the methods he used to deal with a world he felt to be restrictive, domineering, and hostile. Later it became a way in which he could attempt to denature his own ever-present anger through joking. His use of verbal irony was often inappropriate, for he misjudged his audience, arousing misunderstanding, confusion, and hostility in others, which in turn served to reinforce his own fears. It need not surprise us that irony, a potentially useful defensive device, can become chronically maladaptive.

This patient's irony was often hostile, as exemplified by his remarks about my health. The lines separating irony from sarcasm are not well defined. Although irony need not be predominantly sarcastic or hostile, it virtually always contains traces of such elements (Muecke makes a persuasive argument that sarcasm is generally recognized as only minimally ironical [1969, pp. 33–34]). Even Socratic self-irony has its sources in a demanding superego, and it may contain a good many sadistic elements, usually well concealed. It is difficult to demonstrate beyond doubt the extent to which all irony is derived from anal-sadistic sources, but the use of reversal and its capacity to express and yet often mitigate the effects of hostile impulses are highly suggestive. There is less doubt that, in its adult and highly complex form, the determinants of irony will be found in all stages of psychosexual development, especially in such ego functions as intelligence and the capacity for controlled regression, the latter giving access to primary process and whatever else makes joking possible. Ultimately it seems reasonable that some of the more positive roots of irony are to be found in that phase of psychosexual development in which sphincter control becomes established and verbal skills are employed in conflict with the parents. "No" and "Yes" games occur pretty early, while control of one's self and others appears as an overt issue. Irony, especially irony in a more general sense, represents to a considerable degree an attempt to achieve a kind of psychic control over a variety of conflicts, including those inherent in existence itself.

To continue our speculation about the developmental aspects of a generally ironic attitude toward life, we may wonder what it means to a child who is trying to understand "reality," to be subjected to the experience we call "toilet training." He is encouraged to relax, to let himself go, at the same time to control himself, to do it only at certain times and in certain places. His parents give him the impression that delivering the stool is a great accomplishment, that he is giving something of great value. But then they teach him that it is an object to be avoided, to be flushed away as soon as possible. What is he to make of that? He is faced with the curious circumstance that something that appears to be part of his body, is not, and is moreover regarded as disgusting and even harmful. How difficult this is to encompass! It is no wonder that "the terrible twos" are exactly that. The child cannot help but wonder about the nature of life itself. It should come as no surprise that the toilet, in our society at least, is a favorite place for contemplation, and it requires only a little irreverence to see Rodin's great sculpture, "The Thinker," in that light.

It would be absurd to claim that all of our interests in science, in hypothesizing, in philosophy, in psychoanalysis itself were merely derivatives of early preoccupations with the nature of the stool. To put it so would be perhaps disrespectful and certainly reductionistic. But to reject altogether the role of the anal phase in the development of higher thought would be indeed a flushing away of a potentially valuable idea, discarded through a misunderstanding of psychoanalytic concepts, especially that of sublimation, a process that may be envisioned as the transformation of a dung hill which is, after all, fertile, into a flower garden. One of the flowers may be the capacity for an ironic view of the world.

It is also possible to trace this capacity to some of the most fundamental processes originally described as characteristic of the dream work, and especially of primary-process thinking. Reversal, the representation of a quality by its opposite, is a commonplace in the dream work; so is condensation, the economical use of one image to represent a cluster of ideas or subjects. Thus we have present from very early life, the raw materials that make irony possible. It should also be possible to detail the various ego functions contributing to irony, especially its more complex varieties. Even the simplest ironic remark requires an active synthetic function of the ego, along with reality testing, and especially in the case of self-irony, self-observation, which brings superego functions into action. To be playful requires a considerable capacity for controlled regression, and to be so with words implies a highly developed skill. Briefly, irony is as much a compromise formation, a manifestation of Waelder's (1930) "Principle of Multiple Function," as any other highly developed human activity.

That some people lack a sense of irony is what makes spoken and literary irony possible. It is also fortunate, in that most of what people do in their daily lives "could not be carried out in a spirit of irony" (Muecke 1970), just as it would be difficult to live in a mood of constant introspection, a fact that becomes evident to patients beginning analysis. But for those who do employ irony, there are advantages as well as dangers. Like any valuable tool, it may be used profitably, or it may be misused with danger to the user and to others.

It hardly needs to be emphasized that the ironic stance has its dangers for analysis. Irony may be used by analyst and patient alike to defend against depth of feeling, to create a coldly verbal, intellectualized atmosphere, with the analyst so detached that he avoids even decisions that are not only permissible but essential in the conduct of an analysis. Nor should the patient be allowed, without intervention, to transform the analysis into an exercise of wit, at the expense of emotional commitment. Correspondingly, the analyst needs to be aware of the dangers of being carried away by pleasure in his own irony, to the exclusion of genuine concern and understanding of his patient.

Often we are asked by those outside the profession and by our colleagues as well, "How can you bear to practice analysis, just listen, day after day?" Muecke suggests that for the individual who recognizes that internal conflict is inevitable, "the only alternative is irony: a sense of irony will not make him any less a victim of these predicaments but will enable him in some degree to transcend them" (1970, p. 77). We might conclude that the ironic analyst must establish an ironic stance toward his own irony.

SUMMARY

Irony is a more important element of analysis than we generally recognize. First, verbal irony characterizes the discourse of certain patients who employ it as a defense, both adaptively and as a resistance, especially against the expression of intense affect associated with the transference. The frequent employment of irony reflects a significant character trait, a habitual mode of dealing with conflict. It is also a frequent manifestation of a particularly active self-critical faculty. Ironic employment of a "double audience" is also relevant to analytic technique.

Second, situational irony is inherent in many aspects of psychoanalysis, as a process and a point of view. It implies the acceptance of the inevitability of conflict, ambiguity and paradox, never quite capable of perfect resolution. It emphasizes critical examination of mixtures of motives of both analysand and analyst, and it requires perpetual questioning of what might otherwise be taken as accepted doctrine, including the principles of psychoanalysis per se. An ironic stance requires some degree of detachment in conjunction with deep commitment, itself an ironic circumstance.

Third, the capacity to understand and employ irony can be traced to childhood, relatively early in the course of development of speech and sphincter control; some of its early determinants are to be found in the anal phase of psychosexual development; it reflects as well the capacity to use certain early defenses and mechanisms originally described as characteristic of the dream work. Its later fate as a prominent feature of character is very much a matter of ego and superego development, including such components as intelligence, verbal skills, the capacity for joking and for play, i.e., controlled regression. Sources of identification in the family and the culture are of obvious importance.

Finally, an understanding of irony has an important place in the theory of technique, especially with regard to transference and resistance. An ironic stance and understanding on the part of the analyst are valuable, even essential; but irony may become a questionable defense for him as well as for his patient.

REFERENCES

Bird, B. (1972). Notes on the transference: universal phenomenon and hardest part of the analysis. *J. Amer. Psychoanal. Assn.* 20:267–301.

Booth, W. C. (1974). *A Rhetoric of Irony.* Chicago: University Chicago Press.

Caplan, F. (1973). *The First Twelve Months of Life: Your Baby's Growth, Month by Month.* New York: Grosset & Dunlap.

Coles, R. (1974). Irony in the mind's life. In *Essays on Novels by James Agee, Elizabeth Bowen and George Eliot.* Charlottesville: Univ. Virginia Press.

Fowler, H. W. (1954). *A Dictionary of Modern English Usage.* London: Oxford Univ. Press.

Freud, S. (1895). Studies on hysteria. *Standard Edition* 2.

—— (1900). The interpretation of dreams. *Standard Edition* 5.

—— (1916–1917). Introductory lectures on psychoanalysis. *Standard Edition* 15 and 16.

—— (1937). Analysis terminable and interminable. *Standard Edition* 23:211–253.

Jones, E. (1959). *The Life and Work of Sigmund Freud,* vol. 3. New York: Basic Books.

Knox, N. (1961). *The Word Irony and Its Context.* Durham, N.C.: Duke Univ. Press, pp. 1500–1755.

—— (1972). On the classification of ironies. *Modern Philol.* 70:53–62.

Muecke, D. C. (1969). *The Compass of Irony.* London: Methuen.

—— (1970). Irony. *The Critical Idiom.* London: Methuen.

—— (1982). Irony and the ironic. *The Critical Idiom.* London: Methuen.

Plato. Meno. *The Collected Dialogues,* trans. W. K. C. Guthrie. Bollinger Series LXXI. Princeton: Princeton Univ. Press, 1961, pp. 353–384.

Schafer, R. (1970). The psychoanalytic vision of reality. *Int. J. Psychoanal.* 51:279–297.

Stein, M. (1981). The unobjectionable part of the transference. *Psychoanal. Q.*, 29:869–892.

Waelder, R. (1930). The principle of multiple function: observations on overdetermination. In *Psychoanalysis: Observation, Theory, Application,* ed. S. A. Guttman. New York: Int. Univ. Press, 1976, pp. 68–83.

11

Acting Out—Transference and Countertransference: Technical Considerations

Acting out is often discussed as if it were a symptom pathognomonic of the "difficult" patient, or even confined to that vague and subjectively defined category. Although it is true that persistent acting out makes for a very difficult, if not an impossible analysis, it is a phenomenon that occurs in all analyses, sooner or later. While it does constitute a particularly challenging form of resistance, analyzing it can be one of the most productive tasks undertaken by the participants. It places the analyst himself under the greatest strain because it is likely to arouse troublesome countertransference conflicts. But it need not constitute a serious threat to the analysis if the underlying pathology is not too severe and if the analyst can keep his head when confronted with transferential assaults.

We need not, therefore, confine ourselves to a class of "difficult" patients since we do not always agree on the definition of "difficult," and the term implies the existence of another class that might be described as "easy." It is true that some patients find it easier to accept and use the analytic process; others cannot do so with the same facility. There are some patients whose sessions one anticipates with a higher degree of pleasure than others', but they are not necessarily "easier." Their analyses too sooner or later will present problems all the more difficult because they may not have been anticipated. The resistances are more subtle and clever, the traps better hidden, the acting out more "reasonable." The process, therefore, is challenging, but by no means easy, although the ultimate result is likely to be favorable (Stein 1981).

Psychoanalysis depends on listening to and interpreting the patient's associations, including his dreams, fantasies, and behavior, yet it can be argued that its central task is the analysis of resistance, namely, the analytic manifestations of intrapsychic conflict and its effects. Although resistances are defined by their function of impeding the analysis, we have understood for a long time that until they are analyzed, no real analysis has taken place.

Resistances are resolved most tellingly, if not exclusively, in the transference. An analysis that goes swimmingly is easy for a while, putting no great strain on the participants; but aside from increased knowledge on the part of the analyst and a deceptive sense of comfort on the part of the patient, nothing much has happened. It is only when things get really difficult, often downright unpleasant that the analytic process may be said to have begun in earnest. It is now that the analyst must, on the one hand, exert himself to achieve understanding of his patient's struggles and convey that understanding to him, and, on the other, tolerate the patient's discomfort and his own during what may be a long and sometimes agonizing process. Acting out is almost invariably a feature of these crucial phases of the work.

I discuss acting out in this context as a manifestation of the resistance in neurotic patients, not marked by the kind of gross disorganization seen in psychoses, nor in less flagrant forms, in severe narcissistic pathology. Freud (1914) defined it thus: "We may say that the patient *did not remember* anything of what he has forgotten or repressed, but acts it out. He reproduces it not as a memory but as an action; *he repeats it*, without, of course, knowing that he is repeating it" (p. 150). All individuals are capable of acting out under some circumstances, but some show a particular tendency to do so with relatively little provocation. This tendency may be considered a character trait, manifested by a history of repetitive, complex patterns of behavior, generally precipitated by one or another kind of frustration. These patterns demonstrate certain features that are distinctly at variance with what appear to be the dominant modes of the personality. Acting out is likely to be more prominent in severe neuroses but is by no means confined to them (Stein 1973).

Some confusion has resulted from the loose usage of the term. The impulsive behavior of delinquents and criminals, some violent, antisocial and self-destructive activity, much sexual promiscuity, the defiant or merely mischievious actions by which patients attempt to provoke their analysts, may or may not represent acting out. Whether or not the term is applicable depends on the degree to which the phenomenon satisfies a number of criteria. The behavior must be patterned and repetitive, ego syntonic at the time it occurs, marked by some limited and transitory impairment of judgment and reality testing; episodes of acting out might be thought of as periodic, repetitive and "stupid" acts performed by intelligent people. Finally, it should be seen ultimately to conform to the pattern of an unconscious, organized fantasy, generally in the form of a narcissistically dominated dramatic performance.

As an attempt to deal with conflict by action rather than thought, acting out is more subject to the pleasure principle than to the demands of reality; it employs to a greater extent the logic of primary rather than secondary-process thought. It constitutes, therefore, a vivid example of ego regression, in several of its aspects: temporal, in that it reenacts the past in a relatively literal fashion; functional, in its employment of primitive defenses, that is, denial and isolation; in its preference for action over thought, accompanied by a suspension of delaying mechanisms. Finally in its demonstration of topographic regression, for it includes subtle or even obvious interference with conscious awareness, which is replaced in part by modes of thought closer to the dream, a feature that may give some clues to understanding its underlying nature.

When during the course of analysis we become aware of a major episode of potentially disruptive behavior, we are at first at a loss to know what it is. We cannot be sure that we are dealing with a true episode of acting out as an expression of the tranference neurosis until we have taken steps to analyze it, to be sure that it is not simply an impulsive, chaotic action, characteristic of impulse disorders or psychoses; or an isolated symptomatic act, a parapraxis, of far less significance; or a piece of experimental behavior, common in adolescence, as described by Blos (1963).

For example, after some years of analysis, a very intelligent young man engaged in a series of ventures that ultimately were revealed to have been episodes of acting out. He changed his occupation to engage in a potentially profitable but highly speculative series of ventures. Using his family's capital and his own, he invested heavily, hoping to turn a quick profit in a field in which he had relatively little practical experience. Convinced that his essential goodness of character and superior intelligence would ensure his receiving the rewards he deserved, he tried to deny what he knew very well—that without hard work and a certain amount of luck, he might face bankruptcy.

He engaged in a series of cliff-hangers, during which his mood oscillated between desperate anxiety and guilt to varying degrees of elation. His worries were easy enough to understand; on more than one occasion he found himself in serious danger of losing all his own and his family's money. His elation was supported by the fragile conviction that all was for the best, that everything would *have* to come out all right. Not only was he being backed by a generous father (who was understandably apprehensive), but he had the advantage of an all-wise analyst, who would surely help him avoid serious trouble by protecting him from the dangers of the business world. He was sufficiently realistic not to expect me to give him any useful advice about business; his confidence was grounded in archaic, magical expectations.

Behind this touching faith in my powers and his wish to make me proud of him, it was not very difficult to infer a powerful desire to destroy me through behavior that would, at the very least, be a reproach to the analysis, and, at worst, a destruction of it and of me too. At the same time, he would dissipate his father's capital and destroy him as well. It became difficult for me to resist the temptation to blurt out, "Don't be a fool, stop taking those crazy risks!"

Fortunately, it was possible to analyze the dynamic constellation, which included the fantasy that his father and I were so powerful that we could protect him from any dangers and at the same time protect ourselves from his destructive fantasies, the latter all the more urgent because of the very power he attributed to us. He was in any case getting a good deal of gratification, if not pleasure, out of making us apprehensive about his apparently self-destructive behavior. It took over a year of this before the suspense ended. I am relieved to report that disaster was avoided after all, brilliantly, but by an uncomfortably narrow margin.

As we approached the end of the analysis, he realized more clearly that he had been reassuring himself for years with a fantasy that analysis would allow him to achieve a kind of idyllic existence, completely happy, entirely carefree, with no conflicts and no anxieties, like life in a beautiful garden surrounded by lovely flowers and limitless love. This, in turn, could be traced to a persisting fantasy of a "golden age" of childhood, in which he and his parents lived in perfect concord—they never had, of course—and beyond this, to fantasies of what it must have been like in his mother's womb, in Eden before the Fall. This goal could be achieved by the complete elimination of conflict and of the countless vicissitudes of life—in other words, only by death. Understandably, he was reluctant to accept such a disagreeable conclusion.

Later it was possible to demonstrate the role of highly charged oedipal conflicts, which took on regressive, narcissistic forms in this neurotic man whose personality was not seriously impaired and whose object relations were basically intact. In these barely sensed dream-like fantasies, he had discovered a means of achieving all his infantile goals, innocently and apparently without risk. During latency, his attempts to deal with his intense oedipal conflicts had resulted in the development of a set of tic-like movements, evidently magical gestures intended to kill and at the same time to ward off danger. In adolescence, although usually a prudent youth and certainly an intelligent one, he had indulged in foolhardy adventures, frightening to him and to his parents (so far as they knew about them). These were a bit more than adolescent high jinks, or even the experimental behavior described by Blos. They might have led to disaster, and only just failed to do so; finally they led him to seek treatment.

In analysis, it was not easy for him to accept what all of this meant; to recognize that his wish for freedom from conflict was based on an illusion; to accept that such a goal could never be achieved short of death; and to resign himself to the fact that I was not God, or even an all-wise guide for the perplexed. At this point he associated me even more closely with his father, for whom he had a sincere love and admiration, accompanied by the most intense competitive hostility. Faced with these developments, he railed at me for making false promises and letting him down; he went into a period of mourning for his father, who had died a short time before; he regretted his vanished youth and the loss of his beautiful dreams of a lovely garden in which he would find a perpetually young and loving mother.

His pronounced tendency to overidealization could not be readily accounted for by a history of parental neglect, or by evidences of developmental defect. Rather, it was a manifestation of aggressive defense against the most intense oedipal conflicts, including a Cain-Abel fantasy related to his older brother, the structure itself being a corollary of unresolved oedipal wishes. Characterologically, he combined elements of generous son and brother and hostile competitor.

Although at times his acting out was massive and threatening, it could be dealt with by interpretation, without such departures or "parameters" as prohibition, warning, manipulation, or reality testing. As a dramatic manifestation of the transference neurosis, it could be treated, first by pointing out its repetitive, patterned and dramatic structure and its narcissistic preoccupations; second, by interpretation of the transference in terms of the current situation (as emphasized by Greenacre 1950, 1963, 1968, and Gill 1979). Only later could the underlying fantasy be described and traced to its historical sources: variations on oedipal themes; the wish for conquest and reunion with his mother; loving and destructive impulses toward his father and brother, including the wish to castrate them, which was accompanied by the fear of suffering the same fate, in the form of financial ruin.

These conclusions were borne out by the analysis of a dream he reported at the height of the crisis: he was visiting a brothel in the company of an older clergyman. The women were ugly, and their genitals resembled seashells and sharp-edged coral. He awoke in a state of great fear. He associated the razor-sharp coral with some of the messier aspects of his business. The clergyman, representative of the Lord, was I, the guide who would, through analysis, give him the courage to visit a brothel and protect him in this dangerous adventure into the genitalia of the unknown woman, the classical mother–prostitute. Success in business was equated with a forbidden sexual conquest, related to his wish to make a "killing." He was, incidentally, potent and happily married. His belief in his own invulnerability and my magical protection represented not so much a narcissistic character disorder, as described by Kohut (1966, 1971, 1977) and by Kernberg (1975), but rather a narcissistic regression in a neurotic, but well-integrated individual.

During crises of acting out, countertransference forces may be extremely powerful. This creates a temptation to be carried away by rescue fantasies, which play a significant role in the personalities of many, if not all analysts, and to share freely the mature wisdom ascribed to us by our patients, so that we find ourselves advising them how to conduct their lives. It is especially at such times that we are obliged to remind ourselves that whatever special wisdom we have is largely confined to our understanding of mental life, of consciousness, defenses, autonomous and other ego functions, and the analytic methods available for helping patients to deal with them. They generally know and understand much more about their affairs than we possibly can, and we are qualified to deal only with those interferences that arise out of the neurotic illness.

To restrain ourselves, to avoid what are called, perhaps too easily, "acceptable parameters," requires a high degree of patience and self-control. To listen and try to understand, perhaps for a long period, is not easy when we are tempted to warn, protect, or prohibit. This is especially true as we react to the transference implications of the patient's behavior, the overwhelming need for affection, the urgent sexuality, the anxiety, contempt, defiance—all of which may be represented in the acting out. (See Bird 1957, 1972, Greenacre 1950, 1963, 1968, Stein 1973, 1982.) When a patient we are trying to help places himself, apparently quite arbitrarily, in a situation that threatens disaster to his personal life, his career, his finances, and his analysis, we find ourselves inevitably in the grip of very strong feelings. Such behavior looks like sheer ingratitude, and we experience powerful pressures to react accordingly, thus relinquishing our proper function as analysts.

One of the frequent determinants in acting out is the need to test the analyst, to try his nerve, to seduce him into committing technical errors, to fall into a kind of "counter acting out." In order to propel the analyst into active manipulation, some patients will do everything they can to mobilize his guilt and fears of professional failure, calling into action the rescue fantasies that have been under control all along. For the patient, this represents a victory, although a distinctly pyrrhic one, for the analysis is likely to be destroyed. As a consequence, the strain on the analyst is very great, more intense in some respects than it is on the patient, whose suspension of judgment and reality functions allow him to ignore the signal anxiety that should warn him of danger. It is just as well that the analyst has no access to such relief. His capacity to deal with the danger will depend on control of his own anxiety and the mobilization of his skills in evaluating the phenomenon and analyzing it, if it is in fact analyzable.

Thus, rather narcissistically but not without reason, we are inclined to regard acting out as a trap set specifically for us, to provoke and frighten us, to disappoint our expectations, to put us in the wrong no matter what we do. We are reminded of the ordinary behavior of adolescents in relation to their parents, a point deserving special emphasis in view of pervasive tendencies to look for the roots of acting out exclusively in the preverbal phase of childhood. Certainly that is a crucial phase in the development of such tendencies, ranking in importance with the inborn endowment of the individual. But later phases of development, for example, adolescence, also exert a profound influence, often being decisive in whether acting out will lead to clinical and personal disaster or, on the other hand, will constitute an analyzable and clinically useful phenomenon.

It is also not always easy for us in such situations to avoid indulging in righteous indignation and moral superiority. It is tempting to employ our superior wisdom and moral stature, such as it is, to put things right, before we have studied the situation in depth and achieved some understanding and sympathy. At such times, the demands on the analyst for self-control may appear virtually superhuman.

Admittedly, it is all very well to advise patience and understanding while the analysand's actions seem to threaten the fabric of the analysis itself, if not that of his whole life. The quandary may be stated succinctly: the neurotic patient appears to be doing something that may affect him seriously and adversely; we can help him to deal with it, not merely for the moment, but effectively over the long run, only by analyzing its unconscious sources. The process takes a long time, during which patient and analyst may be placed in a series of apparently untenable positions. How then to defuse the bomb without having it blow up in our faces? Neither impatience nor an attitude of laissez-faire will do.

Although at such points we may, through informed speculation, work out some of the underlying meanings of the patient's behavior, just as we guess some of the unconscious meanings of a manifest dream, we are limited in our capacity to interpret, especially in conveying a useful understanding of the transference implications. If we do, after all, interpret on the basis of informed speculation, we are likely to be met with an openly disbelieving response, which is dismaying, or worse, an acceptance, which is flattering. The latter, sadly, is likely to be an intellectualized and compliant response, leading most often to further and more complex episodes of acting out. About all that can be done in the beginning, therefore, is to make clear the repetitive nature of the actions, to place them as far as possible in a historical context then later to tease out the narcissistic and regressive elements, for example, lapses in reality testing and ordinary common sense. Ultimately, the relation to the transference and to archaic fantasy can be explored. If, in the first place, no repetitive pattern can be ascertained, it is probably best to reconsider whether one is dealing with acting out as a clinical phenomenon and to reevaluate the suitability of the patient for analysis.

It is sometimes possible to make use of a principle elaborated by Lewin (1995) and discussed later by Stein (1965). Freud evolved his theory of dream interpretation originally not only for its own sake, but perhaps even more with the purpose of understanding neurosis. With the advent of ego psychology, not very much attention was paid to the possibilities of using our understanding of dream psychology in this context. But it is possible to conceive of the acting-out patient as a dreamer who needs to be awakened from time to time to remind him where he is and what he is doing. Acting out is, of course, not dreaming in any literal sense, for the inhibition of action characteristic of the dream state is not in effect. But the attempts to gratify a complex of archaic wishes, the profound narcissistic regression, the displacements, the predominance of magical thinking, and the transitory suspension of reality testing, all have their analogues in the dream work. Recognizing this may make it easier for the analyst and ultimately the patient to view the phenomenon with more detachment and less exasperation. The risk that the dreamer may walk in his sleep, so to speak, can be better assessed and often alleviated by waking him in a proper fashion, that is, by interpreting. The analogy is worth considering.

We might think of the patient cited earlier as if he were dreaming much of the time. He was in fact a highly imaginative and creatively endowed man, characteristics not unusual in such patients. In his acting out, he entered a highly narcissistic phase, as we all do in our dreams. Interpretation aroused him from his "dream," if only for a time; and, as he became "awake," his acting out became progressively less urgent and more subject to reality testing. His fantasies were not lost, but they had become, to use Ernst Kris's apt phrase, less "poignant." They were no longer likely to dominate the conduct of his life and influence his major decisions.

Another matter: it is questionable whether our main efforts should be directed toward *preventing* action. We are, after all, not in the business of transforming Macbeth, or Prince Hal, into Hamlet. Some acting out, especially in adolescents and young adults contains a good deal of truly experimental behavior, learning by trial and error, as unconscious fantasies are employed for the direction of some aspects of life. We need not feel responsible for helping our patients avoid unhappy love affairs, for example. It may be enough to make it possible for them to live through these troubling experiences, if they acquire some understanding in the process. Analysis is not a substitute for life. Timid and overprotective analysts are likely to be no more successful than parents of the same stripe, and they have less excuse for their errors.

Although some analyses of neurotic patients who are prone to acting out go on far too long and may end in futility, the cause for the unsatisfactory result is to be sought not only in intractable pathology, but also, and perhaps first, in departures from the analytic mode, which have been unrecognized or inadequately thought out. The analyst may have fallen into a trap from which he cannot extricate himself either because he denies its existence or is too anxious or inexperienced to deal with it analytically. As a consequence, sometimes he gives up on the analysis without a serious effort to understand and analyze the transference resistance, a decision that has resulted from the reactivation of his own unconscious infantile fantasies and the intolerable anxiety that may accompany such regression. This may take the form of a sense of frustration, which impels him to conclude that the patient was characterologically unanalyzable. In that case, the opportunity to analyze may have been lost for good, and prospects for other treatment are rendered far more difficult.

This is quite different from a reasoned decision that analysis is not possible, for example, when a patient, having made some analytic progress, becomes afflicted with a serious and persistent chronic illness or suffers a loss that changes radically the circumstances of his life. We cannot avoid recognizing the limits of the analytic process, and we should admit that we can analyze only those individuals, who have the motivation and the capacity to deal with so demanding a task. We must deal honestly with those whose life situation is too fixed or whose psychological resources are not up to the demands. It is then that we should consider significant changes in procedure. In such situations it is often useful to seek the cooler judgment of a colleague, who may enable us to see things in a different light, to repair what may have looked like a hopeless analysis, to advise the employment of another modality, or perhaps arrange a judicious transfer to another analyst.

Even so, after all the potential pitfalls have been considered, neurotic patients with acting-out tendencies should be offered the option of psychoanalysis as a first choice. If this is not possible, or if the advice is rejected, or if analysis proves after a trial to be inapplicable, we should do something else and by all means call it by another name. Less than this is fair neither to the patient nor to the profession. When analysis is feasible, however, the work done with a piece of acting out can become a breakthrough, a crucial determinant in the resolution of the transference neurosis, the point at which everything seems to come together.

To return to our central issue, we may consider exactly how countertransference *conflicts* affect both the incidence of acting out and how successfully it can be treated. In the course of any analysis, episodes may occur in response to unavoidable frustrations, for example, the analyst's holidays and other absences, planning for termination, chance extraanalytic encounters, and the like. In most cases, it is not difficult to bring these circumstances into the analytic situation and resolve them successfully—unless, of course, the analyst himself, out of anxiety and guilt, avoids them and fails to understand their significance. Other intercurrent episodes are less inevitable; analysts are not always at their best. Tempers flare, arguments occur, important facts are forgotten, attention wanders, one has been tactless. It is in these instances that the analyst's "countertransference neurosis" may lead to trouble, especially if he fails to analyze his own errors and repair the damage. To attempt to conceal the error, to react defensively, may effectively disrupt the analysis.

The analyst may also react with excessive anxiety to his patient's characterological hostility or urgent sexuality, leading him to play down these phases of the work and thus encouraging repression at the expense of analytic progress. Such behavior on the part of the analyst may precipitate action by the patient, if only to engage the analyst's attention. Or he may unconsciously identify with his patient's impulsiveness, deriving vicarious satisfaction from the patient's exciting adventures. This is a special risk for a profession that demands such extreme discretion in professional and personal life alike that it may predispose one, absurdly, to moralistic attitudes and stodginess of manner. Such characteristics seldom elude the notice of patients and may, in fact, encourage them to act for the sake of upsetting a person they perceive as rigidly conventional.

Some analysts, without necessarily being moralistic, place an exaggerated value on a "sensible" way of life and consistent reasonableness. It is hard in principle to fault such an attitude, but we should recognize that in practice it may stimulate an opposing reaction in patients, analogous to adolescent behavior, in which transference resistance takes the form of *unreasonable* action. This is understandable; individuals who make a point of being invariably reasonable can make others very uncomfortable and inspire them to all sorts of excesses. It becomes so tempting for patients (and not only patients) to ruffle the feathers of such perfect beings. This is hardly an indication for less reasonableness or more unconventional behavior on the part of analysts, only that its effects on patients should be recognized and brought into the analysis.

In summary, unresolved countertransference conflicts that occur in the course of analyzing patients prone to acting out may lead to a number of difficulties for the analyst, manifested by overidentification with the patient, failure to understand and control his own anxiety, and loss of the analytic attitude, which combines sympathetic understandings and detachment in the necessary proportion. The resultant difficulties are sometimes fatal to the analysis, but need not be. In many cases, they may be corrected by analytic self-scrutiny, often with the aid of advice from a colleague, who can play a role in reaching a decision whether to continue, modify, or transfer. In any event even the "easiest" patient who acts out presents a very complicated problem. If this implies that in order to navigate with any degree of safety the analyst must be a veritable Odysseus, it is no more than a fair statement of the facts.

REFERENCES

Bird, B. (1957). A specific peculiarity of acting out. *J. Amer. Psychoanal. Assn.* 5:630–647.

——— (1972). Notes on the transference: Universal phenomenon and hardest part of analysis. *J. Amer. Psychoanal. Assn.* 20:267–301.

Blos, P. (1963). The concept of acting out in relation to the adolescent process. *J. Amer. Acad. Child Psychiat.* 2:118–143.

Freud, S. (1914). Remembering, repeating and working through. *Standard Edition* 12:145–156. London: Hogarth Press, 1958.
Gill, M. (1979). The analysis of the transference. *J. Amer. Psychoanal. Assn.* 27:263–288.
Greenacre, P. (1950). General problems of acting out. *Psychoanal. Quart.* 19:455–467.
——— (1963). Problems of acting out in the transference relationship. *Emotional Growth.* New York: International Universities Press, 1971, pp. 695–712.
——— (1968). The psychoanalytic process, transference, and acting out. *Internat. J. Psychoanal.* 49:211–218.
Kernberg, O. (1975). *Borderline Conditions.* New York: Jason Aronson.
Kohut, H. (1966). Forms and transformations of narcissism. *J. Amer. Psychoanal. Assn.* 14:243–272.
——— (1971). *The Analysis of the Self.* New York: International Universities Press.
——— (1977). *The Restoration of the Self.* New York: International Universities Press, 1977.
Lewin, B. (1955). Dream psychology and the analytic situation. *Psychoanal. Quart.* 24:169–199.
Stein, M. (1965). States of consciousness in the analytic situation, including a note on the traumatic dream. *Drives, Affects, Behavior,* 2, ed. M. Schur. New York. International Universities Press, pp. 60–86.
——— (1973). Acting out as a character trait. *Psychoanalytic Study of the Child* 28:347–364. New Haven: Yale University Press.
——— (1981). The unobjectionable part of the transference. *J. Amer. Psychoanal. Assn.* 29:869–892.

12

Writing about Psychoanalysis

INTRODUCTION BY BARBARA STIMMEL

Writing about Psychoanalysis I and II are papers long overdue. Freud, powerful role model and daunting competitor, has made psychoanalysis a writing profession. There are those who write and those who don't; that divide sometimes becomes a chasm (unfortunately and unrealistically) when assessing clinical acumen. The writers know more, the readers know less. Stein is quick to disabuse us of such a simplistic and insulting notion. "Some who are very highly regarded as clinicians write little or nothing; on the other hand, many who have written works which have become classics are not known to have been outstanding in their work with patients. There is simply very little correlation between volume of publication and clinical skill" (p. 199).

It makes sense that Martin Stein would be the analyst to take on the task of confronting shibboleths about how our professional literature is written (or not, as the case may be) and is read. These papers were written by a highly regarded clinician who has produced some classics. That being the starting point, we have much to learn from an analyst who has taken as seriously as has Stein the art of marrying what occurs in the consulting room with what appears on the writing pad. These papers are not a "how-to"; rather they are if to, why to, when to, when not to, and, simply, to.

Stein indirectly accuses editors and reading analysts for including and accepting in our literature much that is poorly conceptualized and written. He directly confronts writers with the need to elevate language, expression, and thought so that our literature lives up to our reputations as practitioners who "use words as our primary tools" (p. 192). But the essence of these papers is to help us think through, whether as writers or readers, the entanglements embedded in writing about complex, sensitive, provocative, and confidential instances and ideas. Stein raises the issue of conflict and capability at the same time as he advocates the need for training to include encouragement and education in the skill of translating clinical moments into *written* communications. He wants us to think about the predictable and ever-present problems of transference and countertransference whenever a patient is selected by the analyst to be written about, or conversely, when the decision is taken not to write about a patient after having had the thought to do so. Both carry within them the same possibility for transference enactment. When a patient reads (or hears) his analyst's paper(s) we are confronted with a whole other set of possibilities. Stein shows how these unavoidable transferential tangles are neither to be avoided nor feared but will become a productive part of the working through.

A critically important thread of these papers is the need to maintain confidentiality while at the same time bringing to life the clinical foundation of a theoretical point. Stein worries about the difficulty in "succeeding in conveying to the reader the beauty and complexity of psychoanalytic theory as we experience it in our daily work with patients" (p. 192). It is very much like Martin Stein not only to offer his own beautifully written and complexly organized papers as models for those of us who wish to write and those of us who wish to read serious, carefully crafted, and intelligent papers. He has also taken the time and effort to call our attention to the significant problems in our professional literature, while optimistically assuring us that there are ways to make things better.

Whether you have written, have something in mind to write, wonder whether you will ever be able to sit down and hammer an idea into shape, or look forward to the next issue of your journal for new slants on old problems or, who knows, even new thoughts (!), these papers should be your guide.

ANALYSTS WHO WRITE AND THOSE WHO DO NOT

This study of analysts' writing consists of two parts. In the following paper, I describe the difficulties facing the practicing analyst who wishes to lecture and publish his findings and ideas, whether or not he intends to cite clinical examples. I make some suggestions directed toward overcoming those (largely internal) obstacles. In a second paper, I shall discuss a special problem, concern over how our lecturing or publishing affects the analytic progress of our patients, especially with respect to analysis of the transference.

"No man but a blockhead ever wrote except for money"

—Boswell, *Life of Johnson*

We need not question that the subject deserves our attention. Some analysts write a great deal, some a little, many not at all. Some write pretty well, some acceptably, some appallingly. This range is not peculiar to our field, but since we work primarily with words, we ought to ask ourselves why so little first-class writing is produced, and why so many highly articulate analysts contribute nothing to the literature. What we do publish is often subjected, from the outside, to harsh, even savage criticism, reminding us constantly that we do not write as well as Freud. However complicated the motives of our critics, they have a point. Much psychoanalytic writing is not of very high caliber, being all too often poorly organized and stylistically clumsy, rarely succeeding in conveying to the reader the beauty and complexity of psychoanalytic theory as we experience it in our daily work with patients.

We are by no means unique in this respect, quite the contrary. A review of technical works in other clinical fields, neurology or gastroenterology for example, might lead us to conclude that the quality of our writing is by no means inferior. Even so, we cannot be let off the hook so easily. Unlike neurologists and gastroenterologists (a few of whom do in fact write very well), we use words as our primary tools, and it is demanded of us that we do far better, so that the interested and informed layman will find our writings clear and convincing. Since we are working in a highly technical field, such a requirement may be deemed excessive; but we can demand of ourselves at least that our writing be well organized and written in clear language, in which theoretical demonstration is manifestly derived from clinical observation.

Particularly scarce in our field are clinical papers in which conclusions are drawn convincingly from first-hand observations derived from the raw data of the analytic situation itself. Far more often the presentation of these data is fuzzy, and the conclusions are left hanging in air. Even papers that deal with high-level abstractions are likely to be convoluted, unreadable, and unconvincing; or they may be appealingly simple, having gained clarity of exposition by sacrificing the passion and complexity of the best psychoanalytic thought. We are in fact faced with a number of problems which, while not confined to psychoanalysis, do manifest themselves with special intensity in our field. Some of the reasons are fairly obvious.

Of all the obstacles we face in trying to write a worthwhile psychoanalytic paper, the stickiest and the most familiar is the need for professional discretion. There is no question that in this respect we are at a disadvantage as compared with clinical disciplines that deal with data which may be sensitive, but far less detailed and intimate than ours. When we think of publishing our clinical observations, discretion always becomes a matter of serious concern. It is right that it should be so.

Freud's reports on Dora (1905), Little Hans (1909a), the Rat Man (1909b), and the Wolf Man (1918) were of great importance in giving color and body to his theoretical ideas, but we know that he and some of his patients paid a price for their fame. It is arguable that his most courageous and valuable use of clinical material is to be found, not in these case reports, but rather in his own subjective experiences, as described in *The Interpretation of Dreams* (1900). Had he omitted such personal data, this historic work would have been far less convincing and influential. What he revealed has led to a thriving industry based on the "analysis" of Freud's dreams, and even "analyzing" him, efforts which, while sometimes ingenious and informative, are more often colored by admixtures of reckless speculation and prurient gossip. Such efforts may be of interest, but the real value of Freud's self-revelations lies in what they have to teach us about the interpretation of dreams and the hypotheses based on their systematic study; their value in unraveling the personal mysteries of that extraordinarily complex man is very limited.

In *The Interpretation of Dreams*, Freud betrayed only his own secrets, a major sacrifice, it is true, but one which implicated no one else. He had reasons for giving so much space to his own dreams; none of his patients' reported dreams has a fraction of the interest of his own. For example, the dreams of the "botanical monograph" (pp. 169ff.), "dissecting my own pelvis" (pp. 413ff.), "Count Thun" (pp. 208ff.), or the "open-air closet" (pp. 468–470) make the dream work come to life with a clarity and intensity that could be accomplished by no amount of abstract discussion. His other reason for giving less space to patients' dreams sounds a bit quaint today: "But I was precluded from using the latter material by the fact that in its case the dream-processes were subject to an undesirable complication owing to the added presence of neurotic features" (p. xxiii). He detailed the cost to himself in the "Preface to the First Edition":

> . . . if I was to report my own dreams, it inevitably followed that I should have to reveal to the public gaze more of the intimacies of my mental life than I liked, or than is normally necessary for any writer who is a man of science and not a poet. Such was the painful but unavoidable necessity; and I have submitted to it rather than totally abandon the possibility of giving the evidence for my psychological findings. *Naturally, however, I have been unable to resist the temptation of taking the edge off some of my indiscretions by omissions and substitutions. But whenever this has happened, the value of my instances has been very definitely diminished.* I can only express the hope that readers of this book will put themselves in my difficult situation and treat me with indulgence, and further, that anyone who finds any sort of reference to himself in my dreams may be willing to grant me the right of freedom of thought—in my dream-life, if nowhere else. [pp. xxiii–xxiv; italics added]

Freud did us a great service not only in the substance, but in the quality of his writings. Still, the very excellence of his style, which led him to be thought of as a potential novelist, has exacted its toll on his successors. Probably every analyst wants to write as well as he did; few if any have come close.

Mahony (1984), for example, compares Freud's writing with that of "many current psychoanalytic theorists who expound conceptually deficient hypotheses in a nonprocessive, devitalized language and write themselves into oblivion" (p. 856). We may find the charge too harsh, but it would be difficult to deny its substance. It is possible that the devitalization of the written language of psychoanalysis is not merely the result of the shortage of talented and courageous writers, much less geniuses. Nor is it only that we are working in a field that is no longer entirely unexplored. There is still far more to be discovered and described; the surprises are experienced every day by those analysts who are ready to be surprised. But the medium of expression has narrowed over the decades since Freud wrote and published, especially with regard to the publication of clinical data.

Publishing a detailed case study of an individual, particularly if it permits others to identify him and his family, has become uncommon in practice. It is at the very least an invasion of privacy, and while it need not threaten livelihood or reputation, particularly if the report is written with discretion and respect, it raises serious questions about its effects on the patient in relation to his social milieu. Even if these can be discounted, we must still consider the implications with respect to persisting transferential attitudes toward his (former) analyst. We know that they *do* persist and must be taken into account (Panel 1963). To have one's analyst become one's biographer must acquire a significance difficult to define over the long run.

I have heard a distinguished colleague justify the practice of publishing detailed case reports by citing their value in extending and clarifying psychoanalytic theory and practice, as Freud's case reports had done. When we consider the effect of reading about oneself in the literature, having become a "celebrity," like Dora (see Deutsch 1957) or the Wolf Man (see Gardiner 1971), we may well hesitate to publish a comprehensive and detailed report of a case. It may not be taken for granted that we later settlers have the same rights as those claimed and exerted by the earliest pioneers of unexplored territories, whose errors could to some extent be excused by inexperience and the sense of being surrounded by hostile aborigines.

A striking, and distressing, example of exposure, although based on acquaintance rather than personal analysis, may be found in the *Minutes of the Vienna Psychoanalytic Society*, January 12, 1910, in a presentation by Dr. Fritz Wittels, titled "The 'Fackel'-Neurosis (Minutes 93)." The presentor gave a detailed "analysis" of Karl Kraus, a well-known journalist, with whom he had some personal contact. There was no attempt to protect the identity of the subject, who was mentioned by name, and was in any case known to many of those present. Several of the audience criticized the oversimplifications and the obvious prejudice of the speaker; only Freud, with some irony, pointed out that there were serious questions about the propriety of presenting such material about a living person, remarking that "such a vivisection could justly be reproached as being inhumane" (p. 391). Kraus had been critical of psychoanalysis before; this experience could hardly have contributed to a more sympathetic understanding (Janik and Toulmin 1973, H. Zohn 1984, personal communication).

I have been reminded by M. Horowitz (personal communication) of the part played by the impulse to tell secrets in the conflict associated with the intention to present clinical material. The temptation to gossip, while ubiquitous, is not generally a prominent motive in the preparation of scientific papers, but the need to defend against the unconscious temptation to make improper revelations may well inhibit, rather than stimulate, the conscientious author when he sits down to write.

Putting aside questions of discretion, the length of a "complete" case report and the need to organize such a vast mass of data may still present serious difficulties. Tape has been employed to obtain verbatim recordings, making possible the systematic analysis of word usage and the accumulation of other data capable of being subjected to later study. It has also been used to evaluate technical maneuvers by a close study of the "actual" record (Dahl 1974, Gill and Hoffman 1982). But the very presence of the research atmosphere and instrumentation introduces transference complexities which are at the very least difficult to evaluate. This gives us no reason to reject the instrumentation, or the findings derived from their use, but it should signal the need for caution in evaluating the results. Beyond this, the sheer mass of information acquired during the course of an analysis is overwhelming, especially since it consists not merely of numbers or even detached words and phrases; it contains subtleties of tone and inflection, as well as gestures, which are difficult to record and evaluate even with the aid of sophisticated equipment.

Recently there has been a good deal of progress in the use of computers in compiling concordances, such as that of *The Standard Edition of the Complete Psychological Works of Sigmund Freud* (Guttman 1982), and an increasing number of other works, mostly literary. They are invaluable in textual research, but they will hardly substitute for the interpretive efforts of the literary critic. Thus far, it would seem that the production of first-class descriptions of clinical psychoanalysis calls for the skills of the novelist or critic, rather than the mathematician. Freud was perhaps uniquely qualified; yet even his case reports, so brilliant as demonstrations, leave us only partly satisfied with them as scientific documents.

The detailed, "complete" case report is not, fortunately, the only choice, although theoretically it would be the best, if problems of discretion were not so formidable (and if anyone could read the mass of material). Sometimes we resort to less detailed reports, bringing out only the relevant highlights. This device makes it much easier to protect the identity of the analysand, although it does not dispense entirely with the need for disguise. Generally, we attempt to eliminate potentially identifying material by omitting or even altering some data in order to make recognition by others unlikely. At the same time, we try to retain enough accurate clinical data to render a meaningful account. We are purposely vague about the patient's name and occupation, place his background and schooling elsewhere, even make some changes in the family constellation, if they seem necessary for the purpose. By the time we finish protecting him however, we risk losing the individual by creating a fictional character, less interesting than the original, and capable of misleading the reader. We are therefore limited in how much we can disguise the person without destroying the value of the report. For example, a patient's conflicts may be connected with his possession of a well-known or unusual name, the omission of which leaves a huge gap in the account of his neurosis. Profession may also present a problem, for to disguise a physician as a physicist, or a lawyer as an accountant, creates a false clue, with a potential for arousing tension in the reader, and quite possibly suggesting irrelevant conclusions. We may well envy not only the talent but the freedom of the biographer of figures of the past, who need not disguise his subject at all, and the novelist who creates the character from within his own experience and imagination (and who even so may be sued for invasion of privacy!).

The task of preparing a clinical report, which requires compression and disguise, may remind us of the dream work, particularly that part of it denoted "secondary revision," in which these mechanisms dominate in order to serve the censorship, simultaneously to evade moral condemnation and satisfy the ego's demands for some coherence in the tale as it is finally experienced by consciousness. These clinical reports may be viewed as having some features in common with manifest dreams; the "facts" have been worked over, subjected to secondary revision, and transformed into something more acceptable, for whatever purpose. We are, after all, describing a situation, the analytic hour, which has much in common with dreaming (Lewin 1955, Stein 1965). But in dealing with the written report, the reader is forced to try to figure out what has been altered or omitted, without the aid of the narrator's associations. It is striking that when we hear a protocol presented to a private seminar, the opportunity to ask questions, to invite the presentor to elaborate, to share an atmosphere of free exchange, brings out a vast amount of material, directly or by nuance, which has not been included in the original presentation. Strictly speaking, formal clinical presentations may be thought of as possessing some of the characteristics of manifest dreams, "truthful fiction," while the claim to have rendered the "literal truth" about the events of an analysis may indeed be considered fictional.

We may feel some sympathy for journalists who face similar problems in reporting data which they feel compelled to alter for the sake of discretion and protection of sources, and are influenced at the same time by the understandable wish to add dramatic interest. When we gloss over or omit facts which are, in our opinion, irrelevant or unessential, and which we regard as capable of being misused, are we not also tempted to dramatize, to make the clinical account more convincing and interesting to the reader? Literal accounts, process notes, so-called, are generally impossible to read, and it is not certain that they really convey more information than well-written and edited clinical protocols. Psychoanalytic supervisors have learned by hard experience how difficult it is to pay close attention while a student attempts to give a word-by-word account of a series of psychoanalytic sessions. "Strictly speaking, they [exact reports of analytic case histories] only possess the *ostensible* exactness of which 'modern' psychiatry affords us some striking examples. They are as a rule fatiguing to the reader. . . . This is not the way, it seems, to remedy the lack of convincing evidence to be found in psychoanalytic reports" (Freud 1912, p. 114, see also Mahony 1982). We understand soon enough that such literal renditions often reveal failure to understand the overall trends and underlying meanings of the material. Too often we find ourselves dealing with ignorance in the guise of thoroughness. A chaotic junk shop is not necessarily a more "honest" establishment than that of a dealer in antiques, who substitutes polish for dust.

But where do we draw the line between that editing which is necessary to convey information (rather than "facts"), and the distortion, or even the manufacture, of data to prove a point, to the greater glory of the author? Outright fakery in scientific writing has been publicized a good deal recently, e.g., the writings of the egregious Cyril Burt in the field of psychological testing. But far more often we hear of cases in which one may feel some sympathy with the author, whose mistakes are perpetrated unwittingly; they are purposeful, it is true, and often self-serving, but are likely to be more in the nature of symptomatic acts, "parapraxes," than deliberate falsification. They should not be condoned, for they may be responsible for a great deal of damage, but they do not justify the indignation more justly reserved for massive and deliberate falsification. Knowing where to draw the line requires not only a devotion to truth, and an open mind, but a serious encounter with one's own prejudices. It is a large order.

To convey the sense and atmosphere of an analytic experience means that we must tell a coherent story about it, a truthful one, but a story nevertheless. The preparation of a good clinical report requires a reorganization and selection of data without which the material remains inchoate and incapable of being communicated in a useful fashion. And we remain aware always of the need for discretion.

The difficulties inherent in the writing, and more particularly the publishing, of even condensed case reports, most often leaves us with only two choices: neglecting clinical material altogether or restricting ourselves to brief clinical vignettes. These are limited as a rule to descriptions of analytic events or single sessions, sometimes detailed, giving but the scantiest background information. How valuable a recital of a single hour could be, unaccompanied by any other information, was demonstrated by Bertram D. Lewin in his classroom teaching at the New York Psychoanalytic Institute in the 1940s. One of the students would prepare a protocol of a single analytic session, as complete and literal as possible, which he would then present to the class, sentence by sentence. Nothing was given about the patient's age, diagnosis, chief complaint, nor any anamnestic material, aside from what could be gathered from the exchanges between patient and analyst. Following each sentence or short paragraph, Lewin would ask the class to "associate" to the material just read. The results were surprising. Often, by the time half an hour had gone by, the outline of the case would begin to come clear, and after another hour, the group was often able to acquire a pretty good idea of what was troubling the patient, the state of the transference, much of the dynamics, and more.

This was 35 years ago. I have probably idealized the experience, and have no notes to check that process (no one took notes in that class!). The most striking lesson we learned was that analysis was neither a dry intellectual process nor a matter of inspired and undirected guesswork, but indeed a process that depended on acute intuition and informed imagination, and it could and should be exciting. Lewin (1955) was of course interested in studying the analytic situation via the medium of dream psychology. It was no accident that he evolved this method of teaching.

While this example cannot apply in exactly the same way to formal lectures and published works, it does contain a suggestion: that there is an effective way to convey the matter an spirit of an analytic hour without furnishing a long anamnesis or identifying the patient, even by circumstantial testimony. Agreed, Lewin's method was highly individual, if not idiosyncratic; nevertheless, we have much to learn from it in our attempts to present clinical material in a more acceptable and interesting way.

Lewin furnished the inspiration, if not the literal model, for the sort of device which I and many others have employed so liberally elsewhere, namely clinical vignettes. These brief sketches are most valuable in demonstrating a technical or theoretical principle in a way that no abstract discussion could do by itself. While vignettes present us with some of the same problems as detailed case histories, they are distinctly less obstinate, requiring little if any manipulation of data except, of course, the determination of what to include and what to leave out. I suggest that the use of such vignettes, with all their limitation, can convey a more vivid description of our work and render our conclusions more convincing. They are no substitute for the kinds of data which might be obtained by well-controlled experiments, but so far we have not evolved such methods for studying more than a few elements of mental life, for example, some aspects of the role of day residues in dream formation. It is still not clear how the latter can be correlated with the unique data derived from the analytic session.

Even vignettes must be written with some regard for the identities of the subjects who have been obliging enough to furnish us with useful examples. An individual may be at least tentatively identified by being known to have been in analysis with the author of the report. His colleagues and close friends are inclined to do a good deal of speculating, which may hit the mark now and then, particularly if the subject himself drops a few well-placed hints. In this situation we may feel it necessary to confine ourselves to employing very sketchy vignettes, or combining the data from a group of patients who share certain characteristics.

With all their built-in limitations, their lowly status as "anecdotes," and their deficiencies as "proof," vignettes do make it possible to demonstrate clinical principles, and render high-level theory more vivid and understandable. Well-chosen and appropriately employed, they are generally worth the effort, for they make it possible to write clinical papers without requiring extensive distortions of material to protect the privacy of the individual (e.g., Reiser 1985). And they can be made more informative and convincing by changes in the way we usually present clinical material, particularly if we take the trouble to be clear about the points we wish to make. While they do not eliminate, they do alleviate some of the most obvious problems which account for the reluctance of many analysts to write and publish clinical papers.

But what of all those analysts who write little or nothing? Their more prolific colleagues might assert that those who do not write are likely to be less capable intellectually, perhaps less skillful, that their clinical competence is confined to intuitive processes, to the extent that they lack intellectual rigor, or at least are afraid to have that quality tested. Such claims would be difficult to substantiate, to say the least. Experience in seminars and other meetings at which analytic ideas are expressed extemporaneously fails altogether to support such generalizations, for many colleagues who never present formal papers, much less publish, may be brilliant as teachers, supervisors, and consultants, and sometimes reveal an awesome mastery of psychoanalytic theory and literature. Some who are very highly regarded as clinicians write little or nothing; on the other hand, many who have written works which have become classics are not known to have been outstanding in their work with patients. There is simply very little correlation between volume of publication and clinical skill. Quality may be another matter, but even here the correlation is not clear. In all professions there are those who are impressive lecturers and writers, but are less adept at the workbench—and vice versa.

A source of profound conflict which we have not, to my knowledge, subjected to systematic study, is how an analyst's need to distance himself from the emotional demands of his work operates as a motive for writing, as well as a potential interference. The decision to write implies not only a distinct rise in intellectual interest in the subject, but also the attainment of some distance from it. Professional writers, especially novelists, are very much aware of this issue, since so much of their material is derived from experience with those they have loved and hated with special intensity—parents, lovers, dear friends, and enemies. Much creative work has been written, in part at least, to soften the effects of painful memories: we might think of Dickens's *David Copperfield*, Dostoyevsky's *The Possessed*, Tolstoy's *Resurrection*, and Arthur Miller's play, *After the Fall*, as a few examples among many of creative works which demonstrate the writer's attempts to exorcise his personal demons and to justify himself to a punitive conscience and a critical society.

How often, we may ask, are analytic papers written with the motive of distancing oneself from experience with the analysis of a patient, which may have left a host of unresolved and painful questions? "Did I do all I could to help the patient? Was I not interested enough, or too interested? Should I have agreed to end the analysis when I did? Was I right to take the patient in the first place?" One of the ways we try to deal with these troubling thoughts is by writing a paper with the hope that doing so will bring relief. Maybe it will even turn out to be a "good" paper, contributing something of lasting value. Freud (1905) coped with his doubts about the less than satisfactory case of Dora, by writing an extensive case report and not incidentally, producing a classic. A fair number of clinical papers and others, contain elements of catharsis and self-justification, factors which do not necessarily detract from their didactic and scientific value, especially when they are accompanied by a salutary exploration of the issues and the writer's own conflicts, whether or not he spells them out in the final published work. The analyst's need for distancing, for relief from the intensity of his clinical experience, often stimulates him to write; if unrecognized, it may also have adverse effects on both the writing and his analytic work. It may discourage some from writing at all.

There are in addition more mundane reasons why so many analysts refrain from writing. Some fear they lack the necessary skills. In many cases their doubts are justified, but some are too modest. There is something to be said for such restraint, so long as it discourages the presentation of inferior work, but a certain kind of diffidence may also account for the withholding of valuable contributions by very able and articulate people, the late Otto Isakower having been a notable example. He published a few brief papers, which represented a minute fraction of the seminal ideas he expressed to colleagues and students, many of whom were to build upon his unpublished work (Bertram D. Lewin and myself, among others). Perfectionism seems to be another one of those character traits which is not altogether disposed of by analytic training.

For many people, a major obstacle is the anxiety about how one's papers will be received by colleagues, an apprehension entertained by all but the most self-confident in our small world; undoubtedly such concern plays a major role in the reluctance of many potential contributors to the literature. While criticisms by colleagues may be sharp and not always understanding or charitable, they are not necessarily more savage than the attacks encountered by writers in other fields. Perhaps we analysts are more easily wounded by adverse criticism, an ironic circumstance in view of our training, which prepares us to accept with understanding and equanimity the most hostile remarks by patients. We cannot, of course, explain away our colleagues' attacks by ascribing them to transference, although it is often very tempting to do so. It is, however, almost as satisfying to view them as having been inspired by envy.

It is worth noting that some analysts may simply be too busy with other things more important to them than the writing of papers. Most in private practice see eight to ten patients a day, or even more. Evening time is often taken up with teaching and other professional demands, leaving relatively short periods to spend with families. Psychoanalysis being the most labor-intensive of all professions, and hardly the best paid, younger analysts generally find it necessary to work long hours in order to support their growing households. It should not come as a surprise that this is a sensitive issue among members of a profession which emphasizes the crucial importance of family life, to the extent often of stimulating a good deal of anxiety and guilt among its practitioners. To take the time to study and write may therefore become a source of painful conflict within the family and within oneself. By the time an analyst has reached the age at which he may feel more established, and his children are grown, he has the advantages of a long clinical experience, and we hope, the wisdom of maturity, but is likely to have lost some of the spirited creativity and irreverence of youth—although there are exceptions for which we may feel grateful.

Between the demands of clinical practice and family life, it is often impossible for an analyst in full-time practice to spend the great amount of time necessary to study the relevant literature, and he is hardly likely to have a research assistant to help him. But, we may be asked, "How did Freud manage it?" It wasn't easy for him. For example, the writing of Chapter One of *The Interpretation of Dreams*, dealing with the literature, "had always been a bug-bear" (E. Jones, in Freud 1900, p. xix). And, we hardly need to be reminded, Freud's capacity for concentrated work was phenomenal, a component of his genius, which we find impossible to emulate. As a consequence, writing and lecturing may be placed far down the list of priorities for too many analysts who should be writing. It is understandable, but a pity.

Since so many analysts who are excellent clinicians and teachers do not write, or if so, very little, and that perhaps not very valuable, it is just as well that the principle of "Publish or Perish" does not operate within psychoanalytic faculties, as opposed to university settings. In the latter, research and secretarial assistance are available, one is paid for the time spent in writing, at least in part, and most important of all, publishing is explicitly encouraged, many staff members being offered their jobs with that as a consideration. Even so, it may be difficult for them if they are beset with the many bureaucratic demands inherent in maintaining oneself in academia, which may, in subtle or not so subtle ways, interfere not only with the time available for carrying on the psychoanalysis of a number of patients, but even more with the state of mind conducive to thinking and writing analytically. Those of us in private practice, who have from time to time been engaged in time- and energy-consuming administrative duties can sympathize.[1]

We may hope that recognition of these issues will alleviate some of the anxieties that inhibit or spoil so much psychoanalytic writing. There is no lack of explicit encouragement by a certain number of senior analysts. Some, Charles Brenner and Robert Wallerstein, for example, have conducted seminars; supervisors have encouraged candidates to write up interesting clinical issues, and helped with preparation. All of these efforts should be of value, although we have no measure of the results. Candidates are generally required to render periodic reports on their supervised cases; the quality of these does not usually reflect much potentiality for writing effectively.

In a discussion of an earlier version of this paper, presented at the New York Psychoanalytic Society (September 30, 1985), Charles Brenner reminded us that good writing in this field, as well as in others, depended on clarity of the writer's purpose and the organization of his ideas. This echoed Freud (1900): " . . . the involved sentences of my book on dreams . . . have gravely affronted some ideal within me. And I am scarcely wrong in regarding this lack of form as a sign of an incomplete mastery of the material" (p. xx).

Another factor contributing to dull and unclear writing is the lack of a sense of purpose, or uncertainty about whether it will be read and by whom. This may well account for the dullness of so many reports submitted by psychoanalytic candidates "for the record," who might do much better, and may, when they have recognized more gratifying reasons for writing.

Finally, it is also possible that analysts who value their clinical skills very highly, experience a special problem in putting their ideas, i.e., their interpretations, into written, as against spoken, form. This is a very old issue, long antedating psychoanalysis. Plato (340 B.C.) had Socrates contrast spoken dialogue with written text, very much to the disadvantage of the latter (Phaedrus: 275, p. 521). The written word can do no more than "remind one

[1]I understand from colleagues in other clinical specialties that the situation is not so very different, devoted and expert clinicians often publishing little or nothing, perhaps again for lack of time and assistance.

who [already] knows that which the writing is concerned with." It cannot answer criticism or correct misunderstanding by the reader; it is also capable of being misused by "those who have no business with it." It was like Socrates to have anticipated pop psychology.

Our everyday analytic work is necessarily based on verbal, not written communication. When we interpret to a patient, we look for an immediate response, whether agreement, disagreement, further associations, expressions of affect, such as laughing, or perhaps a period of silence, all responses capable of leading to further understanding. We in turn have the opportunity to react promptly, to elaborate, explain, correct, or even retract what we have said. Even if the analyst is silent most of the time, analysis is in essence a dialogue. In the case of written discourse, or the formal lecture, there is no corresponding opportunity. The reader or listener has no immediately effective way of expressing his reactions, nor is the author able to reply without delay; misunderstandings persist.[2]

Plato had a point; dialogues do indeed have some significant advantages over written communications. While we are not in Athens, with its relatively tiny population of citizens and a culture which allowed for such verbal exchanges, we nevertheless might consider whether we could adapt some aspects of his method. Plato did after all commit the *Dialogues* to writing, and they still make fascinating reading. It is worth noting that they are written as dialogues, i.e., spoken exchanges in which the process of thought, the development of ideas in the minds of the speakers, are described in detail. Arguments are presented, questioned, clarified, elaborated, refuted, defended, revised, withdrawn, or restated in new forms. It is possible to overstate the similarity to analytic exchanges, but they do have something in common—not the essence of the argument itself, but rather the simultaneous development and elaboration of ideas in analysand and analyst. This statement does not, of course, do justice to the affective exchanges occurring during analysis; it is questionable whether words alone can do so. But it should be possible to convey much more of the spirit of analytic exchanges than we are accustomed to read in the literature.

Perhaps we would do better to write in a fashion which, instead of presenting merely observations and explanations, revealed more clearly the processes by which we made those observations and achieved those hypotheses. Such a task would require a candid description of our thought processes, our

---

[2]One has only to look at "Letters to the Editor" in any journal which encourages responses to published articles, for example, *The New York Review of Books*, to be impressed with the manifold possibilities of misunderstanding the written word. The result is often an exchange of intemperate letters. Sometimes, it must be confessed, these make better reading than the original articles, but they constitute dispute rather than dialogue.

errors, the false leads which took so much of our time and energy, the elegant ideas we had eventually to discard. The effort would be a painful one, requiring a degree of self-revelation to which we are not accustomed. We might also overcome our modesty, if that is what it is, and bring ourselves to write more often in the first person, eschewing such unfortunate phrases as, "the analyst replied. . . . " While there are good reasons for our reluctance to expose much of our private lives to our patients, it is by no means certain that these same reasons are equally cogent with respect to the *processes* by which we observe and reach conclusions (Mahony 1982, 1984).

It is a commonplace that we clinicians are likely to learn more from our failures than our successes, a principle familiar to investigators in many fields. It is arguable that the most effective analyses have begun with a series of incomplete understandings and interpretations which are somewhat, but not too far, off the mark. These are then subjected to constant revision, becoming progressively more precise and effective, approximating ever more closely the psychic reality of the patient, but never achieving the ideal of perfect and complete understanding, were that possible, or even desirable.

We have a model in Freud, who demonstrated above all the capacity to learn from false leads and erroneous conclusions, to tolerate ambiguity and inherent contradictions, to allow his personal theoretical system to remain dynamic and fluid. Often we fail to recognize the extraordinary frankness of his writing, from his original reevaluation of the seduction theory of neurosogenesis, and the writing of *The Interpretation of Dreams*, in the early years, to the composition of that remarkable late work, *Analysis Terminable and Interminable* (1937). To discover our own errors, to describe, understand, and correct them, with a scientific purpose (which by no means implies *exhibiting* them), might allow us to create a better psychoanalytic literature. It would not hurt our patients. They know we make tentative hypotheses, which may turn out to be erroneous, even that we are guilty, now and then, of faulty observation. If patients are not aware of these imperfections, it is a sign that something is seriously wrong with the analysis of transference, at the very least.

In conclusion, I have argued that many of the problems of writing which face the practicing psychoanalyst can be mastered by a more extensive and careful use of clinical vignettes, and by more candid and detailed accounts of exchanges between analysand and analyst, including description of the thought processes of the analyst himself. Encouragement and active help for junior colleagues by their seniors have not been altogether neglected, but much more can and should be done, beginning with the period of analytic training and supervision. I have put aside, for the time, the very real problem of the analyst's concern over the effects of his writings on his patients, past or present, whether or not they are subjects of his clinical allusions. This will be the subject of another paper (Stein 1988).

REFERENCES

Dahl, H. (1974). The measurement of meaning in psychoanalysis by computer analysis of verbal contexts. *J. Amer. Psychoanal. Assn.* 22:35–57.

Deutsch, F. (1957). Footnote to Freud's fragment of analysis of a case of hysteria. *Psychoanal. Q.* 26:159–167.

Freud, S. (1900). The interpretation of dreams. *Standard Edition* 4 & 5.

——— (1905). Fragment of an analysis of a case of hysteria. *Standard Edition* 7.

——— (1909a). Analysis of a phobia in a five-year-old boy. *Standard Edition* 10.

——— (1909b). Notes upon a case of obsessional neurosis. *Standard Edition* 10.

——— (1912). Recommendations to physicians practicing analysis. *Standard Edition* 12.

——— (1918). From the history of an infantile neurosis. *Standard Edition* 17.

——— (1937). Analysis terminable and interminable. *Standard Edition* 23.

Gardiner, M. M. (1971). *The Wolf-Man by the Wolf-Man.* New York: Basic Books.

Gill, M. M., and Hoffman, E. Z. (1982). *Analysis of Transference*, vol. 2. New York: Int. Univ. Press.

Guttman, S. A., ed. (1982). *Concordance to the Standard Edition of the Complete Psychological Works of Sigmund Freud.* New York: Int. Univ. Press, 1984.

Janik, A., and Toulmin, S. (1973). *Wittgenstein's Vienna.* New York: Simon & Schuster.

Lewin, B. D. (1955). Dream psychology and the analytic situation. *Psychoanal. Q.* 24:169–199.

Mahony, P. J. (1982). *Freud as a Writer.* New York: Int. Univ. Press.

——— (1984). Further reflections on Freud and his writing. *J. Amer. Psychoanal. Assn.* 32:847–864.

Nunberg, H., and Federn, P., eds. (1967). *Minutes of the Vienna Psychoanalytic Society*, vol. 2. New York: Int. Univ. Press.

Panel (1963). Analysis terminable and interminable—twenty-five years later. *J. Amer. Psychoanal. Assn.* 11:131–142.

Plato (340 B.C.). Phaedrus. In *Collected Dialogues*, ed. E. Hamilton and H. Cairns. Princeton, N. J.: Princeton Univ. Press, 1961.

Reiser, M. (1985). Converging sectors of psychoanalysis and neurobiology: mutual challenge and opportunity. *J. Amer. Psychoanal. Assn.* 33:11–34.

Stein, M. H. (1965). States of consciousness in the analytic situation: including a note on the traumatic dream. In *Drives, Affects, Behavior*, vol. 2, ed. M. Schur. New York: Int. Univ. Press.

——— (1988). Writing about psychoanalysis: II. Patients who read. *J. Amer. Psychoanal. Assn.* 36(2).

Strachey, J. (1953). Editor's introduction. In Freud, S. (1900), *Standard Edition* 4.

ANALYSTS WHO WRITE, PATIENTS WHO READ

When we make a decision to lecture, or to write for publication, we have begun an activity that will affect every one of our patients. If they attend our lectures, or read our published works, they cannot help being influenced. Even if they do not, they will have some reaction to the focusing of our interest on particular phases of the analysis. This will be true whether or not we intend to present clinical material. These considerations inevitably affect the analyst himself, sometimes inhibiting his writing altogether, sometimes constricting its scope, or worst of all, degrading its quality. The analyst's writing is also almost certain to influence whether and with what success his patient may choose to write.

Lest these considerations suggest that we avoid writing altogether, I emphasize that such a sacrifice is by no means desirable or necessary. Problems of discretion will arise, and may in some cases be virtually insoluble, but there are ways of writing that can overcome most such objections. The analyst's interest in writing should be recognized and its effects, if any, brought into the analysis; so long as the writing itself is done with due regard to the conduct of the analysis and the welfare of the patient, it need have no adverse effects on either.

Having discussed some of the problems facing the psychoanalytic clinician who intends to write (Stein 1988), it is my intention to explore yet another reason why it is so difficult to present our primary data for others to examine, and why we often do it so clumsily. To listen to a colleague in a professional seminar relate his exchanges with a patient can be a stimulating experience; to hear or read a boiled-down version as part of a lecture is quite another thing. The experience is often frustrating, if not actually boring; we find ourselves wondering what the author has changed or omitted. Certainly, if we have heard the report before, presented in a private seminar or supervision, we become aware of the inhibition and distortion affecting the formal presentation.

I suggest that one of the more important factors, although by no means the only one, is the concern about the possible impact of our writing on our patients. According to Strachey (1958), this consideration made Freud reluctant to publish his ideas about technique. "He certainly disliked the notion of future patients knowing too much about the details of his technique, and he was aware that they would eagerly scan whatever he wrote on the subject" (p. 87). There is no doubt that as he gained more experience, certainly by 1920, he tended to avoid explicit clinical citations of any length. Why he found it necessary to do so, and how we ourselves are affected by such considerations, has been subjected to relatively little formal discussion. This is so even though we have, or should have by now, a good deal of understanding derived from our work with patients, many of whom are members of this or allied professions and are therefore likely to have read what we have written.

In my previous paper (1988), I considered some of the other factors that interfere with the presentation of clinical data and affect the production of even the most theoretical works. These include the need for discretion and the use of disguise, inhibitions derived from the history of psychoanalysis as a clinical discipline, problems of language, a dearth of the writing skills necessary for the explication of complex, nonquantifiable data, lack of time, fears of criticism by colleagues, and finally, an inherent preference for spoken dialogue as opposed to written argument. What I did not include in that list was concern over how our writing may affect our patients. While hardly the only, or even the chief, inhibitory or distorting influence in psychoanalytic writing, this is the most interesting from the point of view of transference, and countertransference as well.

For a patient to discover that his analyst is about to deliver a lecture in public is likely to create some inner disturbance, especially if he himself is an analyst or practicing in a related field. The same is true, to a lesser extent, of others who are, or who may have been in analysis. Patients ask themselves, "Shall I attend or stay away?" If currently in treatment, they may try to induce the analyst to make the decision and when he refuses to express a preference, ask themselves, "Does attending the lecture mean that I am 'acting out,' being uncooperative?" The analyst's refusal to give or withhold permission makes it more difficult for the patient to adhere to the belief that rule-breaking is really the issue, except with regard to that mass of unwritten laws and precepts which are thought by many to be the essence of a "real" analysis. It may be disconcerting to recognize that staying away may be just as much a form of "acting out" as attending. The analyst's neutrality has given freer rein to his patient's fantasies, which may be uncomfortable, but analytically useful. Either way, there is likely to be some disturbance, although it should not be of such a character or degree that it offers severe difficulties for the analysis. It is vital, however, that the issue be subjected to meticulous scrutiny, including watchfulness for clues in symptoms, dreams, and parapraxes which reveal such factors as hidden competitive, voyeuristic, and exhibitionistic impulses.

It may be anticipated that even when clinical descriptions are avoided, presenting anything at all is likely to effect some disturbance in the state of the transference. Any appearance of the analyst in an extra-analytic setting becomes a source of conflict for his patient, not to mention himself. The occasion is likely to stimulate the ever-present desire to know what the analyst is like outside the rarefied atmosphere of the office. Some patients are very frank about their hunger for knowledge about the mysterious person who sits behind them and murmurs a few words now and then, while others go to great lengths to deny any interest at all. We are nevertheless inclined to take it for granted that all patients have to cope with *some* curiosity about our lives outside the office. While this assumption on our part may he regarded as a manifestation of a professional tendency to exaggerated self-importance, the phenomenon of transference curiosity is ubiquitous if not universal, and our assumption of its presence is based on more than narcissism. We are familiar with the intense eagerness of children to know more about their parents, especially concerning matters the latter are least willing to talk about. Correspondingly, the analytic situation becomes a ready-made stimulus to the revival of transference curiosity, often highly erotized. The total absence of this phenomenon in an analysis is as much a resistance as provocative prying into the analyst's private affairs. Sometimes the anxiety associated with voyeuristic impulses causes the patient to experience a kind of pseudo-imbecility, so that when he hears or reads a paper by his analyst, he cannot understand it, even though he may be well qualified to do so by intellect and professional training. This phenomenon has something in common with attempts to recall a particularly traumatic primal scene experience (Mahler 1942).

The prospect that one's analyst may appear in public arouses conflicts revolving about both idealizing and competitive tendencies. A patient may be both eager and afraid to see how his analyst conducts himself. Perhaps he will be pompous, make a fool of himself and embarrass his patient, who up to now has regarded him as a sensible, even wise mentor. If the analyst does indeed perform badly, his patient may imagine he is somehow responsible, by upsetting the speaker in advance or even by fixing an intense and disconcerting gaze on him during the lecture. Some patients experience a disturbing fantasy: if they attend, they will be impelled to create a disturbance in the lecture hall, thus drawing attention to themselves and away from the lecturer; the analyst will be publicly embarrassed by his analysand's behavior, rather as a proud mother feels when her child has a tantrum in the supermarket. The fear of attending a bad performance or of spoiling a good one is by no means rare in patients who experience severe envy and competitiveness, often disguised by the most reverential attitude. They are often the "well-behaved patients" I have described elsewhere (Stein 1981).

Hearing the analyst lecture or reading his writings also furnishes the patient with a golden opportunity for the expression of hostile criticism. Freud (1915–1917) related one such experience: "A sceptical woman patient had a longish dream in the course of which some people told her about my book on jokes [1905] and praised it highly." Her ingenious dream (*le Pas de Calais*, "from the sublime to the ridiculous") represented an opportunity to compete with

Freud by making a joke and ridiculing his ideas at the same time.[1]

To cite from my own experience: a patient came across a paper in which I had discussed the work of a colleague, describing my substantial disagreement with his ideas. She was very troubled, because she saw a side of me she had never allowed herself to contemplate before, that I might be capable of being harsh, if not actually vicious. She was gratified to have discovered a secret, even though its nature was troubling. I cannot say this interfered seriously with the analytic work, although it required some effort to analyze its manifold meanings. Fortunately, she was able to distinguish between the analytic personality with which she was familiar and the more critical, less benign person she detected in my writing.

Another patient attended a lecture of mine and, after some hesitation, admitted he had found it "disappointing." I saw no need to confess that my reaction had been the same. Again, he had been in analysis for some time, and was able to deal with his detection of my clay feet without losing his ability to regard me as competent enough for his purposes. How he would have reacted if the lecture had been really imbecilic, instead of being poorly organized and rather dull, I cannot say. Certainly he would have had more trouble with it. As it was, he was pleased to see himself as capable of doing better, and my performance was not bad enough to destroy altogether his confidence in me as an analyst.

A woman who had received a notice of a lecture I was to deliver found at the last moment that she could not bring herself to attend. If I were to perform brilliantly, that would be disturbing; her intense competitiveness would come to the fore. If, on the other hand, I did badly, she would feel terribly disappointed. Having stayed away on that occasion however, she kept her ears open during the following days to learn how her friends, uninhibited by transference, had reacted.

These are only a few examples of the ways analytic patients may react to the news that the analyst is going to speak in public; it would be easy to cite many more. We may as well accept that once an analyst publishes a paper containing any clinical data, it is virtually certain that sooner or later it will be read by some of his patients, who will imagine that they themselves have been portrayed. Often enough these suppositions do reflect the truth, that the analyst has learned something from his patient's analysis, which he has now

---

[1]An element in the dream was the word "channel," to which the patient associated a joke she had heard: "On the steamer between Dover and Calais a well-known author fell into conversation with an Englishman. The latter had occasion to quote the phrase: 'Du sublime au ridicule il n'y a qu'un pas. [It is only a step from the sublime to the ridiculous.]' 'Yes,' replied the author, '*Le Pas de Calais*'—meaning that he thought France sublime and England ridiculous. But the *Pas de Calais* is a channel—the English Channel" (Freud 1915–1917, pp. 118–119).

cited to make a point. Not infrequently, however, the patients are in error; the paper they have heard or read may have been completed before they and the analyst met for the first time; or the latter may have had someone else in mind. In any case, the analysand's belief that he has taught his analyst something of value is gratifying, for it is regarded as a gift and experienced as a contribution to the enlargement of the analyst's professional skill and reputation. Patient and analyst have become collaborators in an activity outside the bounds of the analytic process, a development that brings about its own set of problems.

A clinical report by Silverman (1985) demonstrates how the analyst's attempts to deal with his patient's resistances forced him to analyze certain conflicts within himself. The emphasis on the countertransference made it necessary to reveal rather more about the author than we generally find in psychoanalytic papers. It also made it possible for him to write a fairly lengthy and effective case report which gave relatively little identifying material about the patient, at the same time bringing out very clearly how working with him had taught the analyst a good deal about himself and the process of analysis.

The collaboration of observer and subject in the field of ethnography has been discussed by Clifford (1983). Among other questions, he asked whether the informant, the member of the tribe who assisted the scholar, should receive credit as co-author. We may ask as well, "Should our patients receive such credit?" The answer is that they should, and such credit is often implicit. We are all grateful to Anna O., to Dora, and the other patients who taught Freud so much. Naming and identifying the patients who inspired us to write is another matter; ideally, they remain anonymous donors to whom we express gratitude, but we do not identify them.

Certain patients express explicitly the wish that I might write about their analyses. This desire reflects not only the expected exhibitionistic components, but the unconscious fantasy that my writing would be a most intimate collaboration, the equivalent of sharing in the conception of a child. I suspect that this fantasy is more common than we generally recognize in the context of analytic writing. It is likely to be especially significant because of its origins in the ubiquitous incestuous preoccupations of children, who so often entertain fantasies, sometimes conscious, of impregnating or being impregnated by parents.

We need not assume that such fantasies are confined to analysands. Professional writers often preface their works with dedications and acknowledgments in terms that suggest, to the psychoanalyst at least, that someone—a spouse, an editor, an agent—played a role in the production, which could be regarded as a kind of impregnation. Analysts may well have in common with professional writers the fantasy of the book as offspring, to be brought forth in pain and travail. Just as the analyst's interpretations may be viewed as impregnating the patient's mind, so, too, the associations of the patient may impregnate the mind of the analyst. We might be impelled to ask, "Is the offspring legitimate? Should the parentage be acknowledged, and if so, how?" How many analysts experience such conflicts as a source of inhibition of writing and publishing, I do not know, but it is a factor worth considering when preparing a clinical paper, i.e., one to which patients have contributed pretty directly. The very need for discretion in identifying one of the parties to the conception may introduce elements of guilt more appropriate to an illicit sexual liaison than to the preparation of a scientific paper. This may be less evident, but at a more subtle level still applicable to papers which are confined to more abstract theoretical discussions, since even they are or should be based ultimately on what the writer has learned from his work with patients. Rather than assuming that parthenogenesis has been at work, it would be wise to acknowledge, at least to oneself, these conceptual debts.

It seems almost superfluous to emphasize once again that the analyst's writing creates complications in the analysis of the transference. While we no longer expect to analyze the transference out of existence, we do hope to be able to resolve ("cure"?) the transference neurosis, that complex of fantasies, affects, and symptoms which represent the "transferring" of the patient's infantile conflicts onto the image of the analyst as object. We need not doubt that collaboration of patient and analyst in an activity not strictly analytic complicates this task. We can be sure that our writings, whether or not they include clinical data, have significant and complex meanings for our patients and for ourselves in relation to those patients. To ignore this would be a mistake.

Familiarity with the analyst's writings, even if they are predominantly theoretical, or in the field of "applied" analysis, may foster the tendency to carry out those very ideas in action. One patient was explicit: he said, "I'll have to read your Pepys paper again to see what you're thinking about this." He was troubled by fantasies of sexual experiences outside of marriage; perhaps my (1977) treatment of Samuel Pepys's philandering would give him a clue to my attitudes toward sexual freedom. It was a fairly obvious resistance to analyzing some of the thornier areas of his own very punitive conscience.

A psychotherapist who was beginning his private practice, was very worried about his ability to set up an office and attract patients. One day he arrived, lay down on the couch, and said, in a mocking tone, "It would be more valuable to write papers on how to set one's fees, than on subjects like 'irony!' " This was his way of acknowledging that he had seen my paper on the subject (1985) in a current issue of *The Journal of the American Psychoanalytic Association*. His resentment was real; while I had interpreted the nature and sources of his anxiety, I had refrained from giving him more directly the benefit of my long experience in practice. His associations then led to his experience with his parents, who had advised him on all sorts of things, such as politics and sports, but had carefully avoided any discussion of the really important issues in life: sex and money. The publication of my paper gave him an opening to attack me on similar grounds, and to give us some leads into the genesis of the transference neurosis.

Several patients who had read my paper, "The Unobjectionable Part of the Transference" (1981), proceeded to make themselves "objectionable" in a very special way. Having concluded that they themselves might have fallen into the category of "well-behaved patients" characterized in that paper, they began to modify their behavior, to show that they could discard the kind of resistance I had described, i.e., that which took the form of being extremely cooperative, compliant, and too ready to accept interventions. They became less prompt about attending and paying their bills, demonstrated anger more openly, even nastily on occasion, and questioned the cleverest of my interpretations. We soon recognized that they were still being "good" patients, their apparent disobedience being in accord with my "rules," as they derived them from my paper. It would be difficult to cite a better example of irony in psychoanalysis (Stein 1985). Recognizing the nature of this opposition, which was still paradoxically a kind of conformity, became very useful in approaching deeper levels of hostility embedded in the transference, hostility which was now openly displayed for the first time after years of analysis. Previously, we had merely talked about such impulses; now, rather than remaining interesting abstractions, they became subject to meaningful analytic work. Such resistances occur regularly during termination, of course; my having written about them seems to have brought some transference issues to the fore in a fashion and in an order not quite the same as if I had never done so. The writing had indeed created an interference, although not an insuperable one, one which could, with effort, be turned to use.

By no means does this imply that such results can be best attained by having patients acquire their ideas by reading one's works; ideally it would be better if they did not, and transference issues were dealt with during the ordinary course of analysis. But while to prohibit reading would be futile and destructive, a stimulus to acting out one way or another, encouraging patients to read one's writings, or for that matter, works by others, is a questionable practice, at best creating a difficult intellectualizing resistance, and at worst leading to an unresolvable transference mess.

One patient described her reactions when a previous analyst, in an attempt to explain an interpretation, asked her to read aloud a paragraph from a book the analyst had written. She became extremely anxious and did not understand a word she was reading. The analysis was broken off a few months later, the patient feeling very inadequate and discouraged. This incident did not lead directly to the end of the treatment, but it might well have become a factor in an unhappy termination.

It is uncertain how many psychoanalysts write with the wish to have their writings read by their patients. This may well be a motive in those who write for the popular market, but these would be a small minority. Generally, the practicing analyst is aware that having his papers read by his patients is a fertile source of resistance. Most often, we wish to be noticed by our colleagues, and would be just as pleased if patients did not come across our writings, even if it means foregoing the brief and misleading satisfactions derived from flattery from the couch, or the rather less gratifying experience of textual criticism from that same source.

I have heard, at second-hand, of a patient who had read everything her analyst had written. After his death, these memories were added to those of the analysis itself, supporting what sounded like a persistent idealized transference. How often this occurs, I do not know, but I am sure it is not unique. The implications are troubling.

It is not only the analysand who is affected by the analyst's writing, for the very preparation of a psychoanalytic paper exerts its effects even more certainly and immediately on the analyst himself. It may be the patient, however, who first senses that his analyst is interested in some special phase of the process. Perhaps he becomes aware that the latter is more responsive to accounts of parapraxes, dreams, or somatic symptoms, that he reacts more promptly to certain types of associations, shows unusual curiosity about special types of data, or reveals in other ways that he is in a state of alertness at the appearance of particular phenomena. Sensitive patients pick up the signals very quickly, noting even changes in voice or breathing, not to mention such indicators as books and papers piled upon the desk. It is difficult, if not impossible, to conceal such signs of intense interest, and it is by no means certain that it is worth the effort.

Once, when I was preparing a paper on a special aspect of dreaming, a patient who had become aware that I had a keen interest in the subject brought in many dreams, with abundant associations, often leading to satisfying interpretations. Both of us recognized this was a seductive enterprise. We hardly required the confirmation contained in her remark one day, "I have a dream for you today, you'll love this one!" I was not prepared to renounce my interest in dreams; what I had to do was to recognize the nature of the resistance and to keep in focus the other aspects of the analysis, so as to avoid being drawn into a procedure based too heavily on dream interpretation, to the detriment of other aspects. It might have been anticipated that when we began to plan the termination of her analysis and she experienced some of the more hostile elements of the transference, she brought almost no dreams, and the few she recalled were virtually impossible to analyze. The resistances would have occurred anyway; her awareness of my particular interest gave them a special form.

In his discussion of countertransference, Silverman (1985) does not tell us whether an intention to write a paper was a factor in his attitude toward his patient. It may well have been an afterthought, but even if it was, could it have been dormant, but still capable of influencing the analysis?

I have no doubt that similar influences operate whenever the analyst is "working on something," whether it is for the purpose of lecturing, publication, teaching, or exploring any special line of thought that interests him at the time. We see analogous effects with great clarity in the work of candidates who are being supervised. They listen, not always deliberately, for what they expect will interest the supervisor. The analysis is inevitably influenced, but it need not be impaired, so long as this factor is taken into account by both participants in the supervision. A recent paper by Arlow (1985) is particularly relevant in this connection.

A patient engaged in a field related to psychoanalysis is most likely to be affected by his awareness of whether or not his analyst writes. If the latter does publish a good deal, he may feel encouraged to do likewise, as an expression of identification, or the need to compete, or both. He may be impelled to show up his analyst by writing works on a higher level of theory, to be more original and lively and to acquire more popularity, or he may suffer a sense of despair over his inability to compete. He might, on the other hand, be afraid of arousing his analyst's envy, writing better than one's analyst being one way of living out the oedipal conflict, with all of its potential triumphs and terrifying risks. An analysand may be impelled to write by the wish to make his analyst proud of him for furnishing such convincing evidence of a "successful" analysis. To what extent this favors good writing is another matter. Pleasing one's analyst in this fashion may appear to be a favorable development, but it contains the elements of resistance, and as such is subject to all the vicissitudes of the transference.

In the following example, the writer is not a colleague, but the principles apply. A novelist who had published a great many popular books developed the impression that I was not especially impressed by what he had written. I had, in fact, read none of his writings, but had seen favorable reviews and heard good reports about his work. After a few months of analysis, he started to work on a complex historical novel, altogether different from the relatively brief, direct, and vigorous stories he had written so successfully before. It soon became evident that he was trying to impress and please me, whose literary taste, he imagined, made it impossible for me to appreciate the books he had written for the popular market. Fortunately, his astute literary agent was able to deter him from proceeding with what sounded like a very pretentious effort, and persuaded him to return to his more familiar genre. Some years after his analysis, I satisfied my curiosity about his novels, which I found lively and well written.

Wishes to impress, please, humiliate, or glorify one's analyst hardly constitute sound bases for good writing. None of these motives is likely to lead to works of true originality, but rather to writing in forced and pretentious styles. It is as if the writer must give up his "voice," in attempting to develop a new one to please his analyst. The novelist I cited had not, to my knowledge, read anything I had written, but he was familiar with the way I spoke, the periodicals I kept in my waiting room, and other clues to my taste to which he felt he had to conform. In the case of colleagues, such influences are even stronger, so that there is a good chance that what they write will be dominated by attempts to confirm the principles they ascribe to me, perhaps in the form of polemics—or the reverse. Such efforts are quite different from those which reveal the more desirable influence of good teachers and supervisors who, having been experienced in different settings, become more appropriate role models. Personal tributes and polemical works have their place, but they are likely to be of higher quality if they are not dominated by heavy residues of an analytic transference.

If psychoanalysis presents any danger at all to writers or other creative individuals, it is that the writer may be impelled to please or defy his analyst through his *writing*, rather than directly and more appropriately within the analytic situation itself. This can happen, as illustrated above, but it should not be an intractable problem. It is a fine example of acting out in the transference, in which the patient, who has been trying to please or defy some figure out of his past, now tries to please or defy his analyst. This is much more likely to happen if the analysand perceives his analyst as a writer himself, or even as one with critical pretensions. This should not be too difficult to analyze if we are careful not to fall into the trap of becoming a critic.

If a patient who is a colleague or a candidate in training finds that he disagrees with the ideas expressed in his analyst's writings, he may find it very difficult to express these differences. Worst of all, he might be impelled to suppress his disagreement, casting it out of the scope of his attention, so that it never reaches awareness during the session. To avoid interfering with his patient's creativity and spoiling his analysis at the same time calls for a good deal of tolerance and understanding on the part of the analyst, which must be matched by courage and trust on the part of the analysand. It is particularly important that such scientific disagreements be treated with respect and not as if they were inevitably manifestations of acting out, and therefore lacking in substance. This is a non sequitur in any case; the outcome of a piece of acting out *may* turn out to have substantial value. An analysand's scientific disagreement with his analyst is bound to be influenced by the transference; he may nevertheless be making a valid point. Clarity may be achieved only after relevant transference conflicts have been adequately explored and analyzed.

Ultimately, the effect of the analyst's writings on the analysis, deleterious or not, will depend not only on what the analyst has written, but to an even greater extent on how his patient has perceived his motives and attitudes. He may view his analyst as sincerely interested in the scientific advancement of psychoanalysis, combining this with clinical concern and personal regard, or, he may view him as personally ambitious, self-absorbed, indifferent and condescending.

Clearly, it would be unfortunate for a patient to acquire the idea that his analyst is more interested in his own investigations and their exploitation than in his, the patient's analytic progress. We are familiar enough with the definition of analysis which embodies its role as a method of investigation; indeed we recognize that this aspect is linked inextricably with its therapeutic efficiency. We cannot assume however, that our patients find this so easy to accept. If the analyst becomes so preoccupied with his own special interests that he loses his perspective, the patient may very well sense before he does that something is wrong. He may try to deal with it by silence and acting out, which are at least obvious forms of resistance, or worse, he may oblige by bringing in material which will support what he has sensed are his analyst's ideas. Such a reaction is potentially damaging not only to the analytic outcome, but to the value of whatever the analyst is engaged in studying. Misleading one's analyst by compliant confirmation, tempting him to reach hasty and fallacious conclusions, may be regarded as a most exquisite example of masochistic revenge. Let the analyst beware!

CONCLUSIONS

One of the more subtle and important factors that dissuades analysts from writing and publishing clinical papers, and may impair the quality of what is written, is concern over the reaction of patients. This consideration is not limited to questions of discretion, vital as they are, but includes complex transference and countertransference issues. These must be brought into the analysis and be subjected as well to the analyst's own self-scrutiny, both for the sake of the analysis itself and what is to be written about it.

REFERENCES

Arlow, J. (1985). Some technical problems of countertransference. *Psychoanal. Q.* 54:164–174.

Clifford, J. (1983). On ethnographic authority. *Representations* 1(2):118–146.

Freud, S. (1905). Jokes and their relation to the unconscious. *Standard Edition* 8.

——— (1912). Recommendations to physicians practicing analysis. *Standard Edition* 12.

——— (1914). Papers on technique. *Standard Edition* 12.
——— (1915-1917). Introductory lectures on psycho-analysis. *Standard Edition* 15 and 16.
Mahler, M. S. (1942). Pseudoimbecility: the magic cap of invisibility. *Psychoanal. Q.* 11:149–164.
Silverman, M. A. (1985). Countertransference and the myth of the perfectly analyzed analyst. *Psychoanal. Q.* 54:175–199.
Stein, M. H (1977). A psychoanalytic view of mental health: Samuel Pepys and his diary. *Psychoanal. Q.* 46:82–115.
——— (1981). The unobjectionable part of the transference. *J. Amer. Psychoanal. Assn.* 29:869–892.
——— (1985). Irony in psychoanalysis. *J. Amer. Psychoanal. Assn.* 33:35–57.
Strachey, J. (1958). Editor's introduction. In Freud, 1914, *Standard Edition* 12, pp. 85–88.

13

How Dreams Are Told: Secondary Revision—The Critic, the Editor, and the Plagiarist

Secondary revision is a highly provocative concept arising out of Freud's attempts to explain the construction of dreams, but it remains relatively ill-defined. It includes three related, yet by no means identical aspects of the process by which the dream acquires its more or less final form during the experiencing, the remembering, and the telling. It represents one of the most interesting hypotheses dealing with the fluid world between sleeping and waking, a field which still presents us with a host of unanswered questions.

Secondary revision not only reflects the higher levels of the dreamer's mental functioning superimposed on his biological substructure, but it also operates as a sensitive indicator of the cultural factors which have helped mold his personality. These factors include both the subculture of the analytic situation and the impact of society in the larger sense. I make reference to individual dreamers in analysis and to the world of dreams recorded in the past from our own and other cultures.

THE CONCLUSION

Now reader, I have told my dream to thee,
See if thou canst interpret it to me
Or to thyself or neighbor: but take heed
Of misinterpreting: for that instead
Of doing good, will but thyself abuse:
By misinterpreting evil ensues.
Take heed also that thou be not extreme,
In playing with the outside of my dream:
Nor let my figure or similitude

Put thee into a laughter or a feud;
Leave this for boys and fools; but as for thee,
Do thou the substance of my matter see.
Put by the curtains, look within my veil;
Turn up my metaphors, and do not fail:
There if thou seekest them such things to find,
As will be helpful to an honest mind.
What of my dross thou findest there, be bold
To throw away, yet preserve the gold.
What if my gold be wrapped up in ore?
None throws away the apple for the core:
But if thou shalt cast all away as vain,
I know not but 'twill make me dream again.
The End

Although "The Conclusion" expresses ideas about dreaming similar to Freud's, the language gives it away as having been written much earlier, over 300 years ago in fact. It comes at the end of Part One of *The Pilgrim's Progress*, by John Bunyan, not strictly speaking a book on dream interpretation. It has nevertheless a curious bearing on our subject, the role of secondary revision in giving final form to the tales told by dreamers.

I shall discuss how the dream, experienced in a state of sleep, is then transformed into a tale that can be remembered, told to oneself and to another person. Inevitably, this will bring me to the borders of literature, and I shall take the opportunity to refer not only to the dreams of individuals known to me as patients and otherwise, but shall employ as well some classic examples of dreams recorded long ago. As analysts, however, we cannot rest content with listening to and enjoying these dream tales, or even critically studying the texts, as a literary critic might, but are obliged to seek out their underlying meanings, the unconscious elements which are both concealed and expressed in the manifest dream. We try to understand how the dream is transformed into a story, and what that process tells us not only about the nature of the dreamer's deepest conflicts, but more particularly, his resources for dealing with them which include, as I shall point out, his cultural origins.

We may begin with some questions about how we observe dreams in practice. When a patient reports a dream, how do we know what he has really dreamed? To what extent has the dream been modified, condensed, or elaborated during the lapse of time between waking and the recalling and telling of it? If we were to insist that the dream be treated as if it were a precisely demarcated process of thought and affect, occurring during a finite period of sleep, we would be operating with false premises and setting ourselves a task for which we have never had adequate methods and for which answers may not be available. We can measure the length of dreaming *periods* in an individual sleeper by following evidences of electrical activity in the cortex, but this tells us only that the subject was probably dreaming at certain times. If we waken him, he may be able to relate his dream, true, but can we be sure that the very process of awakening did not introduce changes in the text, which will now appear in his report of what he dreamed? (Mack, in Panel, 1984).

Most of the dreams told to us are "dreamlike," full of contradictions and inconsistencies, mixed up in time and space, making little sense at first. A patient related a dream he described as "weird": "There were two men, handsome, well-built, but without arms or legs, as if they had been amputated. They looked identical, like twins. They seemed to be suspended in air, and fighting with each other, but playfully, as if embracing." The dreamer made no attempt to explain how they could do so without limbs. Given its "raw" quality, this account could never be mistaken for a realistic narrative. With the aid of the dreamer's associations, it was relatively easy to relate the dream to masturbatory conflicts and fantasies of castration, confirmed by the dreamer's subsequent remarks. Perhaps most dreams are "weird" in this sense, demonstrating clearly Freud's three original aspects of the dream work: condensation, displacement, and the choice of means of representation.

Even under ordinary conditions, however, certain dreams of both adults and children appear to have a logical structure, with a beginning, a middle, and an end, and to convey rather commonplace ideas. If we accept the surface message, we may find little evidence of unconscious conflict or grossly unacceptable wishes. These well-organized dreams may portray "cure," or perhaps sudden good fortune, like winning a lottery, or sexual success (as in the case of the dream of Samuel Pepys, below). On the face of it these dreams make sense and tell coherent stories; at times it is difficult to be sure whether we are listening to an account of a dream or to that of an actual event. It is tempting to take such stories at face value and be satisfied with the dreamer's interpretation as sufficiently meaningful. Being faced with no new and unpleasant material, he is likely to be pleased by such an approach. Often these interpretations are banal or abstract and metaphorical, conveying some sort of moral lesson or philosophical message.[1]

What has happened in these instances to the unconscious contributions to the dream of "the terrible, savage, and lawless form of desires," ascribed to the dreamer by Plato, and Freud after him? And why dream at all, while one can daydream pleasurable ideas and consciously reject painful ones? It is difficult to accept that dreaming, which occupies so much of our interest and

[1]The latter, "anagogic" interpretation (a term introduced by Silberer), Freud regarded as altogether superfluous, and likely to divert attention from the more significant psychoanalytic interpretation (Freud 1900, p. 524).

energies, deals with banal anecdotes and inferior movie scripts. Freud did not believe it, and we are inclined to follow him in choosing to extend our inquiries beyond the readily available message of the unplumbed manifest dream.

It was in order to deal with the many questions raised by the apparent rationality and logical organization of certain manifest dreams that Freud evolved the concept of secondary revision. His account was not an exhaustive one, nor did it constitute the clearest section of his work, for it contained many ambiguities and undefined areas. This is in accord with the nature of the subject itself, for while we may pretend that we can be clear about the line of demarcation between sleeping and waking phenomena, these are in fact not always so easily distinguished, even by the well-balanced among us. It is generally impossible to say exactly where the dream work proper ends and secondary revision begins (Stein 1965).

Freud's discussion may remind us therefore of an exciting but unfinished sketch by a great artist, containing thinly painted and overpainted areas which reveal tentative and half-concealed figures. Such sketches make special demands on the viewer, stimulating questions and speculations; these unfinished works are often more fascinating and productive of new ideas than those which have been completed. I have no intention of trying to complete Freud's sketch in order to ascertain where the limits of the process are to be located; they are too fluid for that. Rather, let us see where a study of the sketch itself leads us.

Aside from a brief allusion in a letter to Fliess (dated July 7, 1897; Freud 1887–1902, pp. 211–213), secondary revision was first anticipated in the statement: "It is hardly rash to assume that the unintelligibility of the dream's content . . . has led to its being recast in a form designed to make sense of the situation . . . this misunderstanding must be regarded as one of the factors in determining the final form assumed by dreams" (Freud 1900, p. 243). The solution is foreshadowed in the passage: "Even the judgements made *after waking* upon a dream that has been remembered, and the feelings called up in us by the reproduction of such a dream, form part, to a great extent, of the latent content of the dream and are to be included in its interpretation" (1900, p. 445). But Freud did not tackle the problem in earnest until he reached the section on secondary revision. He first included it as part of the dream work, but later recognized that it could not be so narrowly confined (1923, p. 241). The dream, faced with the demand to be put into words and told, if only to oneself, is modified to make it more acceptable to the common sense and moral sensibilities of the dreamer and perhaps to others to whom it may be told. This may take place during sleep, upon the moment of awakening, or at some later time. Secondary revision, therefore, unlike the dream work proper, is not confined to the sleeping state, but merges into waking and is the major contribution of waking thought to the final version of the dream. The questions raised by this phenomenon were eventually to make clear the need for a more inclusive model of the mind which could encompass the idea of functions which were not defined by their qualities of being conscious or unconscious, a task which was not to be accomplished until *The Ego and the Id* was published in 1923.

Secondary revision has in any case never been easy to define, and the term itself is not altogether adequate to describe its various aspects. Freud's name for the process was *sekundäre Bearbeitung*, first translated, as "secondary elaboration" (1900, p. 488, fn. 1), later to be replaced by the current and somewhat more accurate "secondary revision." Freud described, without sharply distinguishing, three related but somewhat different aspects of the process. Keeping in mind that they are hypothetical functions and by no means sharply separated, I have chosen for the sake of this discussion to give them anthropomorphic titles: "the Critic," "the Editor," and "the Plagiarist."

THE CRITIC

The first type of revision occurs when "the dreamer is surprised, annoyed or repelled in the dream, and, moreover, by a piece of the dream-content itself" (Freud 1900, p. 488). Citing the statement, "This is only a dream," Freud pointed out that this occurs most often as a prelude to waking, and that it constitutes a criticism of the dream, made generally because the censorship has been taken unawares by some disturbing image or affect. There are other remarks that may be included under this heading, e.g., "I had a weird dream" (as in the case cited earlier), "This dream is unimportant," or "I had a dream; it was ridiculous; I only had it to get your attention," or, in a different vein, "I have a dream for you; you'll love this one!" These remarks may occur during sleep, upon waking, or when the dream is communicated to the listener. They tell a good deal about the significance of the dream and are frequently laden with valuable clues to the state of the transference.

The first example, "This is only a dream," may indeed be an attempt to reject or devalue the experience. In this case wakening may have brought a sense of relief. Typical is the "examination dream," which many of us have experienced at some time or other. For example, a lecturer who was soon to deliver an important address dreamed he had arrived in another city for that purpose, and on the way to his hotel discovered he had left his lecture notes behind. He tried to telephone his wife at home; perhaps she could get his notes to him on time. But somehow he could not get a call through. Would he have to speak from memory, which now became vague even as to the subject of his address? He awoke, still anxious, and then said to himself, "Thank God it was only a dream!" As he sighed with relief, he decided to make some further changes in his half-finished manuscript, and was thus able to put aside whatever deeply buried conflicts had contributed to his dream.

The expressions, "This is only a dream" or, "This is a weird dream" imply another function as well, which Freud failed to mention in this context, although it is implicit throughout his writings on the sense of reality. The statement reassures the dreamer that he is returning to the wide-awake state, the "real" world, and more important, that he is still alive and in possession of his senses, not crazy. These announcements act as vehicles for the resistance, which denies the significance of the dream and thus prevents recognition of the underlying conflicts which have stimulated it. At the same time they signify the triumph of the sense of reality, the return to sanity. (This double accomplishment constitutes a striking example of Waelder's [1930] principle of multiple function.)

The statement, "This is of no importance," may be understood to imply the opposite of what it says. It is a challenge to the analyst to unravel the secret, a challenge which it is usually worthwhile to accept.

The dream that was presented as "ridiculous, only to get your attention," was about death: the text of the dream and the associations to it revealed the dreamer's own overwhelming fears of his desire to join those loved ones who had died; he did indeed want my attention to protect him from the fatality to which he felt so powerfully drawn.

"You'll love this one!" is a frank admission that the dream is a gift to the analyst, who is expected to be gracious enough to receive it as such. If he is obstinate enough to insist on analyzing it, he must be prepared to deal with hurt feelings in response. Again the resistance is served, this time with charm. Picking up this challenge may teach one a good deal about the state of the transference, especially its seductive elements, the so-called "unobjectionable part of the transference," which I have discussed elsewhere (1981).

These critical remarks about the dream are the most obvious manifestations of secondary revision. We are familiar with them, and usually find ourselves ready to take them into account. The resistance is at least openly displayed; we know what we are up against. Other aspects of secondary revision are much less easily detected; which brings me now to the Editor, a far more subtle fellow who, if he is skillful, reveals few obvious traces of his efforts in the final version of the text.

THE EDITOR

The second function included under the heading of secondary revision is the "editing" of the manifest dream, the attempt to clean it up and at the same time render it more logical, reasonable, and acceptable to common sense. Isakower (1954) suggested using the term, "redaction," meaning "reduction to literary form" (*Oxford English Dictionary*, 1971). It was a more precise rendition of the editing activity of secondary revision, but it never caught on. I shall use it to refer to this "editorial" function, to distinguish it from the critical and plagiarizing aspects. It is closely associated with the process of transforming the visual imagery of the dream into words, so that it may be mastered, put into context, and committed to memory. Only then does it become possible to tell the dream to oneself and others.

The most obvious function of secondary redaction, however, is to repair or at least conceal the ravages of forgetting. We know that most dreams are forgotten very quickly, in whole or in part. In the latter case, the dreamer is impelled to fill in the gaps with whatever material he has at hand. He may be regarded, somewhat unfairly, as confabulating, like the alcoholic patient suffering from Korsakoff's syndrome, who makes up elaborate stories to conceal that his memory for events has been largely lost. In these patients, forgetting is chiefly determined by organic deficits; in the dreamer, it is brought about dynamically, by repression for the most part. (While some of the forgetting may be in the service of "clearing the mind" of unimportant "baggage," as emphasized by some experimental investigators, the dynamic role is far more interesting for our purposes.) We are familiar with the observation that it is far more difficult to remember a fragmentary text than a complete one. If, for example, we try to memorize a poem with a few lines omitted here and there, we simply fill them in, with made-up material if necessary. We do the same with the half-forgotten dream. The story is at least more coherent and more easily committed to memory than before, even if it still does not make much sense. The synthetic function of the ego requires that there be a continuous story line; the dreamer supplies one.

Secondary redaction may be undertaken for other reasons, for example, telling a good story or conveying a message; it may serve a moral or didactic purpose, or one of entertainment and distraction. Editing may be employed, therefore, not only to remember better and to arouse interest in the listener, but also to create a "cover story," to discourage deeper exploration of painful issues. "Disinformation" was not invented by governments, although it seems to have become a special prerogative of dreamers in high places.

If we accept the ubiquity of secondary redaction, recognizing that it plays a significant role in determining the final form in which most dreams are cast, it may be possible to understand more clearly the relation between manifest and latent dream. It is secondary redaction that allows the manifest dream (Freud's metaphorical rebus) to appear as if it made literal sense and its logic were genuine. It is meant to be deceptive, and yet furnish clues, like the cipher that conceals a secret message under an apparently sensible but purposefully misleading text. As analysts, we need not regard ourselves as unduly suspicious if we are reluctant to take literally the obvious messages conveyed by manifest dreams. Through secondary redaction, the dreamer has further concealed the disturbing nature of the dream by adding a mass of detail, much of it irrelevant to the central conflict. It was this aspect of secondary revision which gave rise to the term "secondary elaboration," now lapsed into disuse (although Silber [1973] has argued for its retention).

The following is an example of an extensively edited dream:

> I was driving from Cape Cod to New York in my MG. A Mercedes convertible passed me going the other way. It was driven by a very elegantly dressed young woman. I stopped at a restaurant where my brother and his family were having lunch. They'd been driving along in their station wagon. I told them about the young woman in the Mercedes . . . Route One is not the fastest road, but it is the prettiest, and is a feasible alternative to the Turnpike. If I were unmarried and had no children, I could still be driving my MG, instead of the big station wagon I now own. Marriage may be a burden, but nevertheless I prefer it to being a bachelor.

The dream was actually much longer in the telling, taking up most of the session with an exhaustively detailed account of scenery and events along the road, rather like a travel guide in literary form. The conflict between marriage and bachelorhood had been clear enough; there was no secret about that. We were never successful in analyzing the dream more deeply, but we may assume that the latent dream thoughts included much more material of a less acceptable variety; there had been plenty of evidence elsewhere in the analytic work to confirm such a hypothesis.

This typical example of a long, highly organized, and elaborated dream was employed to disguise what was really troubling the dreamer, while it revealed very little that was new. Did this organizing process take place during the dream itself? Was it part of the dream? Does the dream end when the dreamer awakens, or does some kind of dream thinking persist after the sleeper has gotten out of bed and brushed his teeth? The latter is likely enough, for we have seen what changes can occur when a dream is retold later in the analytic session, or on the following day (Silber 1973). This patient was not aware of having organized his dream as if he were writing a story, yet it was clear that he had done so. Since he was a gifted raconteur, it was not surprising that such organization came readily to him, whether working at his typewriter or reporting dreams (Stein 1984). He did convey a message in the manifest dream, but the latter told us nothing we had not known before, including his predilection for telling a well-organized story rather than associating, which was how he dealt with the vast majority of the dreams he related. In contrast to the patient who reported the dream of the two torsos, this dreamer employed secondary redaction to a far greater extent, reflecting the complexity of his character and cultural level and the effectiveness of his defenses which had available the organizing capacities already built into his ego structure. It was evident that he had a very skillful dream Editor.

Fortunately for analytic work, redaction is not usually so complete so that while dreams may appear to make a certain amount of sense in their manifest appearance, enough inconsistencies are detectable to allow an opening for analysis to uncover latent dream thoughts and even those unconscious wishes which instigated the dream in the first place. But when secondary redaction has been thorough, as in this latter example, analysis is limited; the resistance has taken over.

Analyzing dreams is therefore rather like studying a novel in depth. If we read primarily for pleasure, we like to have the work perfectly edited and beautifully polished; if, on the other hand, we wish to learn more about the author and his intentions, we prefer the manuscripts, the corrections, the letters and notes, especially those the writer and his family were least eager to make accessible. So it is with the dream; we try to undo the editing, if we can, to discover not only the content of the dream, but its origins and the processes by which the dreamer created the finished text. In this way we may become acquainted with his underlying wishes and conflicts and acquire as well an understanding of his habitual ways of dealing with these conflicts during different states of consciousness.

It would not be proper to leave the Editor without a remark about the role of the Listener, who by furnishing clues to his reactions, whether obvious or subtle, exerts an effect on the dreamer, thus influencing not only the frequency of reporting dreams, but the way they are finally told. This influence is not confined merely to the appearance of the transference in the content of the patient's dreams and associations; we are all very much aware of that phenomenon. Dreamers in analysis also edit their dreams to appeal to us, to play on our perceived areas of interest, to tease and frustrate by exposing our ignorance of fields in which they are expert, or to embarrass and shock us. We ourselves, by the way we listen and interpret, become accessories in secondary redaction.

Under the heading of secondary redaction I have chosen to include another familiar phenomenon, the dream within a dream. Here the sleeper dreams a dream and dreams about his dream. "The intention is . . . to detract from the importance of what is 'dreamt' in the dream, to rob it of its reality" (Freud 1900, p. 338). The analogy that comes to mind most readily is the "play within a play," as in Shakespeare's *Hamlet*. The Prince employed this device to charge Claudius with murder, rather than facing him directly with the accusation, which would have been far too dangerous. It is as if he had instead imposed a bad dream upon his enemy, the reaction to which, the King starting up as if waking from a nightmare, Hamlet interpreted correctly as evidence of guilt.

Thus the dream within a dream permits the disturbing thought to reach consciousness, yet allows the dreamer to avoid its direct impact. Something of the same sort may also be accomplished by placing the action of the dream upon a stage or in film, the dreamer playing the role of observer, thus separating himself from the protagonist. This device leads us now to the third aspect of secondary revision which I have chosen to call "the Plagiarist."

THE PLAGIARIST

Freud also included under the heading of secondary revision the employment of preformed day dreams or "phantasies" as readymade material for the construction of the dream. This factor "seeks to mould the material offered to it into something like a day-dream" (Freud 1900, p. 492). Dreams may thus reproduce a previously constructed fantasy, either unconscious or conscious. If such a fantasy does become part of a dream, that section gives the impression of being far more coherent than the rest, and if it occupies a large part of the manifest dream, the latter may well appear in highly organized form, as in the dream of the trip from Cape Cod. In this case, it is often difficult to tell whether the dreamer is reporting what he experienced during sleep or while he was awake.

Child analysts are frequently faced with this question. Young children often tell stories in which night dreams, daytime fantasies, and conscious lying are virtually indistinguishable. The analyst must listen very carefully, and in order to get matters straight, may have to ask a good many questions. Somewhat older children report dreams which were indeed experienced during sleep, and yet incorporate typical daydreams almost unchanged. For example, a twelve-year-old girl dreamed that she played a heroic role in protecting a group of people from wild animals. The wish to be recognized and honored was unmistakably gratified, while conflict was kept out of awareness. Since the dreamer was a perfectly behaved child and a prototypical "good patient," the dream was altogether in character, manifesting a highly effective defensive structure. The analyst may speculate about the deeper meaning of the dream, presumably reflecting reaction formation, a way of dealing with the dreamer's intense anger toward her analyst and family members. Children may also report that they can "control" their dreams, remembering the good ones and forgetting the bad, a feat which, if successful, we may well envy.

Secondary revision may also account for the popular impression that creative acts are conceived during a state of sleep and dreaming. There is no doubt that daydreams may exhibit the kind of creative form and content which can lead to the production of a work of art. Whether this can take place during sleep is less certain. Freud argued against such a possibility, maintaining that true intellectual and creative work must have occurred preconsciously, while the person was awake, by a process akin to intuition. The products incorporated into the dream were then presented, falsely, as new creations of the dream itself. The question is still open. Perhaps we may leave it by reminding ourselves that the lines between dreaming and waking thought cannot be sharply drawn. Creativity may operate anywhere along the continuum between full alertness and dreaming, perhaps closer to the latter, probably not during deep sleep, but rather during those intermediate states which are also most conducive to secondary revision, not quite asleep, but not altogether alert either.

Daydreams represent wish fulfillments, carry infantile memory traces, and are less strictly controlled than ordinary waking thought, but more so than the prototypical night dream. The preformed fantasies employed in dreams are frequently derived from outside sources and thus reflect the cultural milieu of the dreamer (e.g. Artemidorus). Freud's patients borrowed from the drama and poetry currently popular in Vienna, while ours are more likely to incorporate material derived from films and television, so that it is not unusual to hear a patient describe a dream as if it were a film: "And then the scene changed to so and so. . . ." Such images, by giving an apparently coherent and dramatic form to a dream, may serve to convey, and yet effectively protect the dreamer from his unacceptable wishes and painful conflicts—and thus further complicate the analyst's task.

A fine example of all three aspects of secondary revision, including a dream within a dream, may be found in *The Diary of Samuel Pepys* (15 August, 1665). He accompanied his report of the dream with an account of his activities, thoughts, and emotions of the preceding day, and described in detail when and how he recalled the dream. While we lack free associations, we do have enough material available to allow us to make some plausible inferences about this experience of a man who was intelligent, curious, honest with himself, a superb reporter, and yet not notably introspective.

Pepys experienced the dream at the height of the Great Plague in London, during which he had good reason to fear for his life. On 14 August, he ended his entry for the day: "Great fears we have that the plague will be a great Bill this week" (i.e., many deaths would have been reported). The entry for the next day begins:

> Up by 4 a-clock and walked to Greenwich, where called at Captain Cockes and to his chamber, he being in bed—where something put my last night's dream into my head, which I think was the best that ever was dreamed—which was, that I had my Lady Castlemayne in my arms and was admitted to use all the dalliance I desired with her, and then dreamed that this could not be awake but that it was only a dream. But that since it was a

> dream and that I took so much pleasure in it, what a happy thing it would be, if when we are in our graves (As Shakespeere resembles it), we could dream, and dream such dreams as this—that then we should not be so fearful of death as we are in this plague-time." [Vol. 6, p. 191]

Pepys had reason enough to try to reassure himself while people were dying all about him. In the "outer" dream, he says in effect that it was after all only a dream, but at the same time consoles himself with the thought that death might consist of such glorious dreams. The identity of the woman in the manifest dream allows us to infer the nature of the underlying wish fulfillment. Pepys frequently indulged in sexually exciting fantasies about Lady Castlemayne, currently the mistress of King Charles II, his employer. He now incorporated one of these fantasies into his dream. The reminder that it was "only a dream," i.e., not real, was reassuring in at least two respects: first, he need not fear punishment by the King (Charles II was not known to be especially jealous, but still!); second, he could comfort himself with the recognition that he was awake, therefore alive. It was in essence a dream of oedipal conquest over the King—father, the penalty for which would be castration or death. Pepys, a lover of life, awakens and accepts that it was merely a pleasurable dream (see Stein 1977).

Here the revision (which included an attempt at rational interpretation) seems to have taken place during both sleep and waking. Death need not be feared; it may even be anticipated, since it can consist of an erotically satisfying dream which will go on for eternity as the dreamer embraces the desirable mistress-mother. The reference to Hamlet's soliloquy reflects the dreamer's intense devotion to the theater and to the play, which he had seen at least three times. (It is tempting, if idle, to speculate to what extent Pepys sensed the passionate and conflicted nature of the relationship between Hamlet and his mother, and whether Betterton, the Olivier of his day, would have brought this out, even implicitly. Unfortunately, Pepys doesn't say.)

This dream, accompanied by the dreamer's account of his experiences and thoughts, illustrates all three phases of secondary revision. There is a critical comment, ". . . the best that ever was dreamed." We find explicit evidence of a dream within a dream. And the dreamer, acting as Critic, Editor, and Plagiarist, supplies us with a logically organized interpretation incorporating a conscious fantasy, pleasurable, and hardly innocent. His fantasies were frequently accompanied by masturbation, often picturing women favored by King Charles. He was especially preoccupied with Lady Castlemayne's beauty, having "glutted" himself with looking at her although, as he wrote, "I know well enough that she is a whore" (Vol. 3, p. 139). A gifted and candid writer, he turned the dream into a good story.

The use of a preformed fantasy for secondary revision was demonstrated by one of Freud's own dreams. In the dream of "dissecting my own pelvis," much of the imagery of the latter part was derived from the novel *She*, by H. Rider Haggard. Having recognized the connection, Freud was able to interpret the dream on a level which demonstrated to what degree he regarded himself as having embarked upon a journey into unknown and extremely dangerous territory, that of human sexuality. To have conquered this territory would be equivalent to an oedipal triumph; like Oedipus, he would pay the penalty, yet become immortal (1900, p. 452). Since dreams are employed in some degree for the gratification of old desires, long ago transformed or disavowed, it is most convenient to have at hand a suitable structure, already manufactured and ready for use, as Freud had available his memory of Haggard's novel.

Discussing the devices employed to conceal the nature and significance of one's ideas in dreams, Freud wrote: A similar difficulty confronts the political writer who has disagreeable truths to tell to those in authority. If he presents them undisguised, the authorities will suppress his words . . . he must conceal his objectionable pronouncement beneath some apparently innocent disguise . . . for example, by a story set in ancient times or in a far country (1900, p. 142).

This was rarely better exemplified than by Bunyan's *The Pilgrim's Progress*, from which I derived the verse I presented at the beginning of this paper. He composed it in about 1678, while confined to jail for political and religious views considered subversive, not without reason, by the Restoration government of Charles II. Bunyan employed the very devices Freud was later to describe, casting his message, "under the Similitude of a Dream." An exciting allegorical tale marked, or marred, depending on your point of view, by a severe Puritan morality, it became one of the most popular books ever published.

To return to the dream itself, the extreme variation in the length and complexity of individual dreams may be accounted for in great part by secondary revision, reflecting among other factors the contributions of the dreamer's culture. The contrast is most marked when we study dream tales familiar to non-Western peoples. In a study of Indian myths in relation to dreams and illusions, O'Flaherty (1984) has pointed out the extent to which dreams reported in classical Sanskrit texts employed familiar myths in the construction of their manifest content. These dreams were complex and elaborate to a degree which may strike the Western observer as strange and even improbable, being full of dreams within dreams within dreams, stories within stories within stories. It is not clear where the "true" reality is, a question which is treated differently in classical Sanskrit tradition, as opposed to our own. Perhaps for them the dream could be the reality and reality the dream.

We, on the other hand, generally take for granted sharp distinctions between the world of the dream and that of "reality." Our Western myths are not only simpler, but are treated very differently. Influenced as we are by the rationalizing scepticism of classical Greek culture, we are inclined to regard our familiar myths as poetic creations which may have been derived at some remove from historical events, but are hardly to be accepted as historical in themselves (Griffin 1986). There are parallels in the treatment of dreams: in the West, we are for the most part not inclined to regard our dreams as "real," to the extent that we apply such a standard to waking life.

We may suspect however, that the *underlying dream thoughts*, especially those derived from the experiences of childhood, will reveal more points of fundamental similarity between the Indian poets and ourselves. An Indian hero who in his dream had seen a god and his wife in the act of coitus, and was punished for his voyeurism, went on to elaborate a dream within a dream which consisted of going through many different lives over a vast period of time, thousands of years perhaps. A Western dreamer would be more likely to experience, or at least to tell, a much simpler dream set in finite time, just as his myths would be much shorter in the telling and linear in organization. Perhaps the Greeks had less time for story-telling, and demanded more directness and less involved plots, dramas to be completed in a reasonable time and place, and not *too* complicated, conforming more or less to the mode which would become explicit in the "Unities" of Aristotle.

O'Flaherty demonstrates that dreams reported in classical Sanskrit literature were heavily influenced by the familiar myths of that culture, and furthermore that there is reason to suppose that these myths may have been in turn based on the dreams of individuals. This is difficult to prove, but it gains plausibility from our discouraging experience in trying to concoct credible dreams out of whole cloth. Freud for one found it difficult if not impossible. Perhaps some poets believed that their fictional dreams were totally new creations, evolved while they were wide awake. But can we take their word for it? Perhaps these constructions were based on night dreams which had been repressed and returned to consciousness as if *de novo*. Did Homer compose Penelope's dream himself while awake or asleep? I am afraid we are left with a chicken-and-egg problem, but are in any case faced with no compelling reason to rule out the existence of a two-way street between group myth and individual dream, each capable of contributing to the other.[2]

---

[2]Arlow (1961) pointed out that personal dreams and daydreams, in contrast to shared daydreams and myths, "are made to be forgotten" (p. 379). This is generally, but not universally true. Even in clinical practice we come across dreams that nevertheless persist for years or decades in the memory of the dreamer (e.g., the dream of the Wolf Man). There are certain personal dreams which are "typical," or more correctly "common," e.g., the dream of sexual relations with one's mother, which appears in clinical practice and in myth as well (Stein 1984).

> Sophocles (c. 400 B.C.) indicated as much. In *Oedipus the King*, Jocasta tries to reassure Oedipus:
> *Oedipus*:
> But surely I must fear my mother's bed?
> *Jocasta*:
> . . . As to your mother's marriage bed—don't fear it. Before this in dreams as well as oracles, many a man has lain with his own mother. But he to whom such things are nothing bears his life most easily. [p. 52]

An Indian wife of the classical period would probably have offered a much less matter-of-fact statement than did the unfortunate Jocasta, by telling some elaborate stories of her own, which Oedipus, not noted for his patience, would hardly have been in a mood to listen to.

Secondary revision, then, unlike the other aspects of dream work, reflects vividly the culture of the dreamer, both as an individual and as a member of his society. It has been said that our patients have "Freudian" dreams, while those of Jungian analysts have "Jungian" dreams, and so on. To the extent that this is true at all, it is so only in a limited sense. The differences, I suggest, may be accounted for not by a different constellation of conflicts, but rather by the operation of secondary revision. The dreamer's treatment has become a part of his culture which thereby influences the final version of his dreams. Secondary revision supplies not only the language (in the larger sense) in which the dream is told, but much of its structure and imagery as well. It employs the orally transmitted myths, the written literature, the dramatic performances, and so much else that constitutes a cultural heritage, including accepted attitudes toward dreams, their presumed connection with reality, and the customary ways of telling them to others.

Whether the *underlying* dream wishes, the unconscious conflicts and the latent dream thoughts, are so different in other cultures is another matter. Even the highly elaborated dream-myths of ancient Indian storytellers deal with the same basic issues we share with the classical Greeks—birth and death, the afterlife, food and elimination, omnipotence and weakness, parricide, incest, sibling rivalry, the primal scene, sexual success, castration, and changes of gender. The unfamiliarity we experience in reading the dreams of classical Sanskrit poets is determined not by their content, but rather by their highly elaborated form. I suggest that the obvious differences that strike us so forcibly depend on the degree to which secondary revision is used, itself influenced by the circumstances under which the dream is experienced, the expectations of the dreamer, and the identity of the recipient of the dream story, who may be spouse, analyst, or in the old days, an army that needed encouragement in the face of battle (Stein 1984). The underlying themes are alike. Were it not for the contribution of secondary revision, all our dreams might be appallingly uniform, reflecting only our shared biological heritage, without conveying the rich diversity of individual experience and cultural influence. The unadorned dream might consist merely of eating, incest, parricide, and death, which could be very monotonous indeed. Our dreams are far more complex and interesting, uniquely human, thanks to secondary revision, that manifestation of the receptivity and power of the ego and superego, which among other things encompass the reservoir of cultural experience.

This is a matter of some importance clinically, for in order to analyze a patient's dreams, or for that matter to analyze at all, we should be reasonably familiar not only with his language and his individual history, but with his culture as well. Attempting to analyze without being acquainted with the imagery and rituals that play such a large part in the person's cultural heritage is likely to be a futile effort, limited to simplistic interpretations of little therapeutic or intellectual value. We are not required to see every film or read every book the patient has incorporated into his dreams, but we should be open to learning and understanding the special cultural experience that has enriched his dreams as well as his waking personality. While this caveat applies to analytic work in general, it is a particular issue in the interpretation of dreams, for in the secondary revision of the dream the patient evokes his cultural experience in a way which may make the language of the dream even more baffling to the observer who does not share that experience and who has failed to exert himself to become familiar with it.

Finally, the detection, analysis, and understanding of secondary revision is much more than an aid to the interpretation of dreams. Occupying a range of states of consciousness from REM sleep to waking, it has much in common with imagination and creativity, which are also likely to be most active during states of topographic regression. It is in its own way an example of "regression in the service of the ego," a happy phrase for which we owe thanks to the late Ernst Kris (1943, p. 448). I consider the phrase "happy" because it allows for the simultaneous use of two different models of the mind, the topographic and the structural, thus taking into account the complexity of the phenomena that concern us. Freud's original attempt to describe secondary revision purely in terms of topography, i.e., by use of the systems, *Ucs.*, *Pcs.*, *Pcpt-Cs.*, was much less successful than his efforts on behalf of the dream work proper.

We require a more inclusive model to account for the peculiarities of the process by which we introduce some degree of logic and plausibility into our dreams and our ability to incorporate not only "indifferent" impressions (the day's residues), but whole culture-bound structures. The structural model of the mind, based on the concepts, ego, superego and id, has been essential for the description of these characteristics of secondary revision, as well as so many other complex phenomena. This has resulted in the marshalling of powerful arguments (e.g., Arlow and Brenner 1964) for putting aside, or at least rendering subordinate, the topographic model, in which states of consciousness are central, in favor of an all-inclusive structural model, often referred to as "ego psychology." It is indeed possible to describe the analysis of dreams, including secondary revision, in terms of the structural model without references to the topographic, but the effort tends to deprive the process of much of its complexity and richness of allusion, which are better conveyed by immediate references to levels of consciousness. Each model gives us concepts and terms we require in order to think about the mind, and especially about the dreaming or dreamy mind.

Just as physicists have required both wave and particle theory to ask different questions about the nature of light, we need both models to ask questions about the mental apparatus. These models will have to suffice until we can come up with a unitary theory of the mind, more elegant and explanatory than either of these. I hope we shall, for the questions raised by the ways that dreams are prepared for telling are the prototypes for many unanswered questions about mental life in general.

REFERENCES

Arlow, J. A. (1961). Ego psychology and the study of mythology. *J. Amer. Psychoanal. Assn.* 9:373–393.

Arlow, J., and Brenner, C. (1964). *Psychoanalytic Concepts and the Structural Theory*. New York: Int. Univ. Press.

Artemidorus (2nd C., A.D.). *Oneirocritica*, ed. R. J. White. Park Ridge, N. J.: Noyes, 1975.

Bunyan, J. (1678). *The Pilgrim's Progress*, ed. R. Sharrock. New York: Penguin Books, 1965.

Freud, S. (1887–1902). *The Origins of Psychoanalysis*. New York: Basic Books, 1954.

——— (1900). The interpretation of dreams. *Standard Edition* 4 & 5.

——— (1923). The ego and the id. *Standard Edition* 19.

Griffin, J. (1986). Greek myth and Hesiod. In *Oxford Dictionary of the Classical World*, ed. J. Boardman, J. Griffin, and O. Murray. New York: Oxford Univ. Press, pp. 78–98.

Homer (c. 700 B.C.). *The Odyssey of Homer*, trans. R. Lattimore. New York: Harper & Row.

Isakower, O. (1954). Spoken words in dreams. *Psychoanal. Q.* 23:1–6.

Kris, E. (1943). Some problems of war propaganda. In *Selected Papers*. New Haven: Yale Univ. Press, 1975, pp. 443–450.

O'Flaherty, W. (1984). *Dreams, Illusions and Other Realities*. Chicago: Univ. Chicago Press.

Oxford English Dictionary (1971). New York: Oxford Univ. Press.

Panel (1984). The clinical use of psychoanalysis. O. Renik, reporter. *J. Amer. Psychoanal. Assn.* 32:157–162.

Pepys, S. (1665). *The Diary of Samuel Pepys*, ed. R. Latham and W. Matthews. London: G. Bell & Sons, 1972.
Plato (c. 400 B.C.). *The Republic*, trans. A. Bloom. Chicago: Univ. Chicago Press, 1968.
Silber, A. (1973). Secondary revision, secondary elaboration and ego synthesis. *Int. J. Psychoanal.* 54:161–168.
Sophocles (c. 400 B.C.) *Oedipus the King*, trans. D. Grene. Chicago: Univ. Chicago Press, 1942.
Stein, M. H. (1965). States of consciousness in the psychoanalytic situation, including a note on the traumatic dream. In *Drives, Affects, Behavior*, ed. M. Schur. New York: Int. Univ. Press.
——— (1977). A psychoanalytic view of mental health: Samuel Pepys and his diary. *Psychoanal. Q.* 46:82–115.
——— (1981). The unobjectionable part of the transference. *J. Amer. Psychoanal. Assn.* 29:968–992.
——— (1984). Rational versus anagogic interpretation: Xenophon's dream and others. *J. Amer. Psychoanal. Assn.* 32:529–556.
Waelder, R. (1930). The principle of multiple function: observations on overdetermination. In *Psychoanalysis: Observation, Theory, Application*, ed. S. A. Gutman. New York: Int. Univ. Press, 1968, pp. 68–83.

14

Dreams, Conscience, and Memory

The interpretation of certain dreams, as opposed to the direct examination of behavior, makes it possible to explore the conscience of the dreamer, detect hidden sources of guilt, and interpret them with less likelihood of arousing intractable resistances. Through the recovery of memories and the establishment of an intimate familiarity with one's personal history, it becomes possible to resolve problems of "neurotic" guilt, based ultimately on distortions of repressed childhood memories. The resolution of these conflicts allows a greater role for the operation of "appropriate" guilt, based on genuine transgressions, and the establishment of a more mature ethical structure.

. . . a degree of familiarity with history, in the absence of ecclesiastical teaching, is our only available source for an ethical education.

—*Joseph Brodsky (1987)*

The most familiar manifestation of superego functioning, "conscience," may be defined as "the internal acknowledgement or recognition of the moral quality of one's motives and actions: the sense of right and wrong as regards things for which one is responsible: the faculty or principle which pronounces upon the moral quality of one's actions or motives, approving the right and condemning the wrong" (*Oxford English Dictionary* 1971, p. 522).

I intend to show how the systematic interpretation of certain dreams and the consequent recovery of memories make it possible to explore the conscience of the dreamer, and thus put moral conflict into a perspective in which it can be more satisfactorily understood and resolved. This is an important step in the analysis of the neurotic sense of guilt, the alleviation of symptoms, and the stabilization of an autonomous, well-integrated and effective set of ethical standards.

It is hardly to be questioned that moral conflict and the sense of guilt play a prominent role in the development of character, not always for the better, and that they contribute to the formation of symptoms. We accept as a matter of course that we must pay constant attention to these issues. Yet in practice, perhaps out of concern that we may be accused by our patients, or ourselves, of being moralistic or judgmental, we are too often tempted to phrase our interpretations diffidently and in ambiguous terms. This cautious approach is understandable, but our obligation as psychoanalysts to withhold moral judgment in no way permits us to evade significant moral issues. We are required therefore to explore thoroughly not only the dynamics, but the historical sources of the sense of guilt as well, and convey these to our patients in the course of interpretation.

It is my contention that this task may be made easier by the analysis of certain dreams. A major advantage lies in the role of dreams as pathways to long-forgotten yet highly significant affect-laden memories, making it possible to trace guilt to its distant and often obscure origins. Furthermore, the dream's operation in sleep permits evidence of the most painful, heretofore repressed conflicts to reach consciousness more readily, albeit in distorted fashion. The dreamer feels only partly responsible for his or her dreams; they have some of the quality of play, of "let's suppose." As a consequence, it becomes easier to discuss them in the same spirit, as if we were talking about another person, the sleeper as opposed to the waker. Only later must we face the essential, admittedly difficult task of bringing the two together in an effective interpretation (Goldberger 1989).

Moreover, it is relatively easy to maintain an atmosphere of moral neutrality in analyzing a dream. When interpreting behavior directly, on the other hand, it is far more difficult to maintain neutrality. Faced with an account of some real action about which the analysand feels defiant, ashamed, or remorseful, it may be difficult to avoid conveying the impression of moral repugnance on the one hand, or exculpation on the other. Whether or not such judgments are in fact experienced by us (they are, after all, not always avoidable), our patients are all too ready to delegate their twinges of conscience by projecting them on to us. They are likely to respond by concealment or by self-imposed controls of behavior, which have the effect of driving the issue underground, thus impeding or altogether preventing the analysis of the moral conflict. Like well-behaved prisoners, some patients become "good" for the duration, but are left with a high probability of eventual relapse. Even worse, in the special category of those who are prone to acting out, any but the most tactful attempts to interpret behavior directly may result not in suppression, but rather in exacerbation of the very patterns of action we are attempting to understand. Interpreting a dream, on the other hand, has the advantage of being less likely to precipitate such undesired consequences; it should in fact make it possible to deal with the symptom more directly at a later time, with less risk to the continuation of the analysis (Greenacre 1963, Stein 1986, 1987).

I shall relate a dream reported by a very intelligent woman in her forties, whom Freud, in his old-fashioned way, might have described as being "of the highest moral character." She was also, under an attractive and cheerful exterior, guilty and depressed and was sleeping very poorly. One day I commented that she had almost never reported her dreams and suggested that she was afraid of the emotions they seemed to engender.

The following morning upon entering my office, she exclaimed, "I've finally remembered a dream!—My husband and I were sleeping in a hotel last night, out of town, and I dreamed that I woke up, and tried to arouse him, but I couldn't. I thought he might be dead, and I became frightened and left the hotel in a panic. Once outside, I found myself in a foreign city, I'm not sure which, but it was strange, entirely unfamiliar. I had forgotten the name of our hotel too, so I walked the streets, unable to find my way back. I felt lost and terrified. . . . I'm sure I've had this dream before. . . . " She woke up feeling panicky and discovered that even awake she could not recall the name of the hotel in which they were staying. She continued, "I was so disturbed that I got out of bed and made my way to the bathroom and found the name by reading it on the wrapper of a cake of soap." She felt frightened and guilty, a mood which persisted until now.

By nature thoughtful, she had nevertheless always done her best to avoid introspection, suppressing not only dreams but imagination as well, and had spent all of her leisure time in frenzied activity, seeing friends, telephoning, and exercising. The one major exception to this inhibition of imagination was to be found in her work as an artist, but even here her production was confined entirely to the abstract. It was at first very difficult for her to sign her work, and although it was generally recognized to be of very high quality, only after much discussion could she bring herself to exhibit and sell it. She felt it was like appearing naked, and might reveal secrets that even she was unaware of. Understandably, to remember and put a dream into words was a new and disturbing experience.

It was easy to conclude that her dream expressed a wish to be rid of her husband, with whom she had had a number of quarrels. At the time, they were in fact concerned about his health. How much simpler it would be for her if he were to develop a fatal illness! She was actually devoted to him, but her dreams took less account of that than of her hostile fantasies. She soon experienced her punishment, however, finding herself lost in an unknown city, unable to remember where she was or where she was staying, an impression so powerful that it persisted well after she awoke. She had not only cast herself into the wilderness, but was truly lost. She had become a "street-walker," literally. This fate was equivalent to losing her own personality, her psyche or "soul." The idea that she might imagine her husband's death was not entirely unfamiliar, for hints of this had surfaced before. But there was more to be found in the dream. Why the peculiar punishment of becoming a wanderer who had lost even the memory of where she lived? Why should her expressions of guilt take this form?

Exploring her associations further led to memories of the childhood circumstances which had contributed to the persistence of her guilt and masochistic life pattern. Her father, now dead, had been an intelligent and sensitive man who suffered from severe attacks of psychosis, condemning the family to poverty and social isolation. In the course of his psychotic episodes, he would leave home and disappear for weeks at a time, eventually to return looking like a derelict, dirty and unshaven. The patient's perpetually enraged mother could never accept the fact that her husband was really ill. She insisted that he was bad and irresponsible, in her word, "disgusting." Even worse for the child, her mother maintained that it was her birth that had made her father the way he was. The child found it impossible not to share her mother's attitude, and suffered from an overwhelming sense of guilt and persistent embarrassment that made her feel like an outsider among her schoolmates. She had been a bright, well-behaved little girl, but inevitably a very angry one, who found the conflict intolerable. Often she became aware of thoughts that things would be so much simpler if her father were never to return! Her anger with her parents, her wishes for her father's death and later guilt over misjudging and rejecting him, all contributed to her attitude toward her sick husband, so graphically portrayed in her dream. Her attempt to reject completely her personal history, especially everything her parents represented, gave her the sense of being "nobody," an artificial person who could not be recognized by others who met her in the street. Distinctive enough in appearance, she nevertheless felt that whenever she met an acquaintance, she had to introduce herself anew.

It became clear that she punished herself by identifying with her father as the runaway, the wanderer, the lost soul. (There was no evidence that her own symptoms were of a psychotic character.) She also became more clearly aware of the disturbing parallels between father and husband who, while unlike in so many respects, shared a tendency to emotional instability and behaved in a way which could cause her painful embarrassment. A loyal and considerate wife, she was horrified by the sense that she might be tempted to behave like her angry, scolding mother. While the idea that she wished for her husband's death was not altogether new to her, it had never been discussed so directly, nor supported by such vivid and convincing evidence of links to parallel memories of childhood.

Her reaction to this interpretation was a remarkable one: it became a valuable clue to her characteristic defenses. The following day she entered my office smiling, appearing almost triumphant. She began by saying that she had

had a dream and had forgotten it, but upon greeting me she recalled an image she experienced upon wakening: "I saw in front of me the musical chord, C-E-G-B flat, the dominant seventh. I felt wonderful! This chord is one which can always be resolved." She added, "The first dream was for you, this one is for me!" Her triumph was emphasized by her knowledge that she was a practiced musician, while I was, by comparison, a musical illiterate. In effect, she announced that she had no need of me to resolve her guilt; she could do so by herself. She had not only gotten rid of husband and father, but disposed of me as well, in a characteristically disarming and graceful fashion. Thus by creating the image of the self-resolving musical chord, she had dealt with me and my disturbing interpretation cleverly and effectively.

In the course of her treatment, bringing in a dream was itself an unusual event. But why the fear of dreaming in the first place? In her case it was clear that guilt was the issue. If she were to have dreams which revealed such evil thoughts and fearsome punishment, she would rather ignore them altogether. It was most painful for her to recognize that she had been unjust in siding with her embittered mother and rejecting her father so completely, especially as she began to recognize the degree to which, in spite of his recurrent illness, he had contributed to her remarkable intellectual and artistic development. It was easier to deal with such painful conflicts while she was wide awake in my office, where she could express them in measured language, quite removed from the raw brutality of the dream thoughts. Through words, her desires could be denatured and pushed aside. The frenzied activity of her waking life permitted virtually no opportunity for introspection, but during unguarded sleep, she was subject to the full force of her terrible rage and guilt. By understanding the influence of her history, she was now able to achieve a measure of analytic understanding of the nature of her conscience, and take a vital step in moral development. She could begin, little by little, to lead her life in a less masochistic and self-denying fashion, and acquired more effective control of angry and provocative outbursts toward her troubled husband. Her capacity for understanding and sympathy could be more successfully manifested, and things became rather better all around.

Possessed as she was of a highly developed conscience, the guilt experienced by this patient, and so vividly portrayed in her dream, was an example of one of the more pervasive emotional responses experienced by human beings. "Neurotic guilt," as I have chosen to call it, may be defined as that affect based on the memories of offenses associated with childhood, generally forgotten, and recalled (if at all) only in distorted fashion. These memories have become reified during development, remaining dormant until triggered by some current experience, perhaps unimportant in itself, but to which they attach themselves. A frequent consequence is the infantilization and blunting of the conscience, manifested by failure to react with the guilt which should be attached to a genuine transgression. It is a prominent symptom in obsessional neuroses and depressive reactions, constituting a source of great suffering to the individual who is afflicted not only by disturbances of affect, but also by substantial confusion of moral values and defects in judgment. Its contribution to a viable ethical system is, if anything, negative; the sole value of neurotic guilt may be in its role as a clue to previously unrecognized conflicts within the psyche.

In 1900 Freud, in an almost offhand way, suggested that "character" is based upon the accumulation of memory traces of impressions (p. 539). If we add the contribution of genetic endowment, we may follow him in thinking of "character," including its moral aspect, as being acquired through an accumulation of memories. It would follow that the recovery of memory traces, correction of their distortions, and their integration into ego and superego structures (especially the latter) would be vital steps in a treatment which has as one of its goals the establishment of a well-integrated system of ethics. Such a system must include an active conscience which operates as an appropriate and useful signal of transgression, free of the confusion engendered by guilt of neurotic origin. I have pointed out elsewhere (Stein 1966) that when acuteness of moral evaluation is impaired, depending as it does upon accuracy of self-observation, we may expect serious disturbances in the individual's capacity to make judgments about external reality as well. This is hardly surprising when we reflect that children do not at first distinguish very sharply between what is bad (morally wrong) and what is incorrect (wrong in logic). Some people never do make the distinction. The maxim, "Honesty is the best policy," is therefore not a meaningless cliché, at least when applied to mental life.

It may be accepted that the psychoanalytic method possesses a morality of its own, the principles of which are invariable in its field of operation. Both parties who agree to honor the analytic contract bind themselves to tell the truth as well as they can, to conceal as little as possible, to face issues however painful, and to respect the other's integrity, this last condition applying most forcibly to the role of the analyst. While the analysand is necessarily influenced by the implicit ethical structure of the analytic situation, it should go without saying that there is no place for the imposition upon him or her of the personal standards of the analyst, those which the latter applies to life outside the analytic situation. Nor does it by any means imply unquestioning conformity to society at large.

Among the goals of analytic treatment, therefore, is the maturation and integration of conscience as an active moral sense which is autonomous without being isolated or inaccessible to further education. The analyzed individual should be capable of being more honest than before, at least with him/herself, to develop a conscience based not on unresolved transference conflicts and anxieties, but rather on an increased capacity for self-observation and understanding of his or her dynamics and history. In this respect the individual will have identified with the analyst *as analyst*, or perhaps more accurately, with what the analysand has perceived as the analytic stance, the maintenance of curiosity about the workings of the mind and most other matters as well, and the rejection of self-deception. But the conscience of the analysand will have become his or her own, not the analyst's—and it will be an *educated* conscience. The analysand will be able to take away what he or she wants and needs, and to modify that system when appropriate, rather as the pupil of an experienced artist retains what the pupil has found useful, discarding what is no longer needed, in order to develop his or her own style. It is by this means that the transference will have established its most profound and lasting influence, in an open, not a rigid system. One of the ways of approaching this ideal state is through an understanding of the moral implications of dreams.

The dream I have related with its associations and historical context reveals the presence of neurotic guilt clearly enough: the dreamer had little enough to reproach herself with in the context of adult behavior. It is not always the case that matters appear so clearly, for individuals vary just as much in how they express themselves in dreaming as they do while awake. There are people who have the greatest difficulty in ever expressing a hostile thought, or becoming aware of a vengeful fantasy, yet experience and report dreams which seem wildly at variance with their overt personalities. In their sleep, they murder their siblings, cut up animals, and indulge in the most extreme acts of sadism. In waking life, they may be eminently reasonable, kindly to a fault, at the same time inclined to be depressed and masochistic, and subject to unexplained sensations of guilt.

It takes a great deal of patience and analytic work to demonstrate to these patients the role sadism plays in their lives, especially since their capacity for reaction formation is so effective in preventing behavioral manifestations of such impulses. Their twinges of guilt are likely to be intermittent, but their capacity to lead lives of unnecessary suffering seems unlimited. Their sadistic impulses are manifested most irritatingly in their ability to provoke guilt in others. Here dealing with their dream life may be the only immediate clue to those unconscious memories and fantasies that have contributed to the distortions of conscience which account for such behavior. Ultimately, these elements can be integrated with relevant memories of early experience and become part of the analytic process. It is not easy, but more often than not, it can be done.

We may turn now to the consideration of certain classes of "typical" dreams, those which share a common form and are repetitive enough to be quite familiar, like old friends—or enemies. The classic traumatic dream, in which the sleeper relives over and over again an accident or a narrow escape, has long been considered an attempt to master a situation in which one had felt helpless and overwhelmed. While Freud was inclined to ascribe the wish fulfillment of such dreams to the death instinct, I have argued elsewhere that the relief experienced upon waking contains the wish to be restored to life and sanity (Stein 1965, 1989).

In the present context we may see traumatic dreams from yet another aspect. Upon awakening, they are generally accompanied by terror and a sense of relief that the danger is really past, that the dreamer is still *alive*. They are, in addition, often marked by an intense sense of guilt not readily relieved by reassurance. This was a conspicuous feature of the traumatic dreams of soldiers in frontline combat and a distressing aspect of the stubborn neuroses which afflicted so many of them. It was frequently possible to establish that the guilt was engendered by the sense that the dreamers had survived at the expense of others who had died. They were indeed trying to reject part of themselves, the self-interested part they saw as capable of sacrificing others to save themselves. Their persistent guilt expressed the reaction to the idea, "If I were even to *dream* of such an action, I couldn't accept that part of myself which harbors the desire to survive while others die. I would be a lost soul." It is expressed most succinctly as, "If I were to do such a thing, I couldn't live with myself."

An even more familiar example is the examination dream, which seems for the most part to afflict those who, in their school days, were superior students. The dreamer is to take an important examination, but finds him/herself altogether unprepared, or perhaps shows up a day late, or cannot remember the room in which the test is to be administered. Still in the dream, the individual suffers the most intense anxiety and guilt over the lapse. Upon awakening, the dreamer recalls with great relief having long ago passed that particular examination. The conventional interpretation of such dreams emphasizes the person's need for reassurance in facing some trail in the near future. The dreamer has been through it before and did not fail; quite the contrary, he or she had passed it and can do it again. This interpretation is correct, so far as it goes, but it fails to deal with other aspects of the dream's meaning. Both dreamer and interpreter are likely to be left with a vaguely defined sense of discomfort, accompanied by the impression that there is something more.

Freud (1900) had written, with feeling based, I am sure, on personal experience, "The ineradicable memories of the punishments that we suffered for our evil deeds in childhood become active within us once more and attach themselves to the two crucial points in our studies—the '*dies irae, dies illa*' of our stiffest examinations. The 'examination anxiety' of neurotics owes its intensification to these same childhood fears [of wishes]" (p. 274). It is implied that these dreams were derived from memories of exhibiting one's sexual charms, a common and sometimes engaging activity of little children who, at first free of self-consciousness, later become aware of their role as seductive beings, especially when they have been discouraged, if not openly rebuked, by their parents.

A striking example of a closely related phenomenon was afforded recently during the course of a newspaper interview with Alec Guinness (1987). He reported a dream which has recurred once a month during his highly successful career on the stage. He finds himself before the footlights, "not knowing a single line, dressed in the wrong costume, with both audience and fellow artists reacting in total, total astonished silence." Finally, he breaks into a desperate little tap dance. He continued, "My inadequacy nightmares are always about theater, never about film. . . . I prefer the life of the theater. . . . I was equally attracted and repelled by the limelight. . . . when an adolescent, I envisaged thunderous applause for my every gesture."

This led me to recall a patient who dreamed over and over again of appearing at the concert hall, only to find that she was hours late, had prepared the wrong music, or forgotten it altogether. She would awaken in a panic, consumed with guilt, and only slowly experience the relief of recognizing that the performance was still ahead of her and that she was in fact perfectly prepared. An unusually conscientious performer, she had never been late for rehearsal or forgotten a note. There was indeed no shortage of guilt-laden memories related to adolescent and adult sexual experiences, but we found other factors that were relevant to her performance guilt.

Each time she gave a particularly good concert and was rewarded by the enthusiastic response of the audience, she reacted with pleasurable excitement, followed almost immediately by a feeling of depression which included a profound and unexplained sense of guilt. We arrived at the explanation by an event which resulted in considerable embarrassment on my part, if not on hers. During a session in which she described, in moving fashion, an emotionally charged sexual experience, I found myself irresistibly impelled toward sleep. She became aware of my lapse, and so did I. It was not that I was bored; on the contrary, I was *overcome*; her superb performance had charmed me to sleep. This gave us the clue to what she strove to do with her larger audiences. She desired to overwhelm them, to put them into a charmed state, or, as it is so often expressed by performers, to "kill" the audience—the ultimate goal of every virtuoso, as epitomized by Alec Guinness. There is no harm in that, unless it is taken literally by the unconscious ego, which transmits the message unchanged to the superego. If this occurs, which is far from uncommon, guilt strikes in the form of an examination dream or stage fright.

My patient's examination dreams had become transference dreams, now re-enacted during the analytic session: she had become excited by and afraid of her wish to seduce and destroy *me*. She recalled that as a very little girl, she had been an enthusiastic performer who did her best to charm her parents, who were too self-absorbed to appreciate her efforts. She was deeply hurt and, for this and other reasons, was enraged enough to have fantasied their deaths, as mine was now no doubt intended, in a kind of *Liebestod*. Overwhelming charm is one way to bring about such a result; it conveys not only love, but the wish to dominate and destroy by magic the objects toward whom it is directed, including the analyst (Rittenberg 1987). The dream of being examined, i.e., of exhibiting oneself, therefore includes the desire to impress, to charm and dominate, even to kill; hence its association with guilt. Such dreams, while not always easy to analyze in depth, are still more accessible than the symptom alone, particularly when the interpretation can be correlated with transferential exchange and historical reconstruction, as in this instance.

It is hardly necessary to mention that we come across guilty reactions based on the knowledge that one has committed actual transgressions serious enough to justify them. For that matter, hardly any of us are so virtuous as to have *no* genuine reason to experience a sense of guilt now and then. It is vital to be able to distinguish between "normal" guilt, evoked by the conscious or preconscious knowledge that we have committed a real offense, and the "neurotic," founded on (generally repressed) memories of the past.

In psychoanalytic practice, we do not very often come across truly corrupt individuals, the sociopaths and habitual criminals; if we do, we are not likely to get a successful analysis going. There are, however, those patients on the borderline who are worth a try, and here again, the analysis of dreams may furnish a view into analyzable elements of inner conflict.

Neurotic individuals, not as a rule inclined toward serious crime, nevertheless often carry within themselves the consciousness of guilty secrets based on episodes of lying, petty larceny, or minor frauds. During analysis, the first hint of such secrets may appear in a dream, which, if picked up and interpreted, will result in confirmation in the form of a confession. This in turn makes it possible to analyze the underlying conflicts and to demonstrate to the patient the role of repressed memories, unconscious fantasies, and the need for punishment which have resulted in symptom formation, along with an uneasy and unreliable conscience.

Freud was explicit on the moral implications of dreaming: "If we look at unconscious wishes reduced to their most fundamental and truest shape, we shall have to conclude, no doubt, that *psychical* reality is a particular form of existence not to be confused with *material* reality. Thus there seems to be no justification for people's reluctance in accepting responsibility for the immorality of their dreams. . . . It is in any case instructive to get to know the much trampled soil from which our virtues proudly spring" (1900, pp. 620–621). A moral statement, not a moralistic one, making no concession to those who assume, mistakenly, that psychoanalysis does away with guilt; rather, it attempts to trace it to its sources and subject it to scrutiny by the observing ego.

It is not only the strange, "crazy" quality of so many dreams that troubles us, but what they reveal on an even deeper level about those profound desires which disturb the conscience. Freud did not claim to be the first to point out the role of forbidden wishes in the genesis of dreams. He cited Plato, to whom he gave credit in spite of his reservations about philosophers (1900, pp. 67, 620). Plato had Socrates say, "What we wish to recognize is the following: surely some terrible, savage and lawless form of desires is in every man, even in some of us who seem to be ever so measured. And surely this becomes plain in dreams" (IX, 572b). Of the tyrant, the truly evil man, he says, " . . . what he had rarely been in dreams, he became continuously while awake. He will stick at no terrible murder, or food or deed" (574e, 575a). The worst man "is awake, presumably, what we describe a dreaming man to be" (576b) (Plato, translated by A. Bloom, 1968). (Was he in some uncanny way anticipating Caligula, or more plausibly, reflecting on some past or contemporary tyrant?)[1]

I have remarked elsewhere (Stein 1984) that aside from Plato (who was not altogether consistent), there were, in the ancient world, only occasional interpreters who, rather than ascribing dreams to supernatural sources, tried to explain them in terms of human memory and daily concerns, the role of wish fulfillment being at least implicitly recognized. Some striking examples are to be found in the works of Homer and others. During modern times it has become no longer fashionable to view dreams as coming from God, but there still remains a stubborn tendency to seek ways of evading their moral and other personal implications, especially the role of wish fulfillment. New advances in brain neurophysiology, which are certainly relevant to our understanding of dream formation, have, for example, been employed by such investigators as Hobson and McCarley (1977) and Crick and Mitchison (1983), not so much to supplement and clarify the psychological understanding of dreams as to trivialize or discount it altogether. Such reductive approaches fail to take into account the multiple determinants of psychological phenomena, rather as if one were to account for blushing by describing the complex physiology of changes in the blood supply to the cheeks, while ignoring the role of embarrassment. Hobson's recent publication, *The Dreaming Brain* (1989), in which he again discounts the psychoanalytic understanding of dreams, has been subjected to a sophisticated and critical review by the philosopher, Brian Farrell (1989), who points out the simplistic and reductive nature of Hobson's arguments.[2]

[1]Plato regarded dreams as indicative of a man's ethical attitude, believing, however, that they registered a stage in his education, rather than his morality per se (van Lieshout 1980).
[2]Hobson's work had previously been subjected to criticism by Vogel on physiological grounds, and by Labruzza and Reiser on the conceptual level (reported by McDonald, 1981).

But questioning the ubiquity and central importance of wish fulfillment and the moral implications of dreams, with more relevance to problems of interpretation, has come from psychiatry and psychoanalysis as well. Kuper and Stone (1982), employing the theories of Lévi-Strauss to examine Freud's analysis of the dream of Irma's injection, suggest that the structural analysis of dreams may furnish "an alternative to psychoanalytic dream interpretation, focusing particularly on the internal dialectic of the dream—the movement from the initial premise to the resolution" (p. 1225). While this is an interesting way of looking at the manifest dream, essentially from an ego-psychological view, the authors impair their argument by ignoring Freud's concept of secondary revision, which dealt with this very issue at greater depth and with more subtlety by allowing the unconscious dream work its proper role (Stein 1989). Moreover, their argument skirts the issues of wish fulfillment and moral conflict, treating the dream as if it were a purely intellectual exercise.

The Irma dream, which has been exposed to so much critical scrutiny by these and other authors, contains a description of Freud's attempts to deal with a series of painful moral conflicts. He accused himself of lapses in clinical judgment, envy of friends and colleagues, disloyalty to his wife, improper sexual interest in his patients, and much else of which he found reason to be ashamed. These charges he answered very inadequately, leaving himself with a persistent burden of guilt and, fortunately for us, a pressing need to understand his dream. Concern about his moral deficiencies also appears in several other dreams, e.g., "Uncle with the yellow beard," "Undressed, running upstairs," and "*Non vixit*," to select only a few (1900). By analyzing these, he learned to face some of the darker aspects of his own character and to relate them to memories of childhood. Somehow he was courageous enough to describe these painful moral conflicts in his writings. It is not too much to claim that, among many other sources, psychoanalysis arose out of one man's attempt to deal with his sense of guilt, not by self-punishment, nor by confession, but by the active exploration of his dreams and thereby his memories as part of an unsparing self-analysis (Stein 1987).

A very different view of unconscious conflict and the role of guilt was advanced by Heinz Kohut in 1977. Referring to the present day as the age of "Tragic Man," as opposed to the age of "Guilty Man," which encompassed Freud's lifetime, Kohut minimized the role of moral conflict in psychopathology and in modern life generally. He made relatively few references to dreaming in his later works (e.g., 1977, as opposed to 1971), and was for the most part inclined to downgrade the significance of psychic conflict, the use of free association, and the latent dream in the understanding of personality. This was consistent with his advice to rely upon the analyst's empathic introspection, at the expense of the thorough exploration and evaluation of memories of those events and fantasies which are part of the individual's history and are re-enacted in the transference (Stein 1979). Kohut's approach was essentially ahistorical, a trend very much in line with the temper of the period during which he wrote, the late '60's and the '70's.

It is true that the *content* of the manifest dream has changed, for it is above all culture-bound. All dreamers employ the images, myths, and prejudices of their period and society in the construction of their dreams. Modern humans no longer picture Father Zeus, the avenger, in their manifest dreams; they are more inclined to bring in their Chief Executive Officer or their analyst. Yet the underlying dream thoughts and unconscious desires have been far more uniform over the ages. The basic conflicts we detect in the dreams reported by ancient Greeks are altogether familiar, and we come across parallels daily in our experience with patients (Stein 1984, 1986). Sophocles has the power to move us today; the conflicts he described are very much with us, even though we express them in different terms. The question of fundamental changes in the principles of interpretation can be answered only with the aid of a long view; it cannot be taken for granted or decided on the basis of generalizations over a half-century or so, which is, after all, a relatively brief period of history. It is too early therefore to sound the knell of "Guilty Man," the dreamer troubled by the power of desires, fearful of punishment by the reigning deities or the personal conscience, however portrayed. "Guilty Man" can and does coexist with "Tragic Man."

To return to Joseph Brodsky: the brief passage I cited at the beginning of this paper referred to morality in relation to society, and to a knowledge of history in the broadest sense. Brodsky claims that great immorality in politics, e.g., treason, is fostered by an ignorance (or gross misunderstanding and denigration) of history, a condition predisposing to major distortions of the content and meaning of past events and the uncritical acceptance of doctrinaire accounts. When distortion is officially cultivated, as is so often done to justify betrayals by individuals and genocide by groups, it is often called the "rewriting of history," in itself a disingenuous term employed to conceal its dishonest purpose and tendentious quality. (It is not to be confused with "revisionist" history, based on the discovery of new sources and methods of research, which attempts to undo past omissions and distortions. It too, needs to be "revised" every few years.)

Herodotus, one of the founders of Western history, although by no means a moralist, approached his task with the hope that it would hold lessons for his readers. Called by some "the father of history," others called him "the father of lies." There is no real contradiction. By recording all the myths and folk tales he could collect, the "lies" so-called, as well as stories and personal recollections of contemporary events, he furnished us with a view of history which is closer to our own "psychoanalytic anamnesis" (Schafer 1980) than is the more "factual" history of Thucydides. Each has its virtues, but when

Herodotus records some fantastic tale, which he follows by the phrase, "at least so the Persians say," we hear the echo of our own inner response when we are told a somewhat improbable tale by a patient who had reported a screen memory as if it were fact. Whether literally true or not, it is significant that those who relate it believe it and have been influenced by their belief; they have constructed a "personal myth" of their own, by which they have regulated their lives (Kris 1956). Herodotus knew that the behavior of individuals and societies was as profoundly affected by their folk tales, daydreams, and even their night dreams, the "lies" they believed, as it was by their experience of events (Stein 1984). The dominance of Athenian culture and power, and its ultimate fall, for example, was not only a function of economic, political, and military factors, but was profoundly influenced by the Homeric myths, the "lies," which pervaded Greek political and cultural life for better and worse.

That familiarity with history would ultimately be of social benefit has been an age-old ideal, infrequently realized in practice, but worthy for all that. Although it is reasonable to assume that ignorance constitutes a substantial threat, it would not do to claim that a *knowledge* of history, social or personal, by itself ensures the presence of a sound ethical structure. Like any knowledge, or ecclesiastical teaching for that matter, an acquaintance with even the most unbiased history can be misused. It is worth noting that Brodsky uses not the term "knowledge," but "*familiarity*"—"the state of being very friendly or intimate" (*Oxford English Dictionary*)—thus emphasizing that history, presumably a corrected and reasonably honest history, must be integrated and become part of political human beings in the most fundamental sense, allowing them to think and react historically. Only then, as I read Brodsky, may history contribute to moral education. Ignorance, in any case, does not. To quote the historian, Michael Howard, "The historical process, through the very challenges it poses and the responses it evokes, itself creates the morality of mankind. That seems to me a very good reason for studying it" (1989, p. 689).

The parallel with the analytic process is striking. The ideal "analyzed" individuals have more than just a knowledge of their personal history; they have worked it out in the transference, they feel at home with it, it is part of them; they have attained not simply knowledge but *familiarity* with their past. They have it to use or misuse, but at least it is there, at their disposal.

I do not wish to leave you with the impression that every dream is accompanied by sensations of guilt, or that it must contain a significant confession, to be winkled out by persistent analysis. Even if guilty conflict were ubiquitous on some level, it need not be the predominant theme of every dream, or the one which requires interpretation. If the dreamer is successful in resolving the conflict, no guilt at all may be experienced; sleep is undisturbed and the conscience remains clear. But the kinds of decisions which have to be made in the course of the dream work, about how to gratify archaic desires unacceptable to the waking conscience, are likely to result in conflicts that are imperfectly resolved and leave their residue of guilt.

By dealing with the issue of personal guilt the analyst becomes not the conscience of the patient but, to appropriate Calef and Weinshel's (1980) term, "the conscience of the analysis." Analysts are equipped by training and, we hope, by temperament, to face the disturbing nature of the forces revealed by the analysis of their patients. (We should remind ourselves that these forces are not unleashed by analysis—life has taken care of that.) Analysts must be able to look upon them with clarity and a sufficient degree of detachment—not to explain them away, but to put them in context and to evaluate their significance. By refraining from condoning or collusion on the one hand, or punitive interference on the other, we can aid the working through of neurotic guilt, the kind revealed in dreams, fantasies, and symptoms. On the part of the dreamer, it takes energy and courage to look through the window offered by the dream and to understand how forgotten memories of forbidden desires have contributed to his or her unreliable conscience and unexplained burden of guilt. Will the recovery and correction of memories lead to a more discriminating, less punitive and more effective conscience, one which is less troublesome, but more troubling? If analysis can accomplish *that*, it has done a great deal for the individual and for those around him or her.

REFERENCES

Brodsky, J. (1987). Review of *Conspiracy of Silence* by Barrie Penrose and Simon Freeman. *Times Literary Supplement*, 4, 374:99.

Calef, V., and Weinshel, E. M. (1980). The analyst as the conscience of the analysis. *Int. Rev. Psychoanal.* 7:279–290.

Crick, F., and Mitchison, G. (1983). The function of dream sleep. *Nature* 304:111–114.

Farrell, B. (1989). What dreams are made of. *New York Review of Books*, 36, No. 10:28–32.

Freud, S. (1900). The interpretation of dreams. *Standard Edition* 4/5.

Goldberger, M. (1989). On the analysis of defenses in dreams. *Psychoanal. Q.* 58:396–418.

Greenacre, P. (1963). Problems of acting out in the transference relationship. In *Emotional Growth. Psychoanalytic Studies of the Gifted and a Great Variety of Other Individuals, Vol. 2.* New York: Int. Univ. Press, 1971, pp. 695–712.

Guinness, A. (1987). Interview quoted in *The New York Times*, April 27.

Herodotus. *The Histories*. Translated by D. Grene. Chicago/London: Univ. of Chicago Press, 1987.

Hobson, J. A. (1988). *The Dreaming Brain.* New York: Basic Books.

Hobson, J. A., and McCarley, R. W. (1977). The brain as a dream state generator: an activation-synthesis hypothesis of the dream process. *Amer. J. Psychiat.* 134:1335–1348.

Howard, M. (1989). Structure and process in history. *Times Literary Supplement*, No. 4, 499:687–689.

Kafka, E. (1990). The uses of moral ideas in the mastery of trauma and in adaptation, and the concept of superego severity. *Psychoanal. Q.* 59:249–272.

Kohut, H. (1971). *The Analysis of the Self. A Systematic Approach to the Psychoanalytic Treatment of Narcissistic Personality Disorders*. New York: Int. Univ. Press.

——— (1977). *The Restoration of the Self*. New York: Int. Univ. Press.

Kris, E. (1956). The personal myth. A problem in psychoanalytic technique. *Amer. Psychoanal. Assn.* 4:653–681.

Kuper, A., and Stone, A. A. (1982). The dream of Irma's injection; a structural analysis. *Amer. J. Psychiat.* 139:1225–1234.

McDonald, M. C. (1981). Does dream theory need revision? *Psychiat. News*, August 7, pp. 4, 30.

Oxford English Dictionary, Compact Edition (1971). Oxford: Oxford Univ. Press.

Plato. *The Republic*. Translated by A. Bloom. Chicago/London: Univ. of Chicago Press, 1968.

Rittenberg, S. M. (1987). On charm. *Int. J. Psychoanal.* 68:389–396.

Schafer, R. (1980). Narration in psychoanalytic dialogue. *Critical Inquiry* 7:29–53.

Stein, M. H. (1965). States of consciousness in the analytic situation, including a note on the traumatic dream. In *Drives, Affects, Behavior, Vol. 2. Essays in Memory of Marie Bonaparte*, ed. M. Schur. New York: Int. Univ. Press, pp. 60–86.

——— (1966). Self observation, reality, and the superego. In *Psychoanalysis—A General Psychology. Essays in Honor of Heinz Hartmann*, ed. R. M. Loewenstein, et al. New York: Int. Univ. Press, pp. 275–297.

——— (1979). Review of *The Restoration of the Self* by H. Kohut. *J. Amer. Psychoanal. Assn.* 27:665–680.

——— (1984). Rational versus anagogic interpretation: Xenophon's dream and others. *J. Amer. Psychoanal. Assn.* 32:529–556.

——— (1986). Acting out—transference and countertransference: technical considerations. In *Between Analyst and Patient: New Dimensions in Countertransference and Transference*, ed. H. C. Meyers. Hillsdale, NJ: Analytic Press, pp. 63–74.

——— (1987). The clinical use of dream interpretation in acting out. In *the Interpretation of Dreams in Clinical Work*, ed. A. Rothstein. Madison, CT: Int. Univ. Press, pp. 57–68.

——— (1988). Writing about psychoanalysis: I. Analysts who write and those who do not. *J. Amer. Psychoanal. Assn.* 36:105–124.

——— (1989). How dreams are told: secondary revision—the critic, the editor, and the plagiarist. *J. Amer. Psychoanal. Assn.* 37:65–88.

Van Lieshout, R. G. A. (1980). *Greeks on Dreams*. Utrecht: HES Publishers.

Credits

The editor gratefully acknowledges permission to reprint material from the following sources:

From *The Psychoanalytic Quarterly*: "Premonition as a Defense," 1953, vol. 22, pp. 69–74; "A Psychoanalytic View of Mental Health: Samuel Pepys and His Diary," 1977, vol. 46, pp. 82–115; and "Dreams, Conscience and Memory," 1991, vol. 60, pp. 185–206. Copyright *The Psychoanalytic Quarterly*.

From *Between Analyst and Patient*, edited by H. C. Meyers: "Acting Out—Transference and Countertransference: Technical Considerations," 1986, pp. 63–74. Copyright 1986 The Analytic Press.

From *Journal of the American Psychoanalytic Association*: "The Cliche: A Phenomenon of Resistance," 1958, vol. 6, no. 2, pp. 263–277; "Book Review: Kohut's *Restoration of the Self*," 1979, vol. 27, no. 3, pp. 665–680; "The Unobjectionable Part of the Transference," 1981, vol. 29, no. 4, pp. 869–882; "Rational versus Anagogic Interpretation: Xenophon's Dream and Others," 1984, vol. 32, no. 3, pp. 529–556; "Irony in Psychoanalysis," 1984, vol. 33, no. 1, pp. 35–58; "I: Analysts Who Write and Those Who Don't," 1988, vol. 36, no. 1, pp. 105–124; "II: Analysts Who Write, Patients Who Read," 1988, vol. 36, no. 2, pp. 393–408; "How Dreams Are Told: Secondary Revision—The Critic, the Editor, and the Plagiarist," 1989, vol. 37, no. 1, pp. 65–88. Copyright International Universities Press.

From *Psychoanalytic Study of the Child*: "Acting Out as a Character Trait: Its Relation to the Transference," 1973, vol. 24, pp. 347–364. Copyright International Universities Press.

From *Psychoanalysis: A General Psychology*, edited by R. M. Loewenstein, L. H. Newman, and A. J. Solnit: "Self Observation, Reality, and the Superego," 1966, pp. 275–297. Copyright International Universities Press.

From *Drives, Affects, and Behavior*, edited by M. Schur: "States of Consciousness in the Analytic Situation Including a Note on the Traumatic Dream," 1965, pp. 60–86. Copyright International Universities Press.

Index